Mrs. Joe's Housekeeping Guide

FIRST AIDS FOR EVERY KNOWN HOUSEHOLD USE

Compiled by
JOE MITCHELL CHAPPLE
From contributions sent in by

TEN THOUSAND WOMEN OF AMERICA

Consisting of
Home Helps for Cooking, Baking and Canning, Preserving, Pickling, Cleaning, Sewing, Mending, Darning, Washing, Ironing, Nursing, Family Remedies, Toilet Requisites, Etc., Etc.

HOW TO MAKE THE MOST OUT OF WHAT YOU HAVE

Money Saving and Time Saving Recipes and Formulas for Every Member of the Family, including the Babies and Children, as well as the Grownups

HERITAGE BOOKS
2007

HERITAGE BOOKS
AN IMPRINT OF HERITAGE BOOKS, INC.

Books, CDs, and more—Worldwide

For our listing of thousands of titles see our website
at
www.HeritageBooks.com

A Facsimile Reprint
Published 2007 by
HERITAGE BOOKS, INC.
Publishing Division
65 East Main Street
Westminster, Maryland 21157-5026

Copyright © 1909 The Chapple Publishing Company, Ltd.

— Publisher's Notice —
In reprints such as this, it is often not possible to remove blemishes from the original. We feel the contents of this book warrant its reissue despite these blemishes and hope you will agree and read it with pleasure.

The original book was missing pages 19 and 20

International Standard Book Number: 978-0-7884-4293-7

Foreword to Home-Makers

THE growth of popular knowledge due to the interchange of ideas is one of the most striking features of modern progress. The home-maker and housewife of old largely acquired her skill by listening to the household lore of her mother, grandmother and aunts, and watching their labors. She also collected recipes and ideas from friends and acquaintances during afternoon calls, and amid the social chat at the sewing society or whist party; these, neatly set down in handwriting, were the outward indication of her interest in all things pertaining to home life.

The desire to learn is deeply rooted in human nature, and the American home-maker is especially fortunate in possessing varied opportunities to acquire information, because we inherit and utilize all the "little helps" brought to this country by the Briton, Gaul, Slav, Italian, German and other peoples who make up the American nation, each contributing the dishes and methods of housekeeping of their native land. In almost every modern magazine and journal the importance of the home sentiment is acknowledged by a department which gives varied information of interest to women. Thus, "Little Helps for Home-makers," has long been a prominent department in the NATIONAL MAGAZINE, and has crystalized into print the experience of thousands of home-loving women, in all sections of the country, and representing nearly every race that has founded homes in the United States. It is not poverty or wealth that makes a happy home—it is the love and skill of the home-maker, and these are very apparent in the paragraphs that have been collected from the magazine pages selected from contributions by ten thousand actual home-makers, and that now appear in book form. Home-making is more than cooking.

Whether plain or elaborate, the cooking recipes are all well tested and secure tasty food, while many aid in those economies which are so vital in these days of extortionate charges and yet are little understood and practised, at least by city housewives. The baking and cooking departments will be found well worthy of attention by those who seek satisfactory results for their efforts in this line. The confectionery list gives information on how to make delicacies which can be prepared by any good home cook. The housework department affords many valuable suggestions, adapted to city homes and to the farm and ranch, remote from stores. Much loss of material and time may be averted, much labor and discomfort dispensed with, by following these directions; the same is true of the information given in the laundry department. Recipes for the best modes of washing, drying, starching, ironing, preserving delicate fabrics from injury, and many other details of a difficult calling, are always of great interest and are sure to prove useful. The list of cements and glues includes some specialties that have made millions of money for their former manufacturers. Canning, preserving and pickling recipes are simple, effective and have borne the test of many years' use.

In our day hygiene is carefully considered and the cleansing of the home is given strict attention. The great variety of surfaces and material to be kept clean and the refractory character of many of the stains demand some knowledge of practical chemistry as well as judgment and skill in using the various cleansing substances now obtainable. Housekeepers, laundrymen and all who have to remove stains and dirt will find suitable recipes in this book which will prove of more worth to them than the money paid for the little volume itself.

"Pharmacy at Home" contains a list of common simples raised in the garden or found in field and forest and gives safe directions for their use in sickness. It also suggests the medicinal uses of the common garden vegetables and fruits, many of which are as effective as far costlier specialties supplied by the druggist. Many families and individuals far removed from drug stores and physicians have found these recipes of great value, for they embody the cream of information that has appeared in bulky volumes, costing from five to ten dollars. The toilet department has in it recipes for articles safe to use and economical in cost.

Still considering the happiness of the inmates of the home, a few directions, taken from the best European authorities, have been added to provide information for those desiring outdoor illumination or stage display; by the use of these pages local talent in out-of-the-way places may make a creditable demonstration. Suggestions as to private theatricals, hunting, and other matters of interest to both young and old are made by experienced and successful experts in the various lines.

True economy is the aim of every home-maker; it is not economy to be parsimonious, or unenterprising, or to hire things done which we can satisfactorily do for ourselves, or to buy articles at extortionate prices which can just as well be made at home. In line with this truest economy "Little Helps" offers a great store of information from the "uses of ammonia" to the hint that a dollar's worth of vanilla beans, cut up and immersed in alcohol, effects an immense saving for a large family while giving them an excellent flavoring; or the fact that toilet, hard and soft soaps can be easily and well made at a small outlay. Many who purchased copies of the first edition have written to tell us that they have already found recipes in its pages that have saved them several times the sum paid for the book. The list of paints and whitewashes includes the once famous White House Stucco Whitewash, whose cost is little more than ordinary whitewash, while it wears for fifteen or twenty years; "this recipe alone," a farmer writes, "is worth the entire cost of the book to me." The practical purpose of "Little Helps" is impressed at a cursory glance and it becomes a valued book in the library, kitchen or any room in a house.

Homely and helpful, the contributions of thousands of home-makers are here presented with the feeling that "Little Helps" will be widely appreciated in every home in the country.

Boston   *Joe Mitchell Chapple*

Little Helps

THE contributors to "Little Helps" feel that their common labors have produced a book of rare value to all who are concerned in making home happy, attractive and economically administered. This is emphasizing most heartily the insistent demand for a second edition, enlarged and revised. It is often remarked that a housewife in a way starves her intellect if she buys everything she uses, "ready made," occupying herself only with the drudgery of arranging and keeping clean. By the use of some of these recipes, any woman may become a home manufacturer, while at the same time saving labor, time and money by her skill. The economies of our forefathers were crude, no doubt, but today we can to advantage imitate their prudence and resourcefulness, and with finer materials and appliances greatly improve upon the fruits of their labors, while eliminating the waste which frequently prevails in a modern household—waste, not only in food and clothing that might be utilized, but in the inventive faculty that almost all women have, but which is often allowed to lie dormant under the present system of housekeeping.

Many of the "little helps" contributed to this book have an almost sacred significance to those who sent them; some have been handed down from generation to generation; most of them call up some sweet memory of the grandmother or mother who imparted them to us when we "set up housekeeping." Some have come from the maiden aunt who was always in demand when sickness or "a rush of work" visited the house; some were tried for a life time by the patient widowed mother, who for years went the rounds among the homes of married sons and daughters, where her "little helps" added much to the sum total of human happiness. Such tested advisers were considered as the court of final appeal on all questions relating to household science. The ink spot on Mary's pretty graduation dress, the oily appearance of father's coat collar, the ache in little Tommy's teeth, all disappeared before the skilful ministrations of these welcome visitors to the home.

Today, as always, women need to know of little economies, simple remedies, easily managed forms of entertainment and all the other trifles that make for happiness in the home. It is well that such drudgery as candle and soap making and spinning are no longer compulsory; it is well that the vacuum principle has been utilized to clean the home easily and hygienically; these are true economies for they leave the housewife free for other occupations more suited to her ability. In city homes, it may be that cement and glue need no longer be largely used, because it is cheaper to buy a new article than take the time required to patch the old one, but in thousands of country homes these hints are just what are needed.

Many men imagine that housekeeping today is merely a process of handing out carefully labelled packages, with full directions printed thereupon—or of opening cans—with a due regard to the avoidance of cut fingers—that contain every possible article of diet. But no matter how gorgeous the label, or how carefully the manufacturer has prepared the contents of the can, it takes a woman's ingenuity to make that which is removed from the tinny receptacle taste like "real garden truck." If any man doubt this, let him sit at the table of a good housekeeper and partake of the meal she has produced from canned goods, and then let him experiment in private and report results. It is said, too, that the art of preserving will soon be lost to home-makers—not so, for it will be better known than ever before; the whole nation is learning how to "preserve to our use the kindly fruits of the earth, so that in due time we may enjoy them." The variety of fruit and vegetables obtainable in wintertime is vastly greater than in old times, when every house mother had to prepare her own supplies. Though all manner of food may be bought "ready cooked," I believe that members of the "fair sex" have an increasingly wide field for the exercise of their powers; and I am convinced that every man or woman who has, or ever expects to have a home, should at once procure this mine of useful and varied home information, "Little Helps."

Modern journalism has long ago acknowledged the importance of the home sentiment by gallant attention to the needs of women readers, and to details of home-making, in almost every publication. "Little Helps for Home-makers" has long been a prominent department in the National Magazine, and has crystalized into print the experience of thousands of home-loving women in all sections of the country, representing nearly every race that has founded homes in free America.

LITTLE HELPS FOR HOME-MAKERS

TO KEEP MILK

A cheap refrigerator can be made of a biscuit tin placed in a wooden box which is lined on the sides and bottom with many thicknesses of paper, until the tin is closely packed in. A small piece of ice should be placed in this, leaving room for bottles of milk and cream and the butter dish. Press down the cover and over the whole lay a board cover, lined like the box with an inch or so of paper. If the cover fits well the ice will melt very slowly indeed.

It is said that a teaspoonful of grated horseradish will keep a quart of milk sweet for several days.

POTATOES FOR SWEEPING

Potatoes well washed and mashed or cut very fine if sprinkled over a floor or carpet before sweeping will prevent dirt and aid much in restoring floors and carpets.

A NIGHT LAMP

Cut a thin slice from a smooth cork, halve it and connect the pieces with a thin piece of sheet brass or tin, just large enough to let the little raft thus made swing easily inside a tumbler or goblet. Put through a small hole in the center of the connecting metal a piece of white cord about an inch long; fill the glass two-thirds full of water, and pour upon the water about half an inch of sperm or cottonseed oil. Float the wick upon it and light.

POOR MAN'S CAKE

Five eggs, five level teaspoonfuls of sugar, pinch of salt, flour enough to roll; beat the whites and yolks separately; add the sugar to the yolks, then stir in the whites; roll out very thin, cut in diamonds or squares and fry in hot lard; when done, sprinkle with sugar.

TO PEEL BOILED EGGS

Boil the eggs in salt water; the salt cracks the shell and loosens it from the egg.

DOUGHNUTS THAT KEEP SOFT

Two eggs; beat whites, then add the yolks and beat again. One cup light-brown sugar (do not use granulated sugar as it makes a dry cake); one cup mashed potatoes (left from dinner); one tablespoonful of melted lard; one cup of sweet milk; cinnamon and nutmeg to taste; two teaspoonfuls of baking powder, sifted in flour; make stiff enough to roll out and fry in kettle of hot lard.

TO SAVE ICE BILL

I put a board to fit the bottom of the ice compartment of ice box, to protect it from being broken when ice was put in, and found my ice lasted much longer. Put newspapers on each shelf and when anything is spilled, it is easy to change the paper on that shelf and saves washing every shelf in the ice box.

TO MAKE FRUIT PIES

In making any kind of fruit pie, do not put in any sugar; season it, otherwise, just as usual; take the usual quantity of sugar, make a syrup, and immediately on taking pie from the oven pour in the hot syrup through the slit on the top crust; it is delicious and no loss of juice in the oven.

MOCK-CHERRY PIE

One cup cranberries, one cup maple sugar, one cup water, one-half cup seeded raisins, one tablespoonful flour; boil all together, stirring in flour, moistened with water; when cold, add teaspoonful vanilla and a little extract of almond; bake with two crusts.

ORANGE EXTRACT

Shave off thinly the yellow rind of three oranges; put these shavings into one-half pint of the best alcohol. Cover closely and let stand four days, then strain. This will fill several extract bottles, is a superior article for flavoring, and costs less than that sold in the stores.

BUTTERMILK PIE

This recipe has been in use for over a hundred years and is well worth trying.
One egg, two large tablespoonfuls of flour, one pint of buttermilk (fresh), one scant cup of sugar; beat the egg until light, add the sugar and flour, and enough of the buttermilk to make a thick batter; beat until smooth, then add the rest of the buttermilk; bake with one crust in a hot oven; a little baking powder in the crust is an improvement for this kind of pie.

BAKED HASH

A bowl full of each of the following: cooked onions, sliced cold potatoes, chopped meat and bread crumbs; season with salt and pepper; wet with rich milk, or cream, mix well, put in a shallow pudding pan, dot with butter and bake till well done.

LITTLE HELPS FOR HOME-MAKERS

TO REMOVE PEACH STAINS

Put cream of tartar on the water-soaked stains and place the article in the sun.

SPROUTING POTATOES

To keep potatoes from sprouting, fill the barrels half full and give them a good shaking occasionally; I have followed this plan for years, successfully.

TO PARE PINEAPPLES

Slice pineapples before paring and the task will be much easier and a great deal of the fruit saved.

TO REMOVE MATCH MARKS

Rub the spot with a cut lemon; then to prevent a repetition of the offence, apply a little vaseline and rub the spot dry with a cloth; it will be difficult to again strike a match thereon.

REMOVING STAINS

To remove iron rust from clothing, cover the spots with hot, stewed, unsweetened rhubarb.

Peach stains may be easily removed by soaking in sweet milk an hour before washing.

For coffee and most fruit stains, pour boiling water through the spots.

For chocolate, cocoa or tea stains, wash in cold water.

Cover grass stains with cream of tartar, wet with cold water, and place in sun.

For blood stains, soak in cold water, or water and salt; when nearly gone, use soapy water.

Machine oil, or axle grease, should be covered with lard, washed with cold water and soap, then with hot water and soap.

Red ink stains should be washed with ammonia and water.

FOR THE WHITE SINK

I want to tell how to clean a white sink so that it will look like new; mine got so stained with dish water that no amount of scouring with powders would clean it; one day, I accidentally spilled some hot water with cooking soda and chloride of lime in it, and the spots disappeared like magic; so, once a week, I clean it with that, wipe it out with kerosene oil and my sink is as white as snow.

A NEW DISH

Put in saucepan one cup of oatmeal, cover with cold water, seasoned with little more salt than is usually used when oatmeal is eaten with sugar. Chop, or grate, one-half a cup of cheese; set the oatmeal on back of stove where it will gradually come to a boil; when it begins to boil, stir in grated cheese and butter size of a walnut; stir constantly, until cheese melts; when melted, the mixture is ready to serve. Serve hot on toasted crackers.

AN ANTIDOTE FOR POISON

A physician once told me that a poison of any conceivable description and degree of potency, swallowed intentionally or by accident, may be rendered harmless by swallowing two gills of sweet oil. The oil will neutralize every form of vegetable or mineral poison with which physicians are acquainted.

A NEW DISH

Pull dried beef into small pieces, pour some warm water over it and let stand for two or three minutes; break six eggs, add three tablespoonfuls of sweet milk (cream is much better, if you have it) and beat well; have skillet hot with meat fryings of lard and butter; pour in eggs and then sprinkle beef on top and stir well until done; pour into hot dish and serve.

COATING CURED PORK

After pork has been well sugar-cured and ready to hang up, give each piece a thorough coating of lime and ashes, equal parts, mixed with water; it looks ugly but washes off beautifully, and keeps the meat with its finest flavors, free from insects.

USES OF TURPENTINE

After a housekeeper fully realizes the worth of turpentine in the house, she is never willing to be without a supply of it. It is a sure preventive against moths by just dropping a trifle in the bottom of drawers, chests and cupboards; it will render the garments secure from injury during the summer. It will keep ants and bugs from closets and store-rooms by putting a few drops in the corners and upon the shelves; it is sure destruction to bedbugs and will effectually drive them away from their haunts, if thoroughly applied to all the joints of the bedstead in the spring cleaning time. It injures neither furniture or clothing. A spoonful of it added to a pail of warm water is excellent for cleaning paint. A little in suds on washing days lightens laundry labor. It gives quick relief to burns. It is an excellent application for corns. It is good for rheumatism and sore throats. Try it.

FOR SLEEPLESSNESS

Drink a cup of hot cocoa, without sugar, just before retiring and you will not be troubled with sleeplessness.

HINT IN BEAD-WORK

When doing bead-work with fine beads, dip the needle in water frequently and the beads will slip up the needle easily and also cling together.

VERY FINE MARSHMALLOWS

Two level tablespoonfuls of gelatine, soaked in seven tablespoonfuls of water for one-half hour; two cups of granulated sugar, ten tablespoonfuls of water; cook until it makes long threads from spoon; pour over gelatine on large platter and beat twenty minutes; add one-half teaspoonful of vanilla; have square cake tin well buttered, pour in and let stand one hour or more, till solid; turn out on powdered sugar on board or paper, cut in squares, and keep in tight jars well powdered.

A COOKING HELP

If you burn anything cooking in a pan or kettle, fill the utensil partly full of water in which a little lye has been dropped, let stand to soak a while, then place on the stove until the water boils; you will find that the burnt portion can be easily washed off and that the kettle will be as good as new. Should any of the burnt portion remain, a little sapolio will take it off.

STARCH FOR BLACK DRESSES

To make starch for black lawn, or any solid black fabric and make it look like new, take black diamond dye, dissolve same as you would for coloring; keep bottled; when you make the starch, make it quite thin, strain the dye and pour a little (not too much) into the starch and stir thoroughly; then strain starch and it is ready for the black goods; you will find that you will have something that will please you when laundered.

DELICIOUS JAM

Delicious currant or raspberry jam may be easily made by thoroughly crushing the fruit, leaving none whole, then add, by measure, an equal quantity of granulated sugar; mix with great thoroughness, put in cans and keep in a cool place; the delicate flavor of jam prepared in this manner will surprise those who taste it for the first time, and it is cool work and so easy as compared with the old way.

TIRED FEET

Bathe the feet once a day in warm water, to which salt or borax has been added; then dry and rub with linseed oil.

BLOOD STAINS

To remove blood stains where soap and water cannot be used, as on pillow ticks, etc., make a thick paste of laundry starch and warm water; cover the soiled places and let remain until perfectly dry, then brush off the powder; sometimes it is necessary to repeat the process.

FOR BUGS AND MOTHS

Spirits of turpentine applied freely with a brush, will do away with bed-bugs and moths in walls, carpets, furniture or upholstery.

POACHING EGGS

A couple drops of vinegar added to the water in which the eggs are to be poached will keep the whites from separating.

USES OF LEMONS

The lemon is not sufficiently appreciated from a hygienic standpoint; for instance:

Lemon juice removes stains from the hands.

A dash of lemon juice in plain water is an excellent tooth wash; it not only removes the tartar, but sweetens the breath.

Lemon juice applications will allay irritation caused by the bites of insects.

The juice of a lemon taken in hot water on awakening is an excellent liver corrective, and for stout people is better than any "anti-fat" medicine ever invented.

Glycerine and lemon juice, half and half, on a bit of absorbent cotton is the best thing in the world wherewith to moisten the lips of a fever-parched patient.

Lemon juice and salt will remove rust stains.

For a manicure aid lemon juice is all that is necessary for loosening the cuticle and for brightening and cleansing the nails.

Save your lemon rinds and dry them for kindling; a handful will revive a dying fire.

CEMENTS

GRAFTING WAX:—Rosin, five ounces; beeswax, one ounce; tallow, one ounce; or in like proportion. Melt and mix thoroughly. Apply to scions while warm, but not hot, with a small wooden paddle. It will require no strings or bandages to hold the scions in place.

AQUARIUM CEMENT:—Also useful for mending leaks in tanks, metallic roofs, etc. Take of litharge, fine dry, white sand and plaster of Paris, one gill each, and of finely powdered rosin, one-third gill. Mix thoroughly and make into a paste with boiled linseed oil and some good dryer. Let stand four or five hours before using, but if it stands fifteen hours it loses its strength. Glass laid in this will keep in either salt or fresh water.

ARMENIAN CEMENT:—Dissolve a small amount of gum mastic in full strength alcohol and in another vessel cook an equal amount of gelatine until softened, and dissolve it in brandy or rum; unite the two mixtures and place in a two-ounce vial with two small bits of gum ammoniacum; place the vial in a skillet full of cold water, and boil until the cement is completely dissolved. When used soften in the same way by gradual heating. It will unite metals and glass to each other or to polished steel.

LABEL CEMENT:—Mix dry, finely powdered white sugar, one ounce; finely powdered starch, three ounces; finely powdered gum arabic, four ounces. Rub well together in a dry mortar, then add little by little cold water until it is about the consistency of melted glue. Or it may be kept in the powdered state and mixed as required for use.

CHINA CEMENT:—Beat thoroughly together equal quantities of white of egg and cold water. Make into a thin paste with powdered quicklime and use at once.

CEMENT FOR KEROSENE LAMP RINGS:—Mix three ounces of powdered rosin, one ounce of caustic soda and five ounces of water. To these add five ounces of plaster of Paris. It will set in about three-quarters of an hour. It is impermeable to kerosene and quite strong.

CEMENT FOR LEATHER BELTS, ETC.:—Soak equal parts of common glue and isinglass for ten hours in just enough water to cover them. Bring gradually to a boiling heat, and add enough tannin to make the mixture ropy, like the white of eggs. Fit and roughen the surface to be joined. Apply the cement warm and clamp together until dry.

TO PASTE LABELS ON METAL:—Have the surface perfectly clean, and brush that part to be covered with a mixture of equal parts of muriatic acid and alcohol. Paste the label lightly and apply with care.

CHINESE BLOOD PASTE:—To three parts of well-beaten blood from the butchers, add four parts of sifted air-slaked lime and a little alum. The thin pasty mass (which must be used immediately) will waterproof pasteboard, straw matting, ordinary boxes, boats, etc., giving great strength. Two to three coatings should be used on a boat or aquarium.

IRON CEMENT TO JOIN PIPES:—Take coarse iron borings, powdered, three pounds; sal ammoniac, two ounces; sulphur, one ounce, and sufficient water to moisten the mass. Use as soon as mixed, ramming it tightly into the joints.

CAST IRON CEMENT:—Sal ammoniac, one-half ounce; sulphur, one-quarter ounce; fine iron filings, one pound. Mix with water to a paste to fill cracks or holes in cast iron stoves, furnaces, etc.

JAPANESE CEMENT:—Fine rice flour paste.

LIQUID GLUE:—Soak over night eight ounces of fine glue in half a pint of water, dissolve by heat and when nearly cool add slowly two and a half ounces strong nitric acid. This glue will be much stronger if isinglass is substituted for one-half the glue.

MUCILAGE FOR LABELS:—Soak five ounces of first-class pure glue in eighteen ounces of water, and boil until dissolved. Add three ounces of gum arabic and nine ounces of rock candy.

MOUTH GLUE:—Good glue, one pound; isinglass, four ounces. Soften in water, boil and add half a pound of sugar. Boil until it thickens and pour into greased moulds. Will dissolve in the moisture and warmth of the mouth and will fasten things quite strong.

TO FILL CRACKS IN PLASTER

Use vinegar instead of water to mix your plaster of Paris; the resultant mass will be like putty and will not "set" for twenty or thirty minutes, whereas, if you use water, the plaster will become hard almost immediately, before you have time to use it; push your "vinegar plaster" into the cracks and smooth it off nicely with a tableknife.

TO CURE SHEEP-SKINS FOR MATS

Wash the skins thoroughly in a good lather of the best soap and soft warm water, rubbing and scrubbing out all dirt. When cool, rinse out the soap in cold water. Dissolve one pound of alum, and one of salt in two gallons of water, place the skin in this and soak over night. Before it is quite dry sprinkle each skin on the fleshy side with a mixture of equal parts of alum and saltpeter, rubbing the powder well into the skin. Try if the wool holds firmly; if not, let it remain a day or two, then rub in more alum. Fold the skins with the wool out, and hang in the shade for four or five days, turning them over once a day until quite dry. Scrape the flesh side with a blunt knife, and finish it with pumice stone. After being washed and before being cured, they may be dyed with aniline or other dyes. Lamb skins thus treated make nice mittens.

FOR A HORSE'S COUGH

Give in his mash the mucilage of boiled flaxseed, with a little licorice dissolved in it or some honey. Feed no musty or dusty hay, give him apples, carrots and laxative food, and if the heaves are indicated add a tablespoonful of ground ginger to his feed.

The surest cure for either cough or heaves is to ventilate well, and feed cut feed; *i. e.*, hay cut fine, well wet and mixed with bran, middlings, or cornmeal.

LITTLE HELPS FOR HOME-MAKERS

GRASS STAINS

To remove grass stains, dip the cloth into molasses and wash out in clear water.

WHITEWASH

1. Slake a half bushel of choice lime in a barrel; add one pound of common salt, half a pound sulphate of zinc and a gallon of sweet milk.
2. To a pailful of lime and water ready for the wall, add one cup of flour made into a hot clear gruel, and a handful of fine salt.

WASH FOR BARNS AND SHEDS

Skim milk, two quarts; fresh slaked lime, half a pound; white burgundy pitch, two ounces, dissolved in six ounces of linseed oil; Spanish white, three pounds. The lime duly slaked and cooled is to be mixed with a pint of the milk, and to this the oil and pitch is to be slowly added; then the rest of the milk, and the Spanish white. This should give two coats of white to twenty-seven square yards of surface.

PAPERHANGER'S PASTE

Beat up four pounds of good sifted flour—winter wheat flour is the best—in cold water to a stiff batter, and see that there are no lumps. Add cold water until it is about like pudding-batter and put in two ounces of powdered alum. Have boiling water ready, pour it by degrees, boiling hot, on the batter, stirring all the time; when the paste is no longer white like flour it is cooked and ready. Do not use it hot. It should make about three-fourths of a pailful of solid paste. Put a little water over it to prevent it from skimming, and thin with water as needed.

TO TEST WATER

Place in a clean glass jar a half pint of the water of your well, and drop in three or four lumps of loaf sugar. Expose to the sunlight in a warm room. If pure it will remain clear for a week or ten days. If it is turbid it must be contaminated.

TO INCREASE THE FLOW

If a well is curbed with sewer pipe properly tamped, and covered in water and air tight, by using an air pump to exhaust the air from time to time the increased pressure will enlarge the water channels and increase the supply in the reservoir.

BLACKING

Ivory black, four ounces; brown sugar, three ounces; sweet oil, one spoonful; small beer, one pint.

WATERPROOF BLACKING

Beeswax, two ounces; beef suet, four ounces; rosin, one ounce; neat's-foot oil, two ounces; lampblack, one ounce. Melt together and mix well.

WATERPROOF CLOTHING

Dissolve two and a quarter pounds of alum in twenty gallons of boiling water, and in a separate vessel, two and a quarter pounds of sugar of lead in ten gallons of water. When both are thoroughly dissolved mix the two solutions. The soft woolen or cotton fabrics, shawls, etc., are dipped and thoroughly worked over in this mixture, until every part is penetrated. They are then squeezed or wrung out, and dried in the air or a warm room, then washed in cold water and dried in the air, when they are ready for use. Cloth, shawls, blankets, etc., thus treated while still porous, shed water like a duck's back. For small jobs, divide the above proportions by five, which would give to four gallons of water a little less than half a pound of alum, and the same amount of sugar of lead to two gallons of water.

MADE MUSTARD

Mix smoothly with boiling vinegar four tablespoonfuls of ground mustard; one tablespoonful of flour; one tablespoonful of sugar; one teaspoonful of salt; one teaspoonful of black pepper; one teaspoonful of cinnamon; one teaspoonful of cloves. Let it stand several hours before using. This will keep many weeks.

HINTS FOR ROUGH CARPENTERING

NAILS:—There should be kept on hand at least a pound each of lath, shingle, ten and twenty penny nails. In driving these into spruce or hard woods, the nail point should be greased or oiled, a precaution that greatly lessens the labor, and averts much bending of nails, splitting of wood and unregenerate thought and ejaculation. In drawing old nails it is sometimes an advantage to hit the nail a sharp tap before trying to pull it out. Do not buy poor rusty nails or imperfect screws. A few of every common size should always be kept in stock.

ZINC ROOFS AND CONDUCTORS:—A solution of acetate of lead and black lead spread upon zinc colors it a light-brown and protects it against oxidization.

SHINGLE ROOFS:—Whitewash each course of shingles down to the line, and wash them with some hue after all are laid and the shingles will last several years longer.

TO CLEAN WELLS

The well should be examined frequently by means of a mirror, which will reflect the sun's rays to the very bottom. If covered or shaded, two or more mirrors can be used to deflect the rays to the well's mouth. Before going down a well, a candle or lighted lantern should be carefully lowered and watched. If it cannot burn in the well, the gases are fatal to human life. To remedy this, drop quickly to the bottom an iron bucket full of blazing shavings and drop in three or four quarts of fresh slaked lime.

WATER IN CISTERNS

Add about one ounce of hypermanganate of potash to every fifty gallons of water, and all impurities will be precipitated to the bottom of the cistern. Muddy water may be cleared by adding about an ounce of alum to every fifty gallons of water.

Hard water is easily rendered soft by the use of lime water. Slack a quantity of good lime in a barrel of clean water, and when the lime settles, bottle the clear lime water. A cupful of the water will soften a barrel of hard water, precipitating the lime held in solution to the bottom.

CLIPS FOR BASTING

Instead of basting long seams, use the little clips used by businesss men for holding papers. A few of them placed along a seam will hold the edges together while it is being stitched. Keep a box in the work-basket for such uses.

ALUM FOR MENDING PURPOSES

For mending hard substances, like metal or glass, there is nothing more satisfactory than melted alum; simply melt the alum over an intense heat and apply while hot.

An ivory handle to a knife, which was loose, was mended this way over forty years ago, and still is in use. This can be used to fasten loose collars on glass lamps also.

HOME-MADE SOAP

Every housewife knows that dishwater will make the hands dark, but if she will use home-made soap after this recipe, she will have as white hands as heart could desire. It is also excellent for washing any kind of clothes, as it takes out all stains.

Five pounds of grease (clean tallow or half tallow and half lard); one can of Babbitts potash dissolved in one quart of water; two tablespoonfuls of borax; three tablespoonfuls of powdered ammonia; melt grease and cool it and mix together; stir ten minutes, then mold in a box and cut before cold.

TO KEEP RUST FROM TINWARE

For preserving tinware and preventing it from rusting, rub the article well with fresh lard, covering every portion; then heat it thoroughly before using; if treated this way, it will never rust, no matter how much it is left in the water.

HOW TO HULL WALNUTS

Another way to hull walnuts is to run them, when green, through a hand cornsheller, setting a pail under the place where the cobs come out, to catch the hulled nuts. This way is more rapid and saves staining hands and dress.

CHRISTMAS SUGGESTIONS

For years I have made a practice of remembering some children at Christmas time who get presents from no one. As the pocketbook is not always equal to my love of giving, I have originated some things of which I have never heard from anyone else.

PICTURE SLIPS:—During the year I save all good pictures of animals, birds, fruits or good plain views of buildings or any suitable thing; one soon learns to know what can be used. Now take your picture and paste on pasteboard the same size (a good way to get rid of old boxes), then cut in strips an inch wide; if the picture is that of a horse, cut in five strips, and at the end of each strip place a letter—H on top piece, O on next, and so on till all the letters in "horse" are used. Use the same method for bird, flower, or whatever the picture is. The children who have nothing love to put these together.

PICTURE PUZZLES:—Instead of strips you may cut them out in all sorts of shapes, but be careful to make them easy for little folks; the pictures best suited for these are the colored ones to be found in magazines. You would be surprised, and touched, too, to see how much pleasure these simple little gifts give to the children.

STORY BOOKS:—Last Christmas I made another gift that greatly pleased both myself and the school children who received them. I knew some children whose stock of story books was very limited; yet they were often asked to recite in school; being children who spoke quite plainly, I conceived the idea of making them books. I used wall paper (any kind will answer) cutting it in suitable sizes for use; on these sheets I pasted little stories, poetry, cute sayings, some picture rebuses, and the like; when all pasted, I put the sheets together with a cord, using pasteboard covers, pasting a picture on the front cover, leaving the back one plain. The children say: "We won't have to ask teacher any more for pieces to speak."

PICTURE BLOCKS:—For quite small children, I use small pictures of animals, babies, flowers, anything that will please the little tots; cut out straight and paste on smooth wooden blocks the same size of picture, and about one-half inch thick. My twelve-year-old boy saws out the blocks for me—if you have no boy, perhaps your neighbor's boy will help you out.

MOTH KILLER

If moths get into the closet, saturate a cloth twelve inches square with formaldehyde; place cloth in the closet and close up tightly for twelve hours. The same plan may be used in chests, trunks, or boxes, where clothing is stored. The fumes will kill moths as well as their eggs; also germs of any kind. No odor is left in the clothing.

PLENTY OF HOT WATER

I find one of the best ways to always have plenty of hot water on hand is to keep it in my milk pails on the back of my range. I use lard pails to keep it in; when they are washed each morning, I fill them with fresh water and leave them on the stove while I do my cooking, and in this way have plenty of hot water for my dishes, besides having my pails scalded and sweet for the next morning's supply of milk; repeat this each day and you will seldom, if ever, have sour milk; occasionally put in a little soda or saleratus in each pail of water. I have only a cellar in which to keep our supply of milk (no ice) and I find this way very satisfactory.

NEW IDEA WASHCLOTHS

The nicest washcloths I ever used were made of six or eight thicknesses of white mosquito netting; white mercerized cotton can be quickly put around the edge with a crochet hook, button-hole stitch.

A SEWING HINT

When sewing, the index finger soon becomes roughened from the needle pricking through. To prevent this, use two thimbles, one on the left index finger and the other in the usual way. What a comfort! No pricked finger, or little spots of blood to come through on some fine fabric!

A COOKING HINT

Turn the colander upside down over the fish or meat sauteing in an iron spider; the small holes allow the steam to escape and still prevent the grease from spattering.

STAINED WALLS

For removing stains from painted walls, a mixture of wheat bran and water is excellent; it should be allowed to stand till it becomes sour, then wet a cloth in the mixture and fasten it close to the stained part and let it cling there till dry; if the discoloration is still visible, a second application will be necessary.

TO KEEP WOODEN TUBS

One of the best methods of keeping wooden tubs in good condition when not in use, is to turn them upside down and pour water over the bottom. This is much more effective than the old way of covering the bottom with water on the inside.

By adding to every tub of rinse water, one bucket of hard, or "well" water, you will find that clothes will "take the bluing" more readily, thus requiring little bluing and improving the appearance of the clothes.

COCOANUT PIE

Use the recipe for cornstarch pie (see p. 2) and add one-half of a ten-cent package of prepared cocoanut and you will have a very nice cocoanut pie.

GENERALLY USEFUL HINTS

Pieces of cloth or paper, dipped in turpentine, will keep moths and carpet bugs away.

Tansy put among blankets is good to keep moths away.

Chamois is very fine to mend corsets.

Very cute little baskets can be made by cutting around large oranges, only leaving enough for handles, then scrape out the inside, filling with desserts made of tapioca, or anything you choose, and putting wihpped cream on top and two little pieces of jelly, or candied cherries.

For floor wax, shave a five-cent cake of beeswax fine and add one quart of gasoline; let stand over night and it will be ready for use; this is the best and cheapest wax ever used. Caution: Do not have a light in the room with the gasoline.

Sift a little flour over cakes before icing and it will prevent the icing from running off the cake.

Perhaps some of you do not know that you can skin rhubarb, then slice into glass cans, fill with cold water, and always have a supply of fresh rhubarb on hand. Seal the cans as for canned fruit and store away in your cold storage room.

Vaseline stains are hard to remove; before washing, they should be soaked in kerosene.

Try paraffine oil for furniture polish; it is fine.

Black ribbon can be freshened by rinsing in hot coffee, or in alcohol; wrap it around a glass bottle to dry.

"Smile a smile and while you smile, another smiles;
And soon there's miles and miles of smiles;
And life's worth while
If you but smile."

APPLE FUDGE

When making chocolate fudge add two or three tablespoonfuls of juice from apple sauce. This makes a pleasant flavor.

TO CORK GLUE OR CEMENT

After a bottle of glue or cement has been opened, rub mutton tallow or cold cream on a sound cork before inserting it, and the cork will not stick fast and break when an attempt is made to draw it. Moreover, the glue will remain liquid. Glass stoppers should be treated in the same way.

TO SOFTEN PUTTY

The best way to remove the putty from a broken glass and window frame is to touch it with a brush dipped in nitric or muriatic acid. After an hour or so the putty will be soft and can be easily removed.

A UNIQUE CISTERN

Almost every house is fitted with eaves-troughs for the purpose of conducting the water to a convenient point, where it is either allowed to run to waste or run into a cistern, from which it must be pumped when wanted. Every housekeeper knows how infinitely superior is rain water to any other, for many purposes, especially for all sorts of cleansing. But how many of them know that, at a very slight expense, they may be able to draw rain water from a faucet in the house?

First procure a suitable tank. I use a common gasoline tank. If you can get a larger one, or care to go to the expense of having one built, so much the better, but the gasoline tank holds 110 gallons and mine never has a chance to run dry.

Place your tank on a frame, close to the house, as high as you can, and still be able to run the water into it from the eaves-troughs. Bore a hole through the wall where you wish to have the faucet; put the faucet on a short piece of pipe, run this through the hole, and with an elbow and another piece of pipe connect to the bottom of the tank, and the thing is done.

It will be a good thing to prepare a strainer to run the water through as it runs into the tank. Fill the strainer with pebbles and charcoal.

SPILLED MILK

If milk, either sweet or sour, is spilled on carpet, matting or clothes, do not use any water in cleaning them, but simply wipe the milk up with *dry clean cloths* until it is all absorbed. This will leave the material perfectly free from any trace or stain of the milk.

RECIPE FOR PASTILLE

Pastille for killing flies, mosquitoes, and other insects. Mix one part benzoin, one part balsam of tolu, five parts charcoal, one and a half parts insect powder, and half part saltpetre. Add water to, knead into a stiff paste, then roll the mixture into pastilles and dry them. One of these pastilles will burn for some time, give a pleasant odor and the fumes will kill all insects in the room.

COOKING IN THE FURNACE

Just inside the furnace door I have a wide shelf. On this one can set a kettle and cook corned beef and pot roasts that require long cooking. Vegetables can be cooked also, thus saving the kitchen range fire.

BROWN POTATOES IN FIFTEEN MINUTES

Half fill a fry-pan with lard or other grease and place over a good hot fire. Peel the potatoes, and if small put them in whole; otherwise, cut them in two, lengthwise. When you can stick a fork into them, they are done, and you can pour off the grease. This is a quick and satisfactory method of cooking potatoes. They do not absorb any of the grease and have a very superior flavor.

A BELT THAT WILL STAY IN PLACE

A belt shaped in the back is sure to keep in place. Put lining on cloth crosswise and allow a slight flare at the bottom.

TO PUT OUT AN OIL FIRE

It ought to be more generally known that wheat flour is probably the best extinguisher of a fire caused by the spilling and igniting of kerosene oil.

FOR BEE STINGS

When stung by a bee, bruise a plantain leaf and bind on, renewing two or three times if necessary to reduce inflammation.

TO REMEDY A CURDLED CUSTARD

Beat a pinch of soda into custard cooked a moment too long, and it will entirely change its consistency.

LITTLE HELPS FOR HOME-MAKERS

TO SCALD MILK WITHOUT BURNING

Before putting milk into a sauce-pan, boil rapidly a few spoonfuls of water (just enough to cover the bottom of the pan), and the milk will never burn, however fierce the fire.

LACE CURTAINS

After washing and boiling lace curtains, lay a blanket on the floor in some empty room, spread the curtains on this (stretching them carefully) and they will keep their place without any further fastening until dried.

TO LINE ROUGH SHOES

When boots and shoes are rough and uneven inside, cut some inner-soles from light-weight oilcloth to just a right fit; slide these into shoe, having the oil side next the shoe-sole. The warmth of the foot will cause these inner-soles to stick firmly to the leather and leaves a nice smooth surface next the foot.

TO RELIEVE CHOKING

Give the patient a raw egg to swallow. The white of the egg seems to catch around the obstacle and remove it. If one egg does not give relief try another. The white is all that is necessary to use.

TO REMOVE GRASS STAINS

Apply alcohol to the spots, rub well, and the stains will disappear.

MENDING LACE CURTAINS

No matter how many or how large the holes may be in your lace curtains, here is an excellent way to repair them, either stretched on the frames or just before hanging them: Make a good *cooked* paste of flour and water; have your patches ready, taken from discarded lace curtains. The patches must be larger than the holes. Rub paste well into them, one at a time, fit smoothly over the holes, and put them in the sun to dry. When you hang your curtains you will be astonished at the effect.

ONE-CRUST PIE

In baking a shell for a one-crust pie, put it on the outside of the pie-pan and it will not blister.

TO TEST BLUING

Many bluing compounds are composed of iron and Prussian blue, and contact with alkali in the soap in the clothes precipitates the iron, causing rust spots. Test the bluing by adding to a small portion a little soda, then heat it, and if it turns red and dark it contains Prussian blue; if, when a little nitric acid is used and the mixture heated, it turns yellow and then white, it is indigo. These simple tests are valuable, as they may prevent the ruin of a much-prized gown or fine table linen.

TO STOP A LEAK

To stop a leak, mix whiting and yellow soap into a thick paste with a little water; apply to the leak and it will be stopped at once, until a plumber's services can be secured.

TESTING FLOUR

There are several methods of testing flour, which should be known to every purchaser. If flour is white with a yellowish straw tinge, it is good, while if it has a bluish cast, or has black specks in it, it is inferior.

Wet and knead a little of it between the fingers; if it works soft and sticky, it is poor; if elastic and firm, it is good. If a little flour is thrown against a dry smooth surface and it falls like powder, it is not of the best quality. If flour squeezed in the hand retains the shape given it when released, it is of good quality.

MEMBRANOUS CROUP

Mix two parts of pulverized alum and one of granulated sugar or thick syrup. Give one teaspoonful and repeat as often as necessary, according to the case. This preparation cuts the phlegm in the throat, a process which is the first movement toward curing the croup. This is reliable.

PREVENTS CHILBLAINS

A very simple and effective remedy for chilblains is common chalk. Try it and be convinced. Since prevention is better than cure, try putting on a fresh pair of stockings every afternoon—and be convinced again!

CORNSTARCH AS MITTENS

When doing your washing, before you go out in the cold to hang up your clothes, wipe your hands dry and rub them well with cornstarch. Your hands will not suffer with the cold.

GOOD USE FOR PAPER BAGS

Canned tomatoes should be kept in the dark. Put each can into a bag (saved when they come from the grocer's). By doing this with all canned goods, and marking the contents on the bag, the mark is easily seen and the can kept free from dust.

SAVE YOUR DRY LEMONS

If you have some dry, hard lemons, do not throw them away. Put them in a pan of hot water, set it where the pan will maintain the same heat without boiling, and let lemons soak for two hours. When taken out and dried, they will be as soft and juicy as though they never had grown hard.

TO TAKE OUT IRON RUST

To take out iron rust, fill a dish with boiling water and put the spot of iron-rust over this, covering it with salt. Now drop on this enough hydrochloric acid to wet the salt, and drop the material at once in the hot water, when the spot will disappear.

TO RESTORE ARTIFICIAL FLOWERS

To freshen and restore faded and soiled artificial flowers, dissolve in gasoline enough tube oil paint of the desired color to give the right shade. Dip the flowers freely in this, shake out and let the gasoline evaporate. Straw and felt hats may be restored or colored in the same way. Beware of using the gasoline near a lamp or fire.

VINEGAR IN DOUGHNUTS

For doughnuts made with sour milk or cream, add a generous half-teaspoonful of vinegar to the batter before adding the full amount of flour.

PRUNE DESSERT

Soak prunes over night. Boil slowly until very tender. Sweeten to taste. When they have cooled in their own liquor, pierce one side with a pointed knife, remove the stone and fill with chopped nuts and raisins, mixed. Serve with whipped cream.

GRATED COCOANUT FOR BUTTER

A cup of grated cocoanut or finely chopped nuts may be used instead of butter in making cake.

CHICKEN OIL FOR CHICKEN SALAD

In making chicken salad, use the oil that comes out of the chickens when boiled, instead of olive oil. This adds greatly to the flavor of the salad.

FOR THE HAIR

Put one tablespoonful each of salt, glycerine, borax and powdered sulphur into a quart can and fill with soft water; let stand one week, shaking the can at least once every day during the week. Add a few drops of bergamot or any other scent, after straining the above.

TO KEEP MEAT FRESH

To keep beef fresh in hot weather, put the meat (after removing bones) in an air-tight glass jar, and set where it is cool. It can be lowered into the well or cistern. I have kept steak in this way for a week through the hottest weather.

TO KEEP EGGS

Eggs may be kept almost indefinitely if turned often enough to prevent the yolk from sticking to the side. Instead of storing the eggs on a shelf, put them in a stocking hung to a nail and the whole stockingful may be turned as easily as one egg.

TO TAKE CASTOR OIL

Beat castor oil in three tablespoonfuls of boiling milk until cool enough to drink. Take a sip of hot milk after the dose, and there will be no disagreeable flavor. Salts may be given without the knowledge of patient by dissolving in strong, rather sweet, lemonade.

FOR SPRAINS

Place the sprained parts in a vessel filled with buttermilk for a period of thirty minutes, and repeat this three or four times a day. Within a week from the time I began using buttermilk the swelling was gone.

ENAMEL PAINT TO MEND CHINA

An easy and most satisfactory method of mending china and other broken articles is to apply enamel paint to the edges, press them firmly together for a moment and then set the article aside to dry for a day or two. The paint may also be used to cover scratches and broken places on the surface of china.

LITTLE TIME-SAVERS

A small stiff-bristled scrubbing brush, such as can be bought for five cents, should be in every bath-room and kitchen, within easy reach. When you step in the mud with your best extension-soled shoes, hold the shoe under the faucet and, while the water is running slowly, brush briskly between the sole and uppers. It can be done so quickly that the shoe will not be injured in the least by the water, and after wiping dry with a soft rag and rubbing lightly with vaseline, they will be like new, and with a very few minutes' work.

Another should be used to clean the grater after grating chocolate, potatoes, etc. A minute's work will remove every particle, and leave the grater clean and dry.

TO FIND WAIST MEASURE

To correctly find one's waist-measure so as to be able to put belt or girdle on shirt-waist, cut shirt-waist somewhat shorter than full-length pattern; make waist and then try on; tie a tape around waist, placing fullness in back, front and sides just as desired. Then take a lead pencil, mark the waist all around just below tape. Cut off even with marked line, after taking off waist. Put on belt, remembering to have measured distance from middle of back to under-arm seam, so as to know exactly where to let fullness be. This is an excellent idea, and of great benefit to home dressmakers.

AID TO DIGESTION

A few drops of essence of peppermint in a glass of hot water after meals is a great aid to digestion, and will gradually cure stomach troubles. It is a most harmless remedy to give to children who do not seem to assimilate their food. A few drops on sugar is the easiest way to give it to children—unless you can make the large white mint drops.

TO RESTORE COLOR

To bring back color when taken out by any acid, make a weak solution of baking soda and water and into this dip the article which is faded; the color will be restored. This is especially effective in shades of yellow.

RESEATING CHAIRS

Twelve years ago the "split" bottoms of our sitting-room chairs began to give out, and we rebottomed them with common binder twine. Left in the natural state, these would probably have worn out in two or three years at most, but they were immediately painted with a good coat of thick straw-colored paint which was allowed to dry thoroughly before using. Today these seats show practically no wear, though they have been constantly used.

CURTAIN CLEANSING

Clean from loose dust by brushing with a stiff brush. Then take a coarse linen towel, place in warm water until thoroughly wet, wring out and lay on ironing board. Lay the curtain on this and place a piece of fine cheese-cloth over it. Then proceed to iron with a very hot iron until dry. The cheese-cloth is used to prevent scorching of curtain. If this method is carefully followed, you will find that the curtain is not only clean, but that it has the same degree of stiffness as when new.

KEEP KITCHEN STOVE NEAT

As I use white enamel ware in my kitchen, I do not care to have the top of my coal range blacked. Once a month I black my range entirely. Between times I rub it off each morning with a block of wood (2 x 6 x 8) covered with sheep's wool, first rubbing into the wool one teaspoonful of lard and one teaspoonful of kerosene. Rub when the stove is medium warm, and rub rapidly, and you will be surprised how clean your stove will be.

WASHING BLUE GOODS

Before washing blue goods, soak two hours in a bucket of water in which an ounce of sugar of lead has been dissolved, and dry before washing. This will set the color permanently.

TO REMOVE MILDEW

Place article in a solution of about ten cents' worth chloride of lime to one gallon of water with one teaspoonful of soda added. Remove in a few minutes and wash in clear water.

TO BLEACH HANDKERCHIEFS

After washing, let them soak over night in water in which a bit of cream of tartar has been dissolved.

FELT MATS

Mats made from old felt hats are useful in protecting tables and shelves from hot dishes.

TO KEEP A VEIL DAINTY

Don't iron a veil that has become wrinkled. Roll smoothly on cardboard and steam over a kettle.

WHOLESOME PANCAKES

When frying two or more pancakes on the griddle at one time, be careful not to allow one to touch another. If this precaution is observed, the cakes will be lighter and more wholesome.

RELIEF FOR SORE JOINTS

To take soreness from corns or enlarged toe joints wet a cloth with pure cider vinegar and bind on over night.

SCRATCHED FURNITURE

A scratch may be removed from hardwood furniture by rubbing with salt butter.

WALL-POCKET FOR KETTLE-COVERS

A great convenience for the kitchen is a wall-pocket made of wire netting, for holding pot-lids and such like. You can make it as long and as deep as you like—mine is one and a half yards long and one and a half feet deep.

TO TAKE OUT COCOA STAINS

I have tried many things to take out cocoa stains, and have found that to wet the stain with camphor before it is washed will take out the cocoa.

INSTANT RELIEF FOR CRAMP

For instant relief in case of cramps in limbs, dip hand in cold water and rub under the knee of cramped limb.

NEW WAY TO WHIP CREAM

Whip cream in a Mason jar by shaking it up and down for about five minutes. This saves much whipping in the ordinary way and also saves the cream, as not a drop escapes.

NEAT SHOE-LACES

If the tips come off the end of a shoe-lace, melt a little sealing wax or paraffine and dip the ends of the lace in it, rolling between the thumb and finger till it is cold and shaped. It will be as good as new and last for some time.

TO BANISH FLIES

A little oil of lavender sprinkled about the room through a common atomizer will banish flies.

TO CLEAN A CARPET SWEEPER

Empty the accumulated dirt, place the sweeper on the floor bottom up and sweep the brush lengthwise with the broom.

SUBSTITUTE FOR GREASE

A turnip rind (the inside) rubbed on the griddle will answer for grease, and there is no smoke or odor, no sticking or any taste of the turnip.

STARCH FOR WINDY WEATHER

A spoonful of salt added to the starch on a windy day will prevent it from blowing out of the clothes.

HOW TO CAN FRUIT

A safe rule for canning fruit is to use one pound of sugar with four pounds of fruit, with enough water to keep from burning. The following table should be preserved for handy reference:—

FRUIT	Time for Boiling Min.	Amount Sugar to quart Oz.
Cherries	5	6
Raspberries	6	4
Blackberries	6	6
Strawberries	8	8
Plums	10	8
Whortleberries	5	4
Pie-plant, sliced	10	10
Small sour pears, whole	30	8
Bartlett pears, halves	20	6
Peaches, halves	8	4
Peaches, whole	15	4
Pine apples, sliced		6
Siberian or crab apples	25	8
Sour apples, quartered	10	5
Ripe currants	6	6
Wild grapes	10	8
Tomatoes	20	None
Gooseberries	8	8
Quinces, sliced	15	10

BUTTONHOLES

To work buttonholes in dresses of Sicilienne or similar materials, melt some paraffin and place a drop on the wrong side of the goods just where the buttonhole is to be worked. Smooth it down with the finger and work the buttonhole as usual. When completed, place a piece of manila paper on the wrong side and press with a warm iron. The buttonhole will be perfectly smooth and all trace of the paraffin gone.

DRESSES FOR GROWING GIRLS

When making dresses for growing girls, or from goods that will shrink, run a tuck by hand or with a loose tension on the machine, on the right side of the goods very near the bottom. Turn up the hem and tuck will be on the wrong side. When ready to lengthen take out the tuck and no stitches will show.

CORN-MEAL CAKES

To make corn-meal mush, or any fine-grained cereal, when fried, as pleasing to the sight as to the taste, pack it in well-greased pound baking-powder tins. When cold, turn out and cut into slices. These little rounds can be prettily piled on a dish at serving time.

TO KEEP SANDWICHES FRESH

Sandwiches prepared in advance of the serving time can be kept as fresh as when first spread by wrapping them in a napkin wrung out of hot water and then placing in a cool place.

DRESS SHIELDS

To make dress shields for thin waists, cut white flannel the size desired, trim edges with lace and use same as rubber shields. They will keep the waist dry and they look nicely.

FOR BABY'S BIB

Cut a dress shield in two pieces, bind the raw edges and tack under a baby's fancy bib. It will absorb the moisture and keep the little dress from getting damp.

TO FRESHEN CANNED PEAS

Canned peas are made fresh by pouring off old liquid, washing and adding new water, butter and a bit of sugar.

SKIRT BRAID FOR PETTICOATS

Sew narrow cotton tape on white petticoats as you would skirt braid on a dress. When frayed, it can be easily renewed.

TO IRON BETWEEN BUTTONS

When ironing between buttons on a shirt-waist, place the buttons down on a folded towel and iron on wrong side. The result will be very pleasing to both ironer and wearer.

PERFUME BAGS

A perfume bag to keep moths away is made as follows: One-half ounce each of cloves, nutmeg, caraway seeds, cinnamon and three ounces of orris root. Have these in fine powder and place in small bags. These bags placed amid clothing will impart a pleasant odor and will keep moths out.

TO PREVENT MILK FROM SCORCHING

When boiling for a pudding or soup, first grease the bottom of the vessel with butter. It will save all worry and trouble.

TO KEEP CUT FLOWERS FRESH

To preserve cut flowers and at the same time save changing the water, fill the vase two-thirds full of clean sand. Stick your roses or other flowers so they will remain just as you put them; then add water and see how much longer they will keep fresh. Sometimes the stems of roses and carnations will root in the sand.

STOCKINGS

New stockings wear much longer if washed before wearing. It tightens the threads, making them firmer.

VALUE OF WHOLE CLOVES

Sprinkled among furs and woolens, and under carpets and rugs, they will be found as effective, if not superior, to the ill-smelling moth preparations. And if the housekeeper who superintends the canning of her fruit will put a quarter-teaspoonful of whole cloves on top of the thin cloth which many wisely place over the hot fruit before putting on the lid, she will not be annoyed with the molding of her fruit.

SUGAR SYRUP

For buckwheat and other griddle cakes many who prefer a home-made syrup of sugar have trouble with its granulating when it becomes cold. Try putting in it while cooking a spoonful of New Orleans or other molasses, and see if you do not have better results.

DELICIOUS APPLE-SAUCE

A spoonful or more of lemon juice or good vinegar added to apples that do not cook readily will hasten the process and improve the flavor.

WATER IN CAKE

Try using water instead of milk in making cake, and you will find it an inexpensive and very satisfactory substitute, especially in white cakes, as they are lighter in texture and color.

TO SET AND KEEP COLORS

Where green, blue, mauve, purple or purply-red is the dominant note, soak the things before washing for at least ten minutes in alum water, using an ounce of alum to a gallon of water. For browns, brown-reds and tans, use sugar-of-lead in the same proportion. Yellows, buffs and tans are made much brighter by adding a cupful of strong strained coffee to the rinsing water.

TO CUT HOT BROWN BREAD

Draw a clean, strong white thread sharply and firmly across the loaf, pushing it down equally on either side. The result will be clean, smooth slices, free from the stickiness that comes from knife-cutting.

TO KEEP ROSES FRESH

Fill the vase or pitcher with very warm water, and as each rose is inserted cut off the tip of the stem with scissors, under the water, so that no air may reach the freshly-cut stem. Do this every morning, leaving the flowers to cool in the same water until the next day, when repeat the process. All hard-stemmed flowers can be kept fresh in the same way.

FOR THE HANDS

After handling onions or other malodorous things, wash the hands in mustard water. Nothing better.

SCORCHED LARD

It frequently happens that in rendering lard a part of it is scorched, but it can be made as good as any by frying Irish potatoes in it.

I was so unfortunate as to have a large quantity scorched one time, and saved it all by this method. As we often had fried potatoes for breakfast, I would fry them in a skillet full of the lard, then drain it into a bucket kept for the purpose, and when cold it would be white and free from the scorched odor and taste.

CHEESE DREAMS

Cut thin slices of bread at least one day old, spread with soft cheese and press into sandwiches; fry in butter. These "dreams" are favorites with college and boarding-school girls, as they can be cooked over an oil-stove.

SIMPLE REMEDY FOR LOCKJAW

Dr. J. G. Hatch, an old physician of over forty years' practice, recommends the following treatment for lockjaw, having tried it successfully both on himself and on others. If a person is threatened or taken with lockjaw from injuries in the hands, feet, arms or legs, do not wait for a doctor, but put the part injured into the following preparation:—Put hot wood ashes into water as warm as can be borne; if the injured part cannot be put into the water, then wet thick folded cloths in the water and apply them to the part as soon as possible, at the same time bathing the backbone from the neck down with some powerful laxative stimulant—cayenne pepper and water, or mustard and water (good vinegar is better than water). It should be as hot as the patient can bear it. Don't hesitate; go to work and do it, and don't stop until the jaws relax and open. No person need die of lockjaw if these directions are followed.

TO MEND ENAMELED WARE

Mend leaky enameled ware with white lead. Cover the small holes with white lead on the outside of vessel; for larger holes cut a piece of white lawn or muslin a little larger than the hole, pull through on the inside of vessel, and apply the white lead on the outside. Place in the sun or near the stove to dry. Large mends require two or three days to dry, small ones three or four hours.

BUTTONHOLES

In finishing the bands of children's drawers, I work the two outer buttonholes diagonally, first outling the hole with a stitch on the sewing machine, before cutting with the scissors. Buttonholes done in this way are practically everlasting.

TO PRESERVE SHOE-SOLES

The soles of shoes may be preserved by applying shellac.

A HANDY GRATER

A tin-can lid, medium size, driven full of holes with an awl or sharp-pointed nail makes a handy culinary tool for any use to which a larger-grater is put. It quickly removes any scorched crust from bread, cake or pie, and will be found helpful in many ways.

TO KEEP MATTRESSES CLEAN

To prevent a mattress from getting rent by springs, stretch ticking over the springs, hem both ends, sew rings on corners. run tape through and tie to springs.

NEW METHODS OF WASHING

Try this, and you will never wash any other way: Take a pound cake of paraffine and cut into twenty pieces; use one piece of the paraffine and one bar of laundry soap, cutting both up small, and two or three quarts of water. Boil till dissolved and add to the water in which you boil the clothes. Put your soiled clothes into cold water a few minutes and wring; rub soap on the soiled places, put in the boiler and boil twenty minutes; wring out and rinse in the usual way. They will be clean and white as snow, and no rubbing is required.

STORM DOORS

Your screen doors may be very easily transformed into as warm a protection from winter gales as any one need ask for. Fit pieces of building paper to each side of the screens and attach securely with cleats, using screws so that your door may be converted at will from "screen door" to "storm door," and vice versa, and there you are. This saves the work of taking off and putting on heavy doors, as well as the cost.

NEW USE FOR A SCRUBBING-BRUSH

The possibilities of a five-cent scrubbing-brush are unlimited. Having a dress of which only the bottom of the skirt was soiled, the thought came that with care it might be taken on a table, with plenty of space, and with good soap in the water, the hem scrubbed gently, then rinsed, wetting only the portion needed, having irons ready to press at once. Try it and be convinced. Any part of wearing apparel can be cleansed in the same way.

TO CLEAN LAMP BURNERS

If a lamp fails to burn brightly or smokes, remove the burner, place it in vinegar and salt, and let it simmer over a slow fire.

REMEDY FOR BURNS

Cover a soft cloth with a thick layer of scraped raw potato (Irish) and apply to burned part, with potato next the skin. The potato should be renewed so as to keep moist. When other remedies failed, this relieved a hand badly blistered by grasping a red-hot poker.

CLEANING TRIMMING

To clean white or light trimming on dark dresses: cover with cornmeal which has been saturated with gasoline. When the gasoline evaporates, brush off the meal and the trimming will be clean.

TO CLEAN ARTIFICIAL FLOWERS

Cover with flour, let stand for several days, then shake out; if not entirely clean, repeat the process.

A NEW USE FOR OLD STOCKINGS

Have you ever thought of this use for your nice, warm, winter stocking tops, when the feet are too badly worn to admit of further darns? Make them into drawers for the little tots. For a small child one pair of stockings will make a pair of drawers, using an old garment as a pattern. For the older children up to eight years, it will take two pairs. Use black sateen or dress lining for the bands. For little girls' winter wear they are unequalled, saving washing and always neat. They are very little trouble to make, and you will be surprised at the wear you can still get out of your old stockings.

COLD TEA PUNCH

Among good old temperance drinks the following is a fine recipe, often tried. The tea which forms the body of this drink may be Ceylon or Oolong, carefully selected. For the flavoring, prepare early in the morning. Pour one quart of cold water in a small saucepan; add the juice of two lemons, and three oranges, quarter of a pound of sugar, quarter of the rind of a lemon and orange. Let this come to the boiling point. Strain it into a pitcher, mix with the strong tea; let it cool, and serve cold in a punch-bowl with slices of orange and pineapple.

TO DRESS A DUCK

Wring a woolen cloth out of boiling water, wrap the duck and lay aside for several minutes. The feathers and down may then be easily and quickly removed.

THREADING A NEEDLE EASILY

Char the end of cotton or silk thread to facilitate threading a fine needle.

WHEN USING COLD STARCH

When starching by the cold starching process, if the starch is mixed with quite hot water instead of cold, it will not stick to iron, and garment can be ironed in one-half the time.

SUBSTITUTE FOR APPLES

If there is a scarcity of apples when making mince-meat, use finely chopped green tomatoes instead, and when well-cooked none could detect them.

RELIEF FOR SICK HEADACHE

A towel or flannel wrung from hot water and applied to the back of the neck will relieve sick headache in a few minutes.

A GUEST BOOK

A guest book is an easily acquired addition to any home, no matter how humble.

I have a pretty leather-covered book (a cheaper one would do) and in this record the names of all guests who stay over night. To have the names in their own chirography adds to the interest. We have been married but three years, and it does not seem as if we had very many guests, but when the names are all together they make a very entertaining list. You will find more states and cities represented than you imagine. Some say anticipation is better than realization —but in this case you will find the pleasant memories which linger of the guests are the best of all.

"SHORTENING"

A good shortening for pies, cakes, etc., and much more economical and healthy than either butter or lard:—Take equal quantities of leaf lard and beef suet and render out together; put away and use as you would lard.

TO WHITEN FLOORS

A little bluing added to the rinse water when scrubbing will make the floors much whiter.

FOR RELIEF OF EYES

One drop of castor oil dropped in the eye will remove any foreign substance.

FOR IN-GROWING TOENAILS

Scrape the center of the nail from the end back toward the root. Or, when trimming the nails cut the end square; or cut a small notch in the center of the end. Nature will lose no time in remedying the disproportion of the nail by speedily growing to the center, thus drawing the nail away from the oppressed sides. Relief will be obtained in forty-eight hours in the worst cases; and by always thinning the center of the nails a little when trimming them, they will never give trouble.

CUTTING THIN CLOTH

When cutting thin cloth which is slazy and pulls, lay in between two sheets of thin paper and cut out paper and all. This is a great help.

HEAT LEMONS BEFORE SQUEEZING

If you will heat your lemons well before squeezing, you will get almost double the quantity of juice.

TO KEEP PEARLS BRILLIANT

Keep in common dry magnesia instead of the cotton wool used in jewel cases, and they will never lose their brilliancy.

ENGLISH WALNUT GRAHAM BREAD

Add a cupful of chopped English walnuts to your sponge for graham bread and you will find it more nutritious and delicious.

OLD BLACK HOSIERY

When black hosiery is worn out, save the tops to clean black goods or to wipe off furniture. They leave no lint.

NEW WAY TO BAKE POTATOES

Wash and dry large-sized potatoes. Place them in a spider or skillet, cover closely with a pan, and dry on top of stove. They will bake much quicker and with less fire than in the oven, and will be mealy and plump, not dried and shrunken. I have often placed potatoes on an asbestos mat on top of the stove, covering closely with a basin and they bake equally as well.

FOR TIRED NERVES

If overworked home-makers whose nerves are "worn to frazzle edge" would acquire the habit of sitting or lying absolutely still, relaxed and motionless, for five or ten minutes twice a day, they would soon see improvement. The mind must be relaxed, worries dropped, thoughts wandering to pleasant things. You will probably try this several times before you get it right, but after a little practice you will find that it yields large returns, far surpassing the sacrifice of the time it takes. Try it, nervous ones.

FOR STRAINS AND BRUISES

After having done an unusually hard day's work or undergone some unaccustomed strain such as is likely to leave the muscles sore and stiff, mix fifteen drops of the tincture of arnica thoroughly in one-half glass of water and take one teaspoonful of the mixture every hour until relieved. This will give much quicker relief than when applied externally. It is also one of the best remedies to promote absorption, remove soreness and prevent inflammation in any wound or bruise of the soft parts of the body.

HOT WATER FOR A COUGH

For a tight, hoarse cough where phlegm is raised with difficulty, take hot water often, as hot as can be sipped. This will be found to give immediate and permanent relief.

TO RELIEVE ASTHMA

Wet blotting paper in strong solution of saltpeter, dry it and burn a piece three inches square on a plate in the sleeping room. It will afford quick relief.

TO STARCH THIN WAISTS

Thin muslin waists will take starch much better if dried first and then placed in boiled starch and dried again.

EASY WAY TO SPRINKLE CLOTHES

Remove the cover from a quart can, perforate the bottom, fill with water and replace the cover; you have a very good sprinkler.

TO KEEP CHEESE FROM MOULDING

To keep cheese for some time without becoming mouldy, wrap in cloth dipped in vinegar and keep in covered dish.

SOUR PICKLES

A very easy way to make sour pickles for the winter is as follows: Fill quart fruit jars with small cucumbers, mixing in a little horseradish root or leaves. Place a heaping teaspoonful salt on top and fill the can with boiling vinegar. Seal immediately. These pickles keep indefinitely and are as nice as those made with twice the work. They also have that "crumpy" quality so much desired.

TURNING A HEM

If you have a ruffle to hem, the hem may be measured in a tenth part of the time usually required as follows: After the breadths of ruffling are cut off, before sewing them together, lay flat on work-table and measure at each lower edge the width of required hem, allowing for the portion turned under. Then, by the use of a yardstick, mark across the goods with chalk or tracing-wheel, and your hem is all measured, ready to turn.

WINTER PIES

In cold weather one may save much time by making a quantity of apple or mince pies at a time. Put them in some cupboard outside, where they will freeze and remain frozen until wanted. The day you wish a pie for dinner, bring in one in the morning, thaw out, and bake. Pies kept in this way will be as good as if just made.

TO MAKE TURKISH DELIGHT

One ounce Knox's gelatine dissolved in one-half cup of water, grated rind and juice of one lemon and one orange, one-half cup of cold water added to two cups of granulated sugar. When dissolved, mix all together and boil twenty minutes. Pour in a shallow vessel and let stand twenty-four hours; then cut in squares, rolling each in pulverized sugar. By using rose water you get the Turkish flavor.

RELIEF FOR SICK STOMACH

A very simple home remedy for nausea is cinnamon tea. Place a teaspoon of ground cinnamon in teacup, and pour over it a half cup of *boiling* water. As soon as the mixture settles, it is ready for use. This settles the stomach in a remarkably short time.

MAKING A WASH DRESS

In making a wash dress, if you would avoid the unsightly sag which will invariably come in the back of the skirt after a few days' wear, do not gore the back breadths. A five or seven gored skirt model cuts to good advantage this way. Gore the front and side breadths according to the pattern, and set straight back breadths, and see how well your skirt will hang until worn-out.

FOR THE HOME DRESSMAKER

If you are a home dressmaker keep a quantity of sharp black pins on to use in pinning patterns on, etc. Their large heads render them very picked up, while the points, being so very sharp, are easily pricked ti the material, and do not draw the goods as common pins frequently a quantity of these can be purchased for five cents at any department store.

ECONOMY IN MAKING BED LINEN

Sheets are better hemmed with the same width hem at each end. They can then be used either end for the head and will wear more evenly.

If, when making pillow-cases, you make them an inch or so longer than usual, it will allow of cutting off and hemming again when they wear out at the corners and the other parts are still good.

AN HYGIENIC KITCHEN TABLE

Cover an ordinary kitchen table with a piece of sheet zinc, lapping carefully over the edges and tacking neatly on the under side. Easily kept clean, absorbs no grease, always ready to set hot things on. If once tried, the only wonder is how you ever kept house without it.

RED ANTS

To drive away red ants, take liquid corrosive sublimate, pour it on little pieces of cotton batting, lay it where the ants travel, and they will leave instantly. The odor of corrosive sublimate lasts but a short time.

ANT EXTERMINATOR

I was troubled last summer with little red ants in my house. Having dissolved two pounds of alum in three quarts of boiling water, I applied with a brush while hot to every crack and crevice where the ants were in the habit of staying.

To get rid of the larger species, lay about fresh-picked tansy leaves.

SAVE SOAP SCRAPS

Do not throw away bits of toilet soap. Keep a jar to put them in. Make ιgs of fine cheese cloth four by six inches, fill with bran, a few bits of soap, and pinch or two of orris if you have it. Tie the bags at the top; do not fill them ll, as the bran swells in the water. Oatmeal may be used instead of bran. ₂se bags make the nicest kinds of washrags. Another use for bits of soap is ɔut them into an empty jar and pour in alcohol or cologne, not quite enough over the soap. This will make a jelly which will be found useful in sham- ɪg, or in the bath, as it dissolves quickly in the water. Add a few drops of .der or rose to the alcohol and soap just before using.

ABOUT EGGS

When using an egg which has been frozen, break it into the mixing dish place on the stove until slightly warm; beat briskly, and the yolk will be ɪth instead of forming in small curdles.

If you use the whites of the eggs only for a dish, do not remove the yolks from the shells, and they will not form a crust on top.

SUGARING DOUGHNUTS

Put pulverized sugar in a paper bag with new doughnuts, give a little shake, and the work is done, with nothing to clean up.

GINGER IN SAUSAGES

If when making sausages you add a small amount of ginger, it will prevent the formation of gas in the stomach.

TO RELIEVE THE COW

Put nine drops of liquid extract of ergot in half a glass of warm water, and with this bathe the cow's udder thoroughly five or six times a day. The swelling will soon go down. It works like magic when the udder is badly caked.

COAL ASHES FOR CLEANSING

Some of the uses I have found for coal ashes are these:—For china dishes that have been discolored, rub well with a damp cloth dipped in powdered ashes and they will look new. For cleansing brass faucets, etc., it will give a more lasting and better polish than the preparations which one buys, and is also excellent for cleaning and polishing steel knives. The ashes should be sifted through gauze or muslin to remove grit

LINIMENT FOR CROUP

To make a liniment for croup, fill a half-pint bottle one-third full of sweet oil, one-third of ammonia, one-third of turpentine; shake well. Bathe the throat, breast and bottoms of the feet. I have often cured my litle ones with this alone.

BLANKET COVERS

Worn all-wool blankets make splendid covers if darned carefully and patched where necessary. Then cover with light or medium weight outing cloth and tie with wool.

TO PREVENT LOCKJAW

As soon as a wound is inflicted get a light stick (a foot-rule or knife handle will do. I have used a flat celluloid paper cutter) and commence to tap gently on the wound. If it is a punctured wound (such as running a nail in the foot) do not stop for the hurt, but continue tapping until it bleeds freely, and becomes quite numb. When this point is reached, you are safe. *Do not on any account close the wound with a plaster.* Protect from dirt by covering with a clean cloth—that is all that is necessary. I have tried this remedy for rusty nail in foot, puncture from hay-fork tine in leg, and for many other wounds of like nature, and never knew a single instance where the wound became sore or inflamed. For a hard bump on the head, where the above method could not be administered, I have prevented all soreness by *vigorously rubbing* with the hand for a few minutes.

SALTPETER PAPER

Five cents' worth of saltpeter and one pint of water; put in a flat tin and heat until dissolved. A package of best toilet paper must then be soaked, about six sheets together. Take up and twist, but *do not wring out,* and lay to dry. When dry it is stiff and coated. If anyone suffering with cold in the head or asthma will burn one of these candles in an old tin with a little earth in the bottom, upon retiring at night, with bedroom door and windows closed, they will be greatly relieved.

NEW WAY TO SCALE FISH

Use a currycomb when scaling a fish. It is easier to handle than a knife, and prevents the hands from smelling fishy and the scales from working under the nails.

TO CUT HOT BROWN BREAD

Take a piece of common wrapping cord or thin wire and put around the loaf where you want to cut it. Cross and draw through. You will never use a knife again.

TO WHIP CREAM

When cream is rather thin to whip, add the white of an egg to each pint of cream; the whipping can be accomplished much more easily, and the flavor of the cream will not be changed in the least.

QUASSIA CHIPS FOR INSECTS

Buy quassia chips from any drug store; boil them for twenty minutes. This tea will keep the lady-bug, cutworms and other insect life from destroying young cucumber plants.

ROOTING SLIPS

In rooting geraniums and other soft-wooded plants, it is best to take a box that can be easily lifted around. Have one side three inches higher than the other; after putting in good sharp sand, fill it with slips and tack a piece of white muslin over the top, leaving it so that the cover can be laid back while wetting the slips, for they must never be allowed to get very dry. Set where the sun will shine on the box at least half of the day, and if you are as successful as you should be, ninety per cent. will grow. The muslin allows the air to reach the slips, and is far better for the amateur than glass.

TREATMENT OF PIMPLES

After bathing the face with soap and water nightly, a five-minute application of hot towels, followed with cold the same length of time, will prove excellent for the pustule condition, keeping it from spreading over the face. Ether rubbed over the complexion at night and washed off with green soap in warm water in the morning, is very beneficial. The following lotion, used by a specialist, is excellent. Shake and rub over affected parts.

LOTION:—Sulphur precip., one dram; acid salicylic, one-half dram; alcohol, two drams. Add enough rose water to make three ounces.

FOR FROSTED LIMBS

Procure a five-cent bottle of vaseline and have druggist mix five cents' worth of "oil of mustard" with same. Place between cloths and apply to afflicted parts. This will not blister and has been well tested and found to be invaluable in drawing out cold.

TO WASH FEATHER PILLOWS

Choose a bright, windy day; fill the washtub with hot suds, and plunge the pillows (with feathers) in them. Put them through several waters, shaking them about briskly, then hang on the line in the open air. When perfectly dry, shake well. They will be light, fresh and sweet. After they have been washed in this way, they should be hung out in the warm fresh air every day for a week, but they must never be put directly in the hot sun.

KIDNEY SUET FOR LARD

Instead of buying so much lard, get kidney suet; fry out slowly, and add a pinch of salt and one of sugar to each five cents' worth of the suet. The result is much superior to lard, and you are sure it is clean and pure.

CURE FOR CORNS

Take equal parts of wheat flour and pure lard; mix thoroughly, and bind on corn at night. Three or four applications may be necessary, but one night's treatment will draw the soreness out.

TO REMOVE IODINE STAIN

To remove iodine stain quickly from white goods, rub with liquid ammonia as long as any spot remains, then rinse in clear water.

A NEW SPADING FORK

If you have a little garden and wish to work in it yourself, just order from your hardware man a flat-tined potato fork, and use it instead of the spade or shovel, and see how much easier your task becomes, especially if the ground be gravelly. I had just moved here and was struggling to make an impression on the hard ground to set out our roses and violets, when one of our neighbors called over the back fence and wanted to know if I didn't want to borrow her fork. I tried it and decided to pass the good news along to other women, and to the men, too.

SAVE YOUR APPLE PARINGS

Dry your apple parings, as they will be found good for making jellies, sauces and syrups.

STORING FURS

Take an empty kerosene barrel and put in a few newspapers on bottom and sides; then put in your goods, and head the barrel on tight, putting in an out-of-the-way place. The furs will be safe from moths for any length of time. When removing them from the barrel, hang in the open air for a few hours, and you will find them as good as new and no odor of kerosene will remain.

SURE CURE FOR CANKER-SORES

Canker-sores when they first appear in the mouth can be readily cured by applying red vaseline. Anoint the sores just before retiring at night, and once or twice during the day. Sometimes a single application will be enough. The writer knows of no better, milder remedy for these painful sores.

OLD-TIME REMEDY FOR DYSPEPSIA

One ounce bicarbonate of soda, one ounce of powdered rhubarb, one ounce of aromatic spirits of ammonia, eighteen tablespoonfuls of water. This is bottled together, and a dessert spoonful taken after each meal. Is splendid for all suffering from dyspepsia.

TO PREVENT "BOILING OVER"

When cooking anything that is apt to rise and boil over, like rice, peas, beans, etc., if a small piece of butter is put in, it will prevent boiling over and is no detriment to the thing being cooked. This is one of the very best helps I have found.

TO PREVENT BED-SORES

Add alum to alcohol used for bathing people who are obliged to be in bed constantly; it toughens the skin and prevents bed-sores.

BUTTER THE DISH

Rub with butter any baking dish in which you expect to cook milk, such as macaroni and cheese, and the food will not stick to the dish, which will be more easily washed.

BAKED PORK CHOPS

Pork chops will be much more tender if, after being prepared as for **frying**, they are baked in the stove oven.

IRONING SHADOW EMBROIDERY

To make shadow embroidery stand out well, lay it right side down on a Turkish towel when ironing. You will be delighted with the result.

WHEN GLUE GETS DRY

When glue gets too dry and hard to use, pour in a little vinegar, and in a day or two it will be as good as new. This can be done over and over as it dries.

PEELING RIPE TOMATOES

Instead of pouring boiling water on ripe tomatoes to loosen the skin, rub over them the back of the paring knife. The skin will then peel off easily.

The skin can be loosened on ripe peaches by pouring on boiling water for a few minutes. This makes less waste of fruit than the ordinary paring.

TO FRY PORK CHOPS

Try dipping pork chops and pork tenderloins in flour before **frying** them, and see how delicious they are.

TO COOK CABBAGE

A crust of stale bread boiled with cabbage will absorb the disagreeable odor.

FOR TONSILITIS

Dampen the end of your finger and dip it into common baking soda, and touch each tonsil; repeat this treatment every hour until the soreness is entirely gone. You will find this a sure cure, however severe the case may be.

TREATMENT FOR AN OLD FLOOR

For filling up cracks in an old floor which you intend to paint, there is nothing better than kalsomine mixed to a paste. It will soon harden and may then be smoothed off with sandpaper and painted over.

A COUGH CURE

To one pint of New Orleans molasses add one teaspoonful of pine tar. Simmer together till well mixed, then add one small teacup of good cider vinegar and one-half teaspoonful of ipecac. Cook slowly till a good syrup is formed, but not too thick to run well from a bottle. We have used this recipe for over twenty years in our home, and can recommend it.

SEALING FRUIT JARS

When canning fruit, if you dip the rubber in the juice of the fruit just before putting on the jar the sealing process will be more effectual.

CREASELESS DOILIES

To prevent doilies and all fancy linens from creasing and mussing when laid away, roll up in a partly stiff paper, and they will keep their shape as though freshly laundered.

ANTIDOTE FOR KEROSENE

If a child should drink kerosene, give it a large spoonful of castor oil with two spoonsful of cream.

TRANSPLANTING SMALL TREES

A small tree or any shrub may be successfully transplanted at any season or at any stage of growth in the following way. Dig a trench entirely around the tree, a foot or more in width and a little deeper, leaving the roots imbedded in a ball of earth. Fill the trench with wet cement, and leave undisturbed till it hardens. The tree may then be lifted and removed at pleasure. After placing it where it is to stand, break and remove the cement and immediately fill the space with earth.

FOUR SUGGESTIONS

The very best way to remove the odor from pans in which fish, onions, etc., have been cooked, is to put into the dish left-over coffee grounds. All odor almost instantly disappears.

Keep an old comb to clean the carpet sweeper with and you will save your hands as well as time.

Tough meat may be made tender by putting a little soda in the water in which it is boiled.

Always flour suet before chopping, as this keeps the particles from sticking together.

LITTLE HELPS FOR HOME-MAKERS 47

TO CLEAN WHITE PAINT

The best way to clean white paint is to dip a piece of soft flannel cloth in warm water, wring it out, then dip it in clean bran, using this to rub the paint. The friction of the bran will remove the stains without injuring the paint.

CURE FOR JAUNDICE

Barberry root or bark is a sure cure for jaundice. Steep well and extract all the goodness possible. Drink freely of this bitter liquid. Many years ago this cured the writer's mother of the severest attack, and of recent years, a lady residing in Lowell, Mass.

HOW TO MEND GLOVES

I prolong the usefulness of my black silk gloves by turning them wroug side out when I first buy them, and strengthening the ends of the fingers with black court plaster; when a place wears thin anywhere, I also put the plaster on the wrong side. The same might be done with white gloves, using white court plaster.

A SUBSTITUTE FOR SCOURING SOAP

When entirely out of scouring soap, I have found that common baking soda sprinkled on a cloth is very efficient in cleaning marble basins and bath tubs.

TO REMOVE GREASE SPOTS WITH TALCUM POWDER

Sprinkle the spots thickly with talcum powder, let stand over night, and in the morning when the powder is brushed off the grease will have disappeared also.

TO KEEP LARD FRESH

To keep lard fresh for several months, stir in about a tablespoonful of honey to every six or eight gallons of lard, after removing the scraps.

OILCLOTH ON TABLE MAT

I have covered the silence cloth with white oilcloth and bound the two edges together with white tape. This saves washing the cloth and keeps it in its original state, and also saves the polish of the dining-table, which is often harmed by the spilling of hot dishes. A great convenience in this arrangement is that the tablecloth can be slipped on without sticking to the padding beneath.

HANDY WHILE SEWING

It will be found convenient and many steps will be saved if a common magnet is attached to a four-foot string or thread, so that when you drop a needle or scissors you need not get up to get it, but can easily pick it up with the magnet.

SEA AND CAR SICKNESS

Sea sickness and also car sickness can be avoided by the liberal eating of well-salted popcorn. This has been tried many times, with success, and is a very simple remedy.

TO KILL COOKING SMELLS

To kill cooking smells, throw a few whortleberries on the stove and notice the fine aroma it creates. You will never use anything else, once tried.

AN EXCELLENT TONIC

Watercress contains much sulphur, and is an excellent tonic for complexion and hair. Eat it raw or as a salad dressing.

TO RELIEVE BURNS

Make a salve of powdered alum and water and bind on the burn; the pain will immediately cease.

WHEN MAKING FRUIT PIES

In making fruit pies, brush the lower crust with unbeaten white of egg to prevent the juice from soaking through.

CANNED TOMATOES

Melted butter poured on the top of canned tomatoes just before sealing will keep them sweet.

TO BAKE POTATOES IN A HURRY

To bake potatoes in a hurry, pour warm water over them before placing them in the oven, where they should be an inch or two apart. They will bake much quicker than if put in in the usual way.

LITTLE HELPS FOR HOME-MAKERS 49

FOR WASHING SOILED LINEN

For washing any soiled linen, more especially such as one does not wish to handle, a great improvement on the old "pounder" can be made as follows: Take a piece of pine plank two inches thick; make a round block three inches in diameter; bore a hole in the center to receive the end of a piece of broom-handle two or three feet long as desired (depending on whether a tub is to be used on the floor or on a bench). Now take a tin basin six or seven inches in diameter and two inches deep and nail securely to the block, bottom to bottom. In using, press firmly down on the clothes and then lift each time entirely out of the water. The suction produced by the basin in being lifted draws the water through the clothes and washes them.

MOVING MATTRESSES

In cleaning chambers moving the cumbersome mattresses is the hardest task. It is not because of their great weight, although they *are* heavy, but on account of the difficulty in getting hold of the unwieldy things. Just try roping them with a clothes-line and see how it simplifies matters. Put the rope around, book-strap fashion, knotting in such a way that you have rope handles to get hold of and then see how easily the mattresses can be moved.

FROZEN WINDOWS

To prevent windows from freezing at the bottom, spread a thin layer of salt on the sill beneath the sash, adding more salt when needed.

LEAKY HOT WATER BOTTLES

Hot water bottles that leak and are past mending may be filled with *hot* sand and this will retain the heat as well as the water would. The sand can be bought for a small sum at any grocery store, and after heating in the oven can be poured into the bottle with a tunnel.

TO PREVENT SYRUP FROM THICKENING

Syrup for table use made of sugar and water often "sugars" or thickens, after standing. This can be prevented by putting a piece of alum the size of a pea into the syrup while it is boiling.

MAKES CHICKEN TENDER

When boiling chicken, cook a fig with it and it will make it tender.

CAMPHOR GUM IN CUPBOARDS

Camphor gum laid upon the shelves will keep ants and mice out of cupboards.

TWINE HOLDERS

Save all your pieces of bright-colored twine and knit garter stitch. Knit it long enough to fold over. White may be used underneath. If the holder is to be used for ironing, put in an inside lining. This makes a good pastime for old ladies. My grandmother saves every piece of pretty twine, and knits these holders by the hour.

SURE TEST FOR BOILED ICING

Take a clean straw from a broom, tie a loop in the end and dip in the boiling syrup. When a coating forms over this loop and you can blow it into a good-sized bubble, the syrup is just right. One who has practiced this for years is always complimented on her boiled icing.

MOTHER'S SUET PUDDING

One cup finely-chopped suet, one cup water (cold), one cup raisins (seeded), one cup figs (cut up), one cup New Orleans molasses, one teaspoonful soda, one teaspoonful salt, two and one-half cups flour. Steam three hours. Use any good pudding sauce. I consider this an *uncommon* recipe, on account of not having either sugar, butter, milk or eggs among its ingredients, and one trial is convincing proof of its excellence. It is equally good warmed over by cutting in slices and steaming twenty minutes. Will keep in cool place for a week or ten days.

TO HULL WALNUTS

Take a piece of oak plank one inch thick and in the center bore a hole with an auger the size of a walnut with the hull off. Place board across top of box or barrel, put nut side downward on hole, and with a hammer drive it through. If the hole is the right size there will only a small piece of husk left on the nut which will do no harm if the nuts are left out in the sun and thoroughly dried.

STRETCHING NEW SHOES

It is not always convenient to get to a shoe store when you have a tight shoe that needs stretching. Put on the shoe and take a cloth wrung from quite warm water, and wrap it around the shoe over the foot. It will give the needed room and will not injure the leather.

TO CUT WHALEBONE

To cut whalebone, warm by the fire, when it will cut easily.

EATING ONIONS

If you enjoy eating onions, *afterward* munch a sprig of parsley dipped in vinegar.

FRYING MUSH

Before pouring mush into vessel to cool for frying, wet vessel in cold water mush will turn out without sticking.

WHEN GREASE IS SPILLED

If grease is spilled on the stove, sprinkle it with dry salt, and all odor is avoided.

MOSQUITO-PROOF CHAIR

To protect chair-bound invalids living in warm climates from flies and mosquitoes: Suspend the top of an umbrella or parasol from a hook in ceiling, sawing off the handle just below the catch which holds up the frame. Get about four yards of mosquito-netting, sew the edges together with the exception of an opening at front, gather at top of parasol and leave hanging to floor around the patient's chair.

TO ALLAY FEVER THIRST

In cases of fever moisten the tongue frequently with glycerine, and thirst will be greatly decreased.

MEALY POTATOES

To make old and poor potatoes delightfully mealy and nice, the moment water has been drained from them after boiling, take kettle to the open air and *shake* gently; must be done very quickly.

POTATOES A SUBSTITUTE FOR MILK

A couple of cold boiled potatoes mashed fine make an excellent substitute for milk when making baking-powder biscuit, making them moist and *very light*.

TO TREAT SPRAINS

When a wrist or ankle is sprained, take the white of an egg and thicken it with common table salt. Spread it on a strong cloth and bind it firmly around the sprained member. It will almost immediately harden until it forms a cast around the injured part. Let it remain between twenty-four and thirty-six hours according to the severity of the sprain. Remove, and the sprain will be entirely cured. A music-teacher received a severe sprain in her wrist two days before a concert in which she was engaged to play. She tried this remedy and was able to fill her engagement.

OILCLOTH APRONS

Make oilcloth aprons with bibs for washing, and keep your clothes dry.

SANDWICH·BREAD

To make a round loaf of bread for sandwiches, bake in tin can after having melted off the rim.

TO CLEAN STRAW HATS

To clean old or soiled straw hats, rub with a mixture of three parts benzine to one part of magnesia.

THE SALT BATH

Bathing in salt water is so refreshing, so invigorating, so health-inspiring to the cuticle and to the whole system. It leaves the pores in a healthy operating condition. The most economical and safest way is the sponge bath; and perhaps the best sponge is a good coarse cloth of the right size. Make your washbowl of warm water salty like sea-water. Commencing with the head, saturate your whole body freely with your sponge or cloth. Take time enough, and use plenty of good soap. Wipe dry with a coarse towel. Do all this yourself. Do not let anyone do it for you if you are able to stand up.

Take this bath at least once a week or oftener. It helps the whole system, even to regulating the bowels and kidneys in their action. It is good for the eyes, the nose, the ears, the hair. It relieves all cutaneous affections and is better than medicine.

FOR DANDRUFF

Wash the head, each morning, in *cold water*. You won't catch cold in the head, if you are careful to dry the hair thoroughly before going outside. Indeed, this treatment, if persisted in, will go a long way toward curing catarrh. It is a "sure shot" for dandruff.

LITTLE HELPS FOR HOME-MAKERS

TO FRY SMOKED HAM

Fry in the ordinary way till half done. Then turn grease out of frying-pan into another dish. Put meat back over fire, have ready *boiling* water and cover meat quickly with it, in the frying-pan, allowing it to stand for a minute or two. Turn off water, replace grease, and continue frying till done. The meat will be delightfully soft and nice.

TO CLEAN PAINT BRUSHES

Make a good soap-suds with boiling hot water, then dissolve sal-soda in the water until quite strong. Work the brush in this, changing the mixture if it becomes too thick with paint, always using enough sal-soda, and see if your brush will not be soft and clean, unless it has been used so much that it is a hopeless case.

NATURAL CURE FOR CONSTIPATION

Each night, just before retiring, practice bending exercise, backward and forward, and from side to side; also come to a full squat and rise again, from ten to twenty times. In the morning drink a cup of warm water, in which has been mixed the juice of half a lemon and a pinch of salt. This remedy is especially good for a "lazy liver."

BACKACHE

If you are troubled with pains in the back, try heating a bag of salt in the oven, and taking it to bed with you. Salt heated in this way will retain its warmth for hours. Besides, it has a curative property in itself, which acts upon the kidneys.

FILLING A FOUNTAIN PEN

Next time you fill your fountain pen, after you have filled the barrel and have the tip partly screwed on, turn the pen point down over a piece of blotting paper and finish screwing on the tip in this position. This will *force* out any air bubbles and the pen will not blot.

TO MEND BROKEN CHINA

Bind the broken pieces together with twine, and boil in milk for thirty minutes or more.

FOR INSOMNIA

For insomnia, take a cup of hot milk before retiring.

OVEN COOKING

For next year's canning remember to salt tomatoes and prevent popping, also that apple butter made in the oven requires little stirring. In canning berries I place a pan in the oven to cook while the top of the stove is filled. Fry meat or sausage, also heat dish water in the oven when stove is crowded.

PRACTICAL JELLY-MAKING

Feminine efforts to "hang" the jelly-bag with the aid of chairs, broomsticks and flat-irons are both pathetic and funny. This is how one woman solved the problem and thereby halved the labor of jelly-making:

Take a wooden box at least two feet long and a foot deep; with a hammer split out half of one end and drive a strong nail in the middle of the split edge. Set it up cupboardwise on the table and place a stone jar under the projecting nail. Use a three-cornered jelly-bag of thin flannel or doubled cheese-cloth, and keep it open by pinning the top over a hoop of suitable size—a wooden embroidery hoop is excellent for the purpose. This hoop should rest on the edge of the jar while you pour in your hot fruit; then raise it gently and let it hang from the nail until the juice has run through. Empty and rinse before removing the hoop, turning the bag inside out in the process.

CLEANSING WITH GASOLINE

To secure success in cleansing with gasoline, heat it quite hot by placing the vessel containing the gasoline in another of hot water. Place soiled garment in the hot fluid, cover for a short time and success is assured. Be careful and have no fire or lights near at hand.

PUMPKIN PIE WITHOUT CRUST

For lovers of pumpkin pie with whom pie crust does not agree:

Prepare pumpkin as for ordinary pie. Butter your tins well and sprinkle them with as much corn meal as the butter will take. Pour in prepared pumpkin and bake. Use a little care in removing pieces of pie from the tin to the pie plates.

POTATO SOUP

When I boil peeled potatoes for dinner, I put on plenty of water and cook them thoroughly; then I drain off this water and save it until supper time, when I add a cup of sweet milk and heat to boiling point, adding a generous lump of butter and thicken with two tablespoonfuls of flour rubbed smooth with a little cold milk. Let boil a few minutes, stirring constantly. Serve at once with celery salt for seasoning.

ANOTHER ANT EXTERMINATOR

Thoroughly moisten poison fly-paper and sprinkle with sugar. Put in places most frequented by the ants, and, as the sugar attracts them, great numbers will gather on it and once tasted is sure death to them.

KEEPS SKIPPERS FROM SMOKED MEAT

To prevent skippers in smoked meat, dip the smoked pieces into boiling water for three or four minutes, and while yet moist sprinkle with black pepper, and not a skipper will ever bother the meat.

CLEANING TINTED GLOVES

Put the glove on the hand, take a piece of white flannel and moisten it very lightly with sweet milk. Rub on gently a little white Castile soap and go over the soiled glove until clean. Then rub with a dry flannel cloth.

PLANTING SMALL SEEDS

In planting very delicate flower seeds, fill eggshells with fine dirt, and when nearly full put in the seeds; cover lightly with a little more dirt, keep moist, and when the plants are large enough to transplant, it can be done without disturbing the little delicate roots, as the shell can be broken away instead of digging out the plants.

TO MAKE MEAT TENDER

To make tough meat tender, rub over it at night a small quantity of soda, wash off the next morning and cook.

HOT BRAN BAG

Try using a bag of hot bran, instead of the hot water bag, for the invalid's bed.

SUBSTITUTE FOR CARBON PAPER

Cover one side of a smooth pine board with a thin coat of paste made of common bluing powder and lard. Place in the sun to absorb the lard. When thoroughly dry, place on the board the cloth to which you want the pattern transferred and trace with any sharp pointed instrument that will not injure the cloth—a slate pencil or a wooden skewer will do.

A KNITTING HINT

When doing any piece of knitting the pattern of which requires some of the stitches to be removed to another needle for a time, the worker will find it more convenient to slip the stiches onto a safety pin instead of a knitting needle. When the pin is clasped they cannot slip off, and the pin is not in the way as much as an extra needle.

TO BAKE POTATOES

Before baking potatoes, wash them carefully, pour boiling water over them, and let them stand for three or four minutes. Then wipe them dry. Take small piece of brown paper, dip it in melted fat, and rub all over each potato. They will bake in a fourth less time, and peel as though they had been boiled.

TO RELIEVE DIFFICULT BREATHING

To relieve difficult breathing in case of membranous croup, fill the room of the sufferer with the fumes of vinegar. This can be easily done by pouring vinegar upon hot coals carried through the room on a fire shovel or in a hod. The steam affects the membrane and gives immediate relief.

TO COOK WITHOUT FIRE

The following is so simple that few will try it, but, nevertheless, it is *worth* trying. I took a fifty-pound lard can, (a tight box or old trunk would make a larger cooker) packed it with excelsior (hay or straw would do). Then I soaked some dried peaches one hour, got them to boiling in a tight-lid pail, made a hole in the center of the excelsior, put in the pail of peaches, put a cushion over that and the can lid on and weighted it down. In three hours I took the peaches out, and they were delicious.

To cook beans, soak them over night, then season them and start them to boiling while you are cooking breakfast. Then pack them in your cooker, and do not uncover them until dinner is ready, when you will have a nice dish of hot beans. For those who like oatmeal cooked over night, this is an easy way.

The principle is simple—get the heat and hold it, by packing tightly. Be sure the article to be cooked has reached the boiling point. Don't neglect to put the cushion on, and have the lid tight. Exclude the air and the compressed heat will do the cooking.

ASHES FOR PORTLAND CEMENT

I find by experience that coal ashes are superior to sand for mixing Portland cement. Two, three or even four parts of ashes to one of cement will do good work. Sift ashes for fine work.

QUICK WAY TO LAUNDER CURTAINS

Shake the curtains and spread them out carefully upon the lawn. Pin them down at each scollop with toothpicks. Put on your rubbers, and with the hose spray the curtains thoroughly. This method will not injure them. The sun will soon dry them, and you will be surprised at the result, when you hang them again. This way is especially adapted to heavy curtains.

CHOCOLATE DIP

In making chocolate creams, add a trifle of lard or butter to the "chocolate dip." It will make them easier to manage.

BLACKING A STOVE-PIPE

Have you ever had trouble in blacking the pipe and drum part of your heating stoves? Here is the secret as told me by a hardware dealer:—Do not use blacking, but instead a little sewing machine oil rubbed on with a cloth and polished well. This will work with any sheet-iron or Russia iron parts of stove or pipe.

SAVE ROAST DRIPPINGS

Save all drippings from roast turkey and goose and blend with your lard for fried cakes. Clarify with a potato sliced. This improves the flavor and your cakes will be a golden-brown.

A NEW FRUIT COMBINATION

Prepare, as usual, your pears for canning, but just before filling jars with them, pare carefully all the white covering from several oranges, allowing one large or two small ones to each quart of pears. Separate into sections and drop into the boiling pears, allowing them to remain just long enough to scald through thoroughly. Then fill your jars with pears and oranges, and seal.

A USEFUL PASTE

A useful paste, almost a household necessity, is prepared as follows: Dissolve a small teaspoonful of alum in a pint of warm water, and when it has cooled, add enough flour to make it into a thin paste, stirring it till smooth, then add a pinch of powdered resin and pour on the paste half a cupful of boiling water. When well mixed, and thickened, put into receptacles with covers and store in a dry closet or cupboard. When required to use, soften small quantity with warm water.

SODA IN GRUEL

Just before removing either gruel or hasty pudding from the fire, stir in a pinch of soda. This makes it more easily digested.

NEW APPLICATION FOR BURNS

Milk of magnesia poured onto burns will give immediate relief; then cover burn with plain gauze and keep it saturated with the magnesia. A rapid cure will follow, with little or no scar. Burns caused by electric wires and fire-arms, etc., must be cleansed first with warm water and green soap.

CRABAPPLES FOR MINCEMEAT

Use crabapples for mincemeat. Core and chop without peeling. Much richer than common apple.

COLD COFFEE FOR STOVE BLACKING

Any malleable iron stove if washed in cold coffee will keep black and glossy.

NEW IDEA IN CAKE BAKING

Melt the butter and add to cake or biscuit just before putting into tin, and one need never grease the tin.

TO DESTROY EARTH-WORMS

Fifteen drops of carbolic acid in one pint of water poured over earth in flower-pots will destroy earth-worms.

TO REVIVE WITHERED FLOWERS

Fill a bowl with water so hot that you can scarcely bear your hand in it; throw a little salt in the water and put the flowers in immediately. The effect is wonderful.

ICING FOR CAKE

A good icing that takes no boiling is made by putting a small piece of butter in a bowl with a tablespoonful of hot water. Stir into this powdered sugar until thick enough to spread easily. This will harden and make a splendid cover.

FOR A DAMP CELLAR

If the cellar or house becomes musty from damp weather, do not move out or advertise the place for sale, but put some chloride of lime in a pan, pour over it boiling water, stir to dissolve, then sprinkle about the cellar walls, or saturate cloths with it to use in wiping cupboards, swing shelves or any cellar furniture that would not be injured thereby. Can be used dry. It is an excellent disinfectant and deodorizer.

FOR NEWLY MARRIED COUPLES

It is a pretty custom to speak of the state of marriage as "the sea of matrimony." If a sea, then the home is the ship in which the loving pair sets sail. The husband is perhaps the captain, but upon the wife devolves the duty of keeping the vessel intact, allowing no weak places to develop into leakage as "a small leak will sink a vessel." Leakages of different kinds are likely to occur. We shall look only on the danger of financial leaks. The wife who successfully manages the finances of her home must be familiar with all the details of household economy. One who has learned somewhat in the school where experience rules will give for the benefit of young housekeepers a few hints on repairing leaks. May good health and prosperity attend each married couple who in loving helpfulness assist each other in safeguarding the craft in which lies their hope of happiness. If Darby be the bread-winner, let Joan be the bread-saver. Her task is equally important.

TO MAKE VINEGAR

If you wish to obtain vinegar at small cost, make it from that which is usually thrown away. Procure a large earthenware jar, or keg. Dissolve a pint of sugar in a gallon of warm water. Add a cake of yeast. Cover with a coarse cloth. If air is entirely excluded, fermentation will be slow. Let the jar or keg be the receptacle of rinsings from fruit jars, pans where candy or syrup have been boiled, skimmings from jelly while boiling, etc. When paring apples, put parings to soak for a day or two in warm water, then pour water into jar. After letting fruit drip from jelly bag, to obtain juice for jelly, put bag into crock or large pan, pour water over pulp, shake and mix, then hang and drip again. Pour second dripping into jar. Whenever anything sweet is added, add water also. In two or three weeks, if directions are followed, I predict you will have a large quantity of excellent vinegar. You need never exhaust the supply, if you continue as you began.

SAVE DRY BREAD

If your bread becomes dry, do not throw it away; it is a part of Darby's hard earnings. Dip the dry loaf quickly into water, put in pan, place in oven and leave until crust is dry. The steam from the external moisture will enter the loaf, leaving it fresh as when newly-baked.

TO GLADDEN "SHUT-INS"

Having been an invalid for several months, unable to leave my room, I was greatly cheered and comforted by the gift of a "sunshine bag," forty-five of my friends conspiring together to relieve the monotony of dreary days, and each one sending a little gift, some useful, some merely ornamental, but all most acceptable. Books, perfumery, boxes of note paper, post-card albums, vases, electric night-lamp, bouquet holders, etc. Each one represented the loving thought of the giver, and the hours, before so tedious, were shortened and filled with happy thoughts, as I looked over each article and called to mind the giver. I would like to recommend this as the best kind of medicine for a "shut-in."

TO KEEP DISH-TOWELS WHITE

If you wish to keep your dish-towels white, do not allow the dish water to dry in them, each time they are used, but wash them with naphtha soap. I have found no other soap so good for the purpose.

TO SAVE BATTER

If you have mixed more pancake batter than can be used at one time, set it aside and use next day by adding more milk, flour and soda, allowing an extra quantity of soda for the fermentation of the "kept over" batter.

SHEARS IN THE KITCHEN

Hang on a convenient nail in your kitchen a pair of sharp, medium-sized shears, and with them trim the rind from slices of bacon, clipping the edges as they fry, to prevent curling. Trim the edges of your steak before cooking, and cut out the bones with these shears. When lining pie-tins with pastry, trim the margin with your shears; also cut openings in the top crust to let steam escape. Cut your left-overs of meat for meat pie in strips or cubes; your "croutons" from bread slices with these shears, thus saving many a cut with a sharp knife when hastily used.

TO COLOR PUTTY

After glass is put in and the putty properly smoothed off, take a fine bristle brush and dust on a goodly quantity of dry paint powder, using the same color as sash is painted (lampblack is most commonly used, as that is the color of most sashes). Be careful to have paint powder cover all parts of putty. Tip sash up and dust off surplus. The oil in the putty retains enough of the powder to make it the color of it. The powder also absorbs the oil that is on the glass. This is a much better way than using oil paint.

CURE FOR CROUP

Keep a brick in the stove oven. If the children are suddenly taken with croup, wrap a flannel around the brick, then pour hot vinegar over it, and the fumes of the steaming hot vinegar will clear the air passage. It will have a quicker effect if the head is covered to keep in the steam. Another good home remedy for croup is a small spoonful of sugar with a little powdered alum sprinkled over it. It will quickly relieve croup and bring up the phlegm.

TO STOP HICCOUGHS

For troublesome hiccoughs try a teaspoonful of granulated sugar and three drops of vinegar or lemon juice.

CLEANSING PANAMA HATS

Wash the hat well in Ivory soap, then take an old toothbrush and apply dioxygen; put in the sun for few hours and soon you will see the hat as good as new.

SALAD MAKING

In making salads, do not chop your meats and celery in a chopping bowl—cut into the desired sized pieces with scissors. This is quicker, neater an' cleaner than the old way.

TO COLLECT EARTH-WORMS FOR BAIT

Take water in which walnut hulls have soaked over night and pour it on a spot of ground. In a very few hours the worms will come to the surface in large numbers.

CURE FOR SLEEPLESSNESS

Sleeplessness is often caused by the head being exposed to the cold, whi'~ the rest of the body is warm. In nine cases out of ten, if the head is covere\ with a silk handkerchief, it will induce the much desired sleep.

RUGS THAT "CREEP"

To keep an art square or ingrain rug smoothly on the floor, place under it an old carpet a trifle smaller than the rug. Tack the corners of the under one to the floor if desired; the upper one will cling to it and keep its place much better than if laid on the bare floor.

RELIEVES EAR-ACHE

Put two or three live coals in an old teacup and sprinkle granulated sugar over them. Place a funnel over it, and let the steam and smoke go into the ear through the tube or neck of the funnel. It cannot injure the ear, and always affords relief quickly.

FEATHER PILLOWS

When changing feathers from one tick to another simply press the feathers back from one corner for about six inches, and baste firmly before ripping open the seam. Sew the new tick to within the same distance. Then overhand the seams of the two ticks together, pull out the bastings from the full one and shake feathers into the new tick. When all the feathers are in the new tick, baste firmly before ripping apart. In this way feathers are easily managed without flying about the room.

TO COLOR LACE ECRU

Old white lace or silk gloves may be given a beautiful ecru color by first washing and then dipping them in plain table tea; the stronger the tea the deeper the color.

A GOOD HOUSEHOLD SOAP

To every pound of potash used add one-half pound of borax and a few drops of carbolic acid, according to strength of the acid, stirring in the two last ingredients just at the finish, either in boiled or cold made soap and the resultant soap will be superior to any soap for general purposes, as the housewife is certain of the condition and quality of fat used. If fresh mutton-tallow be used, it makes a good healing soap for workingmen's use.

TO STOP HICCOUGHS

Ten drops of camphor in half a cupful of hot sweetened water will usually relieve a bad case. Repeat in ten minutes if necessary, but usually it isn't. For the baby one to three drops will be enough. Even dropping some on a handkerchief and laying it near the baby's face has been effective.

FLY-PAPER SEASON

When it becomes necessary to use fly-paper try this method and see how much trouble will be saved. Tack the sheets of fly-paper to thin boards. In this way they are not carried across the room by a stray breeze and landed sticky-side down on the floor or furniture.

TO KEEP MEAT FRESH

After butchering and thoroughly cooling, wrap the meat in paper, and bury in a grain bin. This will keep beef or pork fresh for months.

WATER FOR CAKES

Water is much better for making cakes than milk. Hot water should always be used in making sponge cake. A cake made with hot water will not be tough.

TO CLEAN A CLOCK

Saturate a piece of cotton as large as an egg with coal oil, put on the floor of the clock and shut tight. In four or six days you will see the works clean as new and the cotton black with particles of dirt which have been loosened by the kerosene fumes.

HOW TO WASH COLORED BLANKETS

To wash blankets so the colors will not run, use *rain water* whenever practicable (in this country, like the poor, "we have it always with us"), with a half-pint of ammonia to a tub of water. It "sets" the colors while loosening the dirt.

CURE FOR GRIPPE

Garlic eaten raw will cure a cold in the head, grippe or influenza in the first stages, but in cases where prejudiced people refuse to test its virtues, Irish moss lemonade made after the well-known flaxseed lemonade recipe and taken for both meat and drink stands next on the list. Pineapple juice will relieve inflammation of the throat in the most advanced and chronic cases, and cure all ordinary attacks. In both membranous croup and diphtheria, pure pineapple juice, either from the raw or canned fruit, will cure when the entire apothecary shop has been tried and found wanting.

KEEPING POTATOES IN WINTER

To keep sweet potatoes through the winter perfectly, line a barrel with warm dry newspapers, side and bottom, then wrap each potato in paper and pack into it, till full, cover well and keep in warm dry kitchen or any warm dry room. A smaller quantity may be packed in a box in the same way, and kept in warm dry atmosphere. To keep Irish potatoes in the cellar, sprinkle air-slacked lime among them; it seems to keep them dry and healthy. (As they are sorted, sprinkle a little in every layer).

WHEN BAKING

If a handful of salt is put on bottom of oven under pans when baking gingerbread or any cake easily burned, it will prevent burning.

Putting a pinch of salt in the coffee improves the flavor.

SAVE ENAMEL WARE

If any food has stuck or scorched on the bottom of enamelled ware, do not scrape but rub hard soap all over it and put cold water in and cover, setting on the stove to heat, when all can be easily washed off and the kettle be as smooth as new. If very badly scorched, it may need two applications of the soap and cold water.

BRIGHTENS STRAW MATTING AND OILCLOTH

Wash matting twice during the summer with salt and water, say about a pint of salt dissolved in about a pailful of warm, soft water, drying the matting quickly with a cloth. The salt will prevent it from turning yellow. After oilcloths are scrubbed and dried, they should be rubbed all over with a cloth dipped in milk. You will be surprised at the brightness.

TO CLEAN FLOUR SACKS

Put a tablespoonful of kerosene into two quarts of soap-suds and boil up your new flour sacks in the same, and they will be left white, with all the colored lettering gone.

FOR THE ARTIST

When paint has been allowed to harden on the palette, put the board in the oven long enough for the oils to soften, when it can be scraped off with a knife and then cleaned with some sort of scouring soap and polished with boiled oil.

When you are through with your brushes for the day, wash them thoroughly in soap and water.

IN THE LAUNDRY

In doing laundry work whether you wash on a board or with a machine, cool the water so you can bear your hands in it before you put the clothes into it. Why? Because by putting white clothes in hot or boiling water for the first suds, a tinge will be left on them which cannot be washed out.

When you launder fine table linen, never wring it through the wringer; if you do, creases will be pressed in that cannot be ironed out; always wring it by hand.

MAKING A RESTAURANT OF A HOME

Statistics say that only fourteen per cent. of American homes have hired help. If the figures be correct, eighty-six married women out of every hundred are getting their own meals and puzzling more or less over the same problems. Doubtless the majority of them labor self-sacrificingly and unselfishly, keeping house as best they know how or as best they can under their conditions; but often there is a sad lack of applied common-sense. For instance, many consult only the comfort and pleasure of their families, leaving themselves entirely out of the calculation. They are just as foolish and short-sighted as the selfish women.

Any number of these over-kind mothers serve breakfast and sometimes other meals as though they were running a restaurant, allowing each member of the family, young and old, to come downstairs at his or her own sweet will, clamoring for a *hot* meal at once. The results are many, and all bad. The children form habits of selfishness, laziness and irregular rising; good food is wasted or spoiled by standing; the mother becomes literally a servant; the day's work has a broken beginning; and the family has missed the cheery gathering that would have had a strong influence for good upon the whole day. A happy breakfast, during which plans for the day are discussed, means much to the harmony of feeling and action among the members of a home. We need to know where each will be and what each is doing; besides, how do we know what may happen to our scattered flock ere the sun goes down?

Of course when the children are mere babies, it is better for them and for the mother's work that they sleep as long as possible; then the parents can have the first meal together undisturbed; but when a child is old enough to go to school, he should be up at the usual breakfast hour. Indeed, if he has any home studying to do, it is far better to get an hour for it in the early morning when the mind is fresh and the recitation time nearer than to sit up, tired and sleepy, endeavoring to do night work. "Early to bed and early to rise" is the wisest of rules for the school boy and girl. Good health demands a regular, reasonable hour for rising, and we all realize that our *best* work, be it mental or manual, is done before ten o'clock.

But I am pleading for the child's early, regular rising for the mother's sake rather than its own. To serve a meal "on the installment plan" is really a difficult thing. It is also unnecessary (except in unusual cases), and a mistaken kindness to the members of her family. It is rank injustice to herself as well. A housekeeper's work is wearing enough under any circumstances, so there is no sense in prolonging the meal-getting and dish-washing, and thereby adding to her burden of care and worry.

In the average American home, be it mean or "of means," we have no place for either "ladies of leisure" nor for slaves. Our households must be managed in such a way that burdens are shared and equalized as nearly as possible, each member consulting the comfort and welfare of the rest as well as of self. Only so can our homes be the refuge of which we dream, the quiet harbors into which all can float at nightfall for anchorage, where the ugly barnacles gathered out in the open sea can be rubbed off, and a fresh cargo of new courage taken on board.

WHEN USING CANNED GOODS

Much of the danger which we anticipate from using canned vegetables can be avoided by washing them thoroughly. All kinds of course will not admit of a bath, but beets, peas, spinach or string beans I always empty from the can into a colander and hold it under the faucet until they are well rinsed, after which I heat and season them and serve fearlessly.

AUNT DINAH'S RECIPE

(Given before the war)

Yes, chile, dat cake *is* good to eat,
But shuah you doan want no receet,
Still, since dey say you'se goin' orf,
To lib in dat cold frozen norf,
I'll try an' see if I kin fix it
So yo'se pore white trash gal can mix it.

You takes some butter—jess enuff—
Too little makes de mixin' tuff;
Den aigs—now wait, an' le' me see—
Sometimes it's two and sometimes free,
Jess as de hens to lay hab chuse;
One cup or mo' of suga' use;
'Bout half a cup o' milk den add,
An' stir it roun' an' roun' like mad,
But jiss one way, for doan you see
De bakin' else will heaby be.
Raisins and currants, citron, too,
A berry little brandy'll do;
Somehow dat allus seems a waste,
Special if I once gets a taste,
Right smart o' spice, a pinch o' salt,
An' now you'd better call a halt
An' see if somefin dere be not
W'ich in your haste yo' done forgot.
Laws, yes! Some bakin' powder sift in,
Or else your cake will hab no liftin'.
Stir berry hard, turn out an' bake,
An' honey'll hab Aunt Dinah's cake.

FOR WEAK EYES

To one quart of cold water add one heaping teaspoonful of cream of tartar, one ditto of sugar (white). Let settle and bathe the eyes freely, flooding the liquid into them. This is excellent.

TO DARN STOCKINGS

Place a piece of mosquito netting or finer mesh over the hole and then darn through the meshes. It will make a disagreeable task much easier.

TO MAKE A HOLE IN GLASS

Press upon the glass a cake of wet clay and make a hole the desired size through the clay, laying bare the glass at the bottom. Pour melted lead into the hole and it will drop through the glass and leave a perfectly smooth, round hole.

CURE FOR JAUNDICE

Bayberry root or bark is a sure cure for jaundice. Steep well and extract all the goodness possible. Drink freely of this bitter liquid. Many years ago this cured the writer's mother of the severest attack, and of recent years a lady residing in Lowell, Mass.

SAVING ON LONG GLOVES

Long gloves are costly and often wear through on the finger tips after a very little time. If one cuts off the gloves at the wrist, a pair of ordinary length gloves can be sewed to them, and the seam being almost imperceptible, the gloves are practically as good as new at one-third the cost.

TO PREVENT A FELON

On the first sensation like the prick of a briar, wind the finger tight (a few long hairs are best). When very red, press hard with fingers of the other hand, as long as it can be well borne, loosen, repeat if necessary, and there will be no felon.

MOIST COOKING UTENSILS

If on taking up vegetables, etc., one has not time to fill utensil with water, turn upside down on a table, and it will keep moist for hours.

TO PREVENT A RUN-AROUND

When a throbbing pain is felt at the corner of the nail, with needle or sharp point of a knife (do not use a pin) open it close to the nail and squeeze until a little moisture exudes. If, in a few hours, the pain is still there, repeat and there will be no run-around.

TWO WAYS TO COOK EGGS

First way:—Cover the eggs with cold water, put over the fire and when they come to a boil they are done.

Second way:—Pour boiling water over eggs, set on back of stove for half an hour. They are tender and delicious.

TO CLEANSE A SKIRT

Having the misfortune to buy a black bunting skirt which seemed to have been improperly cleansed of the natural wool grease, I tried *completely immersing* and thoroughly washing it in a couple of gallons of gasoline; then I let it drip dry on the clothesline; since then I have had no trouble whatever with it catching the dust. After the first few wearings I felt it was ruined, as it looked gray with dust and the more I brushed the worse it looked, but since cleaning with gasoline, it keeps as free from dust as any goods possibly can, and best of all, the gasoline never wrinkles the goods, as water does, so every crease in the pleats was as perfect as before wetting it.

THE EVER USEFUL MEAT CHOPPER

Having some blackberries that I wanted to use for jam, and my fruit-press being out of commission, it seemed to me a big undertaking to rub them all through a colander, as there were ten quarts of them, so at the suggestion of my daughter, I put them through the *meat chopper*, and it answered the purpose well. No stained hands nor soiled sleeves.

BAKING SODA ON THE TOILET TABLE

If a pinch of baking soda is applied under the arm-pits after washing, it will positively eliminate all odor of perspiration. This is much more economical and effectual than some of the high-priced powders.

FOR BURNS

Save your egg-shells until through cooking. The white left in the shells is one of the best things to apply to a small burn. Apply two or three times. You will have no trouble from these little burns.

CATNIP TEA FOR COLIC

A little weak catnip is very good for the little baby's colic. It is also a slight laxative.

ROSIN FOR WORMS

Give your child a piece of rosin to eat, a little every day, if he is troubled with worms. It is perfectly harmless and will destroy the nests as well as the worms. An old Indian doctor recommended this, and I have found nothing else as effective.

FOR SUDDEN DEAFNESS

For sudden and unaccountable deafness: Dissolve a tablespoonful cooking soda in one-half cupful boiling water. Every morning, for a week or two, take out one-half teaspoonfu' of this, suitably warm, into it drop five drops pure glycerine and pour into the ear, and hold the head over until none runs out. At the end of a week or two, syringe the ear thoroughly with warm water. These two remedies have been successfully tested in my own family.

FOR A SQUEAKING DOOR

Rub soap on bottom of sill; if the difficulty lies in the hinges, dip a feather in kerosene and apply, swinging door to and fro gently.

WASHING HANDKERCHIEFS

Soak badly soiled handkerchiefs a half hour or more in a basin of warm water to which has been added a generous handful of salt. All that is objectionable will be removed, and they may then be washed as usual.

A POINTER FOR THE BOYS

When my twin boys demanded their "rain" shoes recently I was discouraged to find that they wouldn't go on their feet. "They are too little," I said. "Nonsense," said Grandma, "they are only stiff; they have been put away without being properly oiled. Apply equal parts of kerosene and castor oil with a woolen cloth and then see how easily they will slip on." I did so and the boys were happy with their "castor-oiled" shoes.

KEEPING HAT FLOWERS FRESH

When the flowers begin to fade on your summer hat, don't take them off and destroy them, but simply try your water-colors on them, and you will find them quickly restored to their natural beauty. Touch up each flower with the original color, making them much brighter—as water-colors dry much lighter. The water will not take the stiffness out of the flowers. This is a good and inexpensive way to keep your hats looking fresh.

RIDDING A LAWN OF ANTS

To rid the lawn and other places infested with pismires (ants), secure a bottle of bi-sulphide of carbon (at any drug store). Make a hole in the center of a common-size ant's nest with a stick or other instrument—say one inch in diameter—reaching to the bottom of the nest. Into this hole pour three dessertspoonsful of the liquid, and close the top of the opening. Large nests will require more holes and liquid. After twenty years of strenuous efforts with kerosene, hot water, etc., with little success except to deface the lawn, my troubles ended with the use of the above liquid and method of its use. Use for reptiles and ground animals, rats, etc.

PREVENTING TEA STAINS

Put a lump of sugar in the teapot and it will prevent tea staining any damask, however fine, over which it may be spilled.

CUTTING SOAP EASILY

To cut soap easily, first dip the knife in boiling water.

FILLING SALT CELLARS

Salt and pepper shakers can be quickly and neatly filled by the use of a small funnel placed in the mouth of each.

PREVENTS SOGGY PIE-CRUST

Pie-crust will not be soggy if brushed over with the white of an egg before the fruit is put in.

REMOVING INK STAINS

A Chinese plan for removing ink stains from cloth is to wash them with boiled rice. Rub the rice on the stain as you would soap, and wash with clear water. If the first application is not effective, repeat the process. We have found this to work like magic, even upon stains not discovered until perfectly dry.

WHISKEY FOR A BOIL

Keep a cloth saturated with whiskey upon a boil, and it will "head" in from two to three hours.

LITTLE HELPS FOR HOME-MAKERS

A CLOTHES-PIN APRON

It is made of common bed-ticking and has two large pockets. This is much handier than a box or basket, for the apron can be buttoned on, and the pins are always in reach. I put the pins into the pockets when gathering in the clothes and have a special nail to hang it on.

SUGGESTIONS

To prevent the oilcloth sticking to the table, first cover the table with common wrapping paper.

Anything mixed with water requires a hotter fire than if mixed with milk.

Paste made with laundry starch is best for scrap books. It will not grow yellow with age.

To clean alpaca, sponge with strained coffee. Iron on the wrong side.

Whole cloves are better for exterminating moths than either tobacco or camphor.

APPLES IN MANY DISHES

For apple pies select tart, mellow apples. Pare and slice enough to fill a rich crust. Then to a generous half cup of granulated sugar add a tablespoonful of flour and stir thoroughly together, and spread over the sliced apples. Over this dot small lumps of butter before covering with crust. We prefer them without flavoring or spice, which destroys the fine apple flavor.

We boil apples, taking large, perfect ones. First, make a syrup of sugar and water in a basin. Drop the apples, without peeling, into the boiling syrup, and cover with a plate or other tight cover, and place on the back part of the stove where they will cook slowly. When done through, but not broken, remove and pour the hot syrup over them.

Sweet and sometimes sour apples whole, without paring, make spiced sweet pickles nearly as good as peaches.

For breakfast relish take perfect ones and remove the cores with an apple corer. Slice about half an inch thick and fry in butter. After browning on one side, turn, and when nearly done sprinkle with sugar.

For an apple salad, pare and chop, not too fine, mixing with them English walnut meats, also chopped. Cover with mayonnaise dressing.

For a very nice jelly, slice apples without paring, but remove the cores. Proceed as for other fruit jellies.

One year when canning peaches we had a quantity of juice left over. So we made ready some apples and put them into the juice, stewed them down thick, and canned as other fruit. We found it very finely flavored.

In the spring we endeavor to save what apples we may have on hand, by fixing and canning them in self-sealing cans, for sauce or pies for summer use.

When fixing a quantity of apples we always save the clean parings, and after stewing them well, sweeten and strain the juice and add it to our vinegar. It helps us to make cider vinegar.

TO KEEP FLANNELS FROM SHRINKING

Soak flannels in cold water forty-eight hours. Set them on the stove in the same water and let it come to a boil. Remove and let stand twelve hours. After this treatment your flannels will remain just the size they were when you bought them.

OLD PHOTOGRAPHS

There are very few homes which have not numerous old photographs too precious to be thrown away, yet of interest to few besides the immediate family. These generally take up too much space to be kept where they can be gotten at conveniently, and so are carefully put in boxes in the store-room or attic, to be kept from the dust. So when we would gladly spend a few moments looking on the familiar faces and scenes, alas! it is too much trouble to get them out. Here is one solution of the problem: Put the photographs in clear, hot water, and in a short time the pictures can be easily removed from the cards. When dry, either trim down the picture (to economize space) or cut away the background entirely. This last requires care, but can be done without destroying the outline. Mount these in a scrap-book, or better still, a book made especially for kodak pictures. This book (or these books if more than one is needed) can be made very interesting by clever arrangement of the pictures, grouping relatives, school friends, army comrades, babies, out-of-door scenes, etc., in different portions of the book.

SHOE COMFORT

To make new shoes comfortable, moisten the lining of the shoes or the stocking worn with alcohol and wear the shoes while drying. This makes the lining of the shoe stretch to fit the foot and prevents the pinching often caused by the lining alone. By using alcohol there is no danger of taking cold.

KETTLE COVERS

Of all dishes, kettle covers are the most troublesome, when not in use. Try this: Make a large pocket of oil-cloth, binding strong with heavy braid; tack in a handy place near the cook-stove and you can see just the cover you want without handling all the others.

SIMPLE FURNITURE POLISH

The following is the finest furniture polish I have ever known. Take one part turpentine, one part kerosene and one part vinegar and apply to furniture with flannel cloth, and then polish with soft flannel

USE OF FLAVORING EXTRACTS

Flavoring extracts should not be added to sauce until it is cold; if put in while hot, much of the flavor passes off with the steam.

TO KEEP GREEN VEGETABLES FRESH

To keep lettuce, celery, cucumbers, etc., fresh several days, without ice, fold them loosely in a damp cloth. In this way they will keep even crisper than when put on ice.

TO PEEL PEACHES

When canning peaches place a dozen at a time in a pan, pour over them boiling water, let stand two or three minutes, then pour off the water; the thin skin of the peach will peel off easily and the fruit will not be soft or mushy.

LAMP WICKS

A dull knife will trim lamp wicks evenly and without waste. Scrape the wicks from each end toward the middle.

DIGESTIBLE CABBAGE

Cabbage is made digestible by first slicing and then putting in boiling water with a pinch of soda and some salt, and boiling just fifteen minutes.

DEFECTIVE FRUIT CANS

When fruit cans are defective, run white wax—melted—around the top where metal and rubber unite. It has proven a sure remedy, is easily applied with a spoon and can be repeated many times.

TENDER PINEAPPLES

The toughness of pineapples is almost entirely eliminated by slicing the fruit up and down, from stem to blossom end, instead of through the core as is usually done. Thrust a fork into the blossom end to hold the apple steady and slice until you come to the hard, pithy core which can then be discarded. This trick was taught me by an old pineapple grower and makes all the difference in the world in the tenderness of this fruit, which is usually hard and chippy when sliced with instead of against the grain.

PREPARING PUMPKIN FOR PIE

In cooking pumpkin for pies or drying, if it seems watery, run it through the colander, then strain it through a cloth, and it will be found fine and dry.

BUTTONS THAT STAY ON

Place a pin across the top of the button, and sew over that, thus holding the thread so that when the pin is removed the button is not close to the cloth; then wrap the thread a few times around the stem thus formed. The buttons will stay on as long as the garment lasts.

BRIGHT FRYING PANS

Boil a little vinegar in them before washing.

HINT FOR WALKERS

If you are going to take a long walk, first rub that side of your stocking which is next to your feet well with soap, and your feet will never blister.

WIRE CHAIR BOTTOMS

To bottom worn-out chairs, get a piece of common chicken wire netting, cut in the shape of the chair bottom you wish to put it in; only let it be two inches larger all around than the size of the chair; turn in the edges and tack, just as you would a wooden bottom. Your chair will be far more comfortable and the expense is almost nothing. For a rocking chair a light cushion is an addition. Since using the wire I have entirely discarded wooden bottoms for chairs.

KEEPING RHUBARB FRESH

Rhubarb can be kept fresh and crisp several days by standing the stalks in a pitcher, or other vessel, of cold water. By some people it is kept many months, uncooked, by canning in cold water.

HOT CAKES WITHOUT MILK

When boiling potatoes save your potato water, add an egg, salt and a large spoonful of sugar and mix it slowly; then add your baking powder and you will find your cakes lighter and better than when made with milk.

LITTLE HELPS FOR HOME-MAKERS

TO BOIL VEGETABLES

When cooking lima beans, rice, etc., it is very provoking to have them foam and sputter from the kettle onto one's clean stove. Drop into the kettle a small lump of butter and there will be no "boiling over."

OLIVE OIL IN BAKED BEANS

Use five full tablespoons of olive oil to one quart of dry beans. They are delicious and more easily digested than when pork is used.

WHEN THE CAKE BURNS

When baking a cake, if the under side becomes slightly burned, take a lemon grater and rub over the burned portion, so removing it without breaking the cake, as usually happens when a knife is used.

USES OF BUTTERMILK

Should you be so unfortunate as to be poisoned by poison ivy, bathe the affected parts in buttermilk every ten or fifteen minutes until the poison is counteracted. Should the case be a severe one, poultice the blisters with bread and buttermilk poultice. It will give relief very soon and will cure the most severe cases.

Buttermilk will remove mildew from cloth, white or colored. Soak the garment over night, then lay it on the grass in the sunlight. If the stain is set, soak the cloth for two or three days and lay it in the sun.

Buttermilk is excellent for freshening salt pork for frying. Slice the pork and soak over night, or set on stove and let it come to a boil, dip in flour and fry.

TO REVIVE WILTED ROSES

Wilted roses, seemingly fit only for the rubbish heap, may be completely revived and freshened. Put the stems of the roses in a tumbler of water, and then place the tumbler and roses in a vessel of sufficient size to allow the entire bouquet to be covered. Cover the vessel tightly and leave undisturbed for twenty-four hours. By that time the roses will be found all fresh and invigorated as if just plucked from the bushes, with every petal covered with artificial dew. Wilted lettuce may also be freshened and kept in excellent condition for weeks if treated in the same way.

NAIL PUNCTURES

In case you should step on a rusty nail, tack or pin, just set your foot in a basin of kerosene. It will save the doctor's bill and suffering.

CAKE WITHOUT EGGS

One-half cup of butter, one cup of sugar, two cups of flour, one cup of sweet milk, two teaspoonfuls of baking powder, one teaspoonful of vanilla. Mix and bake in layers with any desired filling.

SMOKY LAMPS

To prevent the smoking of a lamp, soak the wick in strong vinegar, and dry it well before using. It will then burn both sweet and pleasant.

TO FASTEN LABELS ON TIN

Allow one-half ounce of tragacanth and two ounces of acacia to stand in one-half pint of water until the acacia has been dissolved, then strain and add two ounces of glycerine, in which seven grains of thymol are suspended. Shake the mixture well and add sufficient water to make one pint.

This separates on standing, but by shaking once or twice it is mixed sufficiently for use.

WASHING SILK UNDERWEAR

Articles made of silk should always be washed in tepid water and the soap used on them should not be caustic. White castile soap or any good white soap will answer. If the silks are to be kept white, ammonia should not be used as it gives a yellow tinge; a little borax, however, may be used. If the silk is of an ecru shade ammonia may be employed.

Never rub silk garments on the board in washing; always rub them with the hands. Make a strong suds of tepid water and add to it one teaspoonful of borax, which has been dissolved in a pint of boiling water. This is enough for two pailsful of suds. Put the silk garments into it and let stand for twenty minutes or half an hour, then wash them with the hands. Rinse in two waters, run through the wringer and hang them out. When a little more than half dried, take them in and spread on a sheet. Roll them up tightly, let them stand about an hour and then press them. Use a rather cool iron and have a clean white cloth or brown paper between the iron and silk.

EGG FOR AN INVALID

Beat the yolk and white separately until extremely light, add a pinch of salt, pour into a china cup, which set in a saucepan of hot water, stirring constantly till scalded, but not cooked. When this is done slowly, the egg just thickens slightly, but puffs up until the cup is almost filled with creamy custard. Set in the oven a moment and serve at once.

FRIED SQUASH

Cut the squash into thin slices, dip into egg, powder with cracker dust and fry in boiling lard. It fries very crisp and makes a delightful substitute for meat now and then.

CURE FOR CONSUMPTION

I lost two daughters by consumption. This recipe is what I think saved the third, who came home from Normal school pale, weak, having no appetite, with a bad cough and a rise of temperature of one and one-half degrees every day.

Break one fresh egg into an ordinary sized tumbler, beat well, add one tablespoonful of granulated sugar, beat again, add the juice of one half a lemon, fill up the glass with water and stir well. To be taken morning, noon and night; after a few days give the patient a glass midway between the others, and so on until from eight to nine glasses can be taken daily. The egg and sugar nourish, the lemon juice stimulates the stomach to digest and the water supplies the moisture the fever is burning up.

Drugs cannot cure consumption. If the stomach can assimilate food and the patient will live in the open air and sunshine only is there hope. Try this in time and the patient will be saved, and you will thank God for the "little help."

RELIEF FOR CROUP

One tablespoonful of lard and one-half teaspoonful of essence of peppermint thoroughly mixed, put in a dish and placed over lamp or Giant Heater to heat, and applied while warm to throat and chest, will relieve a "croupy" child.

CLEANSING FLUID

Dissolve one-sixth of an ounce of saltpeter in one quart of soft water, add one ounce of ammonia (liquid), one ounce of bay rum. Put in bottle, cork tight, apply with sponge.

TO KEEP TINS FROM RUSTING

Tin vessels used in water often rust. This can be prevented by greasing well and baking in oven. They will not rust then, no matter how much used in water. Care should be taken not to burn the vessel.

TO SAVE PLANTS

To prevent bugs from eating your cucumber vines, plant one stalk of garlic in each cucumber hill; nothing will then bother the plant.

SHAWL KNITTED IN TWO COLORS

Wind a skein each of two colors into a ball, knitting as one thread. Cast on eighty stitches and make scarf two yards long. Crochet a scallop for the long edge. Fringe the short ends with a fringe of twenty chain in two colors.

NEW WAY OF COOKING BEANS

Take one pint dry white beans, boil until tender, as for baked beans, then allow the water to boil away and season and mash with potato masher. Pack tightly in a dish and when thoroughly cold, cut in slices and serve.

SEWING HINTS

To prevent machine stitching from drawing or puckering, soak a spool of thread in a cup of water for six hours, then dry before using.

If colored thread is oiled with machine oil it will be stronger and work more easily.

WHEN COOKING OYSTERS

Never salt for soups or stews until just before removing from the fire.

In frying oysters a little baking powder added to the cracker crumbs will greatly improve them.

Escalloped oysters retain their flavor better if covered while cooking.

Half the liquor, heated, or hot milk, may be poured over escalloped oysters when half baked.

It is always better to handle oysters with a fork, as contact with the hands may make them tough.

PERSPIRATION STAINS

Gingham or other colored shirtwaists that have become discolored by perspiration under the arms may be restored by soaking the waist an hour or two in cold water, then use plenty of cornmeal to rub the places—instead of soap—when washing.

WHEN MAKING BERRY JAM

I wash and pick my berries and before heating I take my wire potato masher and mash them thoroughly. When all nicely mashed I stir in my sugar. Then I put on the stove and just let it come to the boil, stirring so it will heat evenly. I let it boil about three minutes and then can in glass jars same as I would any fruit and I find after two years my jams taste just like fruit right off the vine. I never again would stand and stir jams by the hour in the old way.

COOKIES WON'T BURN

Keep your cookies from burning on the bottom. Turn the baking pan upside down and bake on the bottom of the pan and you will never do any other way.

CANNING PIE PLANT

Pick when it is long and good, cut up and put in glass fruit cans, press down, cover with cold water, seal and put away. It will keep fresh until the new crop comes. In sections where the fruit is scarce, it can be easily raised, and is easily kept as described.

PICNIC SANDWICHES

Bake the bread in quart cans and press the chopped meat or chicken in cans of the same size. When both are cold put very thin slices of the meat between two buttered slices of the bread. If your bread and meat are good, you will be proud of your sandwiches.

OIL PICKLES

Twenty-five medium sized cucumbers, sliced thin—not pared; one-quarter teacupful black mustard seed; one tablespoonful celery salt; one-quarter teacupful white mustard seed; one-quarter teacupful table salt; three pints vinegar; one cupful olive oil. Pack in small jar and let stand one week before using.

TO CLEAN LACES

Clean delicate white laces with calcined magnesia: Sprinkle the lace thickly on both sides. Lay it on a sheet of heavy writing paper, place a second sheet over it and put it away within the leaves of a heavy book for four or five days. Then shake off the powder and the lace will be clean.

Laces can be whitened by soaking in soap suds in the sun. They should never be rubbed but soused up and down very gently and squeezed between the hands until they are only damp, not dry.

To clean white silk laces soak in skimmed milk over night, souse in warm soap suds, carefully rinse, then pull out and press down while damp.

Black lace may be cleaned with one teaspoonful of borax to a pint of warm water. Don't dry it near a fire; heat is apt to make it rusty. Gold and silver laces can be cleaned with stale bread crumbs mixed with powdered blue. To a half loaf of bread take one-quarter of a pound of the powdered blue. Sprinkle thickly over the lace and let stand for some time. Brush off and brush lightly with a piece of velvet. Laces are given a creamy color by putting small quantities of strained coffee or powdered saffron in the rinsing water until the right cream or ecru color or shade is produced.

TO BURN OUT SOOT

If newspapers saturated with kerosene are put on top of the cook stove just under the lids and back of the draft in the pipe and fired, the accumulated soot will burn out.

TO IMPROVE RHUBARB

One-half tablespoon of cornstarch dissolved and added to rhubarb when done cooking takes away the disagreeable feeling rhubarb leaves on the teeth, a very objectionable feature of that plant.

CURE FOR "RUN-AROUND"

Mutton tallow and white chalk mixed and bound on the finger is a sure cure for run-around. The same is an excellent remedy for felons if applied when first started.

A CURE FOR BURNS

Turpentine and camphor gum—all the gum the turpentine will cut—applied to a burn will take out the fire, and heal it up, no matter how bad the burn, and will not leave a scar.

ENRICHING GRAVY

If the chicken or meat lacks in richness, the gravy may be made excellent by beating an egg with a little milk and adding to the gravy with the flour.

NOVEMBER SUGGESTIONS TO FLOWER GROWERS

A supply of materials for protecting bulb beds and all tender or half-hardy plants or shrubs, should be secured during this month. As it is the alternate freezing and thawing of early spring which does the greatest damage, the work of covering may be left until very late in the season, but in localities where protection is needed, snow will probably interfere with the work of securing the covering material if not done soon.

A cover to shield from the sun, and so prevent an early flow of sap, or thawing of the soil, is what is needed; care should be taken that it does not pack solid and exclude air. Boughs from evergreen trees are the best covering, but if these are not available any small branches may be put over the beds and leaves thrown over them. Corn stalks, hay, or straw may be used; but the seeds in such materials are a bait for rats and mice which may injure plants.

It is a good plan to get soil for winter use after a slight freeze, as insects go down to avoid the cold near the surface, and fewer will be taken with the soil.

LITTLE HELPS FOR HOME-MAKERS

Prepare a quantity of fine soil for the seed pans to be used early in the spring; keep it moist and warm until every weed seed has sprouted, then set it out where they will "freeze to death."

This method of getting rid of the weeds is better than heating the soil, for the reason that a degree of heat sufficient to kill the seeds will liberate and waste elements of the soil which are essential to plant growth.

To cut away diseased branches of foliage and leave it lying on the ground is a sure way of spreading whatever disease they were affected with. Burning these, and everything in the way of dead vegetation, lessens next year's work to a marked degree, for it destroys millions of weed seeds, insects and eggs, as well as destroying their hiding places.

Ashes from such materials contain a large percentum of phosphate and are one of the best fertilizers for a lawn.

If the ordering of Easter lily (Lilium Harrisii) bulbs has been neglected, do not think it is too late, but find out if Easter comes on one of its late dates next year and order accordingly. There is a great difference in the size of bulbs and a seemingly disproportionate difference in the price, but the one who pays the price and gets the largest and soundest bulbs, will get more beauty from them than could be had from several times the money if invested in a greater number of small bulbs.

Lilies need very rich soil, but if barn-yard fertilizers are used they must be well rotted, and put below the soil surrounding the bulb. As a rule, it is better to give liquid fertilizers after the buds have started than to risk burning the roots.

A pot of freesias, in bloom, makes a delightful Easter gift and November is the time to pot them for that purpose.

If pansy and violet roots are taken from the beds, potted in rich soil and kept in cool rooms with north or east windows they will furnish their full quota of the winter's floral display.

Crowns (pips) of lily of the valley may be taken up and potted; then kept in a dark place where the temperature is just above freezing point until wanted, and will come into bloom very quickly when brought into strong light and warmth.

The garden plants which bloom early in the spring have their blossom germs fully matured before cold weather comes and any of them may be forced into bloom during the winter by taking a little trouble to give them, indoors, the condition of light and warmth which is natural to them at the blooming season.

A few of each kind will give the variety which we need in flowers as well as in other things and amply repay the little time and trouble expended on them.

KEROSENE LAMPS

To prevent explosions great care should be used in looking after kerosene lamps. As the oil burns down in the lamp, highly inflammable gas gathers over its surface, and as the oil decreases the gas increases. When the oil is nearly consumed a slight jar will inflame the gas, and an explosion is sure to follow. A bombshell is no more to be dreaded. Now if the oil is not allowed to burn more than half-way down, such accidents are almost impossible. Always fill the lamps every morning, and then an explosion need never be feared.

ECONOMICAL MEAT DISHES

In the majority of homes, meat is the most costly article of food, yet it is surprising how few housewives give the matter serious consideration or do what they might to reduce this expense. Confounding price with nutrition, they become imbued with the idea that only the high-priced cuts of meat are wholesome, and thus entirely lose sight of the fact that some of the inferior cuts contain equally as much nourishment, and in the hands of the clever cook can be rendered not only as palatable but also as attractive. The appended recipes will illustrate this truth, and at the same time afford acceptable changes from the steak and roast which appear with such monotonous regularity the year round.

Beef Braise: Take a piece of rump of the desired size; pound tender, tie and skewer, then lay in a deep baking pan previously lined with thin slices of salt pork and sliced onion; cover the top of the meat with slices of pork, sprinkle lightly with pepper, add a cup of boiling water, dredge thickly with flour, cover closely and bake in a slow oven, allowing twenty minutes to the pound. Then uncover, take out the meat, skim off the fat and thicken the broth for gravy.

Braised Calf's Liver: Lay the liver in a dish, pour on boiling water to cover, and immediately pour it off, which will seal up the juices and remove the unpleasant flavor which many persons find unpalatable. Lard the rounded side with salt pork. Fry an onion in bacon fat, then put it with the liver in a braising pan or a deep baking dish; sprinkle lightly with salt and pepper, add a bay leaf and a little minced parsley; pour over enough boiling water to half cover, put on the lid and bake two hours in a steady oven. When done, season the broth with lemon juice, pour over the liver and serve at once.

Brown Stew: Put a rather thick piece of beef with little bone and some fat over the fire in a stew kettle; pour over it just enough boiling water to cover, season with pepper, put on a closely fitting lid and bring quickly to a boil, then move to a cooler part of the range and simmer four hours, or until the meat is tender, turning it occasionally and adding, as needed, just enough boiling water to prevent scorching. An hour before dishing the meat, season with salt. Thicken the drippings for gravy.

Veal Fricassee: Cut two pounds of veal—the ribs, the back or knuckle—into small pieces and take out the bones. Place over the fire and cover with boiling water; bring to a boil, skim well, add two small onions, some thin slices of salt pork and a saltspoonful of pepper; cover closely, remove to a cooler part of the range and simmer until the meat is thoroughly done; then add one tablespoonful of flour wet up with a little cold water, and a cup of cream or rich milk. Boil five minutes. Before serving, garnish with rounds of hard-boiled eggs.

Beef Loaf: Put three pounds of chuck steak through a meat chopper; add to it one cup of grated bread crumbs, three beaten eggs, one tablespoonful of salt, a dash of cayenne and one tablespoonful of melted butter. Mix all together and form into a loaf. Put into a baking pan, pour in a little boiling water and bits of butter, cover and bake an hour and a quarter, basting occasionally. Serve hot with tomato sauce or cold with tomato catsup.

Mock Duck: Score an inch thick round steak with a sharp knife. Prepare a stuffing as for chicken and spread over the steak; fold it over and tie or skewer in place. Put in a dripping pan, lay over it a few slices of salt pork and bake forty-five minutes.

LITTLE HELPS FOR HOME-MAKERS

DECEMBER WORK IN THE WINDOW GARDEN

The principal work of December lies in the care of plants already potted and growing and perhaps the greatest care will be given to the bulbs which are expected to furnish blooms for Christmas decorations.

If the buds seem to be well developed but not coming above the neck of the bulb as they should, water them with warm water to which a tiny pinch of nitrate of soda, or saltpeter, has been added. Do not give the stimulant oftener than once a week, and not at all if the buds are coming up well.

It is sometimes a help to place a paper funnel over the plant, leaving the top opening about a quarter of the size of the base, or in other ways to get all the light above the bud, in order to induce it to grow upward.

If geraniums, or other plants which produce their blossoms at the end of branches, show a tendency to grow to one stalk, lose no time in pinching them back, to force a growth of lateral branches and get many blooming points. It is better to sacrifice the first blossoms and have many more, later on.

It is a question of form, too, for the pinched-back plant will become a stocky, bushy plant, much more beautiful than any spindling stalk could ever be.

KEEP LAMPS CLEAN

One very necessary thing in the care of lamps is that the oil reservoir be kept scrupulously clean inside. No oil is so pure that it does not leave a sediment and if this be allowed to accumulate, the oil will fail to burn as brightly as it otherwise would. Lamp reservoirs should be washed out once a week, adding a tablespoonful of soda to a quart of hot water, after which thoroughly rinse and drain, or wipe dry. The burner should be thoroughly scrubbed and brushed, boiling in strong soapsuds, ashes or soda. The wick should touch the bottom of the lamp, and be wiped at the top with a piece of soft paper to remove the charred edges, and if too short can be lengthened by another piece of wick until time is found to prepare a new one.

CARE OF LAMP WICKS

To insure a good light, wicks must be changed often, for as soon as they become clogged they do not permit the free passage of the oil. Soaking wicks in vinegar for twenty-four hours before placing in the lamps insures a clear flame; or wash thoroughly in suds and dry before replacing in the lamps.

To put in a wide wick either in a lamp or oil stove, starch and it will slip in easily; starching does not interfere with its clear burning.

When lighting a lamp turn the wick up slowly and thus prevent smoking. This is well to follow in lighting an oil stove, as the increasing heat causes it to burn stronger as well as heating the chimney too rapidly.

When taking the lamp from a warm room into a cold one, first turn down the wick—and always lower the wick when you wish to extinguish the flame, and wave a book or paper across the top of the chimney—never blow down the chimney, as the lamp is liable to explode if turned up high or partly empty.

CLEANING LAMP CHIMNEYS

A piece of sponge on the end of a stick is convenient for cleaning the chimneys—also holding them over the nose of a boiling tea-kettle for a moment and rubbing with a clean cloth, will make them beautifully clean. Lamp chimneys are made less liable to break by putting in cold water, bringing slowly to the boiling point, boiling for an hour and allowing them to cool before removing from the water.

A convenient arrangement for cleaning lamps is an old server—to hold the articles—provided with a lamp filler, scissors, box of wicks, soda, soap, cloths and a wire hair-pin or two for cleaning the burners.

A WESTERN WIFE

She walked behind the lagging mules
    That drew the breaker thro' the soil;
Hers were the early rising rules,
    Hers were the eves of wifely toil.

The smitten prairie blossomed fair,
    The sod home faded from the scene;
Firm gables met the whisp'ring air
    Deep porches lent repose serene.

But with'ring brow and snowy tress,
    Bespeak the early days of strife;
And there's the deeper wrought impress—
    The untold pathos of the wife.

O Western mother! in thy praise
    No artist paints nor poet sings,
But from thy rosary of days
    God's angels shape immortal wings!

CHOICE RECIPES FOR CHRISTMAS CANDIES

Brown Almond Bar: Put two pounds light brown sugar into a clean granite saucepan; add two-thirds of a cup of cold water and one-third of a teaspoonful of cream of tartar. Put over the fire and when it begins to boil add one pound of shelled almonds, stirring them in slowly. Boil until the nuts will slide off the lifted spoon easily. Then pour into a buttered cooling tin, and when cool cut into strips. To make peanut bar, substitute two pounds of peanuts for the almonds.

Honey Taffy: Pour over one pint of white sugar enough water to dissolve it; add four tablespoonfuls of strained honey. Boil to the hard crack. Pour out on greased pans, and let remain until nearly cold. Then pull on a hook.

LITTLE HELPS FOR HOME-MAKERS 85

Sliced Cocoanut Bar: Cook two pounds of best granulated sugar, two-thirds of a cup of water, and a pinch of cream of tartar, without stirring, to hard-crack in water; then add slowly one cocoanut pared and sliced very thin. Stir thoroughly, then pour into a buttered pan. When cool, cut into any shape desired.

Chocolate Cones: Put one pound of best granulated sugar into a saucepan; add half a cup of water, and with a wooden spatula stir over the fire until the sugar is dissolved. Then remove the spatula and cook *without* stirring until the syrup soft-balls when a little of it is tested in ice water. Pour slowly but in a steady stream into a bowl that has been lightly brushed over with oil or water. Do not scrape the sides of the saucepan or the syrup will granulate. Have ready in a bowl six ounces melted chocolate. Divide the sugar mixture into two parts and into one pour one-third the melted chocolate and vanilla extract to season to taste. Stir until a stiff mass is formed; then shape into small cones and drop them upon buttered paper. Put half the remaining cream mixture into a cup and stand it in boiling water; add vanilla to flavor and stir over the fire until of the consistency of thick syrup. Take the cup to the table, and dip half the cones, one at a time, into it, coating each thoroughly. To the remainder of the creamed sugar add the remainder of the melted chocolate and two tablespoonfuls of boiling water. If too thick, add, a drop at a time, more boiling water, until of the consistency desired. Dip the rest of the cones in it. Although the above process seems a tedious one, the result will make amends for the extra time and labor spent.

Butter Scotch: Put three pounds of light-brown sugar, one-half cup of molasses, four even tablespoonfuls of butter and one-half teaspoonful of cream of tartar over the fire and boil until it is quite brittle when tested in ice water. Add a few drops of any flavoring desired, pour into a greased pan and when cool mark into squares.

Marshmallows: Soak two ounces of white gum arabic in eight tablespoonfuls of water one hour. Stand the vessel containing it in a pan of boiling water, place on the back of the range, stirring occasionally, until the gum arabic is dissolved. Then strain through a fine-meshed sieve. Add seven ounces of best granulated sugar, put into a double boiler and stir over the fire until thick and white. Take from the fire, flavor with vanilla, beat hard and with a quick motion for five minutes; then pour into a bowl containing the whipped whites of four eggs, beating with one hand while pouring with the other. Beat the whole thoroughly, then turn into a pan well dusted with cornstarch. When cold, cut into squares and dust each square with cornstarch. Pack in tin boxes.

Cocoanut Fudge: Boil together until it soft-balls when tested in ice water, two cups of granulated sugar and two-thirds of a cup of sweet milk. Just before taking from the fire, stir in one cup finely grated cocoanut and a rounded tablespoonful of butter. Take from the fire, add a few drops of lemon extract, then beat the mixture until it begins to thicken. Pour out on buttered tins and when cold enough cut into cubes.

Coffee Caramels: Put one pound of light-brown sugar into a clean granite saucepan; add one cup of strong clear coffee, one-half cup of sweet cream and one tablespoonful of butter. Put over the fire and boil, without stirring, until it will hard-crack when a little is dropped into cold water. Then pour into greased cooling tins, and when cool enough, mark off into inch squares.

USES OF KEROSENE

Kerosene is good for many things besides fuel and lamp oil. It should always be substituted for soap in cleaning shellac floors. Use a cupful to a pailful of lukewarm water—hot water spoils the varnish—and wipe dry with a floor mop or soft cloth. After scrubbing oilcloth, if a little kerosene is rubbed on it and rubbed dry, the colors of the oilcloth will be wonderfully freshened. Clean zinc with hot, soapy water and polish with flannel dampened in kerosene. A little used on the furniture will improve it, care being taken with varnished surfaces, as too much kerosene will soften the varnish and cause the dust to adhere more easily. Clean the kitchen woodwork with a soft cloth dampened in kerosene. It is more quickly and easily done than with soap and water—and looks fresher. When so unfortunate as to spill kerosene oil or other grease on the carpet, sprinkle buckwheat flour (wheat flour will do) lightly over it until it is completely covered, and let it lie without disturbing it for a week, brush off, and there will be no trace of oil left; or leave for a couple of days, brush off and repeat.

For removing rust nothing is equal to kerosene. To clean Russia iron, mix blacking with kerosene and apply with a brush as usual; it will look nearly as well as new. When putting away the stove-pipe for the summer, rub well with kerosene, wrap in papers—being careful to stuff each end full of paper—and the pipe will keep nicely. If an article becomes badly rusted, pour the oil into a pan and lay it with the rusted surface in the oil so as to cover it. Leave as long as may be necessary for the oil to penetrate the rust; then wipe off and polish with sand soap or with bath brick, according to the article to be cleaned.

Try a saturated solution of kerosene and salt for chilblains. Wipe your flatiron on a cloth dampened in kerosene to clean and to prevent scorching. Then a little on the hinges of a creaking door—it will stop the annoyance (or the lead of a soft pencil will answer the same purpose, if handier). Saturate a woolen rag with kerosene and polish up the tin tea-kettle—it will make it as bright as new.

When the rubber rollers on the wringer get discolored and covered with lint from the flannels, etc., dip a bit of cloth in kerosene and rub them—they will look like new. Very little oil is sufficient—merely enough to moisten the cloth. To clean sewing machines, cover all the bearings with kerosene oil, work the machine quickly for a few minutes, then thoroughly rub all the oil off with rags and apply machine oil to the parts which need oiling.

Kerosene on salt pork wrapped about the throat when it is sore is good—or rubbing kerosene on the throat, being careful not to blister—and even taking it internally in small doses. Kerosene oil is also an effective remedy for burns—fully equal to linseed oil. It contains the remedial qualities of vaseline, but is a much less soothing application and the odor is, of course, objectionable.

On wash-day, cut up a quarter of a cake of soap into the wash-boiler, and allow it to dissolve, which it will do by the time the water comes to a boil. Then stir in a cupful of kerosene and put in the sheets, towels, pillowcases, etc.—that is, the clothes which are not badly soiled. Boil for fifteen minutes, stirring frequently. Then rinse, rubbing them out in the rinsing water to wash out the soap. This is all the washing they need, and you will find them clean and ready for the bluing. The kerosene dissolves the dirt and whitens the clothes without injury to the fabric.

LITTLE HELPS FOR HOME-MAKERS

BUYING SUPPLIES, ETC., FOR LAMPS

When buying, get one or two extra chimneys or burners, also a yard or two of wicking. This practice saves delay and annoyance when one lives far from the store and kerosene lamps are the only lamps used. If lamps and burners are all alike, only one kind of supplies need be kept on hand.

To trim lamp wicks, slip a piece of old stocking or coarse rag over the middle finger and rub smooth all burned parts of the wick. This will do the work when shears and uncovered fingers or other methods fail.

Always fill the lamps in the daytime; be sure your dealer furnishes good oil, and above all be sure that he does not use the same measure for kerosene and gasoline, as a teaspoonful of kerosene in the gasoline will cause it to smoke—and a less amount of gasoline in the kerosene will cause the lamps to burn cloudily—and the exchange will spoil a five-gallon can of either.

Be sure not to fill the lamps too full, as the heat expands the oil and drives it out, making the lamp dirty and dangerous.

A MOTHER'S SUCCESSFUL EXPERIMENT

Having had two children with very poor teeth, I determined that if I could assist nature in any way to give to my third child a good set of teeth, this I should do. We started him on Mellin's Food and from that to oatmeal gruel, until he was twelve months old, then to the oatmeal and milk with an occasional bit of cracker or bread until he was past two years of age. The result is that my boy, now six years old, has a perfect set of pearly white teeth, which are the admiration of all, as well as a great comfort to both the boy and his mother.

But this was not the only result; he now eats neither pie, fruit, nor melon, and but few vegetables—he says because he ate so much oatmeal when he was a baby. He lives now principally upon breakfast foods, milk and eggs. The result of this is that I am never given one moment's anxiety; no matter how hot the weather is, or what is placed before him, he will never eat anything that will make him sick.

But a six-year old boy isn't always content with "baby foods" even if there are few other things which he likes. Consequently, I have experimented considerably in his behalf, and at last know how to make potato chips that will hurt neither man's nor boy's digestion. Use full grown, new potatoes, else the chips will be soggy. Slice very thin and drop, a few at a time, in boiling lard, turning with a fork until they are crisp and of a delicate brown. This may seem tedious at first, but make it quick work by having the boy, who loves the chips so well, bring in a hod of chips from the wood-pile.

SEASONING A FOWL

To improve the flavor of fowl, when seasoning it, add ginger to the salt and pepper, and rub this into flesh well. For a change, try putting an onion and an apple in ducks in place of the usual bread-crumb dressing.

AGE YOUR SOAPS

My soaps, both kitchen and toilet, last me twice as long as they do most folks and this is the secret of it: I buy a half dozen cakes at a time and dry them thoroughly in the sun for a week or so, turning them occasionally. Then I lay them away in a good dry place and behold! when used, they shed lather satisfactorily, but will not wash away like "green" soap.

TO PROTECT HOUSE PLANTS

To rid house plants of the small black flies, which hatch from maggots in the soil, insert the heads of three or four lucifer matches in each pot.

KEROSENE AS A HOME REMEDY

Toothache: Cotton saturated with kerosene and placed in the tooth often affords immediate relief.

Croup: Kerosene has been used in croup with success. It may be taken internally and applied externally.

Burns: Cloths saturated with kerosene and applied to burns exclude the air and bring desired relief from pain.

Cleansing the scalp: A little kerosene introduced into glycerine constitutes an ointment that will speedily remove dandruff and contribute to a clean and healthy scalp.

A HOME WATER PLANT

A young machinist, wishing to have modern bath conveniences in his new cottage which was too far out to be reached by the city waterworks, accomplished his purpose in this way:

An ordinary, large range tank and force pump were placed in the cellar, the latter attached to wall with pipe leading out to large cistern in the yard. The tank has small air gauge at bottom to denote the pressure at all times, and a check valve at side to which a large bicycle pump is attached when more air is needed in the tank. Also fitted with the necessary piping leading up to the bathroom and the kitchen sink.

Thus the compressed air in the top of the tank becomes the required force for sending the water above.

A large bath water-heater, fitted with gasoline burner, is fastened to the wall in bathroom over the tub, thus economizing space and solving the problem of having hot water at very slight expense, and on a few minutes' notice.

The tank being placed on end, drain pipe put in the corner, and pump on the wall, all complete, takes up but very little space in the cellar. By pumping up to a good pressure, (say sixty or eighty pounds, which takes about five minutes) twice a week, the water flows as freely as could be desired, gushing forth from the faucets as though pumped by an engine at the motor house.

SCORCHED FOOD

When a kettle of meat or vegetables scorches, place the kettle in cold water as quickly as possible and the food will not taste scorched.

SALT FOR THE HANDS

Try rubbing the hands with dry salt after having had them in water for a length of time; afterward rinse them and wipe dry. If used daily after the housework is finished, it will keep the hands smooth, clean and white.

WHEN BAKING BREAD

If you wish to bake five loaves, and your oven will hold but four, steam one loaf, and set in the oven to dry, after the other bread is baked. You will find it much tenderer and better in every way than the loaves which are baked.

PREVENTS FADING

A large spoonful of turpentine put in the water when washing dresses or waists with delicate colors liable to fade, will prevent fading and will preserve the colors fresh and bright.

TO KILL CUCUMBER BUGS

My brother has tried the following mixture for the striped cucumber bug and other pests, for a number of years, and has never known it to fail. He believes that if others would try it faithfully, it would save thousands of dollars for growers of melons and cucumbers.

Three quarts plaster, one pint air-slacked lime, two pounds slug shot, one teaspoonful paris green, two teaspoonfuls hellebore. Mix and sprinkle lightly over the vines.

THE DISH-DRAINER AND STERILIZED DISHES

Few people understand that the best use of the dish-drainer is to avoid handling and wiping dishes.

Dishes should be washed clean first, then put in drainer and scalded thoroughly on both sides, turning as is necessary.

Then the drainer containing the dishes should be put on the back of the stove or in the sun until all are dry.

This method not only saves labor to the housekeeper, but leaves the china absolutely clean and sterilized. If glasses are rinsed in cold water and dried in the same way they will look as if polished.

CUTTING BUTTONHOLES

In preparing to cut buttonholes in a material that frays easily it is well to mark a line the length of hole desired, then stitch close around it on the sewing machine before cutting. This gives firmness and prevents fraying.

WASHING MADE EASY

Moisten white clothes, rub soiled places with naphtha soap, let soak a few hours or over night in cold water. Squeeze a little with the hands, or put through washer in this water. Wring, and put over the fire in cold water with any preferred soap. Scald well, stirring often. Finish in usual way. They will only need a thorough rinsing.

LAXATIVE PRUNES

Make a strong concentrated infusion of senna leaves, (five cents' worth will be enough for two quarts of prunes) strain this through a muslin cloth and boil in the strained liquid as many prunes of good quality as can be well boiled in the quantity of infusion. Stew the prunes in the liquid thoroughly, in the same manner as if for the table, properly seasoning.

When well cooked, put in a glass jar, screw the top down tightly, and set away in a cool place. Two or three or four of these prunes eaten in a day will overcome some of the severest cases of constipation. There is no suggestion whatever of the senna in the taste of the prunes, and the effect is most desirable either in the old or the young.

MIXING COOKING MATERIALS

Get everything needed ready first: pans for cooking, drippings to grease them; measure sugar and put into a bowl; if spices are to be used, measure those and mix into sugar; break the eggs ready for beating; if raisins are needed, pick them over, measure, and cover with hot water.

See to the fire, wash your hands and begin by putting a sieve over a large bowl; measure the flour into sieve; into flour put baking-powder or soda, and sift through together, dry, even if your recipe says to dissolve soda in hot water, milk or molasses. After sifting, mix the dry flour thoroughly with your hands. Then rub into flour the quantity of shortening needed, whether butter, lard or drippings. Rub till the mixture seems like coarse meal, always with your hands. Now add sugar, salt and spices, and mix quickly. Next, grease the pans and wash your hands, as the rest of the mixing is done with a spoon. Turn off the water from the raisins and dredge with flour. Beat the eggs and add to mixture in bowl, next the milk, rinsing with it the bowl in which the eggs were beaten, then put in molasses if that is used. Beat all together with spoon very hard for two or three minutes, and lastly, add the floured raisins.

Every recipe can be put together this way, whether for biscuit, gingerbread, or cake, and for the latter especially, it is a great saving of time.

THREADING NEEDLES

When it is dusk and the sewing machine needle becomes unthreaded, just before the last quarter of a yard is finished, just raise the needle to a threading position, slip a piece of white paper or cloth under needle and see how easily you can thread it.

FRIED SQUASH

Cut a fine-grained, dry, sweet squash into thin slices, pare and fry in plenty of butter and season well. This dish will be found an excellent substitute for sweet potatoes.

CARE OF WOODEN BOWLS

To prevent wooden bowls from splitting, take them when new, before they have been touched with water, apply boiling hot linseed oil over the outside and top edge, all that will penetrate.

BOILED LEMONADE

In making lemonade, boil the desired quantity of sugar and lemon juice together, cool and add as much cold water as needed—a great improvement on the old way.

TO PROTECT NEEDLES

Flannel should not be used in needle books, as it is often prepared with sulphur, which will rust needles. A piece of fine linen or chamois leather is better.

A LINEN LUSTER SECRET

A Bohemian servant taught me the secret of putting a wonderful luster on linen. After the linen had been laundered and dried she put it into a pail of boiling water, wrung it out and ironed immediately until dry. As it takes about two hours, the process may not be practical except for the "best" linen, but is certainly worth the trouble.

SUBSTITUTES FOR ALCOHOL IN MINCE PIES

Instead of cider and other alcoholic liquors, use fruit juices for mince pies. The juice left from canning strawberries, plums, sour cherries, etc., if sweetened, boiled down and canned, makes a rich, delicious moistening for mince meat. If raisins and suet in plenty are added to the mixture, it will be rich enough to please the most fastidious appetite.

COLLARS

For the girl who is preparing her summer outfit let me say: "Be sure to have one dark stock, preferably of black velvet for cool days. Have all the fluffy neckwear you care for, but for the occasional cold 'spells' that are sure to come a velvet collar is more 'comfy,' more becoming and more striking. Let it be plain; and made to wear with numerous 'top-collars.'"

One girl friend with a limited supply of "pocket-book filling" made herself a half dozen fine linen top-collars from the linen of her brother's cast-off cuffs. Some of these are hemstitched, others are bordered with the narrowest and finest of valenciennes, while one is edged with fine tatting.

The linen is very fine, launders easily and needs no starch if ironed before drying, thus making ideal "tops."

FINE DARNING

If a woolen dress be darned with a raveling of the same, the place darned will hardly show. Use lengthwise thread on plain material. If a mixed goods, use thread to match direction of darning. Slightly wear end of thread to make threading of needle easier.

HOW TO TELL YOUNG GAME

To tell young birds from old ones, when shooting or buying in the market, hold them up by the under bill so that the weight will fall on it. If the bill breaks the bird is young; if not, it is old.

BAKING DAY

After taking bread from the oven, do not wrap tightly in cloth as many do; but rub the top of loaves with a little lard or butter, tip on edge on your kneading board so that all possible crust is exposed to the air and if possible place out doors or in the wind to cool quickly a few minutes, then remove to convenient place and let stand until thoroughly cold before putting away in box or can, and you will have delicious, tender crust.

SETTING HENS IN MID-SUMMER

Many experienced poultrymen feel that it is almost useless to try to raise broods of chicks in very hot weather, so apt are the eggs to spoil before they can be hatched. But an old, old lady who has been in the business for years declares that perfect success is attained by setting the hen directly upon the ground. She scoops out a little hollow in the earth, and places the eggs in it without a particle of straw around or beneath them. A shelter is provided, of course. She says the hen suffers less from heat or lice, and if the eggs have been fresh to start with every one of them will be hatched even in the hottest weather.

CAKE FROSTING

One cupful of sugar to each egg; three tablespoonfuls of water to each cup of sugar; a pinch of tartaric acid. Boil syrup made of the sugar and water until it begins to thicken, pour half of it on the whipped whites, beating thoroughly; cook the remainder of the syrup until it ropes like spun glass, then pour into the mixture and beat hard. This icing will not crumble and does not lose its freshness.

TO REMOVE GREASE FROM BROTH

A good way to remove "eyes" of grease from beef or chicken broth, is to pass a piece of brown or white wrapping paper across the top of the bowl of broth before using. The grease adheres to the paper.

MILDEW

To remove mildew, wet the article with soft water and rub it well with white soap, then with powdered chalk; place it on the grass in the sunshine and keep it damp with soft water. Next day repeat the process, and in a few hours the mildew will disappear.

DRYING SHEETS

Much of the labor of ironing sheets is saved if when washed they are hung lengthwise on the clothes line. The selvedge will be found smooth as the rest of the sheet instead of "curled up."

WHITE SPOTS ON TABLES

To remove white spots from polished tables or other wooden furniture, pour upon the spots a few drops of spirits of camphor. Let the camphor remain for two or three minutes, then rub with a clean cloth. The spots, otherwise so difficult to remove, will wipe off.

MIX CAKE WITH THE ICE-CREAM FREEZER

The proper beating of cake was always to me a laborious process, so, by way of experiment, I tried the ice-cream freezer.

Set the butter where it will become soft. See that the cogs of the freezer are oiled so that it will run easily. Put the eggs in the cylinder, place the parts together as you would for making ice cream, turn the crank a minute or two, then open the cylinder and add the melted butter, sugar, milk, flour and baking-powder, or whatever ingredients you wish. Adjust the crank and turn for ten minutes and you will find the mixture as creamy and fine grained as though you had beaten it with a spoon in the ordinary way for half an hour.

PINEAPPLE SHERBET

Two cups of sugar, one can of shredded pineapple, juice of three lemons, one pint of milk, whites of three eggs and water enough to make one gallon. Make syrup of sugar and water and cook three minutes. When cool, add the pineapple, lemon juice and milk into which has been dissolved one package unflavored Jell-O ice cream powder. Now see that water enough is added to make a gallon, and then add the beaten whites of the eggs. Freeze in the usual manner.

WASHING CHAMOIS SKINS

If washed in cold water with plenty of soap and rinsed well in clear cold water, the skins will never be hard, but very soft and pliable.

CLEAN KITCHEN SHELVES

The kitchen cupboard is more easily kept clean and in order if, instead of having paper on the shelves, white table oilcloth is used. Cut the oilcloth the size of the shelf and paste it securely on with either flour, paste or mucilage. The shelf can be wiped off with the dish cloth as often as needed and the cupboard is always clean.

TO MEND OILCLOTH

Trim the edges of the hole to be mended, place an oilcloth patch beneath, and paint the edges on the wrong side. Press down tight against the patch and let dry. Paint all worn places, using the same color as the oilcloth.

FANCY STUFFED DATES

Into a spoonful or two of jelly (quince is very nice for this purpose) stir some English walnuts, finely chopped, a very little crystalized ginger and a trifle of sweet mango pickle, all finely cut and well mixed together. Take the stones from Persian dates and fill each date with the mixture; roll the dates tightly in fine sugar.

TO EXTERMINATE BURDOCKS

The hardest thing to contend with in many localities is the burdock. It is next to an impossibility to dig them out. If the least part of a root is left in the ground it will grow, but if you will take an axe or a sharp butcher knife any time in the summer and cut them off level with the ground, and then pour on about a teaspoonful of kerosene, the plant will die at once and never start again. You can rid a whole field of them in a day.

THE FAIRY COOKER

Two pails are needed—one a deep wooden pail, (a 25-cent candy pail is good) and a three or four quart granite ware pail with a tight-fitting cover. Pack excelsior tightly in the bottom and around the inside of the wooden pail, making a nest for the granite pail. A variety of articles, such as oatmeal, rice, macaroni, tomatoes, soup, etc., can be cooked to perfection in the cooker if they are cooked five or six minutes over the fire in the granite pail and placed at once (while boiling hot and tightly covered) in the excelsior nest in the wooden pail, and the tops of both pails covered with heavy cloths to keep the heat in Oatmeal boiled a few minutes in the evening and left over night in the cooker comes out in the morning like blanc-mange ready for breakfast. Macaroni, rice, tomatoes or soup, cooked on the stove a few minutes after breakfast and placed in the cooker will be found ready for the noon dinner. Meat can also be cooked in this way, but may need a second heating after a few hours and returning to the cooker. No housekeeper who has once tried the Fairy Cooker will wish to part with it, for it saves fuel, needs no watching and cooks to perfection.

WASHING BLANKETS

No blanket should be put away after a winter's use without either a thorough airing, if it has been little used, or a good washing if much used. If carefully washed, blankets, or in fact any woolen clothes, will not shrink a particle. Choose a day when the sun is not too hot and there is a good breeze blowing, so that the articles will dry all in one day. Make a good suds of hot, soft water, Ivory or castile soap, and borax in the proportion of one teaspoonful to every gallon of water. Shake the blankets well to remove all loose fuzz and then soak in the hot suds for about fifteen minutes, then press the blanket against the sides of the tub and squeeze and press well with the hands. Never rub on a washboard or use soap directly upon the article.

The first water must be well squeezed out, not twisted, hence a wringer is better than the hands. Rinse carefully in one or even two waters as hot as the first but containing no soap. A little borax is allowable, however. Again run carefully through a wringer and pull corners well into place and hang where the air will blow directly through it. When about half dry, pat the water out of the lower edge, take down and rehang with the lower side up this time.

Another cleansing way is to use ammonia in the hot water instead of white soap and borax; in other respects the process is the same.

Do not hang blankets out of doors in freezing weather. Dry upon clothesbars about a stove or over a furnace. And do not try to wash blankets when you are doing the general washing. They are enough in themselves for any woman.

To my thinking no woolens should be ironed, but simply pulled and patted into shape.

Blankets, when not in use, should be neatly folded and placed between sheets of soft paper in chests, trunks or upon shelves with bags of camphor to keep out the moths. Refold in new creases two or three times during the year, and air frequently.

TO SAVE BROOM

If you will put a tack in the end of your broom and tie a string on that and hang it up so it will not touch the floor, it will not wear out so quickly.

CLEANING WALL-PAPER

Take the inside of a two-pound loaf of rye bread two-thirds done, add two ounces of naphtha and a tablespoonful of salt, knead together until it becomes a dough, then apply to wall paper.

GREASE ON THE STOVE

If you spill grease upon a hot stove, cover the spot at once with a thick layer of ashes; this will absorb the grease, so you will not be offended by its odor while burning, and a little later you can brush away the ashes, and none of the grease will remain.

SYRUP FOR SWEET PICKLES

To seven and one-half pounds fruit, three and one-half pounds of sugar and one pint of vinegar add cloves, spice, cinnamon (stick) and mace to suit taste. Boil until it makes a thick syrup, then add the fruit and cook until tender. This is nice for peaches, pears, cherries and Damson plums.

SLIPS FROM TEA ROSES

Slips from tea roses can be easily started. Plant deep and place a glass jar over them; leave them so for three months, when they will be nicely rooted and can be transplanted

A CHEAP FLAVORING

A spray of green peach-tree leaves, dropped into a kettle of milk, when it is put on the stove, and allowed to stay until the milk comes to a boil, imparts a most delicate pistachio flavor. This is a war-time expedient, used by a Virginia housekeeper, which is even now found very convenient, when the vanilla bottle is empty, and there is no opportunity to go to a drug store.

SODA FOR CLEANING KETTLES

To remove black from the bottoms of kettles, pans, etc., apply common soda with a damp cloth. It will instantly clean them and keep them bright.

AN IMPROVED SINK PUMP

When the sink becomes clogged, I simply let some water run in it, until about two or three inches deep, then lay the palm of my hand flat over the drain hole and force the water out by working my hand up and down, quickly. The pressure forces all obstructions through the drain pipe. Then pour boiling water through to melt all grease. The above advice was given by a plumber, and has proved good.

TO CLEAN A WATCH

Take the works out of the case. Allow them to lie completely submerged in benzine from eight to twelve hours. If possible, start the watch going, the action of the wheels will work the dirt out. After removing the works, allow the benzine to evaporate before placing them in the case. This is harmless to the most delicate works. I have cleaned my own many times.

KENTUCKY CORN PONE

Sift one quart meal. Salt to taste, pour over meal boiling water, enough to make a stiff dough, stirring all the time. Dip hands in dish of cold water and mould dough in pones. Bake in greased bread pan, in hot oven, till well-browned.

MUD STAINS ON BLACK

To clean mud stains from black dress goods, rub with a slice of raw potato.

A BATCH OF LITTLE HELPS

Borax and water will brighten oilcloth.
Beeswax and salt will make rusty flatirons clean and smooth.
A little soda added to boiling vegetables will hasten their cooking and add to their tenderness.
When you wish to beat eggs quickly add a pinch of salt.
A good cleaner for gold or silver jewelry is a teaspoonful of ammonia in a cupful of water.
By adding a few drops of vinegar to the water when poaching eggs they will set more quickly and perfectly.
A little salad oil gradually added when mixing mustard for the table is a great improvement.
A cloth dipped in the white of an egg will brighten leather chairs and bindings.
A small piece of charcoal in a pot of boiling cabbage absorbs the odor.
A strong solution of nitric acid in an ounce of soft water will whiten piano keys.

LIGHT DOUGHNUTS

When making doughnuts of sour cream or buttermilk, put in enough soda to neutralize the acid in the milk; then to each quart of flour put in one teaspoonful of cream of tartar and see how fluffy your doughnuts will be.

THE BOY'S RUBBER BOOT

When the small boy comes in with his rubber boots full of snow or other dampness, stuff them with old dry newspapers and leave several hours. The papers will absorb all the dampness, leaving the boots perfectly dry.

OILING THE CLOCK

When the clock begins to lose time or rebel at doing its work it needs a lubricator. Put a little coal oil in a small vessel, set it inside the clock and close the door. As the oil evaporates, it will moisten the machinery and overcome the trouble.

A small clock may be laid over a saucer or plate containing a little oil and enclosed in a tin bucket.

GIFT FOR A BRIDE

If you are wondering what you can give that dear friend of yours who is to be married soon, that will really be of use to her, try this: Gather together your best recipes for making all kinds of good things to eat. Be sure to choose only those which you, yourself, have tested. Buy a well-bound blank book and copy these recipes as neatly as possible. It is best to group them, as in any recipe book. If you like, paint or sketch the word "Recipes" on the cover. This little book will always prove an acceptable gift to a housekeeper, young or old.

MENDING CRACKS IN STOVES

Use two parts good wood ashes and one part salt; moisten with water enough to make a thick batter and apply quickly.

FOR SHOE NEATNESS

My laced boots and shoes never looked neat because the tongue was continually slipping to one side. The idea came to me to cut two slits about a quarter of an inch long and nearly a quarter of an inch apart in the end of the tongue close to the top eyelet (on either side) so the shoelace can be run through it before passing into the top eyelet. Now my shoe tongues are always in place. My friends who have tried this method are warm in praise of it.

FOR WHOOPING COUGH

Chestnut leaves steeped in a porcelain dish or bowl are a sure specific for whooping cough, breaking it up quickly. Children like to drink it, it is so pleasant. One man said it cured him of quick consumption.

TO CAN WINTER VEGETABLES

Prepare corn, peas, or beans the same as in cooking for the table. Cover them with cold water and let them boil five minutes. Pour them in a colander to drain, then fill your jars, packing them tightly. Fill the jars with boiling water, to every cupful of which a teaspoonful of salt has been added. Seal the jars tightly and steam four hours. This recipe never fails if correctly followed.

TO KEEP CIDER SWEET

One cupful of whole mustard seed thrown into a barrel of sweet cider will preserve the sweetness of the cider.

COPPERAS FOR PLANTS

Some time ago I read the statement that copperas would make plants bloom in profusion. I asked a florist about it and he told me that copperas is a powerful fertilizer but that it ultimately poisons the earth, and so must be used carefully. It is possible that the potted plants which we sometimes buy and which never look the same afterward have been forced in this way.

MAPLE SUGAR FROSTING

The most delicious frosting you ever ate is made by boiling maple sugar till it forms a soft ball in water; turn it slowly on a well-beaten white of an egg and beat till cool.

SEASONING VEGETABLES

In the southern country kitchen it is the custom usually to "season" the pot of cabbage, string beans, turnip greens, or parsnips, by cooking a generous slice of fat pork (jowl or side meat) with them. The vegetables are "seasoned" all right by this method, but unfortunately they impart their own taste to the meat, and this is not relished by many. Cook the meat in one pot and the vegetables in another. When the meat is about done, pour off its grease and juices, add them to the vegetable pot and cook the vegetables a few minutes longer. It will be as well seasoned as though the meat were cooked with it, and the meat will not be disagreeably flavored. In addition several kinds of vegetables may be seasoned with the one piece of meat, by dividing the juices and grease.

NUT FOOD FOR HENS

Nothing helps so much toward making hens lay in the winter time as nuts. Two pans heaping full of walnuts and butternuts, cracked, are given to a flock of twenty-five hens twice a week, and how it makes them "shell out" the eggs! Remember we live on a large farm, and all the nuts cost us is time to pick them up in the fall.

FOR CATARRHAL COLDS

Dissolve one teaspoonful of powdered borax, one teaspoonful of saleratus and one teaspoonful of pure glycerine in one pint of tepid water, and inhale every ten minutes until relieved. This is a positive and speedy remedy for catarrhal colds.

THE AIR OF A SICK-ROOM

A few drops of oil of lavender poured into a glass of very hot water will purify the air of a room almost instantly from cooking odors; the effect is especially refreshing in a sick-room.

PAPERING OVER WHITEWASH

When wishing to paint or paper a wall that has been whitewashed, the wall should be first washed with hot vinegar. Then apply a coat of thin glue with a broad paint brush. After this dries, the wall may be either papered or painted.

BREAKFAST FOODS

Cook cream of wheat, or any similar wheat food, in a steam cooker as the directions on box cover state, then put in dishes and while the food is still hot place a piece of butter the size of a walnut in each dish, and sugar. Now stir the butter and sugar well in the food and serve. (You may cream if you wish, but it is not necessary.) I find this a great improvement in wheat foods.

WASHING BLANKETS

For one pair of blankets dissolve one-half bar of soap; when thoroughly melted, add one tablespoonful of borax and two of ammonia. Add the mixture to a sufficient quantity of water (already softened with one tablespoonful of borax) to cover two blankets. Let the blankets remain in the suds one hour without rubbing, rinse thoroughly and hang up without wringing; this prevents harshness and shrinking.

LITTLE HELPS FOR HOME-MAKERS

ZINC TO CLEAR CHIMNEYS

Possibly some who use soft coal may not know that a handful of zinc scraps, or if these cannot be conveniently procured, a piece of pure zinc equal in size, thrown upon the fire once a week, will cause the soot that so rapidly accumulates to loosen its hold and fall down, due to some chemical action.

USEFUL HINTS

When attending a party or entertainment where the rubbers are removed, fasten together with a clothespin marked with your name.

Put sugar in the paste to make wall-paper stick to kalsomined walls.

THE HOME DRESSMAKER

In cutting a waist lining lay the pattern across the cloth (not on bias), and it will not stretch as when cut lengthwise of the goods.

CINDER IN THE EYE

I suffered for a week from a cinder in my eye which had become embedded and at times seemed to be out. I tried all the simple remedies without relief, when finally, without faith, I tried a loop of horse hair run up under the lid and out it came. It saved me a journey and doctor's fee and was painless. I have since recommended it in obdurate cases and it has never failed. Properly cleanse the hair before using.

TO SAVE LAUNDRY WORK

Try making baby's little aprons by the bishop pattern, front and back the same, so that they are reversible. Then gather the neck upon a rubber tape (about one-half yard) to slip over the head. They are easy to make, slip on, wash and iron, besides lasting longer than when the wear all comes on one side.

Also, try using a pair of old stocking legs to protect the sleeves while doing up the morning work. They save washing, too.

FROZEN POTATOES

Potatoes which have frozen can be used and be as good as ever if not allowed to thaw. If they thaw the least bit they are worthless. Pare them in cold water and drop one at a time in boiling water.

In the spring when the potatoes are sprouted or withered, pare them early in the morning so they may stand several hours in clear, cold water. Then put them over the fire in cold water and you will have good potatoes with no old taste.

WASHING FLUID

Dissolve one ounce salts of tartar, one ounce salts of ammonia and one can Babbitt's potash in five quarts of lukewarm water. Add half a cake of borax soap shaved fine. Clothes should be dry when put in boiler and should boil twenty minutes. When taken out of the boiler and rubbed for a few minutes, it will be found that all dirt and spots will be removed with very slight effort. This fluid does not injure the clothes.

ESSENTIAL OILS

Oils from which perfumes and toilet waters are made may be easily made at home by taking two tablespoonfuls of pure glycerine and placing the fragrant part of the plant, whether it be blossom, leaf or stem, in it. Put in only as much as the oil will well cover, set it on the back part of the range or where it will keep quite warm, and stir and press it often for twenty-four hours; then press out the parts and put in fresh ones and treat in the same way for twenty-four hours longer, and repeat the process twice more, when you should have a very strong oil of whatever plant you have used. This oil is used exactly as the expensive oils you buy are used in making all toilet waters and perfumes. It never gets rancid and is so inexpensive that anyone may have all they want of it.

ABOUT EGGS

Many housewives do not know that their failure at times to beat the whites of eggs to a light, white foam is due to the fact that the dish used contained moisture other than that of the eggs. Always dry the dish thoroughly before using, as the slightest moisture upon its surface will interfere with the whites becoming light.

When separating the yolk from the white of an egg, break the shell by striking gently against the edge of a dish. The yolk is retained in one portion of the shell while the white is allowed to drop over and fall into the dish. Transfer the yolk from one half shell to the other several times and after each change run the finger along broken edge of shell to cut the white away. By the use of the finger the entire white is separated without danger of the yolk being drawn over the edge and broken.

LET YOUR HENS SET

You should not try to keep a hen from setting when nature wills otherwise. A hen will not want to set unless she is fat, and as she seldom leaves the nest for food during the period of incubation, she needs the flesh for nourishment and to keep the eggs warm.

If you do not wish to have chickens, give her porcelain eggs and let her set for two weeks; then shut her up for a few days. After this she will be in a better condition and will lay more eggs than she would have done if prevented from setting, nor will she desire to set again until she becomes fat.

CANKER IN THE THROAT

For cankered throat and mouth, tea leaves are the best thing.

ZINC-COVERED KITCHEN TABLE

One of the most convenient and useful pieces of kitchen furniture imaginable is the kitchen table covered with zinc. The old-time oilcloth covering will be discarded after one trial of the zinc.

It is so easily cleaned. Just wash with soap and water, and occasionally clean with paper saturated with kerosene to give it the gloss and smooth surface desirable. Never need think whether dishes are hot or cold as with oilcloth.

To make the table, take a good plain table for the purpose, and if the man of the house is at all handy he will have just what is wanted with little trouble. The zinc must be flattened smooth on top, then turned down at edge, hammering to make it turn, then turned under and tacked. This leaves a smooth, easily cleaned edge.

SURE CURE FOR CROUP

At the first symptom of croup, which is always a sharp, shrill cough, let the one who has the care of the child take it into bed with her, placing her open hand upon the sufferer's chest, the thumb and fingers lightly yet firmly clasping the throat, and keeping it in this position until the cough loosens, which it will do in a very short time.

I have used this remedy repeatedly and have never failed to rout the dread disease. It is so simple that people hesitate to try it, but one fair trial will convince the most skeptical of its efficacy.

ODORS

Do you know that the fishy smell on knives and forks after salmon and other oily fish have been served, can be removed by rubbing a slice of lemon over them? That to remove the odor of onions from the breath you should eat parsley; from the hands rub with celery? That a pleasant household deodorizer is made by pouring spirits of lavender over bi-carbonate of ammonia? Put it in a wide-mouthed bottle and cover tightly when not in use, when you wish to use it open the bottle and let it remain so for a few minutes; this mixture is also good to inhale in case of severe headache. Do you know that you should never have groceries or provisions having strong odors near the flour barrel? Nothing absorbs odors quicker than flour. That if you like the odor of violets about your clothes, have a good-sized piece of orris root put in the wash boiler where the clothes are boiled, and a delicate perfume will be the result? That when a knife has been used to cut onions, if you wipe it with a damp cloth, then rub thoroughly with dry salt, the objectionable odor will have entirely disappeared? That milk and butter should be kept away from strong odors?

CURE FOR HICCOUGHS

I have put in twenty-five years as a druggist and chemist and during that time have had occasion to treat a large number of cases of hiccoughs. The following mode of treatment will give an almost instant cure provided the case has not run more than six or eight hours. Stop up both ears tightly with the forefingers, then drink (from the hands of a second party) five or six ounces of water, taking very small swallows, and twenty chances to one the hiccoughs will disappear before the last swallow has been taken. It is absolutely necessary to plug up both ears air-tight for this treatment.

WASHING LACE CURTAINS

Before putting the curtains to soak, stitch a strip of muslin or cheesecloth around the edge of the curtain and you will find the scallops will be round instead of pointed as when you pin directly through the fabric.

SOGGY PIE-CRUSTS

When the pie-crust is prepared brush the lower crust with the beaten yolk of an egg and sprinkle with bread crumbs that have been grated. This is especially fine for fruit and liquid pies.

MENDING GRANITE WARE

When your granite pans and kettles begin to leak, instead of throwing them away, try mending them with putty. I used a kettle all summer for canning fruit that I had mended in this way. Be sure the putty is fresh and do not use the vessel until it is thoroughly dry.

BEST WAY TO COOK BACON

Put the bacon, sliced thin, on a common toaster and place the toaster in a baking pan a little longer than the toaster; put this in a hot oven and as it cooks, the fat drains into the pan.

A CURIO CABINET HINT

A cupful of water placed on each shelf of the cabinet in which curios are kept will provide sufficient moisture to prevent the carved ivories, woods, shells, and the like from cracking. The water may be kept in one of the curios, and thus be inconspicuous. In a furnace-heated house this is a wise safeguard. Change the water every few days.

LITTLE HELPS FOR HOME-MAKERS

CHICKEN CHOLERA

Take equal parts of pulverized alum, rosin, saltpeter and red pepper. Feed one tablespoonful in three pints of scalded meal until the chickens are well.

MASHED POTATOES

When mashing potatoes, after the milk and butter are added and they have had their final stirring, add a small teaspoonful of baking powder and stir well and see how light they will be.

FROZEN ONIONS FRIED

When I found some large onions had frozen, the head of the house informed me that frozen onions were very sweet and nice when fried. I thought so, too, when I had eaten them. I cut them into thin slices, salt and pepper, then fry brown in hot butter.

MAKING FRUIT BUTTER

I would like to suggest a very easy way of making pear butter, peach, etc. After the fruit is prepared and sweetened, put the same in the oven. In this way it needs only occasional stirring. It will cook down and keep just the same as butter made on the top of the stove and is made with a great deal less work.

CLEANING SEWING MACHINES

Take the machine apart, boil the parts in soda water, replace, and oil well. Or, with gasoline, flood every oiling place on the machine, run it rapidly, repeat if necessary, wipe off with a cloth, then oil with machine oil.

BEEF POT ROAST

To make an ordinary piece of beef into a fine pot roast, have the kettle very hot, and brown the meat on all sides before adding the water, which should be boiling. Cook slow.y till tender, making a brown dressing in the kettle after the meat has been removed.

A SILK HINT

When stitching thin silk, or any goods inclined to pucker, place a strip of paper on the under side and stitch through with cloth. The needle cuts the paper, and it is easily pulled away, leaving the seam free of any inclination to pucker.

OATMEAL COOKING

A piece of butter the size of a pea, dropped into the oatmeal pot, will keep it from boiling over.

STEAM OUT SPLINTERS

When a splinter has been driven into the hand it can be extracted by steam. Fill a wide-mouthed bottle nearly full of hot water, place the injured part over the mouth and press it slightly. The suction will draw the flesh down, and in a minute or two the steam will extract the splinter, also relieve the inflammation.

ICE FOR THE INVALID

A small piece of ice held in the mouth is often gratifying to a sick person, and in order to have some at hand and thus save the attendant a trip to the refrigerator try the following: Take quite a deep bowl and cover with a piece of flannel depressed to form a hollow about half the depth of the bowl. Tie this in place. Now fill this with bits of ice broken to about the size desired and cover with another piece of flannel. This can be kept in quite a warm room for hours without melting; while, if the pieces freeze together, a stout pin will readily chip off a piece.

TO CATCH FURNACE DUST

Many persons make the mistake of closing the registers before shaking the furnace fire. Instead, leave them open, place wet cloths over them, and the dust that arises from the ashes will cling to the cloths. If the registers are closed the dust will settle underneath, and when they are afterward opened puffs of dust will rise and spread over the contents of the rooms.

STAINS ON MARBLE

To remove stains from marble mix equal quantities of powdered chalk, carbonate of soda and pumice-stone powder, and sufficient liquid cloudy ammonia to form a soft paste; spread evenly over the marble and leave it for two or three hours, then scrub thoroughly with soft soap and hot water and wipe with flannel cloth. Should the stains still be visible, they should again be covered with paste, which should remain for a day, when the marble should again be scrubbed.

CLEANING COMBS AND BRUSHES

To clean combs and brushes use gasoline, which removes all oil and does not impair the bristles, as ammonia, borax and such things do.

ANOTHER DUST SUGGESTION

A party of ladies, helping to decorate a friend's home for a wedding, chatted about "this thing and that," and drifted at last to the subject of house-cleaning. One said she so much dreaded getting the dust from the top of her wardrobe. I remarked that I kept a newspaper on the top of mine—that it not only kept the dust out of the smallest crack, but could also be replaced at any time by a clean paper.

A PANCAKE "POINTER"

The disagreeable smoke which usually fills the house while pancakes are being baked may be greatly lessened in this way: To grease the griddle use a slice of raw turnip on the end of a fork, and dip in melted grease. The smoke is absorbed by the turnip.

FOR BURNS

Take equal parts flour and cooking soda, and water to make a thick paste; bind on the burn quickly and it will relieve smarting and prevent blisters.

MENDING GRANITE WARE

I have been delighted to find that I could mend my granite or agate basins by chipping off the enamel so that a small circle of the iron base is exposed around the hole to be soldered—which I do by using the sharp corner of a chisel. I then sandpaper the iron and give it a coating of zinc solution and proceed as with tin.

YOUR MATTRESSES

Housekeepers who have to have mattresses made over every few years may save this expense by having at hand a large darning needle or a straight sacking needle and some upholsterer's cord or twine—a small tightly twisted cord—and whenever a "tacking" is broken, use your needle and twine right away. Put the needle through the same place as the original tacking, and fasten with the leather pieces, pulling the string tight and fasten securely in a square knot. You will be surprised to see how much longer your mattress will last and it will not grow "lumpy" and uncomfortable to lie on.

MOTHS IN CARPETS

To destroy moths in carpets, take one-half cup salt dissolved in hot water, saturate edge of carpet, lay on cloth and iron till dry.

KNOW YOUR PLANTS

February is the month when floral catalogues are sent throughout the land, and every flower-lover who reads the descriptions and sees the beautiful illustrations of new varieties of plants is tempted to buy them. As a rule these novelties are all that is claimed for them, if they are properly cultivated; but often they are purchased by people who know nothing of their nature and needs, and who give them little care, and then, because results do not equal those described by the florist who spent time, study and expense on them, he is accused of misrepresentation.

Be sure, before buying any plant, that you know what its needs are as to conditions of soil, temperature, light and other essential points, and that you can supply them. If this is not possible—well, let someone with money to spare do the experimenting, while you grow those you understand; for a thrifty plant of the commonest kind is more ornamental than a sickly specimen of the rarest novelty.

One source of failure and disappointment is found in the floral articles published on every hand, and this is true for several reasons. One is that many of them give the name of the writer, but no hint as to whether their home is in Maine, or in Texas; another is that when such information is given, the reader pays no attention to it, and a third is that many a writer is not writing from an experimental knowledge.

A writer living in the Southern states may describe to the most minute particular how success was achieved in growing a certain class of plants, but the one living in the North who follows those instructions is foreordained to failure.

In the Southland, where an early spring and a late fall give a long season in which plants may grow from the seed and complete their natural period of bloom, there is no need to take time by the forelock as must be done farther north, where the flower-lover, if wise, will have many a seed-pan tucked in among the window plants before this month ends.

The seedling plants which have been transplanted two or three times before being put into the open ground have a start which insures a fairly long season of blooming before being spoiled by frosts.

Fuchsias and other wood-stemmed plants which have been wintered in the cellar will show signs of life, and should be brought, gradually, to the light and warmth. If they need pruning (as most of them will to secure symmetrical form) do it at once, thereby forcing new branches to start and greatly increasing the number of blooming points on the plant.

Look over the cannas, dahlias and other stored roots, and if any show signs of decay remove them, for even one or two that are bad now means that all touching them will be spoiled by planting time.

SOAP ODDS AND ENDS

Save your small bits of soap in a low jar; when the jar is full, reduce to small shavings and add a teaspoonful of your favorite toilet water. Pour boiling water over this and let it stand; when settled pour water off and behold! you have a dainty toilet soap.

NEW WINTER SALADS

No dinner, however unpretentious, is complete without a salad. This dish, when properly concocted, is at once an appetizer, an aid to digestion, and the connecting link between the heavier courses of the dinner proper and the dessert. The housewife who caters wisely is alive to this fact, and is ever on the alert for something wholesome in the way of a salad which is at the same time a little out of the ordinary, in order that there may be no tiresome monotony in the favorite dish.

Various mixtures are employed for marinating salads—a rich mayonnaise, the plainer French dressing, or a simple dressing of oil and lemon juice—the kind depending wholly upon the nature of the salad.

Mayonnaise: A good dressing for general purposes, which possesses the further virtue of its keeping qualities to commend it, is made as follows:

Beat the yolks of eight eggs till smooth; add one cup of sugar, one tablespoonful each of salt, ground mustard and black pepper, a dash of cayenne and one-half cup of cream; mix thoroughly in order that all the ingredients may be incorporated. Bring to a boil one and one-half cups of vinegar, add one cup of fresh sweet butter and bring again to a boil, then pour it over the other mixture; stir well, and when cold, bottle. Keep in a cold place.

Italian Chicken Salad: Take a sufficiency of the white meat of cold fowls and pull into flakes; then pile it mound fashion in the center of a shallow salad dish and pour over it a rich dressing. Have ready two fine heads of lettuce crisped in ice water; strip off the outside leaves, shred the inside and arrange neatly in a ridge around the chicken. On top of the lettuce place a chain formed of the whites of three eggs cut into rings. Serve a portion of the lettuce with each helping of chicken.

Spiced Salmon Salad: Stand a can of salmon in a pot of boiling water and boil hard for twenty minutes; take out can, open, and drain off the oil; then turn the fish into a deep bowl, stick around it a dozen cloves, sprinkle lightly with salt and pepper and cover with vinegar. Let stand six hours. Drain off the vinegar, dress the fish with mayonnaise or any rich salad dressing, and arrange for individual serving in rings of tomato jelly. Garnish with thin slices of lemon.

Oyster Salad: Have ready a head of fine lettuce crisped in ice water, select the best leaves and arrange for individual serving in pretty salad saucers. Also have ready one quart large oysters plumped and chilled. Marinate the oysters with a salad dressing, let stand five minutes, then arrange in the lettuce cups, dress with lemon juice, garnish with sliced lemon, and serve with cheese straws.

Baked Bean Salad: Turn a sufficient quantity of cold baked beans (canned ones may be used) into a salad dish; add a minced onion and one tablespoonful of tomato catsup; stir lightly, dress with mayonnaise and serve.

Ham and Vegetables: Heap two and one-half cups of ham in the center of a shallow salad dish and pour over it a mayonnaise dressing; around the ham arrange a border of cold-boiled potatoes cut into cubes, and on the outer edge a border of pickled beet cubes. Garnish with fringed celery.

To fringe celery stalks, cut them into two-inch lengths; stick several coarse needles into the top of a cork; draw half the stalk of each piece of celery through the needles several times, then crisp in ice water.

Swedish Herring Salad: Soak two herrings over night; boil one dozen medium-sized potatoes in their jackets; when cold, peel and cut into dice; chop a large onion fine; bone, skin and dice the fish, season with pepper and add enough vinegar to moisten. Transfer the mixture to a large, flat dish, pour over it a cup of rich, sweet cream that has been thoroughly chilled, garnish with hard-boiled eggs and sliced beets, and serve at once.

Sweetbread Salad: Soak one pair sweetbreads in cold water one hour, then drain and put into boiling water to which has been added one-fourth teaspoonful of salt and two teaspoonfuls of lemon juice. Cook slowly for twenty minutes, then plunge at once into ice water. When firm and white, cut into slices, mix with one cup of chopped celery, marinate with French dressing, stand on ice until thoroughly chilled, then serve in nests of crisped lettuce. Dress with mayonnaise.

Lamb Salad: Dice a sufficiency of cold boiled lamb; add half the quantity of chopped olives; wash, crisp and arrange for individual serving the inside leaves of a head of lettuce. Arrange the meat mixture in the cups, dress with salad dressing and garnish with pickled capers.

Hot Cabbage Salad: Shave the cabbage fine and put on to cook in just enough water to prevent burning. When tender, add half a cup of cream or rich milk; bring to a boil, season with salt, pepper and a tablespoonful of butter and add enough vinegar to give it the desired flavor. Let boil up, add a beaten egg, stir well and serve.

Fruit Salad: Arrange alternate layers of pineapple and bananas in a salad dish, sprinkling each layer with sugar and grated nutmeg. Turn over all a glass of sherry, and serve.

INK STAINS

To remove ink stains from cotton or linen: Rub the spot as soon as possible, thoroughly, with lemon juice and salt; place over a bowl and turn boiling water on it until the bowl is half full or more, keeping the goods taut. Now turn a saucer over it and let steam five minutes, then rub and wring out. Repeat the process until removed. If a trace is left it will disappear in the wash.

KEEPING RIBBONS IN PLACE

To keep a child's hair ribbon in place: Place a small elastic band (as a security for the ribbon) around the hair several times; then under one portion of band draw through one-half of ribbon's length, and bringing ends forward tie in the usual manner.

FROZEN EGGS

In cold weather it often happens that a nest of frozen eggs are found hidden away in the haymow. Pour boiling water over them and set them aside till the water is cold, and on breaking the eggs, the yolk will be soft, and beat up like an egg that had never been frozen.

WHEN COOKING SAUERKRAUT

To prevent scenting up the whole house when cooking sauerkraut, cook it in a covered dish in the oven. We use a bean jar.

TO REMOVE RUST

I had much trouble with the tank in my kitchen stove. Water would rust in it so I could not use it. It became coated with layers of rust. I boiled washing soda in it for a few weeks, and cleaned it so perfectly that it has never rusted since; that was several months ago. I boil my discolored tinware in sal-soda water. They come out silvery-white.

USES FOR A MEAT CHOPPER

I find my meat chopper useful for many things other than chopping meat. Use the vegetable plate and chop seeded or seedless raisins for cake; green tomatoes for piccalilli; apples for mince pies; nut-meats for cake, ice cream or candy, or lemon for pie. And farmers' wives will find that rendering lard is made easy by using the meat chopper instead of a knife to cut the lard. With the small plate in the chopper, put through dried bread or crackers, dried celery leaves, sage and parsley. If these are put away in fruit jars they will keep perfectly for a long time. Horseradish is as good as though grated.

SOME NEW WAYS TO COOK WINTER VEGETABLES

The only vegetables the great majority of housewives have at their service during the winter months are those which may be safely stored or preserved by canning. Consequently, they must depend for variety in this feature of the daily menus, not so much upon changes in the vegetables themselves as in the methods of cooking and serving them. By so doing, monotony, which is the great destroyer of the appetite, is avoided.

The following recipes may be of some use to the housewife who is on the alert for new ways of cooking the same old things, thereby beguiling her family into believing that they are being treated to a change of diet:

Potatoes a la Italienne: Select a sufficient number of fine potatoes of uniform size and bake done; then cut a round from one end of each and carefully scoop out the inside; mash well and mix with one-third the quantity of boiled rice; season the whole with grated cheese, cream, salt and pepper. Fill the shells with this mixture, rounding up the tops, dot with bits of butter, return to the oven and brown. Serve without delay.

Sweet Potato Puff: Steam six medium sized sweet potatoes without paring; when done, peel, mash and mix with one tablespoonful of melted butter, one teacupful of hot cream or rich milk, one teaspoonful of ground cinnamon, sugar, salt and pepper to taste; then beat the whole until smooth and light. Whip the whites of two eggs to a stiff froth, and fold into the potato mixture; heap high in buttered ramequin, and stand in a quick oven until puffed high. Serve immediately without re-dishing.

Mock Cauliflower: Remove the outside leaves from a firm white cabbage of medium size and drop it into boiling water; boil fifteen minutes, then change the water, adding fresh boiling water. Cook tender, drain in a colander and stand aside until cold. Chop fine, add two eggs well beaten, one tablespoonful of butter, three of cream and salt and pepper to season. Mix all together, turn into a buttered baking dish, and brown in the oven. Send at once to the table.

Turnip Balls: Wash and peel firm turnips; then cut with a vegetable scoop; drop the balls into boiling water, to which a little sugar has been added, until tender, taking care to preserve their shape. Just a few minutes before taking from the fire add a little salt; drain, cover with drawn butter sauce and sprinkle lightly with minced parsley. Serve very hot.

Tomatoes with Minced Chicken: Butter a baking dish; put in the bottom a layer of cold cooked chicken or veal minced; sprinkle with salt, pepper and bits of butter; then put in a layer of canned tomatoes from which the juice has been drained, and sprinkle lightly with sugar; repeat the layers, seasoning as directed, until the dish is full; then cover with bread crumbs, dot thickly with bits of butter, and bake covered until cooked through. Remove cover and brown quickly. Serve with tomato sauce, using the tomato liquor for making it.

Corn Oysters: To one cup of canned corn add three eggs, yolks and whites beaten separately, one cup grated bread crumbs, three-fourths of a cup of sweet milk, one-half teaspoonful of salt and a little white pepper. Mix well, and drop from a teaspoon into hot fat to more than cover, and fry a nice brown.

Fricassee of Parsnips: Scrape or pare the parsnips and, if large, cut into halves. Boil in milk until tender, then cut lengthwise into bits two or three inches long, and simmer for a few minutes in a sauce made of two tablespoonsful of the broth, one-half cup of cream, a bit of mace, one tablespoonful of butter blended with the same quantity of sifted flour, and salt and white pepper to season. Serve as soon as taken from the fire.

TO DETECT CHALK IN MILK

Dilute the milk in water; the chalk, if there be any, will settle to the bottom in an hour or two. Put to the sediment an acid, vinegar for instance, and if effervescence takes place, chalk is present in the milk. I have tried this a number of times, and have been able to bring the guilty parties to justice.

A MAGIC MITTEN FOR NUMB HANDS

About fifteen months ago, my fingers, and finally my hands, sometimes one, sometimes the other, would become numb at night. This numbness seemed to be caused by a nervous tension in the fingers. The mitten was a chance discovery and gave instant relief. Make the mittens the exact size of the hand, with pasteboard fronts and cloth backs, without a thumb. They will stay on nicely without tying. They hold the fingers straight while one is sleeping.

TO POLISH A STOVE

Put a quantity of stove polish into a dish, add equal parts water and turpentine and a few drops of varnish, mix this well together; apply with a small paint brush. Let the polish dry, and then rub briskly with a stove brush. This will give a glossy polish that will last from one spring until the next. This should not be used on the top of a cook-stove that is in use, for the odor would be offensive when the polish was first put on. It is an excellent polish for stoves that are not used through the summer.

THE KITCHEN WORK-STOOL

At any of the large department stores a "work-stool" can be purchased for about eighty-five cents. The one in my kitchen is in almost constant use. "I can't sit down to wash dishes," so many women say; but that is because the chair they use is too low, and the water runs up their sleeves. Also, "it looks lazy." The stool should be about eight inches higher than an ordinary chair and the water will not run up the arms, and as one is already half standing, it is easy to rise to attend to other duties, so one does not look lazy.

AN EXCELLENT DRY-CLEANER

By the use of dry Ivory soap and gasoline, one may obtain results which he may never attain through the use of gasoline only, especially where the article is both grease-spotted and dusty or grimy from ordinary use. Thoroughly rub the soiled spot or garment with the dry soap. Allow to stand for several hours or over night. Then sponge with gasoline and rub dry with a clean cloth. In sponging, begin at outer edge, even better a short distance from spot, rub lightly, gradually working to soiled place, and using more gasoline, always rubbing the right way of the goods. In this way one can usually avoid the ugly rings so often encountered in cleaning. Be sure there is no water in the gasoline or there will be spots. Where the gasoline is perfectly pure, this method cleans the most delicate goods beautifully.

FUEL ECONOMY

Take all pieces of slate from coal cinders, sprinkle well with cold water, and they will burn like fresh coal.

A PIE IDEA

I find it a great help, when mixing pie pastry, to cover several extra tins; set them away in a cool place; then when I want a fresh pie all I have to do is fill the crust, bake it, and I have a pie with about half the labor of the old way. This does away with mixing pastry every time you want a pie.

PREPARING BEEF TONGUES

Buy the tongue, asking the butcher to trim off the roots. Wash it thoroughly, then take a stone crock deep enough to hold it, rub it (the tongue), all over with molasses, about two tablespoonfuls for one tongue; next sprinkle a very little powdered saltpeter on both sides; last, put in a dish and cover thick with dry salt. I use table salt. Turn it over every day for a week; longer won't hurt it. Keep it cool. To finish, take an empty barrel, put in the bottom an old pan with some ashes in it and make a smoke of cobs, lay a stick across the top, run a wire through the top of the tongue and suspend as high as you can in the barrel; cover with some old carpet or burlap and keep the smoke going a day. Then you can hang it up in the cellar, and cook it when you please. If you and all your guests don't say it is delicious cut thin for tea, or for a sandwich, you will be the first to say otherwise. It will pay you to try it. A smoked tongue costs seventy-five cents in market, hard to get and a poor, dried-up thing. You can omit the smoke if you choose.

MENDING BROKEN CHINA

When china is broken do not put it in water. Tie firmly together, put in a basin, cover with skim milk, set on the back of stove and boil one hour. Let it stand in the milk until cold and it will never come apart.

HOW TO BEHEAD A BOTTLE

When far from town and in need of jelly glasses take some bottles or glass jars; saturate a thick cord in turpentine, tie cord around bottle below neck and ignite cord with a match. Let cord burn till a little click is heard. If directions are followed, the bottle or jar will be cut off evenly where the cord passed around it.

COOKING HINTS

Put a tablespoonful of vinegar in the water before poaching eggs and they will remain whole. Cook graham mush closely covered; it cooks quicker and tastes better. Add a little sugar—about the same quantity as you use of salt—when frying potatoes; they brown nicer and taste better. When roasting a fowl lay in roasting-pan *breast downward;* the white meat is much softer and more juicy.

TO FRESHEN RIBBONS

Wash ribbon in warm soap-suds, wring out, and iron at once with hot iron; when ironed, take in hands and crumple and crush; iron again and you will be surprised at the soft, glossy ribbon you will have.

ONE FOR BOSTON

The best way to make codfish fine and smooth for fish-balls is to run it through the meat grinder, as the grinder will take bits of skin and tough pieces that are ordinarily wasted. The first time this was tried in one family the fish balls were pronounced "the best we ever had."

REMEDY FOR CATARRH

In a country where nine-tenths of the human family are afflicted with catarrh in some form, a simple and inexpensive catarrh cure should be one of the greatest of "little helps." If those so afflicted will try for sixty days the old "German Remedy"—which consists simply of washing the feet each night in cold or cool water, rubbing dry with a coarse towel and putting on a pair of fresh, clean stockings every morning—they will as heartily believe in it as I do, although the remedy is so simple most people will not try it.

WASHING CHAMOIS SKIN

In washing chamois to keep it soft and pliable, rub it vigorously in lukewarm water, using any brand of soap you wish. Then rinse twice in same temperature of water and lay on clean cloth to dry. The principal thing is to rinse all the soapsuds out before drying.

TO REMOVE RUST FROM CLOTHING

While rinsing clothes, take such as have spots of rust, wring out, dip a wet brush in oxalic acid, and rub on the spot, then dip in salt and rub on, and hold on the hot tea kettle and the spot will immediately disappear; rinse again, rubbing the place a little with the hands.

TO WASH PRINTS

To wash a dark percale or sateen dress—put two or three quarts of flour starch into sufficient water in a tub to wash it nicely. Rub well, rinse and hang in the shade to dry. Enough starch will remain in the goods to make it appear like new when ironed on the wrong side.

TO POLISH GALVANIZED WARE

To clean galvanized iron (as buckets, tubs, etc.) dampen a cloth in kerosene and rub until the dirt disappears, then polish with old papers, and they will look as well as new.

TO SAVE EGGS

Stir your cakes the same as usual except that you leave out the eggs. After your baking powder is added and tins greased, the very last thing before placing them in the oven, stir in one tablespoon of clear snow for each egg you would have used. Your cakes will be light and tender.

CORNSTARCH IN CHOCOLATE

For a dainty cup of chocolate or cocoa to serve with wafers: Take a pint each of milk and water, two squares of Baker's chocolate and sugar to suit the taste. Dissolve two teaspoonfuls of cornstarch in a little cold milk, and stir into the boiling chocolate. Serve a spoonful of whipped cream, sweetened and flavored with vanilla, in each cup.

MORE LEMON HINTS

Hot lemonade, taken at bedtime, is good to break up a cold.
The juice of one lemon in a goblet of water, without any sugar, taken at least half an hour before breakfast, will clear a bilious system with great efficiency.
Lemon juice will also take out mildew.

CELERY LEAVES

To have always on hand a supply of celery leaves for soups, trim off the green leaves before serving the celery, wash, drain and place in a warm oven for a few hours; when thoroughly dry, crush them and put in a tin can with cover. A pinch of this powder gives a more delicate celery flavor to pressed meat and stews than does celery seed.

REMEDIES FOR BURNS

When badly burned by concentrated lye, bathe the part at once with vinegar. In a second, relief is obtained, and pain is almost banished. Syrup or molasses applied to a burn from fire, is soothing as well as excluding air. While common soda is good for excluding air, it does not give the relief that syrup does.

FOR IRONING DAY

When ironing, if your flatirons do not heat fast enough, try placing a dripping pan over them, and they will get hot much quicker.
Put all common towels, cloths, etc., through the wringer, set close. This mangles them nicely.

LITTLE HELPS FOR HOME-MAKERS

INEXPENSIVE CLOTHES RACKS

Saw barrel in three equal parts, then wrap with clean strips of cloth and take a loop in the center to hang up by. These make excellent racks for shirtwaists and skirts to keep them in shape and from wrinkling.

CURE FOR EAR-ACHE

Place a pipe-stem against the patient's ear, putting a thin rag over the bowl to prevent ashes scattering and blow the smoke into the ear.

TO WASH LINOLEUM

Never scrub with a brush, but wash with tepid water and a dash of soap powder. Rinse with clean water and when dry rub with furniture polish.

SAWDUST FOR GRIMY HANDS

If the wives of those men whose occupation necessitates the handling of grimy and greasy machinery, or other things that make almost hopelessly dirty hands, will provide some fine sawdust to be used at "wash up" time, they will find it more than a "little help"; it will save time, soap, towels and laundry bills.

CLEANSING A WHITE NET VEST

I have made a very valuable discovery in the preservation of the dainty articles of a woman's wardrobe. At a recent reception I wore, for the first time, a dress with a white net vest. The result of an accident left my dainty front bespattered from top to bottom with tomato juice. I feared the use of any liquid in the process of cleaning lest it should leave a stain on the snowy whiteness of the fabric, and could resort to nothing strong on acount of the delicate texture, so I determined to apply a thick paste made of talcum powder and water. After this had remained on the spots over night and was perfectly dry, I brushed it off with a clean, dry tooth brush. To my amazement the spots showed signs of disappearing. Encouraged in the effort, I repeated the application. With each brushing the stain grew more obscure. I persevered through five applications, at the end of which time my dainty garment appeared in its pristine freshness, with no reminder of the calamity which had overtaken it.

The success of this experiment suggested to me some ugly spots which defaced a white voile skirt. Although these spots were of a year's standing and other remedies had failed to remove them, it took only one application of this talcum and water paste to remove every vestige of stain. This last mentioned victory was so remarkable that I was induced to write to the friends of the National, that they too, might share in the benefit of my discovery.

FOR BAKED APPLES

When baking apples, run the corer only part way through, leaving a bottom to the hole as it were. Into this little cup place the sugar, spice and a bit of butter without danger of their running through into the pan, and they will cook into and flavor the whole apple. Besides, the fruit will keep its shape better than when the entire core is taken out.

THE UNEXPECTED GUEST

The unexpected guest for dinner sometimes creates commotion to the inexperienced housewife. Here is one way to be always ready. The prepared soups of today—such as Campbell's—are served by simply adding hot water. Keep some on hand all the time. When the unexpected guest appears simply add soup to the bill of fare, and it doesn't take a minute to do it.

WHEN MAKING JELLY

If jelly is boiled long after adding the sugar, the mixture will leave a coating on the sides of the kettle, as it boils down or evaporates, which may be scorched by the heat of the stove and will destroy both the flavor and color. This I learned from experience after being at a loss for some years to know why my jelly did not always have the fine flavor and beautiful color I sometimes obtained. To make perfect jelly, clear fruit juice should be reduced one-third, and the juice obtained by cooking the more solid fruits should not only be boiled away one-third, but also long enough to evaporate the water used in cooking the fruit. Measure the juice and turn it into a clean kettle, add an equal quantity of granulated sugar, and boil gently five minutes, not allowing it to rise in the kettle. Jelly made thus will be perfect in consistency, flavor and color, providing the fruit used is fresh and just ripe—not over-ripe.

BABY'S PLAY DRESSES

Make the babies' play dresses of dark material, very plain and with three buttons and buttonholes in the bottom hem, buttons in front and buttonholes behind. These are buttoned between the legs and keep the underclothes clean or may be used as aprons over white dresses. These are better than overalls, especially on small children, as it is much easier to give the child necessary attention

PARING PINEAPPLES

When preparing a pineapple for the table, try slicing it first and then paring it. In this way, with a good paring knife, you can remove the eyes, without waste.

CURE FOR IVY POISON

Three grains of hyposulphite soda to one ounce of water, eight drams to one pint.

If applied soon as inflammation appears, the cure is complete in less than two hours, and even when neglected until pustules and suppuration set in, it gives immediate relief, and recovery is rapid.

As hyposulphite of soda is perfectly harmless, being that used by photographers in fixing negatives, it can be used much stronger than proportions above. In some cases a stronger solution is best. This is also good for prickly heat.

TO KEEP THE WORKS OF YOUR WATCH CLEAN

Open the front case of watch and with a soft match, cut chisel shaped at the end, rub a little vaseline all round the seat of the case where the lid fits. Close the front, open the back and treat in the same way. Only a very small quantity is required, just enough to grease it thoroughly all round. This will make your case dust and water proof at those points. At the end of two or three months open case and if much dirt has collected take a match, cut in the same way, and scrape it all off clean and give it another coating of the vaseline. This is the only known plan to keep a watch clean where the cases do not fit perfectly close.

TO KILL BUGS ON PLANTS

I have been following a suggestion made to me, and find that saltpeter (prepared by dissolving one tablespoonful in a bucket of water) will not only kill bugs on vegetation but seems to act as a fertilizer to the soil. Spray and then repeat two days later. Two sprayings proved sufficient for the worst cases

TO CLEANSE COMBS

I lately learned such an easy and simple way to cleanse hair combs. Put a teaspoonful or so of baking soda in a wash basin, pour on hot, or good warm, soft water. Throw in combs, let lay a little while, then take small brush and cleanse; soon they are clean and sweet as if new.

BOTTLING CIDER

To bottle cider, to keep it perfectly sweet indefinitely: Scald the cider, and when just at the boiling point, put into self-sealing bottles, fruit jars or common bottles. If the latter, scald the corks, and cover with beeswax or resin. The bottles must be filled to overflowing, and sealed or fastened immediately. It must be bottled not later than two weeks from the mill, or it will not keep so well, and not much earlier or the flavor will not be as good.

A FEW SUGGESTIONS

Before potting slips, cut the end of the slip, and insert an oat. It will root better.

After seeds are sown in the ground, moisten well and place a cloth or paper over them. The ground will keep moist and the seeds will sprout soon.

If your pen is rusty hold it in the flame until hot and then dip in cold water. The pen can then be cleaned.

When troubled with ants, lay a few pieces of wormwood around, and they will soon disappear.

If cake or cookies have become dry and hard put a slice of bread in the jar and notice the change.

SHORTCAKE CRUSTS

When making shortcakes, instead of baking the desired thickness, then splitting, my way is to bake in two layers. Spread butter over the upper side of the lower layer, and on top of this place the other one; then when baked they come apart easily. This is much better than splitting the hot crust.

PLANT PESTS

At this time of year (late June) when every green growing thing is attacked by various bug-beetle-worm pests, all garden people are at wits' end to find a universal spray. The following is the first "sure thing" we have used: One pint quassia chips; one pint home-made soft soap; one teacupful kerosene oil.

Steep the quassia chips several hours in one gallon of water (hot). Add one gallon of hot water to the soap, and stir it until a strong "suds" is formed, add to this the quassia solution, then the kerosene oil and beat until thoroughly emulsified. To this now add two gallons of water, making four gallons in all. Apply this with any spraying machine or syringe, and it will drive every eating thing from plants and trees—both for indoor and outdoor plants.

DRIVES OUT MOSQUITOES

Mosquitoes are overcome by kerosene. They will drop into a cup held under them; or a cloth saturated with it and hung on the head frame of the bed will drive them away from the occupants of the bed.

MUD FOR A SPRAIN

Apply a poultice of cold, wet earth to a sprain, changing it often so that ti may be kept cold. This draws out the inflammation in a few hours and relieves the pain. Then a few rubbings with alcohol or any common liniment will make the joint as strong as ever.

LITTLE HELPS FOR HOME-MAKERS

HOW TO KEEP CREAM

During the hot weather many find it difficult to keep cream from souring, even in the refrigerator, unless they use it very soon after it is bought. Most of us who do not have cows, buy one-half pint at a time. Take this quantity as soon as it reaches the house, put in a bowl, add a heaping teaspoonful of powdered sugar, six drops of vanilla and soda the size of a small bean. Whip until foamy, but not thick. Put on ice and it will keep a week even in hot weather.

SOME WAYS OF SERVING COCOA

By the cup: Put one-half teaspoonful Bensdorp's Royal Dutch Cocoa and one teaspoonful granulated sugar in a clean dry cup, mix both well, add one-half cup boiling water, stir until cocoa and sugar are dissolved, then add one-half cup rick milk, sweeten to taste, and cocoa is ready. This is much improved by boiling one minute.

By the quart: Mix thoroughly four teaspoonfuls Bensdorp's Royal Dutch Cocoa and the same amount of granulated sugar, add one pint hot water, stir until all is a smooth syrup and boil three minutes, then add one pint rich milk and bring all to a boil. Whipped cream when served is a great improvement.

Directions for making iced cocoa: Four ounces Bensdorp's Royal Dutch Cocoa, six ounces granulated sugar, mix cocoa and sugar well, add one quart boiling water and stir until all is a smooth syrup.

For serving by the glass: Half fill glass with shaved ice, add one or two ounces syrup, a little sugar (say one-half teaspoonful), fill glass with half milk and half water and shake well.

A HINT FOR WASHING DAY

In very cold weather, it is always imprudent for a woman to hang out the clothes while overheated and tired from doing a large washing. This can be obviated by hanging them out the next day.

Take each piece and shake well, then drop it into the basket, straightened out as much as possible, with the corners which you wish to pin to the line hanging over the edge of the basket. When all are in, in the order in which you wish to hang them up, fold the corners that hang over the edge of the basket all together back on top of the part already in the basket. Now, cover all up smoothly with a heavy, damp towel, and set the basket of wet clothes in some cold place where there is no danger of freezing. This gives you an opportunity to cool off gradually while cleaning up the rooms, putting away tubs, etc.

In the morning, remove the towel, turn the ends of pieces back over the edge of the basket, and there will be no trouble in hanging them all out, without getting chilled or suffering from aching fingers, and the clothes will have plenty of time to dry, which they do not have in short winter days, if hung out after the washing is done.

Dry flannels in the house if weather is cold enough to freeze them.

MENDING A LEAD PIPE LEAK

How to stop a pinhole in a lead pipe: Take a tenpenny nail, place the square end upon the hole, and hit it two or three light blows with the hammer, and the orifice is closed as tight as though you had employed a plumber to do it at a cost of a dollar or more.

LACE INSERTION

Now that so much lace is used many may be puzzled about inserting it. Cut the material in the desired shape, and baste the insertion firmly, just where you would like it to be, turning corners neatly, and where necessary to curve or round it, draw the little cord in the edge or gather on a thread where it can be easily shaped as desired, then stitch on the inner edge of the narrow margin, after which slit the material in the center of lace, turning back the edges, cutting down to enough for a tiny hem, then stitch again on the outer edge of the margin. On thin material use No. 200 cotton which is sufficiently strong for all purposes, and will launder any number of times, with no frayed edges.

For goods that are not to be washed the edge need not be turned under for the second stitching, simply turned back, stitched and cut down closely, leaving a very neat appearance.

A COTTAGE CHEESE HINT

In making cottage cheese, sometimes after draining the curds through a cheesecloth bag, the curds are tough and lumpy. When such is the case, run them through the food chopper and they will become light and delicate. Then add cream, salt and pepper, and you will have a dainty dish. Sometimes I make tiny balls and roll them in chopped nuts; sometimes I add pitted cherries and make a salad of it; sometimes I thin it with cream and add caraway seeds, and again I add little onions.

A TRICK OF THE OVEN

If you wish to bake something quickly in a range with no fire started, get together a collection of fine wood or chips, start your fire, and let the top lids of the stove get very hot, put these in the oven on top of the grate, put the thing to be baked upon these hot lids and these will furnish bottom heat, while the quick fire will almost at once furnish top heat. The baking is very rapidly done with little heat in the house.

REMEDY FOR SEA SICKNESS

Take bromide of soda, four drams; bromide of ammonia, two drams; peppermint water, three ounces. Mix well. Use for three days before journey begins. It is not needed afterward. Take a teaspoonful in wine glass of cold water before each meal and also at bedtime.

TO BEAUTIFY THE LAWN

By digging away a strip of sod, about three or four inches wide, from the walks and around the trees and filling in the furrow thus made with fine white sand or gravel, one can mow the grass off evenly and in consequence the lawn is greatly improved and beautified. If the sand is put in sufficiently deep, no weeds or grass will grow through and thereby, at the same time, a clean effect will be brought forth.

TO REMOVE NUT MEATS

Pecan and hickory nut meats can be easily removed without breaking, by pouring boiling water over the nuts and letting them stand until cold. Then crack with a hammer, striking the small end of the pecan.

SIMPLE REMEDIES

California cure for headache. Lay the head upon a pillow and strew the pillow with fragrant roses. Another cure for the same is to walk backwards.

Lavender, when applied to face and hands, will keep away mosquitos in this western land.

For malaria, put lemon juice in all the water you drink.

A tablespoonful of melted butter, swallowed, will cure croup and hoarseness. Melt over a lamp and take when necessary.

For cancer, take violet leaves, (the garden variety is better than the wild violet) steep them in water, drink the hot tea thus made (a wineglassful several times a day), and also apply cotton wool soaked in the hot tea, over the cancer. It has cured very bad cancers, and such a simple remedy ought to be known and remembered.

SWEETENING SOUR FRUIT

Put a pinch of soda into rhubarb or other sour fruit and only half the usual quantity of sugar will be needed.

TO CLARIFY COFFEE

Instead of using the white of an egg to clarify coffee, drop a pinch of salt into the coffee pot before adding the water, and you will have clear, bright, well-settled coffee. This was learned from an old hotel keeper and will not fail.

TO KILL WEEDS

If one will when the dew is on, sprinkle a little fine salt on the leaves of any plant he wishes to kill he will be both surprised and pleased at the result.

SALT FOR BLACK ANTS

In certain seasons the large black ants become very troublesome, getting even into the ice-box if their advance is not checked. Judging from the number of applications I had last year for "something that will drive away the pests with no danger of poisoning the family," it is not very generally known that common salt freely sprinkled where they gather will drive them away, yet such is the case. Try it and be convinced.

WHEN MAKING BREAD

An experienced friend taught me how to make bread up at night and thus save time and labor. Two years ago I conceived the idea of putting the dough into the pans during the night, instead of punching it down as was generally necessary. Since then I have always followed this method, and find it much easier than my neighbors' who make their bread up in the morning. During the winter, of course, it takes more care to have the room heated properly, but during warm weather "it works like magic." When my family was smaller, I found the easiest time for baking pies or cakes was before breakfast when the fire was clear. That baking time now has to be given to packing dinners for four hungry school children, though even yet I snatch time to bake their cakes in muffin pans while the breakfast is under way.

COOKED FROSTING

To make cooked frosting soft and creamy, put only enough water in the sugar to dissolve it; add a pinch of cream of tartar or baking powder. Cook quickly, watching it closely until it will spin in a thread from the spoon. Beat the white of an egg vigorously with an egg-beater for at least three minutes. Beat while pouring the syrup in and for a few minutes afterward. Your frosting will rarely fail to be creamy.

CARE OF NEW BOOKS

Lay the book back downward, on a table or smooth surface. Press the front cover down until it touches the table, then the back cover, holding the leaves in one hand while you open a few of the leaves at the back, then at the front, alternately pressing them down gently until you reach the center of the volume. This should be done two or three times. Never open a book violently nor bend back the covers. It is liable not only to break the back, but to loosen the leaves.

WASHING WHITE SILK

In washing white silk use cold water to keep it from turning yellow.

HOME-MADE PHOTO PASTE

Not many people know that the finest paste for mounting kodak pictures is made with ordinary starch not cooked quite so much as for stiffening. I know a photographer who mounts his most expensive pictures this way.

TENDER OMELETTES

A little boiling water added to an omelette as it thickens will prevent it being tough.

USES OF BORAX

Borax is a bleach and will prevent clothes turning yellow.
Borax fixes colors.
Borax added to starch gives a superior gloss to the clothes.
Borax relieves hoarseness.
Borax cures sore throat.
Borax preserves the teeth and heals the gums.
Borax exterminates ants, bugs, and roaches.
Take a solution of warm water and borax and it will cleanse hair brushes and combs perfectly.
Borax dampened with a little water and rubbed on the scalp cures dandruff.
A pinch of borax added to warm hard-water softens it.
Borax used when boiling clothes whitens them more than any other washing powder.

HANGING UP CLOTHES IN COLD WEATHER

Before hanging up clothes in cold weather, take each piece and shake out, and then take hold with both hands of the end to be hung on the line, and drop into the basket, putting in the pieces just as you wish them hung up. It is best to hang sheets and tablecloths by the hem to save them whipping out. If they must be left out all night, at dark roll them over once or twice on the line and pin securely; in the morning unroll them. If a sudden wind starts up they cannot be damaged. Another help is to have mittens made of white canton flannel. Lay your hand on the cloth and work around with pencil, leaving half an inch for seam, stitch around with machine and they are done.

RELIABLE PIE CRUST

If hot water is used in making pie crust, it will not bend outward and allow the contents of custard or other pies containing a soft filling to run out in the oven. Put the soda and cream of tartar in the flour, stir the hot water into it, and add melted butter or lard. This pie crust is easily worked and is light when baked.

CURES FOR HICCOUGHS

Give one tablespoonful pure lemon juice at frequent intervals, as required; it has cured when doctors have despaired. Another cure is to order the sufferer to keep his tongue out of his mouth to judge of his condition, and not to withdraw it until directed so to do.

A MISCELLANY BOOK

A scrap book of clippings from newspapers and magazines will be found of great help to the housekeeper. These may be recipes, little helps for the household, or anything along a literary line. The housekeeper of modern life has use for all, and if easily accessible, they will be "just the thing" frequently.

MENDING STOCKINGS

The stockings which I buy for my six-year-old are much too long. I cut off the tops to the right length and lay the upper parts away. When he has worn out the knees, as boys are apt to do, I sew on this new top and have another pair of stockings as good as the first, as one pair of feet will outwear several legs.

WINTER CARE OF BEETS

In the fall we put our beets in a barrel in the cellar with alternate layers of earth and beets so they will keep in fine condition. Then any time during the winter when work is not so pressing, and as fast as the fruit jars become empty, we can fill them with beets and have them as we want them; they are excellent when canned.

FRUIT AND BAG SHOWERS

Like "Linen Showers," the "Fruit Shower" is very acceptable to the prospective bride. Held at the home of one of her girl friends, each one brings a can of fruit or a couple glasses of jelly. In this way the bride has quite a start in fruit, without taxing anyone much. The "Bag Shower" is the same plan, each one making a bag of some kind, from a laundry bag to a dainty chamois bag for jewels.

MAKING DRAWN-WORK COLLARS

Do not use embroidery hoops; instead, after pulling the threads, sew firmly to a piece of stiff cardboard, then cut away the card from beneath the threads and you have it ready for work and firmly and equally stretched. Do not remove until entirely finished and your collar will be perfect.

COLD-STARCHED IRONING

Rub the starched pieces with a rag that has been wrung out of water that contains a few drops of kerosene. You will be surprised how much easier they iron. It will also give a nice gloss.

MEAT-PIE CRUST

If, in making meat pie, the crust be left thin enough to drop from a spoon instead of rolling, better results will be obtained.

A HELP FOR THE BOYS

Let the mothers try knitting or crocheting a loop on the wrist of each mitten to hang it up by.

HOW TO FIND THE RIGHT SIDE OF CLOTH

To find the right side of woolen dress goods of smooth surface, hold the goods level with the eyes between them and the light; if it looks fuzzy it is the wrong side. The right side is always singed smooth by the manufacturer.

RELIEF FROM ASTHMA

Persons suffering from asthma may be greatly relieved by smoking sumach. Gather the green leaves while fresh, dry them, and smoke in a common clay pipe.

TO PREVENT OIL STAINS

Put blotting paper in the holder under a bracket or hanging-lamp, and the oil will go on further.

WASHING AN EVENING SHAWL

Many beautiful evening shawls are ruined by home washing, and frequent dry cleansing is costly. If washed by the following method, an umbrella shawl will retain its original appearance.

Soak the shawl in a warm suds of white soap. Do not rub soap on the shawl. Squeeze the suds through it, but do not wring. When clean rinse in a weak suds of the same temperature as the first water. Throw in a heap on a clean sheet to dry, turning occasionally. When dry, pin in shape on a sheet, then sprinkle with cold water to raise the fluffy fiber.

A knitted or crocheted shawl so washed will appear new.

TO REMOVE COCOA STAINS

To remove cocoa stains from table linen or other fabric, soak the article in cold water, when the discoloration will quickly disappear.

AN INSECTICIDE FOR ROSES

Save coffee grounds, dry them out, and put around your roses with equal parts of soot. It is a good fertilizer and insecticide.

WHEN WASHING MUSLINS

To keep delicate colored prints and muslins from fading when washing, soak in salt water for half an hour.

TO RENEW PATENT LEATHER

First rub with a linen rag soaked with olive oil or milk, and polish with a dry, soft duster. Cream and linseed oil in equal parts are a good polish for patent leather boots.

AMMONIA'S USES AND ITS ANTIDOTE

A little ammonia in tepid water will soften and cleanse the skin.

Spirits of ammonia inhaled will often relieve a severe headache.

If the color has been taken out of silks by fruit stains ammonia will usually restore the color.

One or two tablespoonfuls added to a pail of water will clean windows better than soap.

A few drops in a cupful of warm water, applied carefully, will remove spots from paintings and chromos.

To brighten carpets, wipe them with warm water in which has been poured a few drops of ammonia.

Keep nickel, silver ornaments and mounts bright by rubbing with woolen cloth saturated in spirits of ammonia.

If one of you has swallowed ammonia accidentally, make haste immediately to drink lots of water or skim milk or both, at frequent intervals, while someone is stirring up a half-cup of starch and cold water, (two or three heaping teaspoonfuls of starch)—give a teaspoonful or so, every fifteen minutes.

The reason for this: First, the water to "flush" the stomach, thus diluting the ammonia so it will not find lodgment and burn the stomach; then the starch water forms a coating on the suffering gullet which the ammonia burnt like fire, and alleviates this distress until the doctor gets there. Otherwise your patient will likely be asphyxiated long before other help than yours can reach him. It will take quick work.

TO RENEW TARNISHED GILT FRAMES

Take sufficient flour of sulphur to give a golden tinge to one and one-half pints of water, and boil in it five onions; strain, and when cool apply to the parts that require restoring, with a soft brush, and it will come out as good as new when dry.

TO RENDER HARD WATER SOFT

Dissolve one ounce of the best quicklime in a bucket of water; then stir all thoroughly in a barrel of water, and as soon as it settles the water will be soft and fit for use; the lime, having united with the carbonate of lime, which makes the hard water, will be all deposited.

TO DRIVE A NAIL EASILY

A person trying to drive a nail through a piece of seasoned oak an inch and a half thick found it impossible to do so until the suggestion was made that he grease the nail. It then was driven easily without bending.

CARE OF PATENT SHOES

Patent-vici shoes, or dancing pumps, should be stuffed tight in the toe with tissue paper, cotton or old cloth, after taking off, and rubbed with a little vaseline. If cared for in this way they will not crack, even if kept for an entire season. Vaseline is a splendid preserver of any kind of leather, but should be applied sparingly so it will not leave a greasy appearance.

A STOVE POLISH

Mix the stove blacking with vinegar, to the consistency of cream, add pinch of sugar, put on with a brush and polish with old newspapers; it will give a beautiful and lasting polish.

TO CLEAN SILVER

Put one-half pound sal-soda in eight quarts water; when at a boiling heat dip in the pieces of silver, immediately wash in soapsuds and wipe dry with a piece of cotton flannel.

DON'T PEEL PIE PLANT

In cooking pie plant, do not peel it, as the red skin gives a rich color to the sauce.

TURKISH DELIGHT

Take one ounce sheet gelatine and soak in one-half cup water for two hours. Take one pound granulated sugar, dissolve in one-half cup water and when at boiling point add the gelatine. Flavor with one orange, juice and rind, and one lemon, juice only. Chopped nuts improve it. Boil all steadily for twenty minutes. Dip a tin in cold water, pour in the liquid and when cold cut in squares and roll in confectioner's sugar.

HINTS ABOUT CUSTARDS

In making a custard of any sort, the whites of the eggs are not necessary. Use the yolks to thicken the milk, in the proportion of one yolk to a cup of milk. The whites of the eggs may then be used as a meringue for the top of the custard.

To prevent a baked custard from wheying, place the dish containing the custard in a basin of water while cooking.

To prevent a boiled custard from curdling, do not cook more than two or three minutes after adding the eggs to the milk and do not add salt until you have removed it from the stove.

Scald milk with which to make custard pies.

BAKING SWEET POTATOES

After washing sweet potatoes thoroughly, grease the outside with fried meat grease before baking. They will be found a great deal more juicy, and the skin can easily be removed.

DESTROYING AN ODOR

The odor that clings so persistently to a utensil in which fish or onions have been fried may be dispelled by placing in a hot oven for ten or fifteen minutes after washing and drying.

CANKER CURE

To each fluid ounce of sweetened gum-arabic mucilage, add very carefully and mix intimately two drops of creosote. Take about one teaspoonful in the mouth and thoroughly gargle, taking half a teaspoonful internally three times a day. A cure greatly prized by the late Dr. Ira K. Warren.

WHITE SPOTS ON FURNITURE

For white spots on highly polished furniture, apply common baking soda, dampened. Allow it to remain on the spots a short time, then rub firmly and the spots will disappear.

LITTLE HELPS FOR HOME-MAKERS

JEWEL CUTTER'S CEMENT

Add to equal quantities of resin and beeswax four times as much of marble dust or sharp fine sand. For home use take the best resin and bleached wax, for coarser uses the lower qualities are just as effective. Melt the resin and wax, add the sand or marble dust, and mix well, pour out in greased pans, mark with an oiled knife into sticks, and cool.

This cement will quickly mend anything not exposed to heat, alcohol or benzine. Apply hot and while still warm remove excess, and smooth edges. It will fix lamp collars, door, cane and knife handles, tighten loose tools, mend leaks in boats, etc.

TO MAKE SUGAR SYRUP

Fill a clean bottle with granulated sugar and pour in clean cold water, filtered pref r ed. Let stand over night and add more water until bottle is full, and all the sugar dissolved. C lor and flavor to suit. The use of syrup instead of sugar fur tea and coffee will save about ten per cent. and give better beverages.

CORN AND FELON CURES

Baking soda dampened, spread on a thin cloth and bound over a corn, will remove it.

A paste made of equal parts of saltpeter, brimstone and lard, and bound about a felon will cure it. Renew as soon as the poultice gets dry.

BOXES FOR CLIPPINGS

In these days of magazines and newspapers everybody makes a collection of clippings, and they are valuable or not as we have them classified and conveniently at hand.

Select eight or ten pasteboard boxes of uniform size and color, such as can be obtained from dry goods or furnishing stores. They should be oblong, about five by ten inches, and if an inch or two deep will hold quantities of clippings. Label them neatly, as for instance, "Recipes," "Household Helps," "Menus," "Poetry," "Remedies," "Games," "Famous Persons," etc.

The nest of boxes—one above the other—will fit nicely into the corner of a lower shelf on the bookcase where they are easily accessible when the various lists of valuable information are wanted.

REMOVING RUSTY SCREWS

To remove a rusty screw, hold a red-hot iron to the head of the screw for a short time and use the screw driver while the screw is still hot.

STEWED SWEET APPLES

Place enough sweet apples side by side in a bright milk pan to cover the bottom; pour in about a pint of water, sprinkle over half a cup of sugar, cover with another pan and let them steam and boil until tender. When about half done turn each one over; when done, take up in a pretty dish, pour over the syrup and set away to get cold. It is a great improvement on the old baked sweet apple, and saves heating up the oven.

WASHING CHINA SILK WAISTS

To wash black or white china silk waists to look as good as new, use warm soft water. Make a suds of Ivory or any good white soap. Do not put soap on the goods. Wash carefully with the hands, without rubbing, through two waters, having the last also a suds, and do not rinse. When partly dry, iron on wrong side, with not too hot an iron.

PURIFYING A SPONGE

By rubbing a fresh lemon thoroughly into a soured sponge and rinsing it several times, it will become as sweet as a new one.

A HANGING BASKET

Do you know that one of the prettiest hanging baskets imaginable can be made from a cocoanut shell? Select a large cocoanut; if practicable, one shaped like a nutmeg. From the end containing the eyes slice off a section about one-sixth the depth of the nut. This leaves the edge of the basket curving in a little, making it graceful in shape. Bore three holes about three-quarters of an inch from the edge for the cord or little chains by which to suspend it, and also a rather larger hole in the bottom for drainage.

GETTING PRUNES CLEAN

Cooked in the following way prunes will be absolutely clean and delicate. Wash and put to cook in cold water, let boil slowly for five minutes. Drain off this water and with it will go all impurities. Add fresh water and cook in a covered dish until tender. Sweeten to taste.

CURE FOR HEADACHE

The juice of half a lemon in a cup of strong coffee without cream or sugar will relieve the worst headache.

A PENCIL POCKET

The husband will greatly appreciate a narrow pencil pocket not over one inch wide placed on inside of coat, cutting through the facing to the right and a little above the inside breast pocket on the left side of coat. It should be just wide enough and deep enough to hold a pencil and fountain pen. If the husband be a business man who often goes without vest on hot days, he will wonder why he did not have it long ago.

HINTS FOR IRONING DAY

If your flatirons do not heat fast enough, try placing a dripping pan over them, and they will get hot much quicker.

Put all common towels, cloths, etc., when dried through the wringer, set close. This mangles them nicely.

A "NATIONAL" STRAWBERRY STORY

In the spring of 1904 the National Magazine called attention to the free seed and plant distribution carried on by the department of agriculture at Washington, and the following was received from a subscriber:

Late in the season I wrote the department for strawberry plants. The supply was nearly exhausted, but they sent me fifteen plants of the Brandywine variety. These reached me April 30, in good condition. I set them out the same afternoon. May 15, I hoed them. Two plants were dead. From the remaining thirteen plants I picked one pint of nice berries the 30th day of May, and had fresh berries every day from May 30 to June 21.

Those thirteen plants made me a bed from which I picked just thirty-five quarts of fine berries. The first of the season berries sold here at twelve and one-half cents per quart; afterward at ten cents and then at eight and one-third. Now don't you think my subscription to the National was a good investment?

LIGHT DUMPLINGS

To have dumplings in a stew perfectly light, they should be laid on the meat and not dropped into the broth. If there should not be meat enough, make a foundation with potatoes. In mixing use just flour enough so that they can be handled nicely.

TO SOAK KETTLES CLEAN

Do not put pans and kettles partly filled with water on the stove to soak, as it only makes them more difficult to clean. Fill them with cold water and soak away from the heat.

KITCHEN AND PANTRY HINTS

In making tomato soup the milk will not separate if you pour the hot milk into the hot tomatoes—not the tomatoes into the milk.

In heating milk that you are afraid will sour, do not add any salt after the milk has boiled. Salt helps it to separate.

Try putting your dry groceries, such as beans, rice and tapioca, into glass jars. You can see in a glance what you want and your pantry is thus free from mice and bugs, as well as neat looking.

HOUSING VEGETABLES

Pumpkins should be kept in a dry part of the cellar, apples in a moderately dry part, and turnips in a damp part.

LIGHT UNDERCRUST

After a pie is baked and removed from the oven, if it is set on a wire tea-tray or anything that will allow the air to circulate under the tin, the under crust will be light and flaky, and not heavy and soggy as it would be if set on the table to cool.

CURING MEAT

Put a thin layer of salt on a table, or boards, and to every 500 pounds of pork use the following preparation: ten pounds of salt, five pounds of brown sugar, one-half pound of ground ginger, one-half pound black pepper and two ounces saltpeter. Mix well and as soon as the meat is cut up lay on the boards or table (we use a table made expressly for that purpose) rub well over the flesh side and well in the ends. If the pieces are not large, that one going over will be enough, but if large, in a week or ten days (according to the weather) some bare places will show: you then simply put salt on, unless you did not use all your preparation; if you did not, then use that. The sides treated this way and then smoked will equal, if not surpass, your fancy breakfast bacon. Be sure and let the brine drip off. When it is smoked or ready to put away, get powdered borax and rub all over the meat; some rub the skin side, but some do not think it necessary. Hang up any place you wish and Mr. Fly will give it a wide berth. Some use molasses instead of sugar and use a brush and put the mixture all over the meat, but the sugar is just as good and is nicer to handle.

WHEN BAKING CAKE

When a cake, after it is baked, does not come out easily, wring a cloth out of cold water, fold, and lay on table, set the hot pan on this for a few moments and the contents can be removed without the slightest breakage.

LITTLE HELPS FOR HOME-MAKERS

TO KEEP EGGS PERFECTLY FRESH

A good method is as follows: When strictly freshly laid, pack them closely, so that one braces the other, into a small bag, made of strong, loosely woven cotton cloth which has short loops of stout twine sewed firmly at its diagonal ends.

Two dozen in a bag are sufficient to handle easily. When filled, pin or sew the bag carefully together, and hang by one of the loops on a rail driven into a beam midway of a well-ventilated cellar where a current of air circulates freely. Every seventh day change the bag and hang by the opposite loop.

Don't forget to make the change every week, and with abundance of air circulating, the eggs will keep for months, delicate and appetizing as when freshly laid.

TO SOFTEN DRIED LEMONS

When lemons have become hard from keeping, cover them with boiling water and set on back of range a little while. They will become soft and pliable.

MEALY POTATOES

If potatoes are immediately placed in the oven for a few minutes after taking them from the boiling water in which they have been cooked, they will be much more palatable.

TO COOL THE OVEN

If when baking, the oven gets too hot, put in a basin of cold water instead of leaving the door open. This cools the oven, and the steam arising from the water prevents the contents burning. When cooking in a gas oven, a basin of water should always be kept in the oven.

CHOPPING RAISINS

By first washing the raisins in *cold* water before putting them through the chopper, they come out in fine condition to use, not adhering in masses as usual.

COOKING HINTS

Let the kettle in which mush has been cooked stand for five minutes before taking up. Then no hard residue will be left sticking to the bottom of the kettle to be soaked off and thrown away.

A quarter of an apple cooked with a quart of cranberries takes off the crudeness, but does not diminish the tartness.

TO BOIL EGGS

Pour *snapping* boiling water over the required number of eggs. Set them on the back part of the stove (where they will simply keep hot) for ten minutes. Cooked in this way, the whites are not tough.

If you wish hard-boiled eggs, let remain twenty minutes.

But if you wish to use eggs in decorating a salad or anything of the kind, cook in the old way, as for this purpose you need to have the whites firm and hard, or you cannot cut them properly.

TO UTILIZE OLD COLLARS

When you find linen collars are past wearing, put them in hot water and rub the starch out; then peel off the outer linen pieces, hemstitch them, and put them on bands for the little girl to wear with school frocks. These turn-overs are easy to make, launder beautifully, and wear as long as those made of new linen.

THE OLD WAY AND THE NEW

Every country housekeeper knows the enormous waste from the lard supply in "cracklings" in the old way of "drying up" lard at hog-killing time. The *new* way turns all the fat into lard. Cut the fat from the skins, free it from all lean particles and bloody shreds, and where there is only a small quantity to be rendered mix the leaf lard with the other fat. Wash first in quite warm water and rinse twice in cold water, put it on the stove in closely covered vessels, stirring frequently until the fat is boiled perfectly done and tender. Have ready some good, home-made, sound wood-ash lye, strain from all sediment and add half a teacupful of the lye to each gallon of the fat, first removing it from the fire to cool somewhat or it may boil over. Return to the fire and cook gently. If the fat is thoroughly done, it will soon be reduced to a creamy consistency, the fat entirely dissolved. Cook the lard uncovered after the lye is added. When the lard is done it will be perfectly clear with a very thin, brown, gummy scum on top, no cracklings at all. Remove this scum and let the lard remain on the stove at the scalding, but not boiling, point for two or three hours. Pour into perfectly dry, hot earthern jars—holding only one gallon each is the best size. Let it cool uncovered and then cover closely and keep air-tight. Keep in a cool, dry place. It is better to keep lard in small vessels, because only the small quantity is exposed to the air while using, the bulk of the year's supply remaining air-tight, and in no danger of becoming rancid.

TO WHIP THIN CREAM

When cream is rather too thin or difficult to whip, add the white of an egg to each pint of cream; the whipping can be accomplished much more easily, and the flavor of the cream not changed in the least.

BAKED EGGS

Break in a buttered gem-pan the number of eggs to be cooked, being careful that each is whole; put upon each a few rolled cracker crumbs, a small piece of butter, and sprinkle with pepper and salt. A teaspoonful of cream is a great improvement. Bake in the oven until whites are firm.

TO POP CORN

To pop corn that has become dry and hard, shell the corn and soak in cold water for fifteen or twenty minutes; drain off the water (have a very hot fire) and put in a small quantity of corn or your popper will overflow. The kernels will be large, flaky, tender and crisp.

TO FRY LIVER

Before frying liver, try dipping the slices in hot water; the flavor is much more delicate.

SUET IN COOKING

Buy nice fresh suet of your butcher. If you buy quite a quantity at a time you will not to have to prepare it so often. Cut it into small pieces—as you would leaf lard—and soak over night in cold water. This takes away the tallowy taste. Turn into a colander and drain, then put in a kettle on the stove and let the fat try out slowly, stirring quite often to prevent burning. When all tried out, strain through a cloth, using scrap-squeezers in order to get all the fat from the scraps. Set away the suet to cool as you would lard.

To have success in using suet one must know how to use it. A good rule for making pie crust is as follows:

For each pie allow one-quarter cup of sour milk or buttermilk—sometimes in very cold weather it is best to allow one-third cup. Add soda in proportion of one teaspoonful to one pint of sour milk. Also put in salt. When the soda is dissolved, stir in flour to make a rather thick batter, then stir in same quantity of melted suet that you used of sour milk. The suet must be warm, but not hot, and be sure to thoroughly mix it in the batter as fast as you pour it in. If not, it will cool in little lumps so you cannot roll the crusts, and you will think you do not like to use suet; but if it is mixed well as fast as poured in you will have no trouble. When thoroughly mixed add as much more flour as is needed to make it stiff enough to roll, and proceed as with any pie crust. After rolling out top crust turn on a little melted suet and spread it around with a knife, then sprinkle flour over and spat it down with the hand—if you use the rolling-pin it is apt to get sticky—and just before putting the pie in the oven pour cold water over it, which will make the crust flaky.

Try using suet and see if you do not like it better than lard. It is much more healthful, as well as less expensive, and just as convenient to use.

A FISH BONE IN THE THROAT

Swallow a raw, unbeaten egg and the bone will be carried down.

TO DRIVE AWAY FLIES

Take five cents' worth of essence of lavender and mix with same quantity of water. Use a glass atomizer to spray it around the rooms. The odor is especially disagreeable to flies.

NEW WORDS FOR THE LITTLE FOLKS

During vacation a child may acquire a great number of new words in this way: Let mother select new words from the reader and after carefully writing and printing them on a piece of cardboard about three by nine inches, tack it up on the wall where the child will see it. He will learn to recognize these words at sight and never know that he has been studying. Two or three words a week learned in this way will make a great improvement in his reading in the fall term of school.

A child's vocabulary may be increased by taking a new word, perhaps a long one, and explaining its meaning to the child. Use it yourself in a sentence, then have him do so. In a week the word will be his. In this way children may easily acquire a large number of words which will help them more clearly to express their ideas and they will speak better English and use fewer "slang phrases."

REMEDY FOR RHEUMATISM

Dissolve one tablespoonful of saltpeter in a quart of water and take a drink of the water—about one tablespoonful—three times a day. This has been tried and is known to be an excellent remedy for rheumatism.

A MAGAZINE CLUB

Ten ladies, who like good reading but can afford a subscription to only one or two good magazines a year, met and each decided to subscribe to one good magazine, each person selecting a different one. Then after receiving and reading each number, it is passed on to another member until each one of the club has read it, when it is returned to original subscriber. Each magazine when received is marked with owner's name on back, and list of club members in order of passing on. The idea proved very satisfactory. The club might consist of more or less members. It might be composed entirely of teachers, using teachers' periodicals, or other professional workers, and the exchange might be the occasion of holding a little meeting or entertainment, etc.

MAKING STOCK FOR SOUPS

In homes where soup is served daily at dinner, the stock-pot becomes a necessity; not alone for economical reasons, but for the sake of convenience as well; for from good stock an almost endless variety of savory and wholesome soups may be made with little trouble.

The most nutritious and best flavored stock is prepared from fresh, uncooked beef and cracked bones. The addition of the bones becomes a necessity for two reasons: they add greatly to the strength and flavor of the stock, and—which is the chief concern—furnish the glutinous properties almost wholly lacking in the beef itself, two ounces of bones containing as much gelatine as one pound of beef. The bones must be cracked before cooking, in order that the water can more easily dissolve the gelatine and free it from the earthy matter in which it is stored.

To make a satisfactory stock of delicate flavor, take four pounds of shank or shin beef, cut into rather small pieces and crack the bones. Put into a scrupulously clean soup kettle having a double bottom and a closely fitting cover with a tiny opening for the escape of steam. The use of such a kettle lessens the danger of scorching and preserves the flavor of the stock. Pour over the meat and bones four quarts unsalted cold water; the use of hot water would seal up the pores of the beef and thus defeat the end in view, which is the extraction of the juice. Let stand until the juices color the water, then put over the fire and cook gently for several hours or until the meat is in shreds and the liquid is reduced one-half. Season with salt and pepper and strain into a jar. By this method the sweetness of the meat is completely extracted. During the cooking skim frequently and thoroughly. A little cold water poured in now and then will assist the scum in rising. This injunction must not be disregarded if clear stock is desired. When cold, remove the accumulation of fat, which should be clarified for drippings. A transparent jelly will remain in the crock and constitutes the stock which in turn becomes the basis of many wholesome soups.

To use stock, cut off the required quantity, add water, bring to a boil, flavor and serve. Vegetables or cereals to be used in soups made from stock should be previously cooked, for prolonged boiling impairs the delicate flavor which is the life of the stock. Clear soups should be transparent, those to which thickening is added of the consistency of heavy cream.

To make white stock from which to evolve the more dainty or creamed soups, substitute for the beef given in the formula six pounds of a knuckle of veal cut fine and poultry trimmings. Then proceed according to directions given.

In small families the most economical way of making soup is to keep a stock-pot, into which should be thrown the scraps of beef and bits of ham left over from meals, gravies from the roasts, trimmings from steaks, and ends always in evidence before and after meals. Cover with cold water and simmer until a rich broth is obtained, then draw off and season. A kettle having a closely fitting cover and a faucet to draw off the soup should be provided. Every two or three days the stock-pot should be emptied, scalded and aired, else the soup will have a stale flavor.

The best herbs for flavoring stock soups are thyme, sweet marjoram, tarragon, mint, sweet basil, parsley, bay leaves, cloves, celery seed and mace. The

principal vegetables used in soups are onions, potatoes, tomatoes, carrots, asparagus, green corn, green peas, lettuce, beans, parsnips and mushrooms.
Of the cereals, rice and barley are most often used. Macaroni and vermicelli are agreeable additions to an otherwise plain soup.

FOR CHAPPED HANDS

Pour fourteen ounces of hot, soft water over one dram of gum tragacanth. Let stand until all dissolved, which will take about twenty-four hours. Then add two ounces of glycerine, two ounces of alcohol and a few drops of rosewater. Keep in a wide-mouthed bottle.

FRUIT CAKE PUDDING

A nice way to utilize the dried scraps of fruit cake is to grind them up in the meat chopper and stir into gingerbread batter. Baked in a loaf and served with a rich wine sauce it makes a delicious dessert for a cold day

IRREGULAR LOAVES

If your loaves of bread sag over the edge of the baking pan, cut strips of heavy wrapping paper about four inches wide, and adjust around the pan so as to extend above the edge half the width of the paper, or more. Fasten together with pin. This will support the loaf till baked enough to stand alone.
A strip of cloth may be pinned around a pie pan to prevent the two crusts separating.

TO KILL FLEAS

The owner of a valuable tiger cat of great beauty, which the past two years has received a weekly washing with a solution of Sulpho-Naphthol, the most perfect eradicator of dirt and fleas, said she had tried all the other advertised remedies, but none proved so entirely safe and satisfactory as this. It keeps the cat healthy and cleanly, and his fur smooth and glossy.

"BEAUTY IS USE, USE BEAUTY"

This is for some of the Western sisters who have to economize. Take 100-pound salt sacks, rip open, sew four or six together, fell the seams nicely, then dye cardinal red. They make very nice everyday table-cloths and look so much nicer than the unsightly oilcloth so many use. One can make napkins of the same material; cut squares, either hemstitch them or hem on the machine. Sugar sacks make nice covers for comforts dyed with some pretty colored dyes.

SMOKY KETTLES

Grease well the bottoms of kettles before setting over the fire and the smoke can easily be wiped off with an old cloth before putting in the dishwater. The finest porcelain pieces may be thus treated and no harm come to them. Those who burn soft coal will find this "help" invaluable.

FLAVORING EXTRACTS

Buy one-half ounce of any essential oil and use one drop of it in place of the usual amount of extract. The cost is trifling, there is no danger of impure alcohol, it will keep indefinitely and you know that you have the real thing. Peppermint, wintergreen, cloves, lemon, orange and others may be used in this way.

CURE FOR A COLD

It may not be generally known that one teaspoonful of aromatic spirits of ammonia in two-thirds of a glass of cold water to be taken in doses of one teaspoonful every fifteen minutes or half hour, according to the severity of the case, will relieve any ordinary cold, if taken in the early stages.

WHEN CHURNING

The easiest and best way to wash the buttermilk out of the butter after churning is to wash it right in the churn. After the butter is churned and gathered, take out the dash and pour the buttermilk off, then pour cold water over the butter in churn and splash with the dasher, gently pressing the butter. Pour this off, taking clean water again until the water pours off clear. Take out and salt the butter.

When churning cream that is a little strong from long standing, as is often the case in winter, be it ever so carefully kept, try one-half cup of juice from a grated carrot with an equal amount of cold water to one gallon of cream. The results will be butter of a rich, sweet flavor and an even color.

QUICK COCOA

To make delicious cocoa with little time and trouble: Use a teaspoonful each of cocoa and sugar for each cup. Place dry in saucepan and shake well; pour over it hot water. It dissolves instantly and is ready for the milk. Let come to a boil and it is ready to serve. No extra dishes to wash, and no lumpy, sticky mess, as by the old process of dissolving cocoa by itself.

RICE STARCH

In cooking rice—of course everyone cooks it dry in the good old Southern way—save the water it has been boiled in to use for starch. It will exactly give the right stiffness to handsome centerpieces and other dainty articles.

TO PREVENT SCORCHING IN OVEN

To prevent scorching in the oven, place a little salt in the oven beneath the baking-tin.

TO AVOID ACHING FINGERS

To prevent one's fingers aching when coming into a warm room with cold hands, simply hold them with the ends pointing upward instead of down as it is so natural for one to do. Mothers, teach this to your little ones and see how much pain can be avoided.

CLEANING A STRAW HAT

If that favorite white straw hat of yours is yellow or needs cleaning, **try a** mixture of sulphur and lemon juice. Mix to the consistency of cream and apply a thin coating, leaving until dry enough to brush off easily. If at all sceptical, try a wee place and you will find it so beautifully white that you will cover the whole article.

WHEN RENDERING LARD

In rendering lard, cut the leaf and trimming of fat into small bits, put in a large dripping-pan, heaping it up, put pan in a hot oven; the stove does the rest without smoke or odor.

WHEN FRYING EGGS

When frying eggs cover the skillet or they will be tough; this also saves turning, as when covered they cook white all over the top and look nicer than when turned.

A TESTED CORN CURE

Take a lemon, cut off a slice about one-fourth of an inch in thickness, bind this firmly to the toe over the corn upon retiring. In the morning remove the lemon. To your surprise you will find the toe white and all the soreness gone. Apply fresh slices of lemon for three or four nights, and at the end of the third or fourth morning you can remove the corn without any pain whatever.

TO COOK AND SERVE CELERY

Aside from its use as an appetizer, the dietetic value of celery is pretty generally appreciated, yet few housewives are aware of its culinary possibilities, both alone and in combination with other foods, which, while affording the change so agreeable to the palate, in no wise detract from the food value of the plant.

Below are appended a few choice recipes for cooking and serving celery:

Escalloped Celery: Wash, scrape and cut two bunches nicely bleached celery into half-inch lengths, then drop into boiling water slightly salted and stew gently five minutes; drain well, reserving one-half cup of the liquor. Put this over the fire together with one cup of cream or rich milk and two tablespoonfuls of butter. Bring to a boil, thicken with two tablespoonfuls of flour moistened with a little cold milk, cook smooth, season to taste with salt and white pepper, then pour over the celery. When the mixture cools, stir into it two beaten eggs, and pour the whole into a buttered ramekin, cover with grated bread crumbs, dot with bits of butter and stand in a hot oven until set and nicely browned. Serve hot without re-dishing. At the last moment before sending to the table sprinkle grated cheese over the top.

Celery Puree with Poached Eggs: Chop one bunch fine celery into small pieces, then stew gently in one pint of chicken or veal stock. When tender, press through a purée sieve, return to the fire and boil rapidly until reduced to a cup and one-half. Then stir into it half a cupful of sweet cream and a large tablespoonful of butter, boil up once, then thicken to the consistency of cream with flour moistened with a little cold milk; cook smooth, then season to taste with salt and white pepper. Poach the required number of eggs, arrange on small hot plates for individual serving and pour the purée around them.

Celery Patés: Wash clean, then cut into small lengths a sufficient quantity of nicely bleached celery. Stew until tender in boiling salted water; then drain, reserving one-half cupful of the liquor, to which add the same quantity of cream and two tablespoonfuls of butter. Put over the fire, boil up and thicken with one tablespoonful of flour. Pour this sauce over the celery. Have ready paté-shapes baked empty, fill them with the mixture and brown in a quick oven.

Celery Loaf: Chop fine a sufficient quantity of celery to measure two cupfuls, stew tender, then cover with a sauce made of one cupful of milk, two tablespoonfuls each of butter and flour with salt and pepper to season. Stir well, then add two beaten eggs or a cupful of minced veal or chicken. Turn into a buttered mold, stand in a pan of hot water and bake in a rather quick oven. When done, unmold on a hot platter, garnish with fringed celery and serve with tomato sauce.

(To fringe celery, cut the white stalks into three-inch lengths, then draw each end back and forth several times through three or four coarse needles stuck in one end of a cork.)

Celery and Apple Salad: Cut the white portions of a bunch of well-bleached celery into half-inch lengths. Pare and cut three tart, nicely flavored apples into dice. Mix with the celery. Wash and crisp one head of lettuce and arrange for individual serving, pile little mounds of celery and apple in the leaves and dress with salad dressing. This salad must not stand long before serving, as the apples turn dark when exposed to the air. Nuts may be substituted for the apples, using twenty English walnuts for each head of celery, reserving a dozen meats for garnishing. Or the celery may be used alone, in which case double the quantity will be required.

Celery Soup: Cook one pint of celery, chopped very fine, in one pint of cold water, salted to taste, until soft enough to mash, then rub through a colander. Bring one and one-half pints of milk to a boil; add the pulped celery and one-half teaspoonful of minced onion. Simmer fifteen minutes, then thicken with one tablespoonful of flour blended with two of butter. Cook until smooth, stirring constantly. Season to taste with salt and white pepper.

THE ART OF MAKING SOUPS

It is said that ten or fifteen years ago soup was served in very few American homes, while now it forms an essential part of every well-regulated dinner.

Soup has its place at the beginning of dinner, for a reason, not a fad. It is a valuable appetizer, acting as a stimulant rather than a nutrient, and being quickly assimilated, prepares the way for the dishes to follow.

Gouffe says: "Beef broth is the soul of domestic cookery." That is, it is the essence that is to pervade the body of the dish, giving character and atmosphere without substance. But to get that "soul" out of the formula, beginning "take a shin of beef," has proven a difficult problem to many a housekeeper and a seeming impossibility to more than a few cooks.

Edward Atkinson said in the beginning of his well-known directions on how to prepare and cook food: "Take one part of gumption and one part of food." Gumption, simmered gently with the "shin of beef," will produce beef broth, but gumption brings a high price on the market of commodities nowadays, and is often lacking at any. The demand for marketable gumption has brought into being a substitute for home-made beef broth, in the form of Armour's Extract of Beef. With a jar of solid, or a bottle of fluid, extract at hand, the cook has, without time or trouble, and with ordinary or even less expense, the "soul" of her cookery at hand.

Thin, poorly flavored, watery soups are never satisfactory and are actually wasteful, but such need never be served if the right use be made of the materials. Pea, bean, corn, tomato, vegetable and grain soups of all kinds, can be prepared of the left-overs of canned and fresh vegetables, if properly combined with stock made from Extract of Beef. In such cases recipes can act as suggestions only, for the ingredients must vary with the exigencies of the larder. The proportion of extract, however, remains the same.

When clear soup, such as bouillon, rice or sphagetti is to be made, take one teaspoonful of Armour's Solid Extract of Beef to every quart of water. When used for purées, bisques and those soups with substance or bodies to them, take one-half, or even at times all that is required is one-quarter, teaspoonful of Armour's Solid Extract of Beef to every quart of water. Soups that have a stock of their own require but one-quarter teaspoonful of Armour's Solid Extract of Beef to give the desired meat juices and flavor.

The exact measurement of the required seasonings can rarely be given, for adaptation is one of the necessities. Add salt until the soup is "bright-tasting" but not suggestive of sea water; pepper to the brink of pungency, giving the tone of warmth, not a burning taste.

LITTLE HELPS FOR HOME-MAKERS

REFLECTED LIGHT

To increase the light given by a small lamp, place a mirror directly back of it, so that your lamp casts its reflection in the mirror. You can easily see just how much additional light you get from the mirror, by putting a paper between the lamp and the mirror, and suddenly withdrawing it, noticing how much lighter the room is.

WHITE LIGHT

A little salt added to the oil of a lamp that gives out a yellow light will whiten and brighten the light, or wash the wick in strong salt and water and dry, and it will give a whiter light.

A CHEAP REFLECTOR

Make a triangular box high enough to hold your lamp, leaving one side open, and having painted the inside of the box black, line the two sides with cheap mirror glass.

A WATER TELESCOPE

Buy an empty candy bucket of your grocer, and see that the hoops are well secured. Paint green or gray on the outside and varnish thoroughly; paint a dead black on the inside, cut a square or round hole in the bottom, fixing it so that a small pane of very clear and rather thick glass can be set in white lead. If necessary, strengthen the bottom with brass, or hard wood strips. Place the bottom of the pail in the water, and look through it with a cloth over your head to shut out the light, and you can see everything in almost any depth of reasonably clear water. Every boat fisherman should carry one.

MENDING FURS

A good way to mend fur rugs or anything made of fur, is to fasten the edges together with strips of adhesive plaster on the under side.

TO LAUNDER FINE GOODS

If you wish your clothes to iron easy and retain that "new" look so desirable, pour one quart of boiled starch into your last rinsing water.

Mix the dry starch with a little water and before pouring on the boiling water shave in a little white soap. No scum will ever form over the top nor will the irons stick to the clothes.

ARRANGING CUT FLOWERS

To the true flower-lover much of the pleasure from them is secured by their use as cut flowers in all sorts of places, for all sorts of decorative purposes, and the hints here given will be along the line of easy and effective ways of arranging them, rather than descriptive of any finished effects.

The petals of many flowers, like the lily and the fleur-de-lis, are so fragile that it is almost impossible to handle them, after they are fully open, without breaking; if cut before the petals begin to curve outward and allowed to finish after they are arranged, this risk is entirely obviated.

Very few flowers look well when massed closely together; in the style of arrangement which leaves the blossoms loose and natural in appearance the stems must be held in some way. When using opaque receptacles, paper, moss, or almost anything may be tucked in among the stems to support them and prevent the blossoms from lopping over on one side, or on all sides.

For use with glass receptacles having wide tops, a circular piece of wire netting is a great help. Any dealer will cut it to a desired size, leaving a few wires on each side to be bent into hooks and caught over the edge of the glass. This is practically invisible if allowed to drop a little below the edge of the receptacle; and by putting the stems through the meshes of the netting they are kept separated and the flowers remain as arranged.

Pansies, violets and other flowers, having large and heavy heads in proportion to their slender stems, are hard to arrange in any kind of receptacle without something to hold them in position; one of the best things to use is a sponge. Get a large one and soak it in water until fully distended, then cut away one side until it is perfectly flat. Round the remaining surface to a symmetrical shape, stick it full of meat skewers and let it dry.

When wanted, pull out the skewers and put the stems of flowers in the spaces; set the sponge in a plate of water (flat side down) and after it has absorbed the water, add more and tuck in a few leaves and blossoms where needed to hide the sponge or plate.

In using flowers that are produced in spikes, umbels or other compound forms, it often is advisable to sacrifice part of the blossom. To illustrate: the immense blossoms of the hardy hydrangea seem little suited for use in making wreaths, crosses, anchors or other pieces where the flowers must lay close to a flat surface; but by cutting away the florets on one side until a flat surface is obtained they may be used as easily and effectively as any flower known, and have the very desirable qualities of filling space rapidly, and keeping fresh for a long time.

When possible, use the natural foliage of the plant (and plenty of it), for no other greenery will give the artistic effect secured by using that with which nature surrounded the blossoms.

Nearly always the finest effects are gained by using but one kind of flower, and *always* by making the vase subordinate to the flowers.

A vase may be beautiful in itself, but if its lines and coloring are not in harmony with the flowers put into it, the effect can never be artistic, or pleasing to a cultivated taste.

LITTLE HELPS FOR HOME-MAKERS

BONES AND CHARCOAL IN FLORICULTURE

During the winter, when more meat is used than during the summer, a supply of bones should be burned for next year's use as drainage material. Throw every bone into the fire and let it burn until it will break easily. Bones furnish elements absolutely essential to plant growth, aside from serving as drainage material.

Those who burn wood should save, also, a plentiful supply of charcoal. When there is a good bed of live coals, take out all that can be spared and pour water over them until the fire is extinguished. It frequently happens that when the kitchen work is done there will be a fine bed of coals in the stove, or some large embers, and the wise flower-lover will not fail to convert them into charcoal for future use.

The bones furnish large per cents. of carbon, calcic phosphates and calcic carbonates for the plants to feed on, while charcoal rapidly absorbs moisture and noxious gases which would make the soil cold and sour, at the same time that it gives out elements which are decidedly helpful to the plants in the way of producing dark, glossy foliage and vividness of color to the blossoms.

If it is possible to save more than is needed for drainage, powder it and mix with the soil, not only for pot-plants but around those in the garden, also. If there is any to spare, divide with friends who do not burn wood from which to get the charcoal, and let them burn their bones in your fire (if they burn gas). You will get the benefit of the heat, which is intense, and they will have the burned bones for their plants.

If a large metal pail, or a stone crock, is kept where it is handy to put both bones and charcoal into it, the trouble of saving them is practically nothing, and if it were considerable, the results would amply repay it. Knowing how extensively charcoal is used as a filtering agent in many lines of work, and that it is given to dyspeptics to neutralize the action of gases in the stomach, it is easy to understand that it *must* benefit vegetable life, and that the one who allows it to go to waste is wasting what represents marked improvement in the beauty of all plants grown, either in pots or in the open ground.

It is well to know that where large lumps of charcoal or bone are used as drainage material, they may be purified and made fit for use again by putting them into the fire and letting them get red hot, then throwing water over them to stop the burning. As it is not always easy to find charcoal for sale, when wanted, those who buy it will find this hint worth heeding.

Those unfamiliar with the nature of charcoal may ask what becomes of the gases absorbed, and wonder why the plants do not draw them from the charcoal as easily as they would from the soil. The reason is this: The pores of the charcoal are filled with condensed oxygen, and the gases absorbed are decomposed by contact with it. The process of decomposition generates warmth, which is another reason why charcoal is one of the best materials to use around the roots of plants.

TO PREVENT A SNEEZE

When you feel an inclination to sneeze lay the forefinger across the upper lip, close under the nose, and press down hard.

FLORAL POINTERS FOR FEBRUARY

Before this month ends many of us will be making comparisons between the number of plants we see listed in the new catalogues, and want, and the amount of money we can appropriate to their purchase, but the experienced ones will stop short of getting many of the much lauded novelties.

Much of the pleasure in cultivating flowers consists in watching the development of unknown plants, and we want a few of the new ones, but it is the part of wisdom to make it "a few" and let someone else try others.

Sometimes they are all that is claimed for them, very frequently they are worth mighty little, and, *always*, they are high-priced.

When planning for the purchase of plants, a thought must be given to the number and condition of the pots on hand, for it is altogether probable that some new ones will be needed and more than probable that a part of those on hand will need renovating. The price of a novelty or two will pay for enough along this line to add more to the appearance of the plant collection than could be added by a dozen fine plants put into, and among, a lot of shabby pots.

Soft-baked clay pots are the best to get for most plants, when conditions for growth are considered, and the natural cream and terra cotta shades in which they usually come blend harmoniously with all colors found in foliage and flower, among our plants, which is more than can be said for some of the expensive, glazed, highly-colored and gilt-bedecked things sold as ornamental (?) pots.

With ordinary care these pots may be used for years before they become discolored, but when that time comes they should be emptied, thoroughly scrubbed and *stained*—not painted. To prepare the stain, add powder of the color wanted to turpentine, a very little at a time, until the desired shade is secured.

English vermilion added to the turpentine produces a color closely resembling that of the darker pots when new; yellow ochre produces a cream tint, and burnt ochre a brown one, while chrome-green with a very little black gives a beautiful moss-green shade, and either of the stains gives a permanent color to the clay without filling the pores.

In order to pot a plant in the way to induce its best growth, it is necessary to take into consideration the kind of root it naturally produces. To put a plant having long, downward-reaching roots into a broad, shallow pot is to invite failure, while to put one that produces spreading roots which remain near the surface into a deep pot is to make sure of having a quantity of soil below the roots which is in a condition to be worse than useless.

Among the broad and shallow pots now on the market we find one class listed as fern-pots, and these are fine for any plant having roots that spread near the surface.

A second class, even more shallow, are called bulb pans and a third class furnishes the seed pans which are the best possible things in which to start seeds.

The advantage gained by the use of these pans comes from the fact that they may be set into water and left until the soil has absorbed moisture enough. If the water is warm, the soil becomes warmed and, in any case, there is no danger of washing out the seeds or tiny plants.

One fine plant in a suitable pot is far more ornamental, and gives more enjoyment to all who see it, than two fine plants in shabby pots, and the fact should be kept in mind when planning the window-garden campaign for any season.

DELICIOUS SWEETBREAD DISHES

The sweetbread or, more properly, the pancreas of the calf, being a part of the digestive viscera, is one of the most easily digested of animal foods, and is, for this reason, especially adapted to persons in delicate health. Its flavor, which is exceedingly dainty, commends it to the palate of both the sick and the well. The thyroid and sublingual glands are also called sweetbreads, but are not only smaller than the true sweetbreads, but greatly inferior in flavor. The pancreas is triangular in shape and, when taken from a healthy animal, is fresh pinkish yellow in color. The throat sweetbread is oval and grayish yellow. The term, a pair of sweetbreads, usually means the heart and throat sweetbreads. The singular number of the noun is seldom used, even though but one sweetbread is in question. Lamb sweetbreads also make a very dainty dish.

Sweetbreads spoil quickly and should never be allowed to stand, but dropped at once into very cold water to blanch and harden. Let stand an hour, changing the water as often as it becomes discolored; then remove the pipes and membrane, cover with boiling water, to which has been added a pinch of salt and a little lemon juice, and simmer for half an hour. Drain, chill in cold water, drain again and dry in a clean towel. They are then ready to be finished by any recipe preferred.

Broiled Sweetbreads: After chilling and drying the parboiled sweetbreads, lay between two flat pans or boards and place a weight on top. When pressed flat, dip each in melted butter, place in a broiler over a bed of live coals. Transfer to a hot platter, dress with bits of butter, dust with salt and white pepper, garnish with parsley and sliced lemon and serve at once.

Sweetbread Chops: Prepare the sweetbreads according to general directions, then chop fine, and for each two cups of the meat add one-fourth cup of grated bread crumbs. Mix well, season with salt and white pepper and bind together with a hot white sauce made by blending with one cup sweet milk, two tablespoonfuls each of butter and flour, with salt, pepper and lemon juice to season nicely. Stand the mixture aside until cold, then form into chops. Dip each chop into beaten egg and dredge with bread crumbs. Arrange in a frying basket and fry a golden brown in deep hot fat. Drain a moment on clean brown paper. Then stick a piece of macaroni in the small end of each chop to simulate the bone. Serve on a napkin with a garnish of lemon crescents.

Larded Sweetbreads: Prepare the sweetbreads as for broiling. Cut narrow strips of salt pork as long as the sweetbreads are wide. Thread a larding needle with these strips and run several of them at regular intervals through the sweetbreads near the top surface. Place in a shallow pan and stand in a hot oven thirty minutes, basting several times with rich stock. When cooked, transfer to a hot platter and surround with a border of stewed peas from which all liquor has been drained.

Sweetbread au Gratin: Chop prepared sweetbreads fine, then stir into a thick white sauce seasoned with salt, pepper and mushroom catsup. Butter a ramequin and line the bottom and sides with grated bread crumbs. Pour the sweetbread mixture into this, cover with bread crumbs, dot with bits of butter and brown in a hot oven. Serve without redishing.

Sweetbread Croquettes: Cut prepared sweetbreads fine; dust with salt and pepper and add four tablespoonfuls of minced mushrooms or oysters, if the latter are seasonable, and bind together with thick white sauce. When cold, form into croquettes of any desired shape, dip into beaten egg, then in crumbs and fry in deep hot fat. Serve with tomato sauce.

Sweetbread with Eggs: Cut a large parboiled sweetbread into dice. Put one-half cupful of rich milk over the fire in a granite frying-pan. When it boils, add two tablespoonfuls of butter, four eggs slightly beaten and the diced sweetbread. Cook, stirring constantly, until of the consistency of thick custard and the white of the eggs is scattered in flakes through the mixture. Take from the fire, season with salt and white pepper. and serve on rounds of toast, heaping up like little mounds.

Sweetbreads in Cocottes: Prepare as for sweetbreads au gratin, then fill buttered cocottes with the mixture, cover with crumbs, dot with butter and brown in the oven. Serve in the cocottes. Just before sending to the table, place a poached egg on top of each.

Fricasseed Sweetbreads: Cut prepared sweetbreads into thin slices. Prepare a sauce of one teacupful of rich stock, two tablespoonfuls of butter, one of flour and seasoning to taste. Simmer the slices of sweetbreads in this gravy forty-five minutes. Then stir in one beaten egg, two tablespoonfuls of chopped parsley and two of cream. Simmer a few minutes longer, then dish and serve at once.

Sweetbread and Nut Salad: Prepare sweetbreads as directed, then with a silver knife tear into bits. Blanch and dry one dozen almonds and the same number of English walnuts. Chop the nuts fine and mix with the sweetbreads. Arrange for individual service in lettuce cups. Garnish with walnut meats and sprigs of cress.

FOR SENSITIVE TEETH

Dissolve three lime tablets in a glass of water. Take a mouthful, working it about between the teeth, retaining as long as convenient. Do this about three times a day and the sensitiveness will disappear. Country druggists, as a rule, do not keep the tablets, but any city druggist can supply you.

RAISING RADISHES

Select a piece of sandy ground in the corner of your garden for this crop. Each spring before sowing scatter wood ashes two inches or more in depth, and mix thoroughly with the soil. No manure is required and the radishes are always brittle and free from worms.

TEA AND RHEUMATISM

It is said that tea-drinking causes rheumatism. One member of a household was badly affected with this disease, scarcely being able to get around. She quit drinking tea, and has not been troubled with rheumatism since.

PANCAKE BATTER

When making pancake batter, add about one tablespoonful of melted butter to one quart of batter, and you will not have to grease the griddle. The cakes will be improved and your kitchen will not be filled with smoke.

CURE FOR MALARIAL TUBERCULOSIS

A young woman, afflicted with malarial tuberculosis on hands and feet, was under the care of the best physicians for several years. The disease was steadily exhausting her strength, and finally she was confined to her bed with no hope of recovery. Her mother, a nurse, would not think of any change (that would be contrary to her training) so she continued fighting the disease with determination, but without success. She became discouraged, and as a last hope purchased a bottle of Liquozone. The remedy acted as a tonic at once, and in a short time she noticed marked improvement. She owed it to the oxygen in Liquozone, which is a scavenger of the blood, that the girl regained health. And a word of highest recommendation may be welcome to other mothers.

CURING AND PREVENTING BED-SORES

If anyone having the care of a bed-ridden patient will bathe the tender skin with brandy each day, there will be no danger of bed-sores. But if these have developed, put the white of an egg in a cup, and cover with brandy; apply as often as convenient. The brandy stimulates, and the white of egg forms a thin skin. In very bad cases a pinch of alum added to the egg and brandy is desirable, as it draws out the inflammation, and, being astringent, helps to dry up the sore.

WASHING BLACK STOCKINGS

Unless washed with great care, black stockings soon turn a greenish color. Wash with soap that is free from soda and rinse in water to which a teaspoonful of vinegar has been added. When damp, press them into shape, but do not iron, as the heat tends to destroy the color.

NEW USE FOR A SAFETY-PIN

The following device proves satisfactory when closet room is scarce or when hooks are few. Fold a dress skirt so that it is in four thicknesses, then through the center of the four-fold belt, at right angles, run a large safety-pin, fasten the pin and slip over the hook, which will hold, in good condition, several skirts hung in this manner.

PREVENTS RUST IN WATER PAILS

To prevent tin water pails from rusting. Solder piece of sheet zinc two inches square in bottom of pail. The galvanic action of the zinc with the tin prevents the rust.

A GLUE HINT

A teaspoonful of saltpeter added to a large pot of glue will effectually prevent it from smelling bad; besides, it causes the glue to dry faster and harder than it would without the saltpeter.

TO PHYSIC THE CAT

If the cat needs medicine, don't try to force it down her throat or mix it with milk. Smear it on her sides and she will lick it all off clean.

OPENING A FOUNTAIN PEN

If your fountain pen is stuck so you cannot unscrew it, wrap a small rubber band tightly around the nozzle or pen part. This will give you a grip on the pen that will nearly always fetch it. If you cannot get it to come off by using the rubber, try putting a little powdered rosin on the fingers. Rosin seldom fails, but it is rough for the hand.

Rosin on the hand will always fetch a tight watch case or any other smooth, screw-joint article.

SECURING A LETTER

Sometimes one wants to be sure that a letter cannot be tampered with. Moisten the flap with the white of an egg and dry thoroughly. It cannot be pulled open, and steaming has no effect upon it.

THE CARE OF JEWELRY

A few drops of ammonia on the under side of a diamond will clean it immediately and make it very brilliant.

Jewels are generally wrapped up in cotton and kept in their cases, but they are subject to tarnish from exposure to the air, and require cleaning. This is done by preparing clean soapsuds and using fine toilet soap. Dip any article of gold, silver, gilt or precious stones into this lye, and dry them by brushing with a soft brush, or a fine sponge, afterward with a piece of fine cloth and lastly with a soft leather. Silver ornaments may be kept in fine arrowroot, and completely covered with it.

LITTLE HELPS FOR HOME-MAKERS

ARE YOUR DIAMONDS SECURE?

An easy way to learn whether your diamonds are loose or not, is to hold them close to the ear, with the stone downward, and gently tap them with your finger; if loose, you will be able to hear them rattle.

THE CORK IN THE BOTTLE

To remove a cork that has gone through the neck into the body of the bottle, make a loop of twine, insert loop into bottle, turn the bottle until loop has encircled the cork, invert the bottle and draw out the cork. This manoeuver may have to be repeated several times, but one will soon learn to remove the cork quickly.

TO KEEP AWAKE IN CHURCH

To keep awake in church when inclined to be drowsy, lift one foot a little way from the floor and hold it there. It is impossible to go to sleep when your foot is poised in the air. This remedy, though simple, is very effectual and never fails to keep a person awake.

FIXATIVE

Crayon sketches and pictures, black and colored, may be fixed so that they will not rub or soil by spraying them with a solution of white shellac gum in alcohol. Spray with a tin atomizer.

CLEANING AN OLD CLOCK

Have any of the readers of "Little Helps" a clock they value, that seems to be near the end of its career of usefulness; does it skip a beat now and then, and when it begins to strike seem to be in pain? To remedy this condition, take a bit of cotton batting, the size of a hen's egg, dip it in kerosene, and place it on the floor of the clock, in the corner, shut the door of the clock and wait three or four days. Your clock will be like a new one, skip no more, and will strike as of old, and as you look inside you will find the cotton batting black with dust. The fumes of the oil loosen the particles of dust, and they fall, thus cleaning the clock.

TO CLEAN PLAYING CARDS

Soiled playing cards may be cleaned by rubbing over with a cloth dipped in camphor-spirit. For about thirty to fifty cards scarcely more than a thimbleful of camphor is needed. Another good cleaner is made by mixing burned magnesia, benzol and a little camphor-spirit, forming a jelly which is to be kept in an air-tight tin box and rubbed on the cards to clean them.

SLIPPERY NEW SHOES

To prevent small children slipping when wearing new shoes with smooth soles, rub the soles a few times over sandpaper.

TO STRAIGHTEN RUG CORNERS

Make stiff flour starch, take your rug to a sunny place on the portico, turn it upside down, apply the starch to the corners, and leave the rug to dry.

FRESHENING DUSTY CARPETS

In the early spring and fall before house-cleaning time has arrived, the carpets often look so dusty that the housekeeper is in despair. When this is the case let her take a basin of water in which a little ammonia has been dropped, and after she has wrung a cloth out and wiped off the floor, she will be agreeably surprised, as the carpet will look as fresh as when first put down and keep clean much longer than it otherwise would.

SAVES LABOR AND DIRT

To save the taking up of ashes, we have an arrangement which we would dislike to be without. In the bottom of our range we cut a hole in which a three-inch galvanized iron pipe is inserted. This leads into a brick pit directly underneath in the basement, which holds two cart-loads of ashes; so it is necessary to have them removed only once a year. As our grate is moderately fine we never have to dump it, thus saving the disagreeable work of sifting the ashes.

HINTS ON BEE-KEEPING

To stop a strong colony of bees from robbing a weaker neighbor, give it something else to do by raising the cover and throwing into it a generous handful of sawdust or chaff. The little workers will immediately get busy with "house-cleaning," meanwhile forgetting all about the coveted store of their neighbors.

To strengthen and revive a weak old colony, add to it a second or third swarm from one of your other colonies. Such swarms are usually too small, anyway, to give satisfaction in a hive to themselves. To double them, first hive the small swarm in a super or cap. Take the lid off the old hive, which should then be covered by a sheet of common screen wire, and place the cap with the new swarm on top of this. The screen wire serves to keep the two hostile colonies apart until all the inner spaces are permeated with a common scent, otherwise a furious battle would ensue, lasting until one or the other colony is exterminated. The screen can be removed in twenty-four hours and you will have gained a flourishing colony of bees by the simple operation. Two or more new swarms may be put together in the same way.

LITTLE HELPS FOR HOME-MAKERS 155

FOR BIRD-LOVERS

Here is a suggestion for those who have canaries for pets. In a little jardiniere about two inches high, which may be found in any Japanese store, plant some of the bird seeds; in a short time they grow two or three inches of tender, green shoots.

Now put the jardiniere in the corner of the bird's cage, and he will have such a good time, eating off the tender tops!

Let him enjoy it for an hour or so and then take it away and save it for another day, placing it in the sun to encourage the new growth of the little plants.

TO SEPARATE BEESWAX FROM COMB

To separate beeswax from the comb, tie it up in a cloth with a stone in it to keep it at the bottom of a kettle of cold water. Place it over the fire. The wax will rise to the top as it melts and the impurities will remain in the bag.

TO IMPROVE FURNACE HEAT

When, as often happens, a register refuses to send out a stream of hot air, if a lighted lamp or candle is placed on the register for ten or fifteen minutes, the trouble will be remedied. The hot air from the lamp starts a draft that draws the cold air from the pipe.

TO SAVE FROSTED PLANTS

When a killing frost has struck tomatoes, grapes or other tender plants in the early fall, sprinkle with cold water early in the morning before the sun's rays reach the plants, and there will be no damage.

TO FRESHEN MATTING

Dip a mop into water to which salt has been added, wring almost dry and mop up the matting. This keeps matting much better than simply sweeping it will.

TYING LOW SHOES

To tie the lacings of shoes so that they will not come undone at inopportune times and yet be easily untied when the wearer desires, try the following, which never fails when correctly done:

Tie the strings as for the ordinary bow-knot, but just before drawing down the two loops, turn one of them back through the open knot, then draw down securely. It is unfastened like the common bow-knot by merely pulling one string. A little practice makes this an extremely simple process and one is saved the vexation of loose shoes and trailing strings in public places.

SECURE AS A BOLT

After a door is locked with the key, if a stout wire eleven inches long, bent in the shape of a hair-pin, is put over the spindle (back of the knob) with the ends down through the key, the latter cannot be pushed out and a key inserted from the outside. A lady traveling alone can carry this device in her hand-bag and use it at junction and summer resort hotels where the keys are often all alike.

SCORCHED FRUIT

If the kettle of preserves, jam, or whatever happens to be cooking, becomes scorched, set it immediately into a dish of cold water, and the flavor will be unimpaired.

DELICIOUS BAKED POTATOES

Select potatoes of medium and uniform size. Wash them well and drop into a kettle of boiling water to which has been added a little salt and a pinch of soda. Boil four to five minutes according to size and take out and put in hot oven and bake till slightly brown. You will say you never knew what potatoes were before, if you time them just right.

TO KEEP SYRUP IN PIES

Take a strip of thin old linen or muslin about one and one-half inches in width and long enough to encircle the pie with a lap of two inches. Wet this thoroughly, wring almost dry, and bind the edges just before putting the pie into the oven, allowing it to come well over top and bottom edges. The pie will bake perfectly with never the loss of a drop of juice, and while still hot the binding will slip off without marring the flakiest pastry.

PASTE FOR PAPER HANGING

When preparing paste to hang paper on whitewashed walls, to every gallon of paste add one pint of vinegar, and there will be no trouble about the paper coming off. It will also save the labor of washing the walls with vinegar.

TO KEEP SILVER BRIGHT

Fill a paper box with alternate layers of knives, forks, spoons, etc., and common flour, perfectly dry; if the silver is bright and dry when put away, it may be used at any time without cleaning for a year or two. After this time, the flour needs drying off. It saves a great deal of cleaning. All silver can be packed in the same way; if used frequently, wiping with a dry towel is all that is necessary.

TO KEEP MICE AWAY

Camphor placed in trunks or drawers will prevent the mice from doing them injury.

TO CLEAN CARPET ON THE FLOOR

The following solution may be used in cleaning silk and other delicate colored fabrics. For cleaning carpet have ready a pan of the lukewarm solution and a pan of warm soft water. Clean a small place at a time, rinsing with a cloth lightly wrung out of the clear water. Apply the solution with a loufah, sponge, or cloth. The loufah, as it does not lint and wears well, is better. One gallon of rain water, one bar of Ivory soap, one-half pound of borax and three ounces of sal soda. Boil until all the ingredients are dissolved, then add two gallons of cold water and one pint of alcohol. Keep in tightly corked jugs. Will keep for years.

USES OF TURPENTINE

Turpentine is excellent and soothing when applied to scalds and cuts.

It will take ink stains out of muslin when added to soap and also helps to whiten clothes if added to the water in which they are boiled.

Moths will not come near clothes sprinkled with turpentine; they seem to hate its odor.

A few drops of turpentine will exterminate cockroaches and drive red and black ants away.

Tan leather boots can be nicely cleaned with turpentine. Pour on a woolen cloth and rub.

Turpentine is a simple and safe remedy for chilblains, corns on the feet and blisters on the hands.

Use turpentine in the bath water for rheumatism.

To remove stains from marble, take a wineglassful of turpentine and ox-gall, and mix into a paste with pipe-clay. Put the paste on the stain and let it remain two or three days.

Carpets can be cleaned and freshened by going over them once a week with a broom dipped in hot water containing turpentine.

TOMATO SOUP

Two teaspoonfuls of Armour's Extract of Beef, one can of tomatoes, one quart of water, bit of bay leaf, two cloves, one teaspoonful of paprika, one tablespoonful of sugar, one teaspoonful of salt, one-half teaspoonful of soda, two tablespoonfuls of butter, two tablespoonfuls of flour and one teaspoonful of finely chopped onion.

Strain the tomatoes, add the water, and cook twenty minutes, add soda, salt, sugar and extract of beef, bring to boil on quick fire, bind with butter and flour, add seasoning. Serve with croutons.

TURPENTINE FOR STINGS

Turpentine is good for a bee's sting.

TO TEST EGGS

A simple test of the freshness of eggs is to drop them carefully into a pan of water. If one lies flat upon the bottom it is fresh, if it rises on end, it is stale, if it floats to the surface, it is unqualifiedly bad and can be thrown away.

FURNITURE POLISH

Best vinegar one pint, turpentine one-half pint. Mix and apply with a brush.

RED ANTS

A string dipped in sassafras oil, and tied around the legs of the table will prevent ants from getting on the table.

TO CLEAN BRASS

Dampen a cloth with ammonia, rub it briskly over a piece of pumice soap, and then over the brass. This mixture acts like magic.

TO REMOVE OBJECT FROM NOSE

To remove any object from a child's nose, such as a bean, etc., have the child open its mouth, put your mouth to it and blow hard. This rarely fails.

IRON HOLDERS

Take old bed ticking, double to four thicknesses about nine inches square, turn in edges, stitch around outside, also several times through center. Use these and avoid burning your hands.

A CURE FOR CROUP

A towel wet with very cold water wrapped around the neck and chest will cure the worst case of croup in five minutes. This is much better than drugs, as it does not debilitate. Hot water is sometimes recommended, but cold water is *much* quicker and more effective, as it breaks up the congestion at once.

LITTLE HELPS FOR HOME-MAKERS

TO CLEAN A PAINT BRUSH

To clean a dry, hard paint brush, pound it with a hammer until the bristles are broken apart, then use a comb to separate the bristles. Soak in turpentine.

SCORCHED SPOT

To remove a scorched spot from clothing, hang in the bright sun until it disappears.

RICE IN THE SALT

Put a few grains of rice in the salt shaker to keep the salt broken up.

COAL OIL ON DUST CLOTH

Use a dust cloth slightly dampened with coal oil, and the dust will not fly, and the furniture will always shine.

TO STARCH DARK LAWNS

Some people have trouble starching dark lawns because the starch will show. To avoid this, use gum-arabic. To starch a dress, take one heaping teaspoonful of gum-arabic. Dissolve in a little warm water, then add enough water to wet the dress. This makes it crisp and it can be ironed in the same way as other starched goods.

THE SUN SPOILS MIRRORS

Mirrors are spoiled if exposed continually to the sun.

TO REMOVE IRON RUST SPOTS

To remove iron rust spots, put salt on the spot after the latter is well wet with lemon juice and then placed in the sunshine.

ROUGH HANDS

For chapped or rough hands use lemon and glycerine in equal proportions. A little rose-water and alcohol added to this mixture is nice. The alcohol prevents the lemon from souring and will keep it fresh for any length of time.

TO CURE HICCOUGHS

A lump of sugar saturated with vinegar will cure hiccoughs.

INK STAINS

Ripe tomatoes will remove ink and other stains from white cloth.

OLD SILK LEAVES NO LINT

Old, soft silk cloths make the best dust rags for the parlor, as they leave no lint on polished furniture.

TO PREVENT STARCH FROM STICKING

To prevent starch from sticking to the irons, add a pinch of sugar and let it come to a boil.

A CLEAN TEA-KETTLE

Keep a clam or oyster shell in the tea-kettle and lime will not form on the sides of the kettle.

BLUEBERRY PIE

Blueberry pie is much improved by adding the juice of one-half lemon to each pie.

TO DRIVE AWAY ANTS

Sprigs of arbor vitæ scattered around the shelves where food and sugar are kept will drive away black ants.

CANNING BLACKBERRIES

To prevent blackberries, when canned, from being hard, fill the jars with the fruit, then place them in a kettle and cook until the fruit is soft. Remove from the fire, fill with a hot syrup and seal.

DYEING STRAW HATS

Straw hats can be dyed any tint desired by diluting artists' oil paints with gasoline and applying with a bristle brush.

LITTLE HELPS FOR HOME-MAKERS

EASILY FOLDED CLOTHES

Leave the clothes on the grass or clotheslines until the dew has fallen considerably at night, then fold for the morrow's ironing. In no other way can they be dampened so easily and so well.

AN ORIGINAL REFRIGERATOR

When one is living 'n small quarters, say in a "flat" or apartments for light housekeeping, and has no refrigerator, a good substitute is to take a good-sized tin, say an old coal-oil can. Lay some empty pint bottles (beer or porter) lengthwise on the bottom, place your ice on top of them and as the ice melts the water will run into the bottles and keep the ice much longer. You can then place your food, butter, milk, etc., around the ice and have it fresh and cool.

TAPIOCA JELLY

Tapioca jelly is excellent for an invalid. Soak one breakfast-cupful of tapioca in three cups of water over night. In the morning put it in a double boiler, with a cup of hot water, and let it simmer until clear, stirring often. Flavor with juice of half a lemon and two tablespoonfuls of wine. Pour in cups and set away until perfectly cold. Cream and suger may be served with this jelly.

HINTS TO COOKS

To prevent fish from falling apart when boiling, add a little vinegar to the water.
Fish will scale more easily if dipped in hot water.
Grease the inside edge of the pan in which chocolate is being made, and it will not boil over.
Cheese may be kept from molding by wrapping in a cloth wet in cider vinegar.
The "taste" may be removed from wooden pails and bowls by scalding with boiling water and soda.
In making bean soup, add one tablespoonful of butter and one of flour, rubbed together to prevent beans settling to the bottom.

TO KEEP BUTTER

Boil together three gallons of water, one-half gallon of salt, two tablespoonfuls of sugar, one of saltpeter, boil three or four hours and when cool strain into a large stone jar. As the butter is made, wrap in clean cloths, in one pound or half-pound pieces, and keep a weight on, to keep under the water; butter will keep sweet and fresh for months in this way.

A GOOD CEMENT

A cement made by adding a teaspoonful of glycerine to a gill of glue is a great convenience in the kitchen, and is especially good for fastening leather, paper or wood to metal.

SAVING SUGAR IN JELLIES

In making jellies or jam, sweeten to taste and add three heaping teaspoonfuls of cornstarch dissolved in a little water to every quart of fruit. It jellies beautifully, tastes just as good and saves one-third of the sugar ordinarily used.

A NIGHT LIGHT

A candle can be made to burn all night in a sick room or elsewhere when a dull light is wished, by putting finely powdered salt on the candle until it reaches the blackened part of the wick. In this way a mild and steady light may be kept through the night from a small piece of candle.

COLD ON THE LUNGS

For cold on the lungs, use a poultice of roasted onions or poultice of hops and cornmeal.

To heal and expand the lungs, inhale steam from milk and water from the spout of a common teapot.

AN INEXPENSIVE HAMMOCK

A cheap and comfortable hammock may be easily made by taking two burlap sacks, two strong sticks the length of both sacks, and three sticks the width of the sacks. Put one at each end of the long sticks and the third about ten inches from one end. Fasten these to the long sticks firmly. Now take the sacks and pull one on at each end, and sew together in the middle with strong string, and the hammock is finished. A piece of burlap may be fringed and sewed to the sides if desired.

TO FIT NEW SHOE

To break in a new pair of shoes, that they may be comfortable at once to tender or swollen feet, put cold water in a large pan till the bottom is covered for one-half or three-quarters of an inch. Place both new shoes carefully in the water, let them stay ten minutes. Take out shoes, wipe the soles, put them on, and walk around for a short time. The shoes, being damp on the bottom, will conform at once to the shape of the feet and soon will be "as easy as an old shoe."

TO CURE HEADACHE

To cure headache or stop pain in any part of body, wring piece of flannel out in hot water, apply and cover with heavy flannel. Alternate with cold water. This will ease any pain, and is better than headache powders and other dangerous drugs.

REMOVING STONES FROM PEACHES

In preparing peaches for the cans, most people pare them *first*, then cut them in half, and they are quite likely to break in removing the pit. I find that by cutting them in half *before* paring, the pit is easily removed without breaking the peach.

A LAMP HINT

To prevent lamps from smoking, wash the wick thoroughly in warm water with a little soap dissolved in it; then rinse in clean water and let dry; after it is dry soak the wick in strong vinegar for an hour, then dry. If this is done every week, you won't be troubled with smoky lamp chimneys.

WHOOPING-COUGH CURE

Boil one pint of molasses and one-half cupful of vinegar together for twenty minutes. Let cool, then add a dessert-spoonful of paregoric and a spoonful of laudanum, and bottle for use. Dose: a small teaspoonful, when coughing. If taken properly, this will cure a case of whooping-cough in six or seven days.

TREATMENT OF SEVERE WOUNDS

Very often death from lockjaw results from the wound of a rusty nail in some part of the body. There is a perfect and simple remedy for such wounds. As soon as possible, smoke the wound well with a woolen cloth. Twenty minutes in the smoke will take the pain out of the worst inflammation arising from such a wound. This has been fre-uently tested.

RELIEF FOR NEURALGIC PAINS

A certain relief for neuralgic pains will be found in the following recipe. Heat one pint of salt—smoking hot—then put it into a cloth sack and insert into the salt one-fourth of an ounce of camphor gum. Apply at once to the part affected, instantly covering the sack with several thicknesses of cloth, to prevent the escape of fumes of the camphor, which escape like steam or smoke. The effect is almost magical. It is a fine remedy for earache.

TO RENEW GILT FRAMES

Gilt frames can be cleaned by wiping them with a small sponge moistened with oil of turpentine. Wet the sponge only just sufficient to take off the dirt and fly marks, then allow the frames to dry themselves.

USES OF SALT

Salt in solution is an antidote to many poisons.
A pinch of salt added to prepared mustard prevents it souring.
Cut flowers may be kept fresh by adding salt to the water.
Brooms soaked in hot water wear better and do not break.
Weak and tired eyes are refreshed by bathing with warm water and salt.
Lemon and salt removes stains from the fingers. Do not use soap afterward.
Weak ankles should be rubbed with a solution of salt water and alcohol.

SPICED GRAPES

Take six pounds of sugar and put in a preserve kettle with a quart of vinegar, let boil, flavor with cinnamon, nutmeg and mace and spice cloves. Take ten pounds of ripe grapes and put in jars, pour the syrup over boiling hot, seal, and set in a cool place.

KEEPS SALAD DRESSING FROM CURDLING

When salad dressing is liable to curdle, a small pinch of soda dropped in will prevent it from doing so.

TO CLEAN AND MIRROR VELVET

The mirror velvet which is so much used at times is easily renewed at home. Upon a perfectly smooth ironing-board place the velvet, with the pile side up, and cover it with a thin wet cloth. This should be well shaken, to take out the wrinkles caused by wringing it. With a moderately hot iron press the damp cloth, being careful to press in the same direction in which the pile of the velvet runs. When you have gone over the entire surface, smooth the cloth and press directly upon the face of the velvet. Care must be taken not to move the iron a particle except in the one direction. If the pile is long, the pressing may be done as above without the damp cloth. Velvet trimmings, etc., can, by mirroring, be made nearly as fresh as new. To clean velvet, brush it thoroughly to remove the dust, and wash it in gasoline. This is done exactly as one would wash a cotton or linen article in water, by rubbing between the hands. If the velvet is much soiled, rinse in clean gasoline. In using gasoline, its explosive nature should always be kept in mind. It should never be handled near a fire or light, or even in the same room with either.

LITTLE HELPS FOR HOME-MAKERS

KEEP TANSY IN YOUR FURS

Tansy is a sure preventive of moths. If the leaves are sprinkled freely about woolens and furs, they will never be moth-eaten.

DUSTING FURNITURE

Dust carved furniture with a new paint brush, which will find the dust in the deepest parts of the work.

KEEPS STOCKINGS "FAST BLACK"

A little vinegar added to rinse water for black stockings will keep them a fast black.

TO KEEP MACHINE BELT FROM SLIPPING

If the band of your sewing machine is too loose and slips when sewing, put a few drops of castor oil in the groove under it, and it will be quickly tightened.

TO PROTECT TABLECLOTH

In homes where there are children, and all eat at one table, take a piece of white oilcloth about a foot wide and the size round of the table, have the edges pinked or plain, and place under the plates. It can be removed after each meal, leaving the cover spotless, and it is not unsightly.

CORN MEAL, A SUBSTITUTE FOR SOAP

If, for any reason, one does not like to use soap on the hands, an excellent substitute may be found in fine granulated cornmeal. Moisten the hands, then apply a little meal, rub in well and then rinse off in warm water. This will remove soiled places, will not set stains and will leave the hands free from any of the unpleasant effects of soap.

HOW TO BOIL WATER FOR DRINKING

In many kinds of sickness, especially among children, boiled water is a necessity. To boil it would seem to be a very simple thing, and yet but few people know how to boil it properly. The secret lies in taking good, fresh water, putting it into a clean kettle already quite warm, and setting the water to boiling quickly, and taking it right off the stove before it is spoiled. To let it steam and simmer and evaporate until the good water is in the atmosphere, and the lime and iron and dregs only left in the kettle, makes a great many people sick, and is worse than no water at all. Water boiled in this way and flavored with a few drops of lemon juice makes a cool and refreshing drink for little sufferers.

MAKES SOLES LAST LONGER

To make shoe soles last, soak them in linseed oil for one or two days; do not get any oil on the uppers, as the oil makes them stiff. This will make them last twice as long as they otherwise would.

BABY'S SHAMPOO

If you have trouble with the little ones, when giving a shampoo, don't lose your patience because they object so strenuously to having soapsuds splashed in their eyes. Take a napkin by the opposite corners and roll until the remaining corners are formed into a pad. Pass this around the baby's head and tie with knot at nape of neck; all superfluous water and soapsuds will be absorbed by the pad, so formed, and baby will be sweeter and so will you.

BOSTON BAKED BEANS

Pick over the beans carefully. Put them in an earthen dish large enough to give them plenty of room to swell. Sprinkle on them a teaspoonful of cooking soda and then pour enough boiling water over them to cover them when swollen. Let them stand over night. In the morning wash them thoroughly in cold water.

Put them in the bean-pot, use sugar to taste—about four teaspoonfuls to a pint of beans is a good rule. Then lay the salt pork on top. A piece of dry red pepper is good for seasoning. Use a little salt if you do not care to use too much pork. Some object to using pork and in that case they can use a lump of nice butter.

Then fill the pot, not too full of water at first, as it is liable to run over, and put them in the oven and bake from twelve to twenty-four hours, putting in fresh water as it cooks out.

MEALY BAKED POTATOES

Cut a snip off the end of potatoes before placing in the oven to bake. The steam escapes and leaves the potato mealy.

BOILED CHESTNUTS

A comfortable way of eating boiled chestnuts: Pare a bit of shell from the larger end of each nut, and boil for twenty minutes in salted water. They are then eaten conveniently from the sinuating tip of a coffee spoon—chestnuts on the half-shell, as it were, properly accompanied by a draught of sweet cider. With a small, sharp knife, a quart of chestnuts can be prepared for boiling in ten minutes or less.

LITTLE HELPS FOR HOME-MAKERS

AS THE BAKER DOES IT

Wash the top of pies with sweet milk before baking to give them the rich golden brown that bakery pies have.

BEATING EGGS

When you want to beat eggs to a froth quickly, have them almost ice-cold before you break them.

SPICED PRUNES

When stewing prunes add about seven or eight whole cloves to a pound of the fruit. They give a new and delicious flavor that is liked by all

TO CLEAN STRAINERS

When your strainers become clogged, a lump of coarse salt, moistened and vigorously applied, will clean them.

CURE FOR IVY POISON

The best and quickest cure for ivy poison is hot water. Take a soft rag, folded several times, dip it in hot, not warm, water, and apply to the affected part for three or four minutes, just as hot as can be borne without scalding; repeat often, do not rub, touch gently. If done when it first appears, nothing more will be needed; it allays the itching at once.

CLEANSING, ETC.

If when putting up fruit some of the nice juices are canned, you have something ready for seasoning mincemeat for Thanksgiving and Christmas pies, with very little trouble.

Wash white-washed walls with strong vinegar-water before putting on paper.

If light cotton goods are put into cold salt water thoroughly heated, and rinsed while hot in cold water, there will be no more shrinking and this will set the colors, excepting fancy colors.

Putting a little butter in cooked starch will make the irons go more smoothly on ironing day.

Ammonia used on beds and mattresses will keep them clean and free from bugs.

To clean lamp chimneys, rub first with cloth wet in kerosene, then with soft paper or cloth.

TEACHING BABY TO KICK

Make baby's night-gown long and put a draw string in the bottom instead of fastening the bed-covering with safety pins.

TO BAKE POTATOES

Before putting potatoes in the oven to bake, grease them. When the potatoes are done, the skins, instead of being thick and hard as is usually the case, will be thin and tender, and the quality of the potato greatly improved.

BED-MAKING MADE EASY

Put two loops made of strong tape or cloth, through which you can insert your hand, on each side of a mattress, and see how much more easily it can be lifted or turned.

CLEANING CARPET-SWEEPERS

If you want your carpet-sweeper to do good work, take the brush out and comb it occasionally. Do not throw your sweepers away when they fail to sweep, thinking the brush is worn out. The brush will last as long as the sweeper. Just have the man of the house lower the spring that controls the brush. In case a mouse eats the brush a new one can be bought at the furniture dealer's for fifty cents.

UTILIZING A CELLAR-WAY

On one side place three grape baskets, nailed one above the other, and into these put paper sacks, wrapping paper and newspapers, respectively. Below these have a small box in which to put all the wrapping cord. So if there is a bundle to do up, a fowl to singe or any need of paper or cord, you always have a supply on hand.

Also keep brooms here on little racks made of two nails driven in the wall just far enough apart to admit the broom handle between them. The cool air of the cellar-way keeps the brooms soft and pliable.

Have a narrow shelf on one side for shoe-blacking, stove-blacking, machine oil and other small necessary articles, which are best kept out of sight.

DRYING RUBBER BOOTS QUICKLY

When your rubber boots get wet on the inside, fill them with oats that have first been heated in an oven to thoroughly dry them. If very wet, replace the oats two or three times. The oats absorb the moisture.

LITTLE HELPS FOR HOME-MAKERS

CLEANSING GLASS, ETC.

Alcohol will keep ice from forming on the windows.
Discolorations on china baking dishes and custard cups can be removed with whiting.
Vinegar will remove paint from window glass.
Use soda water in washing windows to remove finger-marks, putty stains, etc.

TO CLEAN PANAMA HATS

Take half a teaspoonful of equal portions of precipitated sulphur and oxalic acid, mix and dissolve in half a tumbler of cold water, then dip a clean sponge (not too wet) and pass over the hat until perfectly clean, then place in the sun to dry, after which the hat will look like new. Ten cents will cover the entire cost.

WATERING LITTLE CHICKS

The best way to water little chicks is to fill a flat tin nearly full of pebbles, and pour in water. The chicks drink in the little pools between the pebbles and are kept from getting in the water with their feet.
To be successful with little chickens you must keep them dry and warm.

FOR CONSTIPATION

Mix two cups of fine wheat bran with one cup of pastry flour. Then add one-half teaspoonful of salt, one-half cup of molasses, one teaspoonful of saleratus dissolved in one and one-quarter cups of sweet milk. Mix well. An egg improves but is not essential. Bake in gem tins and eat one gem at each meal or twice a day as needed.

COMBING BLANKETS

We are all partial to soft, fleecy blankets, but alas, they soon lose their beauty by the fleece wearing up in little rolls. They can be renewed by taking a clean coarse comb and combing lengthwise of the blanket, to a smooth, fleecy blanket again.

TEETHING BABIES

If mothers with teething babies will feed them crushed rice, it will help cut the teeth and also cool the fevered gums. And if baby's bowels act too freely, give him a bath in water as warm as he can bear it, with a handful of salt thrown in it. Let him stay in the bath ten or fifteen minutes, keeping the water warm by adding hot water from time to time. Repeat bath two or three times a day if necessary.

A BUDGET OF HINTS

The worst ink stains may be removed by soaking in cold milk and changing the milk as fast as it becomes colored with ink.

To hang up a broom bore a hole through the handle large enough to slip over a nail.

A sure cure for erysipelas is to bathe with tincture of lobelia.

To clean bottles, take warm suds and put in a few shot, shake well and rinse.

To clean paint brushes, soak in spirits of turpentine; if you do not have turpentine, take kerosene oil.

To take out iron-rust in clothes do not use oxalic acid, but cut a lemon in halves and rub on the spot; then rub with salt and lay in the sun and it will all come out. If it is bad, try several times.

To take grease out of silk, rub with buckwheat flour.

When washing linen embroidered with white silk use cold water. Keep hot water away from white silk and it will retain its whiteness.

Rub hinges with a feather dipped in oil and they will not creak.

Linen embroidered with colored silks should be washed quickly in suds made with castile soap, rinsed thoroughly, rolled in sheets and then ironed.

Boil three or four onions in a pint of water, apply with a soft brush to gilt frames, and flies will keep off them.

A spoonful of vinegar put into the water in which meats or fowls are boiled makes them tender.

Melted paraffine poured over the top of jelly will prevent molding.

To remove skins of cooked beets, let them lie a few minutes in cold water and the skins will slip off easily.

To prevent a bruise from turning purple, rub fresh lard upon it.

A little cream of tartar or vinegar improves boiled frosting. It will not grain so readily and will be more creamy.

When crackers become soft from long standing, put them in a pan and bake them over. They will be as crisp as fresh ones.

Chestnuts and walnuts may be kept a year by packing in dry sand.

If you wish to iron a starched or other garment quickly, sprinkle it with hot water instead of cold.

If boiled or roasted meat is to be eaten cold, wrap a piece of dampened cloth around it when it is put away after cooking. It will be more moist and tender after this treatment.

If potatoes for baking are placed on the back of the range or in the warming oven until they are heated through, they will bake in less than half the time when placed in the oven.

A dish of water in a hot oven will prevent food from burning.

A spoonful of sugar put in the water when boiling turnips will prevent their tasting bitter.

To restore a faded carpet, dip it in strong salt and water.

To remove stains from the hands wash in the juice of a ripe tomato.

A teaspoonful of burnt sugar will give an amber color to soup made from white meats.

Half a lemon placed in the water in which dish towels and kitchen cloths are soaked is said to sweeten them wonderfully.

MAKING STOVE-PIPES FIT

If you should have an odd size stove, and your piping is too large for it, cut a slit about five inches up one end, lap over the ends and fasten with a brad. This is an easy, simple and very effectual manner to make the piping fit.

THE SEWING MACHINE

If, when sewing on a machine, the upper thread keeps snapping without apparent cause, reverse the bobbin in the shuttle; *i. e.*, take the bobbin out and put it back the other end foremost.

COOKING CORN MEAL

To prevent corn cakes and bread from having a raw taste, mix the meal with milk a few hours before baking the bread. When ready to bake it, add the salt, egg, a spoonful of flour and last of all the soda, or if sweet milk be used, add baking powder.

Mush, to be good, must be boiled a long time. Boil it thoroughly, being careful not to make it too thick, then place closely covered in the oven where it is kept at boiling heat for several hours.

SAVING SAFETY-RAZOR BLADES

If you own a safety razor (such as the Gillette) strop the blade very lightly on a soft strop before and after using, and the blade will last three times as long.

FILLING A HOT-WATER BOTTLE

The following directions were given by a hospital nurse: Heat the water to near boiling, fill bottle about one-third full, and before putting in stopper, lay bag flat and double it over. This will prevent the accumulation of steam, which makes a bag hard and unyielding.

WASH YOUR COFFEE

How many housewives see to it that the green coffee purchased from the grocer is carefully washed before being roasted? Many otherwise careful housekeepers empty the coffee from the parcel in which it was bought into the pan for roasting, never thinking that they are doing an unclean thing.

Coffee is often dyed to give it a better color, and aside from this, there is such a quantity of real dirt upon it that it really astonishes people who never washed it. Wash your coffee.

REMEMBER THIS ON JULY 4TH

If your boy gets his eyes burnt with powder while shooting fireworks, relieve the pain while waiting for the doctor by pouring sweet oil in his eyes.

HANDY HOME-MADE FUNNEL

Half an eggshell with a hole in the end makes a handy little funnel for bottles. If the eggshell is browned in the stove slightly it will be more durable.

A BEEF'S HEART AND TONGUE

When meat of all kinds is high, as at the present time, it seems to me that the most economical meat to buy once or twice a month is the heart and tongue of a beef. In small towns in the Middle West, the two will cost about forty cents. Wash the heart carefully to remove the blood. Use a vegetable scrubbing brush and rub the tongue until thoroughly clean. Put together in a granite iron kettle, cover with boiling water, season with summer savory, and cook three or four hours. Let both stand in the broth until cold, and slice one-half or two-thirds of each and you will have some of the most delicious of cold meats. Enough for two or three meals for an ordinary family. Carefully remove all the fat from the top of the broth and put in the doughnut kettle. Take about half of the broth for stock for a vegetable soup. Put the meat that is left through a meat chopper, add a cup of walnut meats (also put through the chopper), two cups of cracker crumbs, three well-beaten eggs and the unused half of the broth. Mix thoroughly, season to taste, and if the mixture is not quite moist enough, add milk or water. Bake slowly in a well-buttered, deep and narrow cake tin for an hour and a half and you will have a delicious meat loaf that will last three or four meals. The loaf may be made without the nut meats, but has a finer flavor and is more nutritious with them.

HOT WATER AS A MEDICINE

Hot water, if used with common sense, might save many a doctor's bill, and many a course of drug treatment as well. For bruises, sprains and similar accidental hurts it should be applied as hot as can be borne, by means of a cloth dipped in the water and laid on the wounded part, or by immersion, if convenient, and the treatment kept up until relief is obtained For pains resulting from indigestion, a cupful of hot water taken in sips will often relieve at once. A flannel folded in several thicknesses, wrung out of the hot water and laid over the seat of the pain, and renewed every ten minutes or oftener will aid the relief in severe cases. For insomnia, when "too tired to sleep," as we sometimes say, bathe the neck and temples, the back of the neck particularly. This seems to relax the muscles and veins that supply the brain. The same treatment will refresh during the day, and a headache may often be relieved by it.

POWDERED CHARCOAL FOR BURNS

For scalds or burns cover the burn with finely powdered charcoal; use dry and it will stop pain at once.

HOME-MADE FIRE-EXTINGUISHER

Take twenty pounds of common salt and ten pounds of muriate of ammonia, to be had of any druggist, and dissolve in seven gallons of water. When dissolved it can be bottled and kept in each room in the house, to be used in an emergency. In case of fire, one or two bottles should be immediately thrown with force into the burning place, so as to break them. The fire will certainly be extinguished.

HOW TO PREVENT COUGHING

Coughing is the worst thing for a cough, and in most instances of cough there is more coughing than is necessary to subserve the purpose of the cough, i. e., to remove offending material.

The following directions will help one to avoid coughing in all instances, while in the more mild cases it may stop the cough altogether after a little perseverance. When tempted to cough take a deep breath, filling if possible every air cell, holding it until the warming, soothing effect comes or so long as is reasonable, and mark the mollifying result on the cough, which, even when the latter seems unavoidable, will often be found under control.

Repeat if necessary. The explanation of this is that there is a liberation of nitrogen in the air cells which has a quieting, sedative effect on the irritated mucous membrane.

HEALING PROPERTIES OF WATER

There is no remedy of such general application and none so easily obtainable as water, and yet nine persons out of ten will pass it by in an emergency to seek for something of less efficacy. There are but few cases of illness where water should not occupy the highest place as a remedial agent.

A strip of flannel or a napkin folded lengthwise and wrung out of hot water and applied around the neck of a child who has croup will usually bring relief in a few minutes. A towel folded several times, then quickly wrung out of hot water and immediately applied over the seat of the pain in toothache or neuralgia, will afford prompt relief. This treatment in colic works like magic. Cases on record, having resisted other treatment for hours, have yielded to this treatment in ten minutes. Pieces of cotton batting dipped in hot water, then applied to all sores and new cuts, bruises, and sprains is the treatment now generally adopted in hospitals. Hot water taken freely a half hour before bedtime is an excellent cathartic in the case of constipation, while it has a most soothing effect on the stomach and bowels. This treatment continued for a few months, together with proper attention to diet, will alleviate mild cases of dyspepsia.

SWEEPING MATTING

A carpet sweeper can be used successfully on straw mattings if moved across the breadths.

SASH-CURTAIN RODS

When putting a sash-curtain rod into the run of a curtain, it quite often sticks. This may be avoided by putting a thimble on the end of the rod.

CLEANSING THE BROOM

There is no more fruitful scatterer of germs than the common broom, therefore it should be frequently cleansed. Dipping in hot soap-suds not only makes the broom clean, but lengthens its time of usefulness materially.

CLEANING SOILED BOOKS

Stains on the edges of book-leaves can be removed with sandpaper; a slice of bread will clean covers soiled by handling.

STARCHING FRINGED ARTICLES

When starching toilet covers or anything that has fringe trimming, fold the cover twice and gather the fringe tightly into the hand and hold it firmly while you dip the middle of the cover into the starch. When dry shake the fringe well, comb carefully with a large toilet comb, and it will fall as softly and prettily as when new.

HOME CLEANSERS

Brown paper moistened in vinegar will polish your tins until they shine like silver.

A slice of Irish potato will clean oil paintings without injury, and dipped in soda will brighten silver.

SALAD DRESSING WITHOUT OIL

One heaping tablespoonful of butter, one rounded tablespoonful of flour, put in pan on the stove and stir until hot and smooth, then add one cupful of milk. Now put in a bowl separate from the above one even tablespoonful of sugar, one even teaspoonful of salt, one heaping teaspoonful of mustard, one egg and a scant half cup of vinegar. Mix well and add to the other mixture and cook until thick; if it curdles it may be made smooth by beating with an egg-beater.

PRESERVES WHITE FABRICS

A white dress, or other white article, if wrapped in blue paper, can then be laid away for years without turning yellow.

A DELICATE PERFUME

A good perfumed toilet soap placed in the bureau lends a delicate and lasting perfume to underwear and toilet accessories. Its advantages over sachet powders, which lose their scent in a short time, are easily seen. Sandalwood and violet in in the same drawer produce a delightful combination.

A GREAT SAVING IN IRONING

After sprinkling, fold your napkins, towels, etc., as you want them to be folded when they are ironed, smoothing them with the hands as you fold them. The ironing will then be much easier.

AN INK ERASER

An ink eraser is not always at hand. Apply your moistened finger to the word to be removed, then use an ordinary pencil eraser. The result will please you.

SALT TO CLEAN MARBLE

Always keep a cup of salt on your lavatory. It is invaluable for cleaning the marble, and something one always has at hand.

NOODLES

Two-thirds of a cup of thick, sweet cream and milk, taken from the cream jar, one egg, a pinch of salt, one and a half teaspoonfuls of baking powder, and flour enough to make a stiff dough. Roll this out in three thin sheets and rub with flour, and let dry from nine o'clock till noon, then roll up and cut in thin strips a fourth of an inch wide, shake, rub and drop in boiling soup, and cook ten minutes without lifting lid.

CURE FOR APPENDICITIS

Half a wine-glass of sweet oil (olive oil), taken two or three times a week, is a preventive of appendicitis. A pint taken at two doses has cured a developed case. Olive oil is also beneficial to persons inclined to pulmonary diseases.

NOVEL USE FOR NUTMEG GRATER

Use a nutmeg grater to remove burnt places in a cake.

SLIPPING ROSE BUSHES

Rose bushes can be easily started for growing by pulling off a slip at the joint and planting in the ground with a little sand. Cover with an inverted glass can. Let remain all winter.

THREADING THE SEWING MACHINE

A machine needle may be threaded much easier if a piece of white material is held back of it.

A CONVENIENT SCREEN

A screen may be made very convenient when bathing and dressing a baby by placing a number of pockets on the inside to contain the necessary articles. The screen is also useful to keep off the draught.

SPACE ECONOMIZER

To economize space in a bedroom, fasten a shelf, holding a bowl, to the inside of a closet door with large braces or brackets. Smaller bracket-shelves may be fastened to the door higher up, to be used for soap dish, shaving mug, etc.

TO CLEAN LAMP CHIMNEYS

To polish your lamp chimneys so they will simply shine, first, wash in soapsuds, rinse and dry. Then use an old newspaper to polish with.

TO SALT PORK

In salting pork, sprinkle it generously with ground black pepper and add a little saltpeter. This will keep it fresh and sweet, and it also keeps any bugs or flies from the pork.

FOR NEW BROOMS

Dip your new brooms in scalding water (soapsuds are preferable) and they will last twice as long as ordinarily.

COOKING SOUR FRUIT

Use a pinch of baking soda in cooking sour fruit, and it will not require more than half the ordinary amount of sugar.

A NEW SHOE POLISH

The white of an egg makes an excellent shoe polish for patent or ordinary leather. Clean the shoes of mud, etc., and apply with a cloth. It produces a gloss that would satisfy the most fastidious, renders the leather soft, and prevents cracking.

REMOVES INK STAINS

To remove ink stains from the fingers, dampen the head of an ordinary match and rub briskly on stain.

SMOOTH FLATIRONS

Lard (unsalted) is better than beeswax to make flatirons slip easily. Fold a cloth several thicknesses, put a lump of lard the size of a walnut within the folds and rub the iron over it. Same cloth will last many weeks by folding clean side out and adding more lard when needed.

TO CLEAN KETTLES

Granite kettles or dishes which have been burned, no matter how badly, may be cleaned perfectly by filling above burned depth with two parts soft water and one part washing fluid and placing them on stove to simmer lightly one-half hour, when sand-soap or wire dish-washer will remove it easily. If it does not come off first time, repeat or increase quantity of washing fluid, and in most obstinate cases double the quantity of fluid, and let stand in dish a day or more, which will clean it thoroughly. Do not throw solution away. Put in bottle or jar to use for same purpose again.

SAVING TAILOR'S BILLS

The economical helpmate may save tailors' bills by mending the ankles of her husband's trousers with buttonhole stich.

When they begin to fray out, buttonhole the worn places, using a fine needle, fine black silk and taking a short stitch.

They can be turned up later, as the stitching presses out flat if carefully done.

CLEAN BED-CLOTHES

If a strip of the material of which a "comforter" is made, eight inches wide, is sewed by hand along each end of it, the "comforter" will last much longer, as this strip can be taken off, washed and replaced, thus insuring cleanliness and longer service.

FOR TONSILITIS

Take equal parts of lamp-oil, spirits of turpentine and camphor. Mix well and swab the throat several times a day.

FOR CROUP

Save the lining of a fowl's gizzard, and when dry pulverize and mix with molasses or honey.

A HANDY SOAP-DISH

A handy soap-dish can be made by punching fifteen or twenty holes in the bottom of a tin quart cup in such a way that the suds will not drain out when cup is hung up. Keep cup hung on a nail by the kitchen sink, and pour water through it for dish-washing, etc., thus saving time, inconvenience and soap.

Mak a kettle scraper by folding in the edges of a piece of window screen and fastening with fine wire.

TO BEAT EGGS

If the whites of eggs are chilled before using, they can be beaten twice as well in half the time usually required. A pinch of salt added just before beating prevents the whites from falling, as is sometimes the case when the beaten mass is allowed to stand.

RELIEF FOR INFLAMMATION

In cases of severe inflammation and swelling, tallow if melted and applied hot on a woolen cloth, will give relief and has been known to cure a case of appendicitis. Should be changed often enough to keep hot.

CURE FOR A COUGH

Take a small piece of rosin and crush it fine to the amount of half a teaspoonful; can be taken with any kind of favorite sauce. It will induce sleep and there will be no coughing all night.

CARE OF THE HANDS

Ground mustard is excellent to cleanse the hands after having handled strong-smelling substances. Wash the hands in vinegar after having them in soapsuds and they will be soft and white and not will chap.

To remove fruit stains from the hands, wash in clear water, dry slightly and then hold them over a lighted match.

TO KEEP EGGS FRESH

Eggs can be kept perfectly fresh for a very long time by placing each one separately in a small paper sack and tying securely to exclude the air.

PRESERVING HINT

When putting up fruit, roll your jars in hot water before filling them and they will not crack. Fill while still hot and they will be all right.

FOR NURSING MOTHERS

Apply glycerine and camphor in equal parts to cracked and sore nipples.

REMEDY FOR TONSILITIS

An effective remedy for tonsilitis is two grains of bichromate of potash dissolved in an ordinary drinking glass of water used as a gargle every two or three hours.

In case of croup, one-half teaspoonful of this gargle swallowed will loosen the mucus.

TO PAINT CRACKED WALLS

Mix white wine vinegar with an equal part of water, add plaster of paris enough to make a thick cream, wet the cracks first with the vinegar and water, and then force in the plaster mixture with a flat stick, wiping away the surplus.

When dry, apply paint, and not one crack will show in either wall or ceiling.

TO IMPROVE THE DIGESTION

Prescription to improve the digestion and increase the appetite: Tincture of Nux Vomica, two drams. Tincture of Columbo, one ounce. Compound tincture of Gentian, three ounces. Dose for an adult, one teaspoonful, to be taken in water before each meal.

SALADS FOR HOT DAYS

Cucumber and Tomato Salad: Wash and crisp one head of lettuce. Pare a sufficient number of fine cucumbers and place in ice water for an hour. Pour boiling water over two or three ripe but firm tomatoes, then remove the skins and stand them in pounded ice to chill. At serving time, arrange the light-green leaves on individual salad plates; cut the cucumbers first into thick rounds, then into quarters, heap in the center of the leaves and sprinkle lightly with salt and white pepper. Cut the tomatoes into thin lengthwise sections and use as a garnish. Over all pour a good salad dressing.

Macedoine Salad: For this most appetizing dish use remnants of cold cooked vegetables in palatable proportions, or slice one cold cooked carrot, one beet and one potato; cut a few cold cooked string beans and asparagus tips into half-inch lengths. Toss all together lightly, add a few cold stewed peas and a small onion chopped very fine, marinate with French dressing and stand on ice to chill. Then heap in tiny mounds on crisped lettuce leaves for individual serving; dress with mayonnaise and garnish with radish ribbons. To make these "ribbons," cut a small turnip-shaped breakfast radish round and round into thin narrow strips, being careful not to break the strips.

Cottage Cheese Salad with Tomatoes: Break the cheese into grains, moisten with rich, sweet cream, season with salt and white pepper, and rub with the back of a silver spoon until thoroughly blended Wash fine, ripe tomatoes and cut into thick slices. Place each slice on an individual salad plate and cover it with the cheese, well heaped toward the center. Dress with mayonnaise and garnish with sprigs of watercress.

Shredded Cabbage Salad: Select firm, white cabbage, shred very fine with a sharp knife and sprinkle lightly with salt and white pepper. Rub the yolks of three hard-boiled eggs smooth, then blend with them two tablespoonfuls of sugar, one of ground mustard and one-half cup of butter slightly warmed. Stir this mixture lightly through the cabbage, then add a cup of good vinegar. Cut the whites of the eggs into rings for garnishing the salad, placing in the center of each ring a tiny beet cube cut from cold cooked beet.

Beet and Potato Salad: Cook four medium-sized blood beets tender; plunge them into cold water and remove the skins. Chill on ice; cut into small cubes and sprinkle lightly with salt and sugar. Have ready four cold boiled potatoes, diced and salted to taste. Wash and crisp the inside leaves of a head of lettuce, and line a flat salad bowl with them. In the center of the bowl heap the diced potatoes, surround with a border of beet cubes, and dress the whole with a rich salad dressing.

Cauliflower Salad: Remove the outside green leaves from a small head of cauliflower; cut it into quarters, then let it lie in salt water for an hour, to destroy any possible insect life or eggs not dislodged by washing. Drain, tie in a clean cheesecloth bag, and cook one hour in boiling water to which has been added one teaspoonful of salt. When done, take from the bag, break into flowerets and chill on ice. At serving time, line a salad bowl with crisped lettuce leaves, heap the cauliflower in the center, dress with French dressing, and garnish with tiny cheese balls.

Spinach Salad: Wash the spinach through several waters, or until free from grit, and cut off the stalks; then boil it in a closely covered saucepan without water for thirty minutes. Drain and chop fine with a sharp knife. Add the chopped whites of two eggs and marinate with French dressing. Have ready a sufficient number of individual molds or small cups. In the bottom of each place a slice of cold boiled egg; fill up with spinach, packing in closely. Stand in the refrigerator to chill. Then unmold and serve on a bed of lettuce. Dress with mayonnaise.

A Breakfast Salad: Hull and rinse one quart of fine strawberries. Pare three oranges and break into thin sections, taking care to remove each portion of the white fiber. Place the strawberries in the center of a salad bowl and garnish with the orange sections. Pour over the whole the juice of a lemon and sprinkle with sugar.

VETERINARY MEDICINE

For a horse suffering with an obstinate colic, take two large spoonfuls of ground ginger, pour over it a quart or so of hot water; pour into a long-necked bottle and force into the mouth of the horse, and compel him to swallow the tea. Be careful that the water is not too hot. If not relieved, repeat the dose in ten minutes.

I have used this same remedy for calves when they seemed to be dying, and in five or ten minutes have had them on their feet. I use, however, only *one* tablespoonful of the ginger for a calf.

For scours in calves, break a raw egg into the animal's mouth and force the calf to swallow egg *and* shell; in severe cases, use two eggs. Sometimes I give a tablespoonful of sulphur in the milk at feeding time, instead of eggs.

For a cow in a run-down condition, take a large handful of the inner bark of black birch, cover with four quarts of water, and let steep till the decoction is strong; then give this quantity in a pailful of warm water every morning for a few days.

I always milk in the stable, and to prevent flies from troubling the cow, I cover her with an old sheet or piece of burlap, or any light covering most convenient.

To insure healthy chickens: for every twelve chickens, add to their moist food one tablespoonful of sulphur, once a day; slightly increase the dose of sulphur while chicks are growing, and give it occasionally afterward.

My favorite harness oil: take such a quantity of fresh lard as you think necessary for the amount of harness to be oiled; add just enough kerosene oil to "cut" the lard; add lampblack to make a good clear black, and apply while warm with a brush. This oil will not "gum" and it keeps the leather soft and pliable a long time.

A CLEAN SWEEP

In sweeping carpets and rugs, after sweeping them and gathering up the sweepings moisten cornmeal quite wet with gasoline and scatter over them and sweep again, and you will be surprised how clean and bright they will look. I always remove all the furniture I can from the room and open doors and windows. Do not have fire in room as there is danger of gasoline igniting.

VEGETABLE SOUPS

Purée of Potatoes: Boil four large potatoes, two onions, two stalks of celery and a sprig of parsley in two quarts of water until quite soft: then pass the whole through a colander; return to the fire, season to taste with salt and white pepper, stir in two tablespoonfuls of butter creamed with one of flour, add a pint of sweet milk and let boil up once. Then turn into a soup tureen containing one cup of whipped cream.

Cream of Tapioca: Cover one-third of a cup of tapioca with two cups of cold water and let stand over night. Then add one quart of fresh sweet milk and cook gently for an hour. Add one pint of cream, a minced onion, two stalks of celery cut fine and a small blade of mace. Cook twenty minutes, season with salt and pepper, stir in one tablespoonful of butter and serve.

Tomato Soup: Stew one quart of tomatoes in one quart of water until quite soft; stir in one teaspoonful of soda and allow it to effervesce; then add one quart of boiling milk, season nicely with salt, pepper and butter, and cook five minutes. A thickening of flour and butter may be added, if desired.

Vegetable Soup: Put three quarts of boiling water over the fire in a soup kettle; add three onions, three potatoes, three large tomatoes and a small head of cabbage, all chopped fine. Cook gently until the vegetables are tender, then stir in one cup of cooked rice and one pint of stewed corn. Pass the mixture through a colander, return to the fire and boil up once. Then add two tablespoonfuls of butter creamed with one of flour, season with salt and pepper, stir in one tablespoonful of brown sugar, cook five minutes and serve with toasted crackers.

Asparagus Soup: Cook two bunches of asparagus and a small onion in one quart of water until quite soft, then press through a sieve. Add one quart of hot milk and return to the fire. Let boil up once, season to taste with salt and pepper, and thicken with four tablespoonfuls of butter blended with two tablespoonfuls of flour. Just before serving, add a cup of cream.

Rice and Celery Soup: Boil a small cup of rice in three pints of milk until soft enough to press through a sieve, then add to it the tender white portions of two heads of celery grated; put over the fire with one quart of milk and cook five minutes. Season with two tablespoonfuls of butter and salt and white pepper to taste.

Onion Soup: Cut fine the white portion of a dozen green onions and cook tender in a pint of boiling water to which has been added a little salt. Then add one quart of rich milk. Boil up once, season with salt, pepper and butter.

Cream of Corn Soup: To each quart of grated corn add three pints of water, and cook tender. Then stir in two tablespoonfuls of butter blended with one of flour. Boil five minutes, season with salt and pepper and add one pint of boiling milk.

Cream of Spinach Soup: Pick over and wash clean two quarts of spinach, then cook tender in one quart of water, and rub through a purée sieve. Add to it one quart of boiling milk, place over the fire, add a thickening of two tablespoonfuls of butter creamed with one of flour, cook five minutes, season with salt and pepper, and serve.

THE HANDY CARPET-SWEEPER

A great deal of hurry and worry can be avoided in the daily routine of housework by learning to "save steps." When your old sweeper becomes worn and seemingly useless, don't discard it, but keep it for the lighter work in your upstairs rooms, while your new sweeper may be kept for the heavier carpets downstairs. In that way you will save that tedious rushing up and down stairs which is bound to wear on the best of nerves.

GYPSY-MOTH POISONING

Put a few drops of Sulpho-Napthol in about a tablespoonful of water and apply where the irritation appears on the skin. It will smart at first, but in a few minutes all itching sensation will disappear. If the irritation returns, apply again until completely cured.

A BUDGET OF SUGGESTIONS

When mixing mustard, always use milk instead of water, and the mustard will not dry up so quickly.

Rub magnesia on soiled spots and dainty light colored goods. Put plenty on both sides, and when wanted for use again brush well and the spots will be gone.

Alcohol will remove varnish from fabrics.

To beat eggs quickly add a pinch of salt.

Prevent brass articles from tarnishing by applying a thin varnish of gum shellac and alcohol.

If soda is used in dishwater, no soap is needed.

TO ARRANGE FLORAL PIECES

When arranging floral pieces in which wire frames, covered with lead-foil and filled with moss, form the basis of the work, it is hard to get the surface closely covered, and the edges hidden. I have found wire hair-pins used as staples for fastening flowers and foliage into position the greatest help of anything I have ever tried. The pins pierce the foil and enter the moss, easily, and so make it possible to quickly staple vines, foliage or flowers around the edge of the frame or into vacant spots over the face of the piece. Then, too, a flower or leaf often persists in standing up when it should lie flat, and, when this happens, a hair-pin put across the stem brings it into the required position and holds it there.

LAMP WICKS

Fray the lower end of a lamp-wick about an inch and it will give a brighter and stronger light.

TO CLEAN SPECTACLES

To prevent the sudden clouding of eye-glasses, in change of atmosphere, on entering the warm store or car from the cold street: wash the glasses or spectacles in warm, soapy water. The instrument men in the surveyors' camp on Puget Sound find this a help to their instruments in the fogs of early spring.

UNPEELED APPLES

Do you know that apples for pies are much better if not peeled? In mince pies, especially, as the skin adds wonderfully and both the meat and apples may be cut with the Enterprise meat chopper. When apples are worth one dollar a bushel, this is worth trying.

FRIED MUSH

When making mush for frying put a little milk in the water. It makes the mush fry much nicer.

SNAKE BITE REMEDY

Here are a few ideas that all who expect to go to the mountains for their vacation would do well to remember:

Chloroform is a sure cure for rattle-snake as well as all other snake bites. It will cure even if not used for several hours, though the sooner the better. Bind a cloth over the wound and wet thoroughly with chloroform. Repeat several times. The bottle may be carried inside of one's waist. I never left our tent without it.

For poison oak dissolve one teaspoonful of concentrated lye in one quart of boiling water. Cool and use when ready to go out on a tramp, washing the hands, face, ears and neck with it. One of us forgot to apply it to her neck, consequently the eruption appeared there and nowhere else.

For bee stings and bites of poisonous spiders apply concentrated ammonia.

DELICIOUS CABBAGE

The following directions for cooking cabbage were furnished by a physician who asserted that the dish cooked in this fashion could be eaten by persons with the most delicate digestion, as the boiling water removed the objectionable qualities which usually render cabbage so difficult to digest. The taste is also much more delicate when cooked in this way.

Cut cabbage in quarters and boil steadily in salted water for fifteen minutes. Remove from the water and allow it to become perfectly cold. Then shred in pieces, place in saucepan and cover with milk. Simmer slowly for one hour and a half. Season with butter, salt and pepper. The milk will not curdle if simmered very slowly.

LITTLE HELPS FOR HOME-MAKERS 185

TOMATOES

Tomatoes should be freely used when in season. Served ice-cold on a hot morning, with a little olive oil, salt and pepper, they cool the system and freshen appetite.

Peeled, sliced and stuffed with minced onion and bits of cucumber and their own pulp, in crisp lettuce leaves, with a heaping spoonful of mayonnaise on each we have a salad that is tempting for mid-day luncheon. Peeled, chilled and left whole, with mayonnaise, they are a delicious dinner salad.

A sharp knife should be used to pare them. I do not approve of pouring hot water over them to remove the skins. Put them on ice and chill them thoroughly.

Stuffed tomatoes: Choose firm, round tomatoes, cut a small piece off the stem end and scoop out all the seeds, sprinkle the interior with salt and turn upside down to drain. Equal parts of chopped meat and boiled rice makes a good filling. The seasoning must suit the filling. Onion juice and chopped parsley and a few drops of catsup are generally liked; moisten with melted butter, fill the shells with the selected mixture and bake until tender, but do not allow them to lose their shape.

HINTS FOR LAUNDRY

A teaspoonful of turpentine put in boiler when boiling white clothes will keep them snow white and remove the dingy look about neck-bands, wristbands, etc.

Add a little pulverized borax to starch while cooking; it will give a gloss and prevent it from sticking to irons.

When washing white flannels, blue the water you rinse them in very blue and they will not become yellow. Add borax to water you wash and rinse them in, using rather warm water for both, and your flannels will always be white and soft.

In washing knit or crocheted articles, squeeze instead of wringing, and dry by laying on a clean towel, turning often, and they will be as nice as when new, and will retain their shape. Do not hang on line.

TO CAN RHUBARB

Cut tender rhubarb stems into half-inch lengths without peeling. Pack in cans. Pour in cold water till can overflows and bubbles cease to rise. Seal tight and treat as any canned fruit. Fine for pies in the winter.

POTATO AS A PEN WIPER

Keep a raw potato on your writing desk, and when the pen needs cleansing, stick it several times in succession into the potato; you will find that it works like a charm.

TO KEEP SALT PORK SWEET

Put in your pork barrel a bunch of smartweed, or old man's pepper, found very commonly around barnyards and farm buildings. Cut off the roots and tie up in a bunch. This is an unfailing remedy. Have used it several years. Get the kind with green leaves. The variety with a black stripe in the leaf is of no use.

TO DRIVE AWAY LARGE BLACK ANTS

Get five cents' worth of tartar emetic. Mix up half the quantity with sugar and water to a thin syrup. Put it in a little dish wherever they are troublesome. It will not only drive them away for that season, but they will not come back. We have tried it and the second season has brought no ants.

TO KEEP ICE

To keep ice a long time, take six or eight newspapers, place them in the ice-box, have the ice put on top, then wrap ice much as one would a shoe-box or package; then if the ice-box is not full, stuff well with crumpled paper around edges. The ice will last twice as long and do the same work.

FOR TRAVELING

The berths in a Pullman sleeper are often unbearably hot and stuffy in warm weather, and one tosses about, unable to sleep. To overcome the heat, a *hot water* bag filled with cold water (from drinking tanks in car) and placed under the back of the neck at base of skull, or used as a pillow, will give great relief. One almost feels as if one were even breathing cooler air, and soon gets restful sleep.

The same use may be made of the bag of cold water at home, and one can often go to sleep in overheated rooms by taking a quick cool bath and without wiping (except face and head) get in between sheets with the cold bag under the head.

A little linen slip on the bag makes it more suitable for invalids confined to the bed and for restless, fretting babies.

TO MAKE STOCKINGS LAST LONGER

Stockings will last three times as long if the heels and toes are lined before being worn. Cut strong muslin on the bias, just enough larger to allow for a very narrow lapped seam across the toe. See that it fits perfectly; then cross-stitch to the stocking with thread of the same color Leave the thread a trifle loose to allow for a little stretching.

Treat heels in a similar manner, making the muslin the size of the heel at the bottom of the foot, and taper to a point about four inches high in the back.

IRON EMBROIDERY ON A TURKISH TOWEL

Iron all embroidery and laces used as trimming on a Turkish towel, placing the goods face downward; the work will then stand out beautifully. It is a very easy matter, also, to iron gentlemen's fancy vests in this way. The seams sink into the towel and no glossy streak is left, as is otherwise the case.

WASHING WINDOWS

Wash windows with warm water in which you have first placed a small amount of ammonia, and use a chamois in place of a cloth or sponge; they will not require wiping or polishing if washed in this way.

A GOOD, HANDY PASTE

A cold boiled potato, cut in two and rubbed on back of scraps for scrapbook, will make them stick well, and it is always ready.

ABOUT LEMONS

Lemons may be kept fresh a long time by placing under an earthen-ware crock.

A few drops of lemon juice put into boiling rice will keep the kernels distinct and make them very white.

The juice of half a lemon in a glass of unsweetened water taken before breakfast, will ward off a bilious spell.

Wash the hands and finger tips in lemon to remove all sorts of stains.

A gargle of water and lemon juice will cure a sore throat.

A slice of lemon dipped in salt will scour brass utensils. Rinse well.

Castor oil taken in lemon juice is palatable.

A few drops in fruit juice that will not jell will bring about the desired result.

A lemon in a dish of apples or other fruit will impart a delightful bouquet to the fruit.

After a shampoo rinse the hair in water that has some lemon juice in it. It will cut any grease that remains and render the scalp extra white.

TO REMOVE A CORK FROM BOTTLE

Take a stiff piece of string, double, and insert the loop into bottle, which should be held on its side so the cork will lie on its side. Place the loop over the cork and draw toward the neck, and by slight manipulation the cork can be drawn out.

BETTER THAN MOTH BALLS

To keep moths from furs and woolen garments: take of patchouli leaves, ground fine, one-half pound; lavender flowers, pounded, four ounces; ground cedar-wood, four ounces, and essence of patchouli, one dram. Mix and sift, and sprinkle among the clothing to be cared for, then wrap securely in newspapers, pasting the open ends together. A delicate and delightful odor clings about the garments thus cared for, instead of the odious aroma of the usual moth balls.

A CURE FOR BED-WETTING

A sure and harmless cure for bed-wetting is the weed known as white daisy and also known as bull's eye. It has a yellow center with white petals. You will find it in almost any backyard. It also has a smell similar to tansy. Pull weed—root and all—wash and put to steep in milk. This may be taken freely in cupful doses two or three times a day, and if kept up for several days will effect a cure.

TO KEEP A STEEL RANGE LOOKING NEW

To clean a steel range, first wash thoroughly with soap and water and then polish with a woolen rag wet with kerosene. Never blacken the steel part. If treated in the above way, the range will always look new.

THE REAL WAY TO BOIL POTATOES

After you pare them, place in cold water for half an hour, and then plunge them into salted *boiling* water (never put them in warm or cold water to cook, as they will be water-soaked). Last but not least, drain them in a colander so the cold air may strike them while hot, which has the effect of drying and making them very mealy.

HOW TO WASH A WRINGER

The rubber of a wringer which has become dirty may be easily cleaned with a clean cloth wet with kerosene. It will make it as clean as when new.

HOW TO TELL WHEN LARD IS HOT ENOUGH

To know when lard is just right for frying cakes, pass a match through the grease, and if it lights it, it is just right; if it does not, let it heat a little longer, and try again, but with a *new* match.

LITTLE HELPS FOR HOME-MAKERS

CLEANING ENAMELED BATH-TUBS

Never use sapolio or any kind of scouring soap to clean an enameled bathtub. It will take off the enamel if the use is continued long. Use kerosene on a cloth or ammonia.

TO CLEAN SOILED PHOTOGRAPHS

A photograph which has become soiled by dust, or smoke, can easily be cleaned. Hold it underneath the cold water faucet, and gently wash it with the hand or soft brush, as the water flows over it. Thoroughly rinse in clear cold water, and the picture will look almost or quite as good as new.

SOAP THE NAIL

To keep nails from splitting furniture or delicate wood-work push them into a bar of soap before driving into the wood.

SUGAR ECONOMIES

About one-tenth of all the sugar used to sweeten tea and coffee goes into the dishwater. Try using pure home-made sugar syrups for table use.

Plain Syrup: Fill a large bottle or jar with granulated sugar and pour in all the pure water it will take. Let stand over night and fill up again with water. Serve at table in syrup pitcher or glass jug, with stopper. Coffee, tea and cocoa are much improved by using syrup.

Maple Syrup: Procure pure maple sugar, dissolve with hot water, and add double the quantity of plain syrup. You will have a better article than you can get at the stores.

Fruit Syrup: To each six pounds of sugar and half gallon of water, use one-half ounce of citric acid and extract of Jamaica ginger to taste. If too sour add more plain syrup. A fine summer drink with cold soda water or ice water.

Lemon: To the above proportions of plain syrup and citric acid, add essence of lemon to taste.

Sherbet: To the lemon syrup mixture, add an extra amount of plain syrup and the expressed juice of either pineapple, raspberries, oranges, or grapes.

Capillaire: Make the syrup with orange-flower water, instead of plain water, and use very little citric acid.

Cough Syrup: Mix eight ounces of Stockholm tar with two quarts of soft water and let them stand for a week. Pour off and strain the tar water. Add all the sugar it will dissolve, with citric acid or lemon juice to taste.

Almond Syrup: Blanch half a pound of sweet and seven or eight bitter almonds, and pound to meal in a mortar, add water or rose water and rub with the pestle until the strength of the almonds is extracted. Strain the milky fluid and add sugar until a saturated syrup is formed.

TO REMOVE STAINS

Cream of tartar will remove stains if a little is tied up in the stained part, put in cold water and slowly brought to a boil; afterward rinse in clear cold water.

SMOKED SARDINE SANDWICHES

Split or pound good Norwegian smoked sardines to a paste and lay wet or crisp lettuce leaves, slices of tomato and mayonnaise dressing between three slices of buttered bread or toast. Serve with hot coffee and slices of lemon.

SUPERIOR GRATE POLISH

Get from the drug store twenty-five cents' worth of black liquid asphalt, thin enough for immediate use with turpentine, and after thoroughly washing and cleaning grates, apply with a paint brush. It gives a shiny, jet black polish, much superior in every way to the old methods, and saves both time and money.

TO REMOVE STUMPS BY BLASTING

Where the trees are many and large, blasting the stumps is the cheapest way to remove them. It is best done in warm weather, when rendrock, and other explosives are not likely to get chilled and need thawing. Use a two-inch auger, and bore in downward from the top or side to the center and bottom of the stump. Be careful about crimping your detonating tube to the end of the fuse, insert the detonator in the cartridge and press the explosive and cartridge paper gently around the fuse and let the cartridge down into the hole. Fill up the hole with dry sand, and if anything near is likely to be injured pile boards, branches, old boards, etc., on that side of the stump. Light the fuse and get behind a tree or rock if nearer than two hundred yards. In hard ground the stump will fly into kindling wood, in soft ground it will be thrown out and split into root-sections which may need a horse to extract them.

ENGLISH GAME OR MEAT PIE

Take a deep pie-dish, and line the sides only with crust or pastry dough, putting an old cup bottom up, to support the upper crust. Cut your beef, mutton, veal, pork, poultry or game in small pieces, and strew a layer on the bottom, seasoning with salt, pepper and herbs to taste. Dredge lightly with flour, and add another and another layer in like manner until full. Fill nearly with cold water and put in a hot oven until the crust is nicely done, then set on the top of the range and simmer gently for an hour or so. When done the meat will be tender and surrounded by savory gravy; and if eaten cold will be a mass of titbits and jelly. Potatoes and vegetables should never be put in a meat pie. Veal pies should have slices of ham or bacon.

TO MAKE FINNAN HADDIES

"Findhorn haddocks" were originally smoked at their peat fires by the fishermen of an obscure Scottish village, but have become famous the world over. The haddock seems to be the only fish largely cured in this way, but small cod, pollock, mackerel, eels, shad, trout, bass, pike, etc., can undoubtedly be used to make a like breakfast dainty. Split your fish neatly, wash it in brine, and lightly salt it with fine salt over night. Wash off any excess of salt, dry thoroughly, dredge the flesh side with powdered sugar, and smoke for one night over smouldering fires of corncobs, or hardwood sawdust. If you make a quantity for the market, keep in pickle several days and smoke more heavily.

CARE OF THE HAIR

Everyone can have beautiful hair. "Regardless of color?" someone may ask. Yes, regardless of everything except care and cleanliness.

Instead of washing the hair (which takes off the natural oil and causes it to "fly just everywhere" for several days, until the oil exudes and is brushed over the hair) spread a clean, white cloth, that will not lint, over the slightly parted fingers of the left hand and with the right one rub your brush thoroughly but gently on the cloth. Brush the hair a few minutes and again clean the brush by rubbing on the cloth. Hair treated in this way ten minutes every evening for two or three weeks will be clean, soft and silky.

Should the scalp be dirty, part the hair in several places and brush well each side of the part. This will not only cleanse the scalp but cause the blood to circulate freely, thus stimulating the growth of the hair and prevent its falling off.

Perseverance is the price of satisfactory results.

NORTHAMPTON OYSTER TOAST

Mix biscuit dough, using baking powder, or self-raising flour. Stir in the oysters, cut out portions holding one oyster, with a spoon dipped in water, and fry brown in hot lard or cottolene as one does doughnuts.

To the oyster liquor add milk, season with pepper and salt, and thicken with flour or cornstarch. When nearly done stir in a good lump of sweet butter. Serve the oysters hot, adding the sauce as served.

CAPE COD FISH CHOWDER

Fry small slices of fat salt pork brown, put in your fish in rather small pieces, cover with warm water and boil, add peeled potatoes, and one or two small onions if liked. When the fish and potatoes are done, add milk to fancy and boil a few moments, salting to taste. Many thicken a little with flour or cornstarch, beaten to a smooth paste with cold water or milk, and some add butter. Season to taste.

CAPE COD SEA PIE

Take any kind of game birds, clean and cut into moderately sized pieces, and put in an iron pot in which a few slices of fat salt pork have been browned. Cover with hot water and allow to boil moderately, seasoning with salt, pepper and summer savory. When nearly tender put in a layer of onions if liked, then a layer of peeled potatoes which have been soaked in cold water an hour or so; and when the potatoes are nearly done, cover with very light raised biscuit dough, and let simmer until the dumplings are dry and light. Take up dumplings, potatoes, onions and game in separate dishes, and thicken the gravy to taste. Beef, veal, mutton, or venison can be cooked in the same way.

USES FOR OLD HOSIERY

One often hates to throw away old stockings when the legs are perfectly good and the feet past darning, and there are few now who take the time to make over stockings for children. They are, consequently, apt to accumulate and be in the way, yet it is surprising in how many ways they can be used. After cutting off the feet they make good padding for iron and pot holders, and they may also be used as sleeve protectors. On a chilly morning when it is sure to turn warm a little later, it is a good idea to have a pair of the stocking-legs handy to slip over the arms, under the dress sleeves and pin to shoulders of dress with small safety-pins, and when desired they can easily be drawn off. The balbriggan hose make excellent little dusters and polishing cloths, almost equal to chamois-skin. Cut off feet and cut the legs lengthwise. They are particularly nice for small articles such as are used on the dresser, and it will be found very convenient to have one or two in the top dresser drawer.

NEW WAY TO PICK FRUIT

Attach a fruit can to a long light pole by means of a nail which is driven through the side of the can near the top and into the pole, bending the point of the nail over to keep in place. Such a pole will be found very convenient when one wishes to pick a few of the choicest pears, peaches or apples which are sure to grow on the outer limbs of the tree, too high to reach without a ladder. Hold up the pole and let the edge of the can touch the stem or twig, and the fruit will fall in.

HANDY-BAG FOR SEWING MACHINE

Make a bag five by eight inches of cretonne, or any material you wish. In the top casing put a small embroidery hoop. Hang the bag by cords or ribbon from the corner of your sewing machine. The open top affords easy access for all scraps and bits of thread, and when the day's work is finished the floor is free from the litter so common in sewing-rooms. The little receptacle is easily emptied and ready for the next busy day.

LITTLE HELPS FOR HOME-MAKERS

TO REMOVE COAL SOOT

Coal soot can be effectually removed from woolen clothing by rubbing with a crumpled newspaper.

PRESSING RIBBONS

To quickly press ribbons, laces, or other small articles when you have no fire to heat the iron, light a coal-oil lamp, which is usually to be found in the kitchen, at least, and wind the ribbon or lace about the chimney; the heat will soon take out all wrinkles.

APPETIZING HASH

Try putting a spoonful of sugar in the next hash you make, and see if you are not pleased with the result.

DEVICE FOR HANGING SKIRTS

To insure your wool or tub skirts keeping their shape and minus wrinkles, fold in center of the band, fold again back to front, then in the middle of this last fold insert vertically a large safety-pin through the edges of the band; hang the other end of the safety-pin on the hook in your closet. It is better than a skirt-hanger. Two or more skirts may hang from the same hook and they will always be straight and free from wrinkles.

FISHING THROUGH THE ICE

Many of our readers spear fish in winter, through holes cut in the ice. Their success will be much greater if they can see clearly the bottom of the river, and the fish as they come and go. The hole in thick ice should not be over-large at the top, but an ice-chisel should be used both to cut holes and enlarge them by chopping off the under part of the ice about the hole. A sheet of bright tin secured by a small line and laid on the bottom beneath the ice hole will show clearly every fish that passes over it. But it pays to build a small lodge of poles, covered with a blanket or rug, and large enough to shelter the head and shoulders of the fisherman, the spear being held in the right hand without the cover.

It is very exciting to see the fish of various kinds gliding out of the gloom into the light, and seen as plainly as if in a glass case. For my own part I have always preferred to use the gig, a small steel rod ten feet long, with one end sharpened, and turned into a keen steel hook about an inch across its curvature. This is brought across and under the body of the fish with a sharp deft stroke, and a fish rarely escapes it. It does not bruise and mangle like the average fish spear, but makes a single small puncture, and in the country will furnish many a welcome dinner, when fish are at all plentiful.

TO CLEAN VELVET AND PLUSH

Velvet and plushes if brushed with dry salt will look like new.

GROWING FUCHSIAS

The secret of successful fuchsia-growing is water, first, last and all the time. In pleasant weather they should be sprinkled at least once a day; twice a day is better, and three times will make a big difference in the number of blossoms.

After the fuchsias get to blooming do not be afraid to cut the blossoms freely, whole sprays of them, as the plant will grow better and flower more freely for the pruning.

WILD FLOWERS FOR THE BORDER

The flower garden border for perennials is a great economy of time and strength, as it can rest undisturbed from year to year if well mulched, and not all amateur gardeners know how many of our wild flowers flourish luxuriantly there if properly treated.

I would like to speak of a few which I have found wonderfully receptive to changed conditions. All the violets are very responsive to care. The Canadian white violet, as well as the downy yellow one, form beautiful clumps of foliage and blossoms, the wood violet spreads beyond all bounds, while the prairie violet develops larger blossoms and leaves and, for me, has blossomed again in the fall, extending its season to late October.

I have a "swamp" corner, occupying the space between two large lilac and honeysuckle bushes. The ground is drained by the roots of the soft maple trees and the wiseacres prophesied failure when I made the beginning. But, by a judicious use of leaves and wood ashes it has become a pronounced success. Here, in their season, bloom bloodroot, hepaticas, anemones, spring beauties, wild ginger, dog-tooth violets, mandrakes and their brotherhood, among a host of thrifty ferns. The plants were taken from the swamps with plenty of their native soil, and their subsequent growth has been wonderful.

To succeed with wild flowers one has only to reproduce, so far as possible, their native conditions. The American pasque-flower, the prairie's first spring blossom, must have pebbles or bits of rock to which to attach its roots. The purple avens, whose handsome foliage and crimson bells are among the finest of our spring decorations, requires the same conditions. All the trilliums improve under cultivation, and with mulching are permanent. Shooting-stars and the wild blood-lilies of the Indians reward one for the time expended in seeking them. By judicious selection the wild-flower border will be filled with color and perfume from the middle of March till the last of October when the gentians and asters make their adieus.

Burbank tells us all to be plant-breeders. Without going to that length we can make valuable discoveries as well as find rich entertainment by giving our native plants a foothold among our exotics.

TO FRY TROUT AND BACON

Get a lot of stones, flat on one surface; heat and brush them clean; put a thin slice of bacon and a small trout on each stone, turning the fish until done.

SCHOOL GARDENS

We talk about arranging flowers and often forget the many who have none to arrange and would not know the most common sorts by name if they saw them; but, fortunately, the sad lack of knowledge and enjoyment along this line is being brought to the public, and a widespread interest is the result. To become interested in such a subject is equivalent to trying to better conditions, and among the many plans being put in operation that of the "School Garden" is destined to be the farthest reaching in its results, and destined to achieve those results quickly because of the fact that when a child is interested he will see to it that everyone interested in him shares in that interest.

This work has grown, in a very few years, from the school garden where a love for beautiful surroundings was taught through the work, to thousands of home gardens where both flowers and vegetables are grown from seeds sold to the school children at a penny per packet.

In order to have the children do their home work with an intelligence which will insure the success necessary to a continued interest, they are taught the work in gardens belonging to the school, where the enthusiasm of numbers working together adds to the interest.

As a means of promoting interest in the school garden idea, as furnishing a text-book for use in the work, Mr. H. D. Hemenway (director of the School of Horticulture, in Hartford, Connecticut) has published a little book entitled "Hints and Helps for the Young Gardeners," in which he shows every step of the way, making plain even such little things as the right and the wrong ways of spading soil and the many other little things which the beginner needs to know, whether his years number seven or seventy.

In a perfectly simple way Mr. Hemenway makes plain the "how-to-do" side of growing flowers or vegetables in the house or in the open ground; in a large garden or in a soap box; in winter or in summer; in shady or in sunny places, and in many instances illustrates the idea by pictures of school children doing the work described. These pictured lessons are so plain that any child gets the idea at the first glance.

This book not only shows working methods so plainly that any teacher may, by its help, start such work among his pupils, but by showing how garden work tends toward the physical development of the children; how the turning of back yards (often filthy ones) into little gardens helps the sanitary conditions, as well as the looks, of an entire neighborhood, and the many other ways in which the work reaches out and betters the conditions of life where they most need bettering, he makes every reader want to help start the work or give it aid where already started.

The price of this little book is so small ($20 per hundred) that any board of control can put it into the hands of every pupil, and at the same time inaugurate a system of gardening which will do more good than can be estimated.

GARDEN HINTS FOR MARCH

Every person who intends to have a garden, large or small, for flowers or for vegetables, should decide during March what it shall contain, and my hints for the month are intended for the thousands of readers who live in cities and have but a tiny back yard, or perhaps not a foot of land, and think they cannot grow a few flowers; while they would laugh outright at the idea of attempting a vegetable garden.

The only requirements of a garden are good soil, moisture, sunshine and a little labor, and the one who has a fence, a wall, a door-step, a window-sill, or a bit of accessible roof where boxes may be placed, may order a load of good soil from some farmer and have a good vegetable garden in boxes.

Where the fence is of the close kind frequently seen between back yards in a city, put brackets near the top and place the boxes on them, to bring the garden up where it gets better light.

Radishes may be grown in such a garden and by putting in a few seeds when radishes are pulled for use an almost continuous crop can be maintained, or by sowing seeds of both early and late varieties at the same time the same result may be obtained.

Dwarf peas, string beans of the dwarf variety, onions and other small stuff, including parsley and the kitchen herbs so invaluable to the cook, may be grown as easily as the radishes, while deeper boxes, or barrels, make "beds" in which tomatoes and cucumbers of the finest quality may be grown.

The cucumbers which ordinarily creep over the soil will trail over the sides of a barrel and make it decidedly ornamental, while the Japanese climbing variety grows as its name indicates. Tomatoes, too, may be had in climbing varieties for growing where they can be trained against a fence or trellis.

If the light is right, but the soil is poor, along a fence, dig it out deeply and replace with good, then plant seeds of such things as are wanted. Either pumpkin or squash vines will, with very little training, clamber all over a fence, and their luxuriant foliage and large yellow blossoms make a fine showing. Later, the fruits growing from day to day and changing from green to gold challenge the admiration of all, and at last furnish delicacies for the table.

This is not merely a pretty theory, but a perfectly demonstrated fact and what was done in my neighbor's garden last year may be done as easily in yours this year.

Some of the climbing vegetable beans are as ornamental as the ones grown solely for their beauty and, like the things already named, serve a double purpose by furnishing enjoyment for both eye and palate.

It must be remembered that plants grown in boxes require watering oftener than those in the ground, but if never allowed to dry out they require less care in other ways. Usually they are planted more closely and cover the ground more completely so that weeds have less chance, and the ground, being shaded by the plants, needs less cultivation.

If flowers are preferred to vegetables the same kind of garden is adapted to their culture, but never give up and feel that it is impossible to have a garden of some kind, while it is possible to put an earth-filled box or barrel in any nook or corner, high or low, where it can be tended and enjoyed.

Plant what you will, but for your own sake and that of others plant *something*, even though you live in a flat and have only a window-sill at your command.

SOMETHING ABOUT FERNS

There is practically no limit to the number of desirable varieties to be found in the fern family, and absolutely no limit to the pleasure to be derived from experimenting with them, as the more one studies them the more interest they arouse.

Among commercial stock the Boston fern has become so well known that comment is not needed, but with that, as with other plants, constant experimenting is producing new forms until now we have several distinct ones, ranging from the "Ostrich Plume" with its crinkly, plume-like fronds, measuring three or four feet in length, or the "Stag Horn," with its wide fronds flattened and cut into so many prongs that one glance at it suggests its name, to the "Pigmy" with its long and graceful fronds, not more than an inch in width.

Among newer ferns the "Holly" is desirable because the leaves are thick and smooth, and shaped more like holly than like an ordinary fern, a fact which makes it capable of enduring more dust and dryness, as well as making it much easier to wash and keep clean. Before the leaves get too large for use, it makes an ideal plant for table decoration, but as it grows larger it becomes rather coarse, though never ungraceful.

The "Climbing Fern" is another of the uncommon sorts which I have found very satisfactory in every way. It is a light, graceful fern that will climb a thread as readily as smilax, or may be trained in any form by a little care. This year I have let it grow wild—trailing over the pot in long, swaying branches, and it is even more beautiful than when trained to grow upward.

The plant seems slow of growth at first, but when it gets started it makes a steady growth, and is in every way well adapted to ordinary window culture in any room of moderate temperature. All these commercial varieties are desirable, yet anyone who can make a trip to the woods, in almost any locality in the United States, can find native varieties that will make, under cultivation, specimens very little, if any, less beautiful.

As each locality has its special kinds, it is not necessary to name varieties, but those may be found of small habit of growth which never grow too large for table decoration; large specimens that will make a tropical showing grown singly for use in parlor, hall or veranda; medium-sized ones there are which make effective showing when grown in masses in a corner; in banks on a shelf; in hanging baskets, or wound into balls—in fact there are ferns suited to every nook and corner of the house, or grounds.

While ferns are beautiful at any time they are doubly so in summer, for the reason that they, more than any other plant, suggest coolness, and if we are to enjoy them during the coming summer we should get to the woods as early as possible and dig them up as soon as the coiled fronds peeping through the soil show us where to find them.

Take them up with plenty of soil adhering to the roots, a supply of soil in which to grow them, and pieces of moss and roots of low-growing things with which to cover the soil after the ferns are potted and in a very short time the results will be ample reward for any trouble taken.

Conditions surrounding them should be as nearly as you can make them like those from which they were taken, and in securing these the question of moisture for the foliage is one of the hardest to meet.

Whenever there is a supply of hot water not needed for other purposes I set it among the ferns and let them get the benefit of the steam. At other times I set them out when there is a gentle rain, without wind. Sometimes they are set out where they can get the benefits of a heavy dew during the evening, but my stand-by is a large perfumery atomizer.

By using the atomizer the fine spray can be made to reach the under side of the foliage, as well as the upper, and the work can be done without muss of any kind.

Partial shade, moisture for the soil without making it too wet, and moisture in abundance for the foliage, plenty of air and freedom from insects are conditions requisite to insure success in growing ferns of any variety, after they are once established in their new homes.

TO CLEANSE DATES

The dates come tightly pressed together. First separate them and then place them in a colander and pour boiling water over them. This positively does not harm the dates, but removes germs and dirt.

GROWING STRAWBERRIES IN A BARREL

If you have a limited space for gardening, and wish to grow strawberries, you can grow them in the following manner: Take a barrel, fill with good, rich soil after boring holes all around the barrel with a two-inch auger, having the holes about eight inches apart each way. Set a plant in each hole and you can either grow strawberries at the top of the barrel or you can have a few flowers. The berries will be perfect and clean if you keep them well watered.

TO GROW FINE CAULIFLOWER

Use wood ashes plentifully on old garden soil and you will have no trouble about your cauliflower heading, providing you purchase good seed. It is equally good for cabbage.

TO TAKE RAW EGGS

Invalids sometimes find it very hard to swallow the raw eggs prescribed by physicians. If the following hints are observed it can be done with perfect ease. Put a few drops of vinegar in a cup, break the egg into the cup, being careful not to break the yolk, salt and pepper to taste, put a few drops of vinegar on top of the egg, throw back the head and take the egg in the mouth and it will slip down the throat almost without any effort with no taste at all except a very slight taste of the vinegar. This has been very successfully tried by an invalid who found it impossible to take this most nourishing food until this plan was tried.

TO REMOVE STUMPS BY BURNING

Bore a large auger-hole down into the center of the stump, fill partially with saltpeter, pour in water until full, and plug up the hole tightly. When the hole is dry and empty, start a little fire over it, and the stump will smoulder until it is thoroughly burned out.

FOR OUTING PARTIES

In setting your tent-stakes, always slant them toward the tent rather than away from it, as much as thirty degrees. They will hold much better, both from wind and rain. This can be demonstrated by driving one and pulling on it from the side to which it points, and vice versa.

HINTS ON CARE OF DISHES

In wiping china dishes, do not pile one upon another while hot, but spread out to cool, then pack. Piling together while warm is apt to make the glaze crack.

To make glass dishes less fragile, it is a good plan to place them in cold salted water. Let the water gradually reach the boiling point, and then keep it boiling for a few minutes. Take the pan off the fire and set it aside, leaving the dishes in it until quite cool.

To brighten the inside of a tea-pot, fill with water, add a small piece of soap and let it boil for about half an hour. Thoroughly rinse afterward, that no taste of soap may remain.

Setting dishes in the oven to warm often results in cracking them. Warm them by pouring hot water over them and there will be less chance of breakage.

Dishes which have become brown and burnt from baking in the oven may be easily cleaned after they have stood a while in borax water.

Clean brass pans with vinegar and salt before polishing. This will remove any poisonous corrosion and make them fit for use in cooking.

WASHING FLUID

One-fourth ounce salts tartar, one-fourth carbonate ammonia, one can Gillet's lye. Dissolve in half gallon soft water. Use one cupful to boiler of water.

Put about one pail of water in boiler, add about one-fourth pound of soap, shaved fine, fill up boiler with water enough to boil clothes, add fluid, stir well, put in clothes *dry*. After they have come to a boil, do not leave on fire longer than twenty minutes. It is very important that no clothes should be put in after the water is hot, as that will "set the dirt." If you have more than one boiler of clothes, take out two or three pails of the hot water, add more soap and fluid and fresh cold water. We find it a great advantage not having to soak clothes over night, and so being able to choose one's weather for washing day.

TO MANAGE A CLAMBAKE

In a small excavation, lay a bed of clean stones, having as even a surface as possible. (If the bed is to be used a number of times, it will pay to lay the stones in cement and level the surface.) When stone cannot be easily obtained, brick may be used. A large fire of hard wood is the best, and should be kept up until the stones are nearly red hot, and the wood reduced to ashes. Then sweep the bed clean, and pile the clams upon it, say about six to eight inches thick. On these lay chickens, lobsters, game or fish, and over them potatoes, sweet corn, etc. Cover the whole with a clean cheesecloth cover, and over this a thick layer of clean wet sea weed, eelgrass, or freshly cut wet grass, or hay. A heavy canvas or cotton cover over this will help to keep in the heat. When the clams are thoroughly done, which can be learned by taking one or two from under the cheesecloth cover, remove the sea weed, and (carefully) the cheesecloth cover. All will be beautifully done.

BOILING WITHOUT A POT

Excavate a rather deep depression in solid ground, and line it an inch or two deep with clay worked over and over until of the consistence of putty. Build a fire in and over it, being careful not to break the clay lining. In the course of an hour the clay-lined hole will be red hot; sweep it out clean and you can stew meat, fish and vegetables, or heat water without fear of loss or leakage.

TO HEAT WATER, A LA INDIENNE

Hollow out a small trough, or fold up birch bark to make a dish to hold water, and put a lot of clean stones in the fire to heat. Brush off the ashes with a bundle of twigs and drop one hot stone after another in the water until sufficiently heated. Coffee, broth or a stew can be made in this way also, but with more trouble.

TO PLANK FISH

Split your fish and tack it, skin side out, to a hard-wood plank or barked log, and set opposite a hot fire where the smoke will not strike it. If *very* thick it may be desirable to expose the other side to the fire.

TO BAKE BEANS

Dig a moderately deep hole in solid ground and floor it with stones. Build a big fire in it and when stones and side are very hot remove the ashes, put in your pot of beans, and cover the whole with bark and leaves. Let the beans cook until morning. They should contain more water than is usual when at home.

LITTLE HELPS FOR HOME-MAKERS

TO BAKE BISCUIT

Put a pan on the hot earth where the ashes have been swept away, cover with a kettle or deep pan and pile hot—not red-hot—ashes over the upper pan.

CAMP COOKERY

A convenient cooking place, not the great cheerful flaming campfire, which is quite another thing, may be made in a turfy bank or rise of ground, by cutting a little trench into the rim somewhat narrower than the kettle or frying-pan, and about a foot deep. The inner end must be the deepest and come to a "dead wall." A very small fire in this trench condenses its full heat on the kettle and frying-pan; most of the smoke goes off from the inner end, and it is not too hot to cook by comfortably.

The big fire can be used when it has reduced a good deal of wood to hot ashes to do some fine cooking.

TO BAKE FISH

Draw but do not scale your fish, wipe dry and roll up in greased or buttered brown paper, if you have it, and swathe in green leaves, until covered like a mummy. Dig into the hot embers and bury the fish in them. Cook for twenty minutes. The skin will come off with the blackened covering, leaving the fish cooked in its own juices. If you have potatoes, bury a few with the fish. They will be very black outside, but beautifully white and mealy within. Small birds and animals can be cooked in the same way.

TO FRY AND FRESHEN HAM

When well done, dip your slices of ham in boiling hot water for a few moments, to remove the salt brought to the surface by frying. Place for a moment longer in the hot fat and serve.

A CALIFORNIA CLEANSER

Get a five or ten-cent package of Indian soap bark (also known as Spanish bark) at the druggist's. For a light-weight skirt only slightly soiled a five-cent package is sufficient. Pour on one to two quarts of boiling water and allow to steep for a few minutes. Strain the liquor off into your tub of water (which should *not* be hot, only slightly tepid), put the garment to soak a few minutes, clean by squeezing with the hands until thoroughly clean, rinse in two tepid waters. Press dry with a hot iron, using a cheesecloth or thin muslin to prevent goods from becoming iron-creased or scorched. If material is very thick, partially dry in the air, then roll up in a damp towel until ready to press.

By following these directions carefully, you will have a garment "as good as new," with its original freshness of color unimpaired.

KEEPS YOUR SLEEVES CLEAN

To keep your shirtwaist sleeves clean while washing dishes, sew across the cuffs, where they button, an inch and a half of narrow white elastic, at each end only. Then when the cuff is unbuttoned you can pull the sleeve up and the elastic holds it in place.

A NOVEL BREAD-CUTTER

You will find a sharpened palette-knife the best bread and cake knife you ever used, especially for fresh baked cake or bread.

STALE CRACKERS MADE EATABLE

If you have crackers too stale for the table, place them in the oven with some bits of cheese grated over them. Let the cheese soften and the crackers brown slightly. They are dainty-looking and very nice, either hot or cold, and are particularly good with salad.

INSTEAD OF WALNUTS

In making apple salad substitute peanuts. They are much cheaper, and are delicious.

A NAPKIN PORTFOLIO

Cover two pieces of cardboard with cloth or silk, fastening together with pieces of ribbon (straps on the back and strings on the opposite edges to tie). You will find this very useful in which to keep napkins and fancy table linen.

PARAFFINE FOR CANNING

When sealing fruit cans, instead of dipping covers into melted paraffine, take a small brush and paint the paraffine around the can rubber; this makes an airtight joint and does not require as much paraffine.

TO BAKE BROWN BREAD

Pour the mixture in a well-buttered tin lard pail, or a coffee tin, and immerse it in a similar one of a larger size, partly filled with hot water. Cover both tightly, place in a moderate oven at noon time, and they will need no attention till they are done, at six o'clock. Then cut with a string for the table. One can take two baking powder tins if small loaves are preferred.

DAMP SPONGE FOR IRONING

You will find a damp sponge kept upon the ironing board on ironing day very handy to moisten the dry spots on thin materials.

TO PREVENT FRUIT STAINING

Do not wet the hands with water while they are wet with the juice of the fruit, as it is the water which turns them black when it comes in contact with the acid of the fruit. Dry them with an old cloth before wetting.

FOR PATENT LEATHER SHOES

To keep patent leather shoes from cracking, even in the coldest weather, rub them with lard, and set them near the fire until the lard has soaked into the leather. Polish with a soft cloth.

TO CLEAN TEA AND COFFEE POTS

Put in two tablespoonfuls of baking soda and fill up with water, let it boil about two hours and the pot will come out clean and white as new.

TO SELECT CHRISTMAS PRESENTS

A convenient way to select Christmas presents is to make out a list of friends after Christmas, note what each especially admires, and write each one's choice opposite the name for use next year. This simplifies matters and will prove a great help to the overworked home-makers.

TO REMOVE STOPPLES FROM GLASS BOTTLES

Pour a few drops of sweet oil or glycerine on a stopple that sticks, and let stand a few days. If then it does not move, pour on more. It will not affect the contents of the bottle, but will work into the neck of the bottle and loosen stopple.

ON THE IRONING TABLE

On one side of a piece of wood about four by five inches and one inch thick, bore five or six small one-inch holes, and fill them with beeswax. Cover with unbleached cotton. On the side opposite the beeswax glue emery cloth or paper the size of the block. To use, rub the iron on the emery side first, then on the beeswax side. Use it for one ironing and you will never be without it.

TO REMOVE INDELIBLE INK

Indelible ink can be removed from muslins by application of ether.

TO DRAW THREADS IN COTTON

First rub with white soap along threads to be drawn, and they will pull as easily as in linen.

TO COOK RICE

If a little butter is put in rice while cooking, it will not stick to the bottom of the pan.

FOR TAN SHOES

When tan shoes are worn off so that the color is badly impaired, dissolve a little tan dye very strong, and go over them with this, then polish and they will look like new. Gloves may be restored in the same way.

FRUIT BUTTERS

When making fruit butters try pouring the stewed fruit into a baking-pan and baking in the oven until of a sufficient degree of stiffness. This process does away with the long, tedious stirring that has formerly made this task one so much dreaded by housekeepers. No attention is required except an occasional scraping down of the sides of the pan and the stirring in of sugar toward the last. Delicious butter may be made of the peelings of peaches of good quality. Cook until soft, rub through a colander, and then cook down in the usual way.

PRESERVING EGGS

The eggs must be strictly fresh. To one part of water glass (obtained at the drug store) add nine parts boiled water (cooled). Mix together, place eggs in a jar and pour the mixture over them. This forms a jelly about the eggs. When eggs are strictly fresh and are preserved according to this recipe, they can be used the same as freshly laid ones, and have been known to keep three years.

FURNITURE POLISH

Equal parts whiskey, turpentine and linseed oil. Shake well, wash old furniture, apply polish with a yarn rag, and rub article until it shines. It gives the old-time polish to natural wood and looks like new. Dust does not stick to it.

RENOVATING RUSTY-BLACK GOODS

When black clothing or stockings are turning brown and ugly, rinse in borax water, and it will restore their original color. (Heaping teaspoonful of borax to one quart of warm water.)

CLEANSING CHALK

Keep a box of chalk handy, to clean ribbons, belts, canvas shoes, etc. Rub it on the soiled parts, brush briskly, and it is usually clean; if not, repeat the process. Use chalk according to the color of the article.

CHILDREN'S UNDERWEAR

Have you ever had trouble with the children's long drawers, in getting them smoothly in the stockings? If so, try this method: Sew a piece of tape the required length from one side of the leg to the other, and they will be smooth.

CRYSTALIZED FRUIT

Pick the finest fruit with the stalks on; dip into whites of eggs beaten to a stiff froth; drain, and beat the drippings to use again. After draining, dip them one by one into a dish of finely powdered sugar, lay in a pan covered with a sheet of fine paper, and place in a cooling oven to set the icing. Keep in a cool place until ready to serve.

ANT EXTERMINATOR

Take common hog's lard and put it thickly on small pieces of kindling-wood, or those little wooden trays one gets at the grocer's; lay the wood around everywhere the ants run, and in no time the lard will be covered with the pests, when they can be burnt in the stove. Repeat until you are rid of them, which will be in a very short time.

CALLOUSED FEET

For callouses on the bottom of the feet or rough heels in winter, soak the feet well and rub with a toilet pumicestone. It is a sure cure.

A CAUTION

Do not rub dry salt on the hands after cleaning and dish-washing if you have any cuts or places on the hand where the skin is broken. It may amount to even more than smart at the time. Salt is almost like poison to some.

TO BAKE POTATOES QUICKLY

Put potatoes on an asbestos mat, on top of the stove; cover with a pan; they bake very quickly and are extremely palatable.

ONION JUICE FOR SEASONING

Onion juice is better than chopped onion for seasoning. Cut the onion in half and press it in a lemon-squeezer.

CREAM CHEESE

To ten gallons of sweet milk heated lukewarm, use a No. 2 rennet tablet dissolved in a little warm water; thoroughly mix; let stand ten or twelve minutes; then thoroughly break up the curd, drain off the whey, wash the curd with hot but not boiling water, and turn it in a pan, salting and coloring as if making butter; put to press in a common lard-press for twenty-four hours; take out of press, grease with butter, and turn it every day. It will be ready to eat in from two to four weeks, according to taste.

HINT TO CAMPERS

For use in the country or in camp, flour sacks will be found especially serviceable. Six will make a good tablecloth if one is "handy" with the needle. Rip them apart, spread flat, and sew together, taking two to make a width. Feather-stitching along the seams makes it very pretty. Pillow-slips may also be made from the sacks, and when finished with a neat hem they will be found very useful in furnishing the camp.

FOR OILY HAIR AND DANDRUFF

Pour half a gallon of water on half a pint of salt at night. Let it stand over night. Next morning boil it well for ten minutes, strain and let it stand twenty-four hours. Repeat the boiling and straining, then bottle. Apply it to the scalp about twice a week. Do not use too much—just enough to wet the scalp and not the hair. Massage the scalp well and the hair will be ready to dress in ten minutes.

OKRA AND TOMATOES

Use okra and tomatoes in equal portions. Slice the okra, which must be young, and skin the tomatoes: put into a pan without water; add a lump of butter, an onion sliced fine, some pepper and salt, and stew one hour. This is a very nice dish.

LITTLE HELPS FOR HOME-MAKERS

TO MAKE SCISSORS CUT WELL

If the scissors do not cut well, draw the fingers gently the full length of each blade, and notice the result.

TREATMENT FOR SWEATING FEET

Procure from your local butcher some brown straw wrapping paper, and cut the paper so that the pattern will fit nicely in the bottom of your shoe. Paste two of these patterns together and insert one in each shoe. These patterns should be replaced with new cnes about twice a week. This treatment will be found very effective.

TO PREVENT SNEEZING

Simply place the tongue between the teeth and press it hard enough, and you cannot sneeze, and no one will be the wiser, as they usually are when you press your finger under the nose or perform other *external* acts to suppress a sneeze.

TO PREVENT COLDS, ETC.

To protect from headache and neuralgia of the face, rub oil or cold cream thoroughly into the skin of the face, especially on the forehead and temples, before exposure to the wind or cold air.

OLD RUGS RENOVATED

Color your old and faded rugs by applying any standard dye of the colors required with a water-color brush. You will be pleasantly surprised at the results.

TO LOOSEN RUSTED SCREWS

To loosen rusted screws, apply a red-hot iron to head of screw for a few minutes.

GREEN TOMATO MINCE MEAT

Chop fine eight quarts of green tomatoes, drain off the juice, then add as much water as juice, scald in that water and pour off, then in another water and pour off. Then add scant five pounds of sugar, two pounds seeded raisins chopped, one teacupful of chopped suet or butter, two tablespoonfuls of salt, one cup of vinegar. Cook until the tomatoes are the color of raisins. When cool, add two tablespoonfuls of cinnamon, two tablespoonfuls of cloves, one grated nutmeg.

LITTLE HELPS FOR HOME-MAKERS

FLY KILLER

A square of ordinary wire netting, fastened by small wire brads or nails into the end of a round stick, is a very good fly killer.

TO COOK GREEN CORN

Those fond of green corn cooked on the cob will find it much more delicious and tender if after cleaning it is rewrapped in an inner husk, tied with a string, and cooked thus.

TO REMOVE PIECES OF EGG-SHELLS

If when breaking eggs into a bowl a piece of shell gets into the egg, by just touching with the half shell, it will cling to it and be easily removed.

SPOOL OF SILK HELP

To keep silk on a new spool from falling off the spool when first opened, immerse in water. It will not hurt the most delicate shade.

PICTURE TUBE FOR DOILIES

If you have doilies which you do not want to fold, and they are too large to be laid flat in a drawer, procure a picture shipping tube (or an old broomstick) and wrap the doiley right side out on this, and lay away in drawer.

FOR UNSIGHTLY SPOTS

A lady was lamenting the loss of a new gray tailored suit on which she had dropped some orange juice. The spots were unsightly and of course the dress seemed ruined, when her sister suggested: "Why not try painting the spots the same shade of your dress with your water colors?" This she did with perfect success.

TO REMOVE OIL STAINS

To entirely destroy oil of any kind on all cloth, from bleaching to satin, woolen goods, lace, etc., just sprinkle plentifully with toilet powder and let it remain a short time, then brush it off and repeat. Brush the goods thoroughly and you will notice the spot has entirely disappeared. This also effaces rain-drop impressions on gray broadcloth. Some goods take more powder, but that is owing to the quantity of grease that is absorbed.

LITTLE HELPS FOR HOME-MAKERS

CORK KNOB FOR KETTLE COVER

If the knob comes off the kettle cover, put a screw through a cork on top; this will never burn the fingers and will last a long time.

NEW USE FOR ORGAN STOOL

One of my greatest helps in housework has been an old organ stool. It had seen its best days in the parlor so I covered the top with a piece of carpet. When I peel potatoes I sit on this stool; when I wash dishes I make it higher and use it again. When not in use it takes up very little room.

TO REMOVE SCORCHED TASTE

To remove scorched taste from food, set it immediately in a dish of cold water for a few minutes and empty.

CURLED EDGES OF RUGS

The big rug in my dining-room curled up along the edges until I sewed with coarse thread some big pieces of pasteboard on the under side of it—making the edge of pasteboard just meet the edge of the rug.

ANOTHER FLY DESTROYER

If a piece of flannel is saturated in turpentine, kept moist and hung up in a room, the flies will disappear.

TO LOOSEN A LAMPWICK

If a lampwick sticks and will not work easily, pull out a thread at each edge.

CUCUMBER PICKLES WITHOUT CANNING

Three hundred small cucumbers, eight good-sized green peppers sliced, one large horseradish root, two quarts very small, white onions. Soak in brine that will bear up an egg for twenty-four hours; drain three hours. Scald two gallons of cider or white wine vinegar, and add one-quarter of pound each of black and white mustard seed, one teaspoonful of Cayenne pepper, one ounce of toomerac. Pour over the pickles, and when cold add a pint of ground mustard, wet with vinegar. Pack in large crock and cover with grape leaves.

A HOME-MADE GUEST BOOK

My guest book is made thus: On a cardboard cover, six inches by nine, is printed this verse:

> "Good-night.
> Sleep sweet within this quiet room,
> O friend, whoe'er thou art,
> And let no mournful yesterdays
> Disturb thy peaceful heart;
> Nor let tomorrow scare thy rest
> With dreams of coming ill;
> Thy Maker is thy changeless friend,
> His love surrounds thee still.
> Forget thyself with all thy woes,
> Put out each feverish light;
> Thy God is watching overhead,
> Sleep sweet, good-night, good-night.

Clovers and grasses, done in water colors, decorate the left-hand side of this cover page. To it are fastened pages of blank paper by narrow ribbon passing through holes punched at equal distances from the edge both of the cover and leaves. Tied to this ribbon, which serves also to hang the book upon the dresser, is a tiny pencil with silk cord and tassel. It has hung in my guest room for ten years, and as I turn its pages I see faces and hear voices of many dear friends who have gone into the Silent Land.

COFFEE CANS FOR BAKING BREAD

Try baking yeast bread in one-pound coffee cans. You will be delighted with the nice, evenly browned loaves of convenient size, and the time required for baking will be found less than for those baked in ordinary-sized bread tins.

BOIL FRUIT JUICE WITHOUT STIRRING

Four or five clean, common playing marbles dropped in the bottom of a kettle of boiling fruit juice will by their continual motion make unnecessary constant stirring to prevent scorching.

TO CLEAN TINWARE

For cleaning tinware there is nothing better than dry flour applied with a newspaper.

CREAM OF TARTAR IN FROSTING

A little cream of tartar, the size of a pea, added to boiled frosting makes it creamy and keeps it moist longer.

A HINT FOR GENTLEMEN

A very good protection to keep a gentleman's full-dress shirt from absorbing perspiration during dancing or on warm days, is to make a shield of oiled silk, the exact size of the bosom of shirt, bind with narrow tape, and fasten around the neck and waist with tape.

NEW USE FOR EGG-BEATER

When making apple sauce, time and labor may be saved, if instead of straining the sauce through a sieve, an egg-beater is used for a few seconds. All of the lumps will have been beaten smoothly and the sauce made palatable.

TO REMOVE STAINS FROM GINGHAM

Rub the stains with a little sapolio and wash as usual. All trace of stains will at once disappear and will not affect the colors in the gingham.

TO KILL COCKROACHES

Roaches are killed outright by the poisonous water exhaling from fresh cucumber peelings scattered about the floor at night, and two or three repetitions will exterminate them.

EASY WAY TO WASH COMFORTERS

When making comforters cover each end to the depth of ten or twelve inches with a slip made of white cheesecloth or some pretty contrasting color of cotton challis or silkaline. This can be removed and washed several times before the comfort requires washing all over. When that inevitable time arrives, make a tub of suds with some good white soap, wash each end to the depth of twelve or fifteen inches; attach firmly sidewise to a line, (large safety pins are preferable to clothes-pins for this), prop up high and securely and turn the hose on each side until thoroughly wet through. Select a bright, sunny morning for this work and the result will be a clean, light comforter, with the cotton as soft and fluffy as when new.

TERRA ALTA SALAD

One cup each of tomatoes and celery, and six hard-boiled eggs. Cut (not chop) the ingredients, and use with either a mayonnaise or French dressing as preferred. This salad, as its name indicates, is the top of the world in the salad line.

TO MAKE BLANKETS LOOK NEW

Beat your blankets with a bamboo carpet-beater when nearly dry on the clothes line. It makes them light and soft.

PICKLED ONIONS

Use the small red onions. Peel two quarts and lay in salt water a few hours. Then steam them till they are tender, after which scald in three pints of vinegar, a few cloves and mixed spices. They will keep for any length of time.

TO MAKE A BRISK FIRE

If you wish new coal to burn quickly, wet with water before putting on fire.

WASHING DELICATE EMBROIDERIES

Make good lather, with pure soap and warm water, (Naptha soap is good) one-quarter teaspoonful of powdered borax to each quart of water. Place article in glass fruit jar, nearly fill jar with lather, seal tightly, shake, place jar in bright sunlight twenty-four hours, more if cloudy. Turn jar so sunlight penetrates every part. When time is up, pour off lather, press fabric gently, rinse several times in clear, soft water. Return to jar with clean water, set in sun, change water daily, until material is white.

QUICK COOKING OF BEANS

To cook dry beans in one hour or less: wash beans, put in kettle, with lump of baking soda size of pea, to one pint of dry beans. Pour boiling water over, parboil, pour off water, and again put in soda same as at first, using boiling water each time. You will be surprised at the result. No soaking over night, or fuel wasted in long cooking.

ONE-CRUST APPLE PIE

In baking an open apple pie, if the apples won't bake well, place a tin cake pan over pie, and in a short time the apples will burst open and be flaky.

WHEN MAKING FRUIT CAKE

To keep fruit from falling to bottom of cake, stir in *before* adding flour. This does away with flouring the fruit and is very satisfactory.

LITTLE HELPS FOR HOME-MAKERS

IN THE LAUNDRY

In hot weather, after sprinkling thin white pieces, instead of packing in asket, wrap in newspaper, and they will iron lovely.

Starch collars made on your shirtwaists in cold starch; they will keep their 1ape until waist is dirty.

CANNING BAKED APPLES

Remove core from the apple, fill with raisins and hickory-nut meats, pour over water and sugar and bake. Fill tin cans, cover with hot syrup. When 1early to use, drain every particle of syrup from apples and boil down to a jelly; pour over apples, sprinkle with granulated sugar.

SIMPLE WAY TO CAN RHUBARB

Wash and cut into inch lengths, without peeling. Fill glass jars and set each under the cold water faucet until the jar overflows; screw on tops and put in dark, cool place. Pour off water when needed to make pies or sauce, and use as if fresh.

OAK FURNITURE STAIN

Linseed oil and benzine half and half, with a little burnt umber or Vandyke brown incorporated with the mixture, makes a fine stain. When dried hard, oil or varnish.

GOOD POTATO CAKES

Boil potatoes, then roll them after they are peeled, and add caraway seed, some milk or cream and a little butter, and flour enough to roll, and fry them like griddle cakes. Cut out with a biscuit cutter. It is a great dish in Ireland. They should be eaten hot.

SOAPY WATER FOR STARCH

Have the water used for starch a little soapy, and add a little lard; this gives a nice gloss and the iron will not stick.

FROSTING FOR CAKES

One cupful of rolled walnut meats, one-half cupful of chopped raisins, and one and one-half cupfuls of confectioners' sugar. Stir together and add enough milk to spread well on cake.

GLASS JARS FOR FOOD

Glass fruit jars will be found excellent receptacles for food to be placed in the refrigerator, thus avoiding the foul smells and bad-tasting food that usually result when the food is placed there uncovered. In this way one may place fish and cheese next to the butter and not the slightest taint can be detected.

TO REMOVE A TIGHT LID

To remove a tight lid from a baking powder or similar can, always grasp the can by the bottom, as holding around the sides presses it out of shape and makes the lid fit tighter.

STARCH IN WINTER

To prevent the stiffening, freezing out of starched clothes, add one-half tablespoonful of salt to hot starch and use at any time, drying out of doors if wishing to.

BLOTTING PAPER PADS

Place blotting paper (white) under dresser and side-board covers, also under doilies, to protect highly polished surfaces from marks, as well as to insure immediate absorption of water or any liquid which may accidentally be spilled on same.

TO KEEP CAKE MOIST

I generally cut a loaf of cake in the middle and take as many slices as needed, then bring the two cut surfaces together again, and the cake has no cut surface exposed to the air to dry.

TO GET WALKING SKIRT LENGTH

Baste the seams and put skirt on band. Try skirt on and when fitted perfectly around hips and hung properly, take a book two inches thick or as many inches thick as you want the skirt to be from the floor when finished. Place the book flat on the floor just under the edge of the skirt. Now begin to turn and pin your hem with the lower edge of the hem touching the book. When hem is turned have person who is being fitted turn around very slowly to be sure the skirt touches the book all the way around. For one who will stand straight while a hem is being put in this way the length will rarely need any alteration. If the skirt is a plaited one, baste the plaits in all the way down and turn plaits and all with the hem until you get the required length; then give plaits and hem a good pressing, and when plaits are loosened and drawn out, fold hem at crease made by iron, and sew on braid, and your skirt will hang perfectly even, without any corners to hang from under the plaits.

NEW SHADES MADE OF OLD ONES

The lower part of the shade usually wears out while the other end is yet good. This can be remedied so the shades will look new by carefully taking the tacks out where the curtain is tacked to the pole and hemming the raw edge; if there is fringe, it can be ripped off and sewed on as before. The old part of the shade may be tacked to the pole and when rolled up a little it looks like a new shade.

CANNED TOMATOES

Tomatoes keep perfectly if canned in beer bottles with hot sealing wax poured over the cork. When used for soups, sauces, etc., the extra cooking necessary to make them fine enough to run through the funnel while filling the bottles is not objectionable.

LEMON FOR ENLARGED JOINTS

For those who suffer with enlarged joints or bunions, which quite frequently become much inflamed and very painful if the feet are chilled, or even get very cold, nothing will afford such instant relief as a generous slice of lemon bound on at night with plenty of bandage to retain the moisture. If continued for three nights the soreness will be entirely cured. The peeling should be removed from the lemon and only the soft pulp should be used.

DELICIOUS SAUERKRAUT

The German way: Put one tablespoonful of lard or bacon grease in an earthen crock (half-gallon size) add one tablespoonful of flour, stir together. Put in one pint of sauerkraut, stir all together. Pour in enough water to fill crock. Put plate on top and bake in oven three hours. Most delicious kraut you ever tasted.

A STOCKING HELP

To prevent stockings from being lost or mismated, sew to each one a piece of tape the color of the stockings, and tie each pair together before sending to wash. They can be washed without being untied.

RHUBARB JELLY

Rhubarb may be made into jelly by adding about two tablespoonfuls of lemon-juice to a cup of rhubarb-juice; use cup for cup of sugar and rhubarb-juice; the stalks should be washed, dried and bruised to start the juice, and then stewed to a pulp without adding water, straining through a double bag of cheesecloth. The jelly will be of a beautiful pink color and delightful in flavor.

CANNING FRUIT SUCCESSFULLY

If when canning fruit the *covers are scalded*, dried and set on the edge of the range, to keep hot while the jars are being filled with fruit, the probability of having broken tops will be reduced to a minimum and no second screwing on when the fruit in the jars has cooled will be necessary, as the metal contracts while cooling, so no air space can possibly be left if the rubbers are properly adjusted. Incidentally, if, when a jar is to be opened, it is set in a vessel of boiling water two inches deep (jar bottom side upward) for a few minutes, until the metal top has had time to expand, the cover can be unscrewed easily without spoiling the rubber or prying off the rim of the cover.

SMOKE-STAINED IVORY

To remove smoke stains from ivory, immerse the article to be cleansed in benzine and go over it with a brush.

KEEPS SHOES IN GOOD CONDITION

Shoes may be kept up to the mark by rubbing them with a piece of black cloth dipped in a solution of cream and black ink, polishing with a piece of old flannel.

INK STAINS ON COLORED GOODS

To remove black ink stains on children's colored dresses, etc., cover them immediately with red ink and wash, when you will find not a trace of either ink remaining.

SALMON LOAF SANDWICHES

Chop fine a pound of salmon, add a cup of bread crumbs, one egg, one tablespoonful melted butter; season with salt and pepper; mix and pack in two one-pound baking powder cans which have been well greased; put on the lids, and boil an hour. Shake out when cold and slice for the table.

MEAT SOUFFLE

Meat souffle is simply a bread pudding with the raisins and sugar left out, and a can of potted meat and an onion put in instead; season highly with red and black pepper and nutmeg, place bits of butter over the top, and bake in a pudding dish until light brown. Serve with salad dressing and a lettuce garnish. The ingredients are: one pint of milk, two eggs, one onion, one can of potted meat, one pint of bread crumbs.

TOILET WATER

One quart of water, one scant pint of best white vinegar. Two drams of each of the following: rosemary, rue, camphor, lavender, thyme and orris-root. Let the herbs soak in the vinegar several hours, then strain and add the water.

A DELICIOUS FLAVORING

Boil six peach kernels in a quart of milk which is used for custard; they will give the custard a delicious flavor.

TAKING CASTOR OIL

To avoid the unpleasant taste of castor oil, pour the oil into a glass of root beer or sarsaparilla, and it cannot be detected.

POTTED TONGUE CROQUETTES

Potted tongue can be used for croquettes or meat souffle, and makes a purer food than when eaten without being thoroughly cooked. To make croquettes: Stir into a pint of thick milk, gravy or drawn butter one can of potted meat, one raw egg, one pint of bread crumbs (or enough to make the mixture stiff), one chopped onion, a pinch of nutmeg; season highly, and when cold form into balls, roll in bread crumbs and drop into hot grease to fry a deep brown. Serve on lettuce leaves with salad dressing.

BATH BAGS

To three pounds of clean bran and one pound of orris-root pulverized, add one and one-half pounds of almond meal, two handfuls clover blossoms (red) and eight ounces of white castile soap (grated). Mix thoroughly. Make cheesecloth bags, and put five ounces in each bag. Use one at a bath. These bath bags will keep the flesh firm and the skin nice and white.

FACE WASH

A face wash that is far superior to powder of any sort, does not harm the skin, but rather keeps it from sunburn and makes it smooth and white, is prepared as follows: Five cents' worth of each of the following—bergamot, powdered snowflake magnesia, oil of lemon, bay rum—and a pint of rain water. Shake thoroughly, put into bottles, and apply to face with linen cloth. Always shake well before using.

PREVENTS CROCKING

If you have cloth which crocks, rub it very thoroughly with fine dry salt, applied with a soft cloth.

SAVE YOUR HANDS

Wind the handle of your broom with soft cloth of some kind—outing flannel is good—tack securely in place, and you will find that your hands will not become calloused by sweeping. This is better than taking time to put on gloves.

TO CLEAN WALLS

Rub with old outing flannel. It removes smoke and dirt, making the paper look like new.

TO MAKE PIECRUST

Use equal parts melted lard and lukewarm water, a small lump of salt, pinch of soda and flour to roll. Let it get cold before using.

STEAMING POTATOES

To cook potatoes so they will remain whole, try steaming them, or boiling very slowly. It will take about fifteen minutes longer to steam than to boil them, but one will be pleased with the result.

BAKING SODA FOR CORNS

To take soreness out of corns, bind common baking soda on them at night until the soreness is gone.

TO GET NEW FURNITURE

The furniture of my sitting room was donated from time to time by various friends, and no two pieces matched, the woodwork of the chairs being of all shades. I noticed at the New England Food Fair a demonstration of Jap-a-Lac, and bought a small tin to experiment with. I washed one of the chairs with strong soda water, scraped off some of the darker part ot the surface, and gave it two coats of Jap-a-Lac. It looked so well I got a larger tin, gave the light-colored chairs two or more coats and the dark ones one coat. Now my furniture is supposed by friends, not in the secret, to be a new lot that has replaced my odds and ends.

HANDY FLOOR POLISHER

A man's old felt hat can be put to good service to take up dust from or to polish floors. If you have a long-handled brush much worn, cover with the old hat; or make a thick pad of woolen stuff on the end of an old broom handle, and cover this pad with the felt hat.

A GOOD CEMENT

Take a thick solution of gum arabic and stir into it plaster of Paris until the mixture is of the proper consistency. Apply it with a brush to the broken edges of china-ware and they will adhere firmly. The whiteness of the cement renders it especially valuable.

TO DRIVE AWAY CURCULIO

For one tree soak about twelve cobs over night in turpentine, then hang them in the tree when in full bloom.

CASTOR OIL FOR WARTS

Moles and warts may be removed without your knowing it, so gradually but surely do they go away by the constant daily application of castor oil.

ADHESIVE PLASTER TO MEND BOOKS

Adhesive plaster is the best thing I have found for fastening the backs on books which have become loosened. The gummed flaps of envelopes are splendid to mend the torn leaves.

AMMONIA FOR SILVERWARE

To clean silverware, either solid or plated, use a weak solution of twenty parts water to one of ammonia and soap. Rub with a brush and rinse in alcohol. This is for bright or polished finish. For satin or frosted finish, use the weak solution of ammonia and baking soda. Wet the brush, rub on the soap, then dip brush into dry baking soda and scrub the article thoroughly. Repeat if necessary. Do not use soda on gray silver, it will make it all the same color.

TO MEND RUBBERS

Rubbers may be quickly and easily mended by applying a cement of pure rubber dissolved in chloroform. It must be applied quickly with small brush.

A CLEANING HINT

The unsightly ring left on clothes that have been cleaned with gasoline may be removed by steaming over a tea-kettle.

A SUBSTITUTE CHIMNEY SWEEP

A chimney may be kept clean and safe by throwing a piece of zinc into the furnace or range once a month.

A FLY REMOVER

Flies will soon leave if you saturate cloths with oil of sassafras and lay them near windows and doors.

SUGAR FOR TEAPOT

Put a lump of sugar in your metal teapot before putting it away. You will find the flavor of the tea improved when teapot is next used.

RAW POTATO USED AS GREASER

In frying pancakes, after the first panful has been cooked use no more grease, but slice a raw potato and rub the pan each time. Pancakes fried in this way are more easily digested.

WILL MAKE THE THIMBLE STICK

To prevent the thimble from slipping off the finger when sewing, wet the *ball* of the *thimble finger* before putting on the thimble.

AN IMPROVEMENT SUGGESTION

Almost all nasal troubles can be (at least temporarily) relieved by the use of inhalers of some kind. We would suggest the use of *resin* instead of cotton rags. Take powdered resin and sprinkle upon live wood coals, inhaling as much of the fumes through the nose as possible. All of the preparations of a resinous nature have a healing tendency which the fumes from many of the substances commonly used for this purpose do not possess. I have seen much benefit in the poultry house from fumigation. Burn tar or resin in an iron kettle containing live wood coals, *after the poultry have gone to roost.* Inhalation is also an old veterinary remedy, and can be used with good results upon horses having distemper, or other head troubles.

ECONOMY IN PLANTING POTATOES

When using large potatoes for seed, slice off the outside for planting and save the inside for table use.

FLOWERS FOR TABLE IN WINTER

Flowers were scarce last winter and the usual floral centerpiece for the dining table not always obtainable, until I hit upon the following device: Several sprays of Wandering Jew were placed in a low vase of water. They soon sprouted and furnished greenery for the whole season. The addition of a bunch of geranium blossoms, begonias, fuchsias, or whatever happened to be in bloom when wanted, kept the vase a thing of beauty and joy forever. The south window furnished desirable colors. Water in the vase must be frequently changed.

FOR THE OUT-DOOR CAVE

An out-door cave—or under-house cellar—after a prolonged wet spell, often becomes moldy and generates an offensive smell. A friend of mine tells of how she thoroughly routed every speck or smell of mildew in her cave by building a fire of corn cobs on the cement floor; closing door and windows, subjecting the room to prolonged dense fumigation. Results were satisfactory and productive of great rejoicing.

LINSEED OIL AS STOVE POLISH

Instead of the usual sticky stove blacking for the kitchen range, paint the stove while moderately hot with boiled linseed oil, rubbing it in well.

REMEDIES FOR POISON IVY

Apply sweet oil or bathe the affected parts in sweet spirits of nitre.

TO CLEAN RUSSIA IRON

To clean Russia iron, mix the blacking with kerosene and it will look nearly as well as new.

VARNISH STRAW MATTINGS

A thin coat of varnish applied to straw matting makes it more durable and adds to its beauty.

TO IMPROVE CHICKEN GRAVY

To make chicken gravy richer add eggs found in chicken or yolk of an egg.

FOR CLOSET FLOORS

Paper them with a pretty figured wallpaper, then go over it when dry with Jap-a-Lac, and you will have a neat and moth-proof covering.

OATMEAL MACAROONS

Oatmeal macaroons are very delicious. Take two and one-half cupfuls of Quaker oats, two teaspoonfuls of baking powder, one-half cup of sugar, two well-beaten eggs, two teaspoonfuls of vanilla. Mix thoroughly, and drop in half-spoonfuls on buttered tins. Bake in a moderate oven until crisp and lightly browned.

TO KEEP COOKIES MOIST

Put into your crock a few cookies, then a slice of bread, then more cookies, then bread, until you have them all in. The bread will become dry and the cakes keep moist. Replenish the bread if it gets very dry.

A TRANSFERRED EMBROIDERED PATTERN

If a pattern of an embroidered piece is desired, it can easily be obtained by placing white paper over the embroidery and working a silver spoon over the design. The spoon should occasionally be rubbed on the hair near the ear. There seems to be just enough oil to aid in producing a distinct pattern.

HOW TO OPEN A NEW BOOK

In opening a new book the covers should first be pressed flat to a table, then sections on each side until the center is reached. In this way the binding will last much longer.

PICKLED CORN

Cut off ten cups of sweet corn, add two cups of finely chopped cabbage, also one red pepper chopped fine, then add two cups of vinegar. One cup of water, one cup of sugar, one and one-half tablespoonfuls of salt, one tablespoonful of yellow mustard (ground), one tablespoonful of celery seed. Mix all together, put on stove, boil thirty minutes and it is ready for your glass jars when they are hot. Seal tight.

TO STICK STAMPS

One very often has a stamp from which the mucilage has been removed in some way, and being out of paste or mucilage and in a hurry to post a letter it is often very trying. A good idea is to moisten the "sticky" part of a new envelope, rub it on the stamp and it will stick as good as new. The envelope thus used can be laid aside and used sometime when one has paste to seal it with, or can be used with sealing-wax.

A DAINTY BREAKFAST DISH

Butter thick slices of bread. Separate the yolk and white of an egg, carefully preserving the shape of the former and beating the latter to a stiff froth. Turn this beaten white over the buttered bread, then put the round yolk in the center. Sprinkle with salt and pepper and brown in the oven. A very dainty and extremely appetizing dish.

PAPERING A ROOM

Often when papering a room there are weak places where the plastering is crumbling and shaking off, and it is difficult to make it firm. First cover the weak places with table oilcloth, paste it smoothly and firmly in place, and cover with the room paper. You will find it to be strong and lasting.

A SHORT ROAD TO PERFECT JELLY

This method is good for all fruits but pineapple, crabapples and quinces. Mash the raw fruit until all is well broken, then take a cupful at a time and put in a bag—a salt bag is very good for the purpose—and gently squeeze the juice into a dish; when all the fruit is thus treated, measure the juice and place in a vessel and put over the fire to cook. Measure one cupful of sugar for every cupful of juice, putting on the stove or in the oven where it will become very hot, but do not let it scorch. Let the juice boil for about seven or eight minutes and skim, then add the hot sugar, bring to a boil and cook one minute more. The color and flavor of the fruit is much better preserved by this plan than by the more tedious process. From beginning to end it will take less than an hour to make the jelly.

WET GRASS FOR SWEEPING

Every housewife has her special favorite among the numerous sweeping day "aids." My partiality for keeping down the dust is fresh green grass, pulled while the dew is on it, if possible, if not, slightly dampened. It does the work better than salt or tea leaves, and leaves such a delicious odor of "outdoors" on rugs and carpets.

DRY MUSTARD PLASTER

For a mustard plaster that will not blister, take a piece of flannel and rub into it all the dry mustard it will hold, shake, to remove the surplus, and apply to the part affected.

TO SOFTEN DRIED WET SHOES

Wet shoes dried and then rubbed with a cloth wet in kerosene oil will be soft as when new, and will take blacking and not dirt as shoes rubbed with vaseline will do.

TO TAKE CASTOR OIL

Heat a wine glass in water, pour in the castor oil, hold the nose and the oil will slip down quickly without being tasted; but, to prevent the after taste, before letting go of the nose, rub lips and touch the tongue with a bit of pickle, lemon or the like.

PEELING OLD ONIONS

Winter onions are always strong, and very offensive to the eyes, while peeling. In peeling always strip the peel from the roots up, and this trouble will be entirely overcome.

TO RETAIN THE COLOR OF RED FLANNEL

To keep the color of red flannel, stir two tablespoonfuls of flour into one quart of cold water, let boil several minutes, add warm suds, and wash the flannel in this in the usual manner.

WASHING LINGERIE SHIRTS

Badly soiled turnover cuffs on lingerie shirts can be more easily cleaned by laying flat on the washboard and scrubbing with a brush.

TO CLEAN STEEL

Dip a slice of raw potato in brick dust and rub till bright.

TO REMOVE MUD FROM BOOTS

To remove mud from boots quickly, one will find that a strip of carpet glued to a piece of wood is more effective than a brush.

LITTLE HELPS FOR HOME-MAKERS

TO CLEAN VELVET

Spread the material on a clean board and sponge with turpentine or alcohol, then rub briskly with dry cloth. Afterward steam the velvet to raise the pile, by drawing it over a wet cloth placed over a hot flatiron and brushing lightly.

FADED DRAPERIES

Owing to the tiresome work incident to dyeing draperies, etc., I had been compelled to discard much that, while faded, was still otherwise in good condition, until I accidentally discovered a most simple and effective method to restore the color. After washing cotton dresses, or draperies that were faded, I rinsed them in water to which had been added some dye of the orignial shade of the material. By doing this each time they were washed, they were kept like new. A package of dye mixed with a quart of boiling water should last a long time where light shades are desired.

TO RID HOUSEPLANTS OF APHIS

Take your plant to the kitchen sink and shower its whole top until every aphis and plant-louse is washed off. This is harmless and effectual.

TO STOP HICCOUGHS

Sit erect and inflate the lungs fully. Then, retaining the breath, bend forward slowly till the chest meets the knees. After slowly rising again to the erect position, slowly exhale the breath. Repeat second time.

A YEAST HELP

It is better to put the package of yeast in a drawer or on a cupboard shelf than to keep it air-tight, as yeast is a living plant and should have air, or it loses its raising power.

EXCESSIVE PERSPIRATION

Bathe daily under the arms with common laundry soap. If used faithfully, this will prevent odor, as well as being helpful in excessive perspiration.

TO RID THE HOUSE OF ROACHES

Calomel, borax and flour mixed together—one part calomel to three parts borax, and three parts flour—will rid a house of roaches and waterbugs.

HOW TO WASH LIGHT WOOL WAISTS

Stiffen the light wool waists in half skim milk and half water instead of in starch. They will be found "just right" and so much easier to iron.

WHIPPED SOUR CREAM SWEETENED

If the cream is sour for breakfast, drop in a bit of soda and whip well. It will not curdle in the coffee and can hardly be detected unless too much is used.

ELASTIC INSTEAD OF RODS FOR CURTAINS

Hang the sash curtains on a half inch elastic instead of a rod or string and see how much nicer they look. Cut elastic a little shorter than width of windows, sew a brass ring on each end and hook in place on tiny brass hooks.

NEWSPAPERS AS A STOVE-CLEANER

Keep a quantity of newspapers conveniently near your range or cookstove. After each meal, or whenever anything is spilled on the stove, with a liberal handful of paper rub the soiled places briskly till dry, and you will find that not only will the stove present a neat appearance, but a thorough blacking will be needed less often than otherwise. It also cleans and keeps the nickel bright.

ASBESTOS MATS FOR THE GAS RANGE

Many persons complain of the treachery of gas stoves. The trouble can be eliminated by obtaining asbestos mats for each eye of the gas range. By placing one of these mats under each vessel and turning the gas to medium heat, it can be left as safely as if using a coal range.

STOVE POLISH

Mix stove polish with turpentine instead of water. Apply and allow it to become perfectly dry; then the stove can be very easily polished.

TO REMOVE PUTTY

Apply a red-hot poker to putty and it will soften at once. It can be removed in one-tenth the time it takes to use acids.

INK STAINS ON LIGHT COLORED GOODS

Ink stains may be removed from light goods by dampening the heads of matches and rubbing them on the ink spots until they disappear.

WASHING WOODWORK

To wash windows and woodwork easily, take a pailful of tepid water, put into it a tablespoonful of kerosene; wash thoroughly with a cloth wrung partially dry; then rub with newspapers until bright and shining. In wiping off furniture, wring the cloth out as dry as possible, wipe off all dust, and then take a soft, dry cloth and rub hard and dry. One does not need furniture polish.

FOR CAR-SICKNESS

For sickness caused by traveling in the cars, take a sheet of writing paper and place on the chest next to the body.

TO STOP HICCOUGHS

No matter how severe or how long the spasm of hiccoughs, by eating freely of ice cream you will have no difficulty in stopping it very soon.

TO PREVENT INK FROM BLOTTING

To prevent ink from blotting or running, after erasing mistake, or scratching out with knife, scrape over the spot a small quantity of rosin and rub over and in well with a clean handkerchief on end of finger. Then place over spot a smooth piece of paper, and having removed the rosin, rub hard with some smooth article. You may then insert the desired word with ink without fear of blotting.

WASHING WOOL SHAWLS

Many people having yarn or wool shawls (knit or crocheted) find that they stretch out of shape and present a hopelessly stringy appearance after washing.

Lay your shawl out, perfectly flat, on a piece of cloth sufficiently large to cover it, and baste with heavy thread several times around, until held firmly in place. Cover with another piece of cheesecloth, and baste this enough to hold well in place. Wash in good suds of wool soap, squeezing rather then rubbing; rinse well, pressing out as much water as you can without wringing; hang on line to dry. When properly dry, remove covering, and you will find your shawl in perfect condition—light and fluffy, and not stretched at all.

CURE FOR TOOTHACHE

A cure for toothache is made of equal parts of oil of cloves, laudanum and creosote. This should be used with great care.

LUSTROUS STOVE POLISH

A pinch of sugar dropped into the stove blacking greatly heightens the lustre.

WHITE KITCHEN FLOORS

A white kitchen floor is obtained only by the use of cold water and common soap. Hot water and washing powders tend to make it yellow.

HOW TO KEEP FURS

Sprinkle dark furs well with black pepper, wrap up in brown paper, and put away in hat-box, and you can keep for years with no fear of injury from moths. To keep white furs, use white paper, and when it is time to use again, hang out and shake out well.

TO RENEW LINEN

Linen suits often become badly faded while the fabric is still good and serviceable. To renew or freshen to make over for children, fill wash boiler half full of nice, clean hay, boil an hour or more in sufficient water to cover the hay; strain through coarse cloth into jar large enough to entirely submerge the goods. Wash them and put to soak for twenty-four hours. Be sure it is well covered with the tea (best to weight it down); rinse in cold water and dry in the shade. The result will be a nice shade of green linen. How durable the color is, anyone who has tried to wash grass stains out of cloth will know.

APPLICATION FOR APPENDICITIS

Equal parts of water and spirits of turpentine. Heat and apply hot fomentations, until all inflammation is relieved. At the same time take internally sweet oil in teaspoonful doses at frequent intervals.

GARGLE FOR TONSILITIS

Put a few drops of spirits of myrrh in half a glass of water, and gargle the throat often.

LITTLE HELPS FOR HOME-MAKERS

FROZEN FEET
Make a poultice of soft soap and cornmeal, and bind on feet.

REMEDY FOR POISON IVY
If poisoned by poison ivy, paint the affected parts with iodine.

CRANBERRY POULTICES
Cranberry poultices are cooling, and afford speedy relief to those suffering from erysipelas; poultices made from cooked cranberries, applied hot, often relieve cases of inflammation of the bowels.

BOILING CABBAGE
A couple of little red peppers dropped in the kettle with cabbage will keep the odor from going all over the house.

TO CLEAN A CHIMNEY
To clean a chimney, place a piece of zinc on the live coals in the stove. The vapor produced by the zinc will carry off the soot by chemical decomposition.

EVERLASTING FENCE-POSTS
To make fence-posts durable, take boiled linseed oil and stir into it pulverized charcoal to the consistency of paint; put a coat of this over the timber and it will never decay.

RENOVATING BED-CLOTHES
After washing and thoroughly drying bed-quilts and "comfortables," fold and roll them tight, then give them a beating with the rolling pin, to liven up the batting. It will make them soft and new.

UNPAPERED CAKE-TINS
Do not paper cake-tins, but grease freely with lard, put in dry flour and shake about until it has entirely covered the grease. Put in cake batter, and when it is done it leaves the tin easily without use of knife, and does not adhere in any place. You have no broken cake and no paper to peel off.

NEW USES FOR RUBBER TAPE

If rubbers tear down at the top, draw the edges together neatly with strong linen thread, using the "ball stitch," then on the inside of rubber apply a strip of adhesive tape large enough to extend well beyond the threads. The inside lids of trunks and suit-cases can be repaired with the tape very successfully by passing an iron, slightly warmed, over the tape while held tightly stretched in the proper position. It makes a "hinge" superior to that usually found on a new trunk.

CLEANSING WATER BOTTLES

A little salt and vinegar mixed together is splendid for cleansing the inside of water bottles, etc.

MOTHS' ENEMY

Equal parts of coal-oil and turpentine mixed together is splendid for painting the inside of wardrobes, cupboards, etc., to keep away the moths.

TO STRETCH NET AND LACE CURTAINS

Measure the length and width of curtains before wetting them, then when washed ready to stretch, tack small brads about an inch or so apart all around the attic window-casing, according to the measurement of the curtains, and stretch a pair or two pairs right over the window, where they dry rapidly. This keeps them all the same size and prevents them from being torn to pieces, as they so often are on stretchers. The longer curtains you can stretch by tacking to the floor. Also scrim and Swiss curtains done this way hang much prettier than when laundered in the usual way. The small brads do not mar the casing, and any window with a sunny exposure or otherwise can be used. You can leave the brads in casing to be used for other curtains at any time.

OPENING KEYED CANS

Tin cans furnished with a key can be opened with greater ease if a skewer is passed through the opening of key, thus giving a greater leverage.

TO EXTINGUISH A FIRE

In extinguishing a fire, one quart of water applied to the bottom of the blaze will do more to put it out than ten quarts at the top. A few gallons at the bottom of the flames will rise in clouds of steam when the fire is rising and quench it.

LITTLE HELPS FOR HOME-MAKERS

WHEN BUYING CANNED GOODS

Examine canned goods before buying. If the ends of the can bulge, reject them, as this denotes the presence of gas, which renders the contents unfit for food.

DISH-WASHING MADE EASY

Use a small whisk broom in place of a dish-rag in washing dishes. It saves the hands and can be kept sweet and clean by scalding after using. Use the broom for the pans and kettles, as well as the china, and dry them on a separate towel kept for that purpose. This is especially helpful when one is obliged to wash dishes in hard or alkali water.

NICE PUMPKIN PIE

To improve the taste and flavor of a pumpkin custard, add a small handful of shredded cocoanut; this does not hurt the pumpkin taste, but gives a pleasant flavor.

"LADY BALTIMORE" CAKE

Many persons upon reading Owen Wister's book, "Lady Baltimore," were disappointed because the recipe for the cake, held secret for many years by the aristocracy of South Carolina, was not given. Here is the original recipe for that famous cake, which is truly delicious.

One cupful of butter, two cupfuls of sugar, three and one-half cupfuls of flour, one cupful of sweet milk, whites of six eggs, two level teaspoonfuls of baking powder, one teaspoonful of rose water, or vanilla. Cream butter, add sugar gradually, beating continuously; then add milk and flavoring, next the flour into which baking powder is sifted, and lastly, stiffly beaten whites of eggs, folding them in lightly. Bake in three layers.

Filling: Dissolve three cupfuls of granulated sugar in one cupful of boiling water, cook until it threads, then pour it over stiffly beaten whites of three eggs, stirring constantly. Add one cupful of chopped raisins, one cupful of chopped nut meats (pecans preferred) and five figs cut into very thin strips. Ice top and sides of cake.

QUICKLY MADE HOT BISCUITS

At dinner, when your kitchen is warm, measure flour, put in salt, baking powder (or soda), then rub in the necessary quantity of lard, having it ready to mix with either sweet or sour milk. In the morning it requires but a few moments to mix it and "pick it and pat it and put it in the pan," and how delicious they are buttered while hot. If one will keep this prepared flour on hand, mixing bread ceases to be the bugbear so many consider it.

EXTERMINATING RED ANTS

Sprinkle the shelves with plenty of Cayenne pepper.

TO REDUCE THE FUEL BILL

To cook soup, mush, dried fruit, or anything that takes a slow fire and long time to cook. Try using the hot-air register. First bring to a boil on stove, then wrap clean cloth around vessel with heavy shawl over all, and put on the register. No extra heat from register is needed. Soup-bone treated in this way at seven in the morning will be thoroughly cooked by noon; mush put on the night before will be fine for frying next morning.

FRESH LETTUCE

Lettuce will keep for days if washed and wrapped in a dry towel and laid on ice or on a cold cellar floor.

PLUM TARTS IN MID-WINTER

Take good, ripe plums (they must not be at all bruised) put into gem jars, screw down tops and put into the oven, leaving them there till the fruit cracks; take out and fill jars up with boiling water; screw down tops and put away. These will keep for months and are most delicious.

TO SOFTEN THE NAILS

Rub cold cream on the nails at night; this will soften and improve them.

PREVENTS DISAGREEABLE ODOR

When any liquid boils over on the stove, a little salt sprinkled on will prevent the disagreeable odor.

TO COOK SWEET APPLES

In cooking sweet apples, add a spoonful of vinegar to a small saucepan of fruit, and they will cook soft, as well as sour ones.

TO REMOVE AXLE-GREASE FROM COTTON

Rub a little stale butter on spot, and lay away over night. Rinse out next morning with cold water and any good laundry soap.

LITTLE HELPS FOR HOME-MAKERS

KEROSENE AS A CLEANSER

If one gets fresh paint on a garment, wet a cloth in kerosene and rub it off. Unless the fabric is very delicate, it will not injure it, and will soon evaporate. If a paint brush gets hard with paint or varnish, soak it in kerosene. If one gets axle grease or varnish on their hands, which will not wash off, wash them in kerosene, then in hot water and soap.

RAILROAD BREAD

At dinner time save out about a pint of mashed potatoes and enough of the water in which they have been boiled to make about one and one-half quarts. At bed time, add three tablespoonfuls of sugar, one compressed yeast cake, or any good yeast; let it be in a warm place over night. It should have more or less white foam on the top if the yeast is good. Add a pinch of soda. Then put in the bread-pan a pint of boiling water, two tablespoonfuls of salt, half as much butter or lard. Stir it thick with flour; now add the potato water, and more flour, mixing it hard. When light, put into tins, and bake when the loaves have about doubled in size. This will make four large loaves, which should be done for dinner. Very easy and good.

TONIC FOR THIN PEOPLE

A teaspoonful of olive oil is an excellent tonic for thin people. It is very good for a sallow complexion, as it acts directly on the liver. Taken for costiveness, it acts on the bowels without griping pains.

TO REMOVE STAINS FROM TABLE LINEN

Dissolve five cents' worth of oxalic acid in a pint of water; also dissolve five cents' worth of chloride of lime in a pint of water. When the tablecloths or napkins are washed ready for the boiler, dip the stained parts in the solution, first the chloride of lime and then the oxalic acid; then boil and finish as usual. Years of experience have proved the recipe infallible.

KEEPS THE HAIR FROM FALLING

To stop the hair from falling out and to cure dandruff, put a tablespoonful of flour of sulphur in a quart bottle, and fill the bottle with rain water; let stand until the sulphur settles to the bottom of bottle, then use the water to wash the scalp two or three times a week. You can wet the tips of your fingers and rub the scalp, and not wet your hair, if you do not wish to. There will be no odor of sulphur, as it seems to be deodorized when it settles.

ONIONS IN DIPHTHERIA

A pan of sliced raw onions, placed in a room where there is diphtheria, will absorb the poison and prevent the disease from spreading. The onions should be buried every morning and fresh ones cut up.

TO REMOVE TAR STAINS

Rub tar stains with a few drops of salad oil. They can then be completely removed by the application of benzine.

Cold rain-water and soap will remove machine grease from washable fabrics.

TO KEEP MEAT FRESH

Fresh meat beginning to sour will sweeten if placed out of doors over night.

TO SOFTEN BOOTS AND SHOES

Kerosene will soften boots and shoes that have been hardened by water, and will render them as pliable as new ones.

TO CURE A COLD

Put one ounce of camphor gum in a half pint of good whiskey and inhale the fumes often; also sniff it up the nostrils. I have known it to break up a cold, if used in time.

CLEANS KNIFE HANDLES

Half a lemon dipped in salt and rubbed over the discolored white handles of knives will make them white like new ones.

NEW BATHING HINT

Bathing in water made strong with bicarbonate of soda will prevent any odor of perspiration and help to cure rheumatism.

TOO MUCH SALT

If in cooking, food is too salty, add a teaspoonful of sugar. The sugar counteracts the taste of the salt.

USEFUL AND ORNAMENTAL PEPPERS

The "Coral Gem Bouquet Pepper" makes a beautiful little pot plant for the house in winter, and the peppers are good to season anything in which you would use common ground pepper.

TO LAUNDER LACE CURTAINS QUICKLY

To launder lace curtains quickly, and easier than pinning them to the carpet, wash and starch rather stiff, then pin them on the clothes line by each scallop in one edge, full length; stretch and smooth out nicely and leave them to dry, and when dry lay a damp cloth on the scallops that were pinned on the line and press them smooth. That will be all the ironing they will need, and the curtains will be crisp and look like new ones.

CLEANING SILVER QUICKLY

In cleaning silverware, stir whiting in alcohol to the consistency of cream; put on with a woolen cloth; when dry, rub off, and the silver is cleaned, unless very black, when a second application may be necessary.

TO REDUCE FEVER

Nothing is better to reduce a fever than hot sage tea with a few drops of spirits of nitre in it. The dose of nitre varies from three drops for an infant to a teaspoonful for an adult.

WORTH TRYING

When you put your bread to rise on a cold night, try placing your dish on a warm soapstone.

Put horse-radish through a meat-cutter, instead of grating it.

When eggs are scarce, put a dessertspoonful of cornstarch for every egg in your rice pudding.

Try putting a teaspoonful of baking powder in your buckwheat batter.

In baking juicy pies, put a teaspoonful of tapioca in each pie. It prevents juice from running out.

To open a fruit-can, try placing a warm flatiron on the cover for a few minutes.

When scraping fish, hold it under water, to prevent scales from flying.

When cleansing rice, wash it twice in warm water; it is said to be more effective in removing starch than several washings in cold water.

In frying doughnuts, drop a few slices of peeled Irish potatoes in the fat. It will prevent the cakes from absorbing too much grease.

Try alcohol to remove grass stains.

HOT WATER FOR BRUISES

Bathe all wounds, bruises, cuts, etc., in *hot* water to prevent discoloration.

CURES STOMACH TROUBLE

A cup of *hot* water taken before each meal and on going to bed, is a sure cure for constipation and chronic stomach trouble, if persistently taken. I cured myself of stomach trouble of twenty years' standing.

TO KEEP GRANITE-WARE CLEAN

In a hurry, sometimes you would like to put your nice granite-ware pan over the fire, but you don't like to blacken it. Rub the bottom with lard, and you will be surprised how easily the black will wash off.

TO CLEAN WHITE FURS

Buy ten cents' worth of plaster of Paris, and with the hands rub into the fur until every part is reached; then hang on a line and beat gently (I use a rattan beater), until the powder is all out. Repeat the process, using cornstarch instead of plaster of Paris, and you will find your furs are white and fluffy as when first bought. The work should be done, if possible, in the open air.

SHEARS IN THE KITCHEN

Have a pair of shears in your kitchen, or better yet, narrow-bladed barbers' scissors, (which cut anything, from a piece of thread to tin and zinc) and find out by experience how much better they are than the generally *dull* knife for neat service, in cutting into shape any kind of meat or pork for frying.

Especially useful are the scissors when preparing *fish* for cooking, as they cut through the *tough skins* of either salmon, haddock, codfish, pollock, mackerel, or any frying fish, so very easily and to whatever shape or size desired.

FOR TIRED FEET

Tired, painful feet will find relief by frequently changing from one kind of shoes to another.

CURE FOR RHEUMATISM

Gasoline is a cure for rheumatism and neuralgia. Rub the afflicted parts thoroughly with the gasoline, taking care not to be near a fire or lighted lamp.

ABOUT THE SINK

Should the sink pipe become clogged, take a piece of hose about two and one-half feet long, with a coupler on one end, and couple onto faucet. Insert the other end in pipe (after removing strainer), hold down firmly, turn water on full force, and you will find it does its work well, removing the obstacle.

MAKES TOUGH STEAK TENDER

Should you have a piece of tough steak, pound well, dip in vinegar quickly and fry in very hot butter at once. You will then have tender meat.

WASHING WOOLEN UNDERWEAR

Before washing, turn wrong side out, hang on line out of doors, whisk thoroughly and leave out to air. You will be surprised how much nicer they wash and press.

POTATO USED TO SPROUT CUTTINGS

To insure sprouting of syringa or other shrubs from cuttings, insert the end in a potato before planting.

FROST-BITTEN PLANTS

Jack Frost stole into a room from which the heat had been accidentally turned off, and did his very worst to a window full of plants left to his mercy. Fortunately I discovered, in the morning, before the warm air had been let into the room again, that they were "stiff as a board." It occurred to me that I had heard of the remedy—a dark closet; and as there was one close by, I dragged my luckless "window-garden" into it, shutting the door so that no sudden light or heat could enter. Toward evening I peeped in with bated breath, and was amazed to find my plants restored to their pristine beauty.

NEWSPAPER PILLOW FOR TRAVELING

A newspaper crushed into a soft ball makes an excellent cushion for resting the head on the train, and is most comfortable, owing to the fact that there is a certain amount of spring to a rolled paper, which will prevent one's feeling the jar and motion of a train even better than a feather pillow.

When traveling by night in summer, I carry an old piece of white cloth and several thumb tacks. I moisten the cloth and tack it firmly over the window screen of my berth, and find that this simple device serves to keep out a great deal of dust and soot without depriving me of air.

TO REMOVE FRUIT STAIN

Hot milk is even better than boiling water to take out fruit stains.

BRILLIANT WINDOW-GLASS

Starch rubbed over windows or mirrors instead of whiting will make them even brighter and does not hurt the hands.

ONIONS AS A DEODORIZER

Sliced onions in a pail of water will remove the odor of new paint.

NUTMEG IN CREAMED POTATOES

A little nutmeg in creamed potatoes is a wonderful improvement.

NON-DRIPPING CREAM PITCHER

A speck of butter rubbed on the nose of the cream-pitcher will prevent the cream from running down on the tablecloth.

FOR SNAKE BITE

Apply gunpowder and salt, or an egg thickened with salt.

DRESSING FOR FRUIT SALAD

To the yolks of two eggs well-beaten add one-half cupful of strained honey, one tablespoonful of sugar and the juice of two lemons. Cook until thick. When cool add one-half cupful of whipped cream. Serve with fruit salad.

MEASURING FOR HOOKS AND EYES

Keep a half-yard of "tape hooks and eyes," to baste on dresses when fitting. When ready for the permanent fastening, lay right sides together and baste securely, then, with a long stout thread, begin at the waist-line and take stitches in the edge of both pieces as far apart as you wish your hooks, remove the basting and shift the thread until the pieces are an inch or more apart, place a hook at each stitch on the other, and you may be sure they will be even, and you are saved the trouble of measuring from hook to hook.

NEW WAY TO COOK RICE

Put the desired quantity of rice into a thin cloth, tied loosely enough to allow for swelling, and place it in a kettle of salted boiling water and allow it to stay one hour, then take out and prepare. It will be whole, light and snowy, presenting a most appetizing dish, and is easier cooked, requiring no stirring.

COLORING FADED RIBBONS

To color faded silk ribbons or silk of any description, procure tissue paper several shades darker than you wish your ribbon to be when colored; wash and rinse the silk or ribbon, scald the tissue paper and put the wet material in the hot water, moving it about until the desired shade is obtained. Squeeze from the colored water and press with a moderately-hot iron, pressing hard. Yellowed ribbon can be colored a beautiful pink, using rose pink paper. This is for the lighter colors, as pink, blue and white.

UNIQUE ANT EXTERMINATOR

Take the parings of cucumbers and throw around wherever the ants come. Each time you have fresh rinds throw them among the old ones. Don't feel discouraged if the ants do not leave immediately. When cleaning the closet or other place where the ants come, do not throw the rinds away; put them back again, and continue to add fresh ones as you obtain them. Use for several weeks. To drive away red ants, rub the inside skin of cucumbers over or across their paths, and you will not be bothered with them again.

WHIP CREAM FOR SALAD DRESSING

Whip the cream to be added to salad dressing. A thicker, richer dressing than if plain cream is used will result.

SWEET APPLE PICKLES

Use the spiced vinegar in which peaches or pears were pickled in making sweet apple pickles. These can be made in the winter after the pears and peaches have been eaten, and will be of delicious flavor.

TO MEND A COAT LINING

To mend a coat lining that is worn about the arm-holes, shape pieces like a dress shield, making them just large enough to cover the worn spots. Hold them at the seam full enough so they can be pressed down flat at the outer edges.

DUSTING THE SEWING MACHINE

Use a small paint brush with long handle, and the dust will be dislodged with perfect ease.

SAVES YOUR HANDS

To save burning your hands when taking pies, etc., from the back of the oven, slip a pancake turner under the dish and draw to the front of the oven. The turner is also useful in removing cookies from the kneading board.

SCREEN FOR A CYLINDER STOVE

When the door of cylinder stove is left open there is always danger of pieces of coal snapping out and setting fire to whatever they fall upon.

Take a piece of quarter-inch square-mesh chicken wire a half-inch larger all the way round than the door. On one side cut notches to fit over the hinges of the door when open. On the opposite side cut one notch to slip over the door-catch and secure the screen in place. This screen-door may be blackened with stove enamel.

EGGSHELLS TO CLEAN BOTTLES

Eggshells dried and crushed are the very best bottle cleaner for baby's bottle; use rain water and soap or hard water and soda.

CANNING VEGETABLES

Snap string beans in halves; then pack them in cans as tightly as possible. Turn water in until the air bubbles are all out. Place the covers on and let them stand over night. In the morning again allow water to run over them, and work out all bubbles. Then place the covers on and partly fasten. Boil for six hours, remove from fire and seal tightly. Small early beets, shell beans and peas can be canned in the same way. The secret of success is in packing tightly and getting out all the air bubbles.

To can corn, cut from cob and press it firmly into can with a round stick which just fits into the neck of the jar. Then scrape milk from the cob to fill the can—no water should be added. Cook the same as the other vegetables.

TO CLEAN LAMP BURNERS

When your lamp burners become black and do not give a good light, try boiling them in water in which you have parboiled white beans and with a little rubbing they will be as bright as ever.

LITTLE HELPS FOR HOME-MAKERS

TO REMOVE MILDEW

Rub the article with soft soap, completely covering all the spots, then lay on the grass or hang up where the hot sun will strike it. In a few days wash out the soap and boil it. If you have missed any spots, repeat the process. This is a sure recipe and removed the mildew from a white dress which was perfectly black with it and everything else tried was a failure.

TO COVER BUTTONS

To cover buttons smoothly without the little corners which so often come in the cloth, cut the circle of the goods to be used, about one and one-half times the size of the button; gather as near the edge as possible and slip over the button. Draw the thread tightly and fasten.

TO SWEEP RUGS

The most satisfactory way to sweep a dusty room is to use a broom for a short distance and then gather the dust and dirt with carpet sweeper—continuing in like manner until finished. It is not only easier and more sanitary, but at end of season carpet is almost free from dust.

ELEVEN BRIEF SUGGESTIONS

Worn out mantles from gas burners are superior to any silver polish.
Remove mud spots on black clothes by rubbing with raw potato.
Make starch with soap suds, to give gloss to linen and prevent irons from sticking.
Clean silver with deep engraving with a paste made of whiting and ammonia, apply with a brush.
Use olive oil when salting almonds or peanuts. It gives a finer flavor than butter.
Keep an old tea-kettle on the hot-air register, and have hot water all the time, besides saving gas.
A little grated horse-radish added to milk gravy is nice on boiled beef.
Use milk instead of water when making cornmeal mush to fry; it will brown in half the time.
Put scraps of cold meat through food chopper and stir in cornmeal mush when making it to fry. An appetizing dish for breakfast.
Add a beaten egg and milk to cold boiled rice, form into cakes and fry. Nice for tea.
Rub worn spots on black kid gloves and shoes with a mixture of olive oil and black ink.

NERVE TONIC

There is no better nerve tonic than a cold sponge-bath every morning.

TO ALLAY SORENESS

Oil of peppermint dropped in a fresh cut will allay soreness and prevent taking cold.

TO DRIVE OFF ANTS

Mix five cents' worth of tartar emetic with equal parts of sugar; dissolved in water and placed in small dishes where the ants congregate, it will drive them away. As the water dries, add more.

GASOLINE CLEANSING

When washing silks, gloves, or other articles in gasoline, set the vessel containing the gasoline in a larger one partly filled with very hot water; this warms the gasoline and makes it more cleansing and pleasanter for the person doing the work. Wash each article as thoroughly as you would in soap and water; then rinse in more clean gasoline and hang up to dry.

NEW WAY TO GATHER

Perhaps everyone will not know of this method of gathering: Use two threads, gathering one on the right side; then start from the end on the wrong side and gather back. Pull the threads as in drawing a bag, and the gathers are very evenly laid.

NICE PUMPKIN PIES

Put a little baking powder in pumpkin pies; they will be very light and it improves them very much.

A BROKEN UMBRELLA HANDLE

To fasten metal or any kind of an umbrella handle which will not hold, melt powdered alum and use while hot instead of glue.

EASY WAY TO SPREAD THICK ICING

Have you ever tried to make a thick icing and failed? Always line your cake pan with a stiff paper which has been cut to fit, about an inch higher than the sides of the pan. When the cake is baked leave the paper on. This forms a support for the icing which can be poured into any desired depth, and the paper can easily be removed. A thin layer of melted chocolate spread over a white icing makes a more elaboarte cake with but little work.

LITTLE HELPS FOR HOME-MAKERS

LOOSE LOW SHOES

Low shoes that have become stretched will not slip up and down at the heel in walking, if a strip of velvet is pasted inside. The wear on the stocking will also be lessened.

TO KILL BURDOCKS

Pour a tablespoonful of gasoline in the crown of a burdock root after having cut off all the leaves.

REMEDY FOR HAY FEVER

Keep the inside of the nostrils well anointed with cold cream or simple vaseline, and diligently use a menthol inhaler. This treatment commenced well before the mid-summer sneezing sets in, and continued faithfully throughout the hay fever season, will often cure and always mitigates the symptoms.

TO SET COLORS

Epsom salts dissolved in rinse water will set color and prevent the most delicate tint from fading. Use one heaping teaspoonful to a pailful of water (about six quarts) and have the clothes perfectly clean, else the salts will set the dirt.

WALL-PAPER MATS

Wall-paper makes the prettiest kind of mats for framing pictures. Take, for instance, a plain color with a few dainty flowers here and there and use it as a mat when framing some magazine cover.

TO REMOVE PAINT STAINS

If clothing is soiled by contact with paint, rub a small amount of butter on the soiled spots, letting it remain five or ten minutes. Then take a whisk broom dipped in hot water and brush; the stains will come off.

DARNING COTTON HOSIERY

For darning cotton hosiery, fine darning wool or silk-finished crochet cotton will be more satisfactory than ordinary darning cotton. The mended places will always be soft and not grow harsh and hurt the feet as happens when using darning cotton.

TAKING CASTOR OIL

To destroy the repugnant taste of castor oil beat the oil with the white o an egg until both are thoroughly mixed.

BROOMS

Brooms wet in boiling suds weekly will last longer and sweep like new ones

TO CURE EARACHE

Fill the ear with warm sweet cream, inserting cotton to keep the air out and the cream in. Then apply a hot-water bottle, or flatiron wrapped in paper. In ten or fifteen minutes the worst case of earache will be greatly eased or entirely gone.

This remedy has been personally tested. I used to suffer greatly with the earache, and tried laudanum, onion-juice and other remedies which did not seem to help, and a friend prescribed the cream. It is a very simple remedy and is not injurious to the ear, though effectual.

IN THE PANTRY

Cover pantry shelves with white table oilcloth, the one and a quarter yard width being desirable; cut strips very straight the longest way of the shelf and about three inches wider. Put on with flour paste, allowing one edge to come up about one inch above the back of the shelf, the other to run over and paste under the lower edge of the front; this will last for years, only needing wiping off with a cloth and warm water.

RAINCOAT BUTTONS

Sew small buttons underneath, allowing the same thread to go through both buttons.

SAFETY-PIN BODKIN

When a rubber tape is too large for the eye of a bodkin, pin a safety-pin in the end of rubber or tape, and use like a bodkin.

TO PRESERVE COLORS

To prevent washable fabrics from fading, mix equal parts of vinegar and turpentine and cold water. Wet the goods thoroughly in this before washing.

TO PARE TOMATOES

Ripe tomatoes may be easily skinned without scalding by scraping the tomato with the back of a knife. This saves both heating water and cooling the tomatoes after paring.

FRUIT-TREE GUM MUCILAGE

The gum found on peach, plum and cherry trees dissolved in vinegar makes an excellent mucilage which will keep indefinitely.

BISCUIT PAN

Ask your tinner to cut a piece of Russian sheet iron, which, after being turned under one-half inch on all sides, will be just large enough to slip into your oven. Have an oblong ring riveted to one or both ends for use in drawing it from the oven. This will cost only from twenty to thirty cents and is a great time and fuel saver in baking cookies, biscuits, cream puffs, etc., as the work can be done much more quickly than by using the ordinary pans. Also, cookies and biscuits are more easily removed from this sheet, as there are no high sides to interfere.

HAIR TONIC

Dissolve in one-half pint of alcohol as much castile soap as it will take up. To this add two grains of tannin. Rub this well into the scalp every night and apply a little almond oil to the roots of the hair in the morning. After the hair has ceased falling out, apply once a week.

TO FASTEN LEATHER UPON METAL

Wash the metal with a hot solution of gelatine or pure glue. Having previously steeped the leather in a hot infusion of nut galls, press it upon the surface of the metal, being careful to remove all air bubbles. Place under a weight until cold. It adheres so firmly that it cannot be removed without tearing.

TO POLISH OLD FURNITURE

Wash the entire surface in a strong solution of washing powder, applying with brush or mop to save the hands, and rinse in soft warm water, rubbing dry. Let stand overnight. With a soft flannel or sponge (flannel is best) apply a coating made of equal parts of boiled linseed oil and turpentine, rubbing in thoroughly. After standing at least twenty-four hours, apply a second coat, polish well with the hands, and you have piece of furniture as handsome as new.

IVY POISON

On first finding that one has been poisoned with ivy, barley, wild parsnip, poison oak, or in fact, any of the vegetable poisons, bathe the parts in sweet spirits of nitre (*Spt. arth. nit.*). It will kill the poison as fast as it can be applied. If, however, it runs untreated twenty-four or thirty-six hours, then add to every ounce of the nitre five grains of sugar of lead (*Plumbi acetate*), and apply freely as before, sometimes using several applications to effect a cure.

NEW USE FOR SALT

Salt thrown on fruit juice that has boiled over will stop the smell and make it more easy to remove the burnt mass.

EIGHT LOAD-LIFTERS

Cornmeal sprinkled thickly over freshly-spilled oil will entirely absorb it; renew frequently.

Wipe up your carpets once a month with a cloth wrung out of warm water and ammonia, with a tablespoonful of kerosene mixed in.

A crust of bread put into the water in which greens are boiled will absorb all objectionable rankness of flavor.

Milk added to the water in which palms are washed makes them glossy.

Cut-flowers will keep fresh much longer if a small quantity of alum is added to the water in the vase. Make a solution of the alum by dissolving it in hot water, allowing it to cool, and then adding a tablespoonful to a pint of fresh water.

Stains on woolen goods may be removed by using a mixture of equal parts of glycerine and yolk of an egg. Spread it on the stain, let it stay half an hour or longer, then wash it out.

Tea and coffee stains may be taken from a tablecloth by soaking the spots in glycerine and letting stand for several hours; afterward wash with soap and water.

ONIONS FOR A DELICATE STOMACH

Slice common onions very thin, and cover well with boiling water. Allow to stand about one minute, drain off the water and cover with very cold water, stir the onions well and again drain. Cover the second time with cold water and allow to stand for a short time, and the onions will be found crisp, mild, delicious and grateful to the most delicate stomach. The strongest onions will lose their biting properties under this treatment.

Heat very hot the kettle in which onions have been cooked, and the disagreeable odor will entirely disappear.

MEDICINE-GLASS COVERS

Cut a square of clean pasteboard (preferably white) which will project about one-fourth of an inch over top of glass. Then make a tiny pillow-slip to fit of linen or white cotton. It will be easy to remove at any time for washing. A square of thin glass can be used in place of the pasteboard, and the slip will prevent clinking.

A PALETTE KNIFE

Every housekeeper who owns a palette knife wonders how she ever did without one. It is a time and material saver. Being flexible, it can be shaped to the sides of a bowl, removing all of the mixture that has been prepared in it. It is also an excellent thing for removing cookies from pan or in egging and crumbing croquettes, cutlets, etc.

COMFORT FOR EYE-GLASS WEARERS

If the nose becomes irritated from eye-glass, rub the portion of the nose whereon the glasses rest with alum three or four times, and you will have no more trouble.

PASTE THAT WILL KEEP A YEAR

Dissolve a teaspoonful of alum in a quart of warm water. When cold, stir in flour to give it the consistency of thick cream, being particular to beat up all the lumps. Stir in as much powdered rosin as will lay on a silver dime, and throw in half a dozen cloves. Have on the fire a teacupful of boiling water; pour the flour mixture into it, stirring well all the time. In a few minutes it will be the consistency of mush. Pour it into an earthen or china vessel; let it cool; lay a cover on, and put it in a cool place. When needed for use take out a portion and soften it in warm water.

RICE FLOUR CEMENT

This cement, much used in China and Japan, is made by mixing fine rice-flour with cold water and simmering over a slow fire until a thick paste is formed. This is superior to any other paste either for parlor or workshop purposes. When made of the consistency of plaster, models, busts, bas-reliefs, etc., may be formed of it, and the articles when dry are susceptible of high polish and very durable.

A HANDY HOLDER

A very convenient way to always have a holder handy is to fasten one to the apron band by means of a tape the length of the arm, and it will be with you all the time while you are at your work.

SMOOTH MAYONNAISE

In making a mayonnaise, add a pinch of soda to the vinegar, and you will never be troubled by the curdling of the dressing when cooking.

USE FOR OLD WAISTS

A white shirt-waist that is worn out around the collar and arm-holes makes a neat under-body that will wear for some time if the neck is trimmed out square or round and bound and trimmed with narrow lace, cutting out the sleeves and trimming them also. A waist opening at either front or back may be used.

GRASS-STAINS REMOVED

Molasses rubbed on grass-stains on white dresses or undergarments will remove the stain

TO RESTORE SCORCHED LINEN

Mix the juice of two onions, one-half ounce of white soap, two ounces of fuller's earth and one-half pint of vinegar; boil together and cool before using; will remove scorch from muslin or linen.

TO COOK CRANBERRIES

Select and wash three pints of berries, and put into stew-pan with one and a half pints of sugar and one pint of water. Stir thoroughly to dissolve the sugar. Cover closely, set on back of range where it will *heat*, for an hour or more—if the berries pop it is too hot—do not stir them, as you desire to have the berries heat gradually in the syrup, without breaking. Uncover, draw forward, let boil rapidly eight minutes, when the berries should be clear, red and transparent. Cooked a little longer, the juice will jell.

BABY'S TABLE

Line the table of baby's high-chair with oilcloth and lighten the task of keeping it clean. Fasten it on with paste.

FOR CHILBLAIN SUFFERERS

Rub into one spoonful of lard as much gunpowder as will make a stiff salve. Rub the feet well at night, leaving some salve on; bind closely with a cloth to keep from soiling bed linen and you will find almost instant relief. If soreness remains, continue treatment several times, and relief will be certain.

LITTLE HELPS FOR HOME-MAKERS

REMEDY FOR SPRAIN

You will find the following simple and easily obtainable remedy unfailing for sprains: A raw egg mixed with table salt till it is the consistency of a thick paste, and applied directly to the skin. Leave it bound on the injured part until the plaster is perfectly dry, or over night. In order to be effective the egg and salt must be applied as soon after the injury as possible or before the bruised blood has settled in the injured part. The entire egg is to be used.

TO REMOVE PIN-FEATHERS

After the feathers are off, roll the bird thoroughly in powdered resin for a few minutes; dip carefully in hot water and hurry to the air with it. A gentle rubbing will free the bird from down and pin-feathers.

TO FRESHEN SALT FISH

Salt fish is more quickly freshened and more appetizing if washed in sour milk.

TO CLEAR THE VOICE

A raw egg beaten with a little lemon juice will strengthen and clear the voice.

FLAKY PIE CRUST

Never turn pie crust over in rolling it out and the pies will require less lard and be richer and more flaky.

BAKING NUT CAKE

If you add nuts or chopped fruits to cake, to prevent them settling to bottom in baking, pour half of the dough in baking-tin, then half the fruit well floured, then add remaining half to rest of dough and pour in. The result will be pleasing.

CANNED PIE PLANT

Select stalks when the plant is young and tender, peel and cut in small pieces, mash in a stone crock, a little at a time, with a wooden potato masher, till the juice runs quite freely. Have glass fruit jars ready (and be sure to have new rubbers and good covers) and fill with the crushed plant, being sure to have it well covered with juice. Seal carefully and keep in a cool, dark cellar.

SHIRT-WAIST BELT

A belt made from a half-yard of narrow elastic and fastened with hook and eye you will find is much more satisfactory than using a tape to hold a shirt-waist down.

TO SWALLOW A POWDER

When there is difficulty in getting the patient to swallow a powder, simply beat the white of an egg thoroughly, mix with the powder and put in patient's mouth. It will be swallowed without trouble.

TO WHITEN THE FACE AND HANDS

To whiten the face and hands and keep them white, soft and smooth, once during the day and after supper wash well with good white soap and warm water, then wash them in buttermilk (fresh buttermilk is best) wipe lightly on a soft cloth and rub both face and hands thoroughly until perfectly dry with fine cornmeal. Meal which has been sifted twice is all right. This works like a charm on any skin.

TO PREVENT HAIR FROM FALLING

If the hair falls out, rub common table salt into the scalp for a few weeks, say three times a week, when it not only will stop coming out, but will promote a new and healthy growth.

PROFUSE PERSPIRATION

People affected with profuse perspiration should rub common baking-soda upon affected parts, and it will lessen the amount and act as a purifier.

TO CLEAN RUSTY IRONS

Do you know that rusty grates, and irons, or other fire-irons can be cleaned of rust and made bright by dipping meat skins or bacon rinds in molasses, and rubbing the iron?

MOTHS IN A CARPET

Wring out a crash towel, and spread it smoothly on the carpet where moths are suspected or detected; iron it dry with a hot iron, repeating if necessary. The hot steam will penetrate the carpet (not injuring the color at all) and kill both moth and eggs.

TO DRIVE AWAY ROACHES

If sliced cucumbers or the rinds be placed where roaches are troublesome, the pests will be driven away or poisoned.

ANT EXTERMINATOR

To exterminate little red ants, use a strong solution of alum washed into every crevice, upon and under shelves, and wherever it can be put without injuring the polish of woodwork.

TO REMOVE INK STAINS

One day my small girlie tipped over my bottle of ink on the dining-room table. I was in despair. Tablecloth, table-mat, tray cloths, napkins, all were saturated. I had a bottle of oxalic acid solution which I kept for the purpose of taking out iron rust. I turned it all in an agateware basin and set it on the stove. When boiling hot I dipped the stained pieces up and down in the liquid until every thread of linen was wet, then I rinsed in hot water and proceeded to wash in the regular way, boiling all in soap suds. Every trace of the ink was gone and my table linen looked as nice and white as if nothing had happened. I have tried the method with smaller ink spots many times since, and find it works well with white goods every time.

SEA-FOAM CANDY

To one-half cup of water, add two cups of sugar and one-half cup of syrup (honey drip best). Let this boil until it hardens in water. Be sure to cook long enough; can't cook too long. Take from stove and stir into the well-beaten whites of two eggs. Beat until stiff, add nuts and pour into buttered tins.

TO POLISH JEWELRY AND SILVERWARE

Dissolve one-half of a five-cent bar of cocoanut oil soap in one pint of ammonia; add a small quantity of water; shake well before using and apply with a tooth-brush. Brush until bright and clean, rinse in cold water and dry quickly with sawdust or soft silk cloth. Hardwood sawdust preferred.

TO EASE TIGHT SHOES

A shoe that is uncomfortable and pinches badly can be made to fit perfectly by placing the foot with shoe on where you can pour hot water on all the places that hurt. Let the shoe dry on the foot; it will shape to the foot and cause no more trouble.

TO HANDLE FEATHERS

In removing feathers from one pillow to another, take a tin can with both ends melted out (or better still, make a large pasteboard tube), tie or sew firmly an end in each pillow, and shake feathers through.

NEW USE FOR SANDPAPER

When flatirons and kettles become dark or rusted, try sandpaper combined with a small amount of muscle to make them look like new. Also on new-burned cooking vessels, the discolored work-table, butter bowl, broomhandle and other unvarnished woodwork.

SIMPLE REMEDY FOR GOITRE

That much-dreaded affliction, goitre, may be easily cured in its early stages by the patient and persistent use of salt and water.

Make a solution of salt and water as strong as possible, using so much salt that there is always some remaining undissolved at the bottom of the dish. Wring a thick cloth out of this and bind on the throat at night, with a dry towel over it. The wet cloth should be thick enough to retain the moisture all night. This treatment should be followed faithfully for some months, it may require six months or more to complete the cure. Some years ago I had a clearly-defined goitre which was completely removed by the above treatment, and it has never returned.

NEW USES FOR GLYCERINE

Hot lemonade for a cold, if made with glycerine instead of sugar, will make the remedy more valuable.

When washing oilcloth, put a teaspoonful of glycerine and a lump of borax, about the size of a cranberry, into two quarts of water. This solution cleans and leaves a polish which makes the oilcloth look like new and does not affect even the most delicate colors.

Shoes dressed with glycerine will keep black and soft. When shoes are wet, before putting them away to dry they should be stuffed with paper and when nearly dry rubbed with glycerine.

TO WASH THE HAIR

To one quart of soft water, add one heaping teaspoonful of baking soda; wash hair thoroughly in this. If very dirty, wash through two waters, then take one quart of water, add one tablespoonful of salt, wash again and rinse in clear water twice; let the hair dry before brushing and it will be very soft and nice.

A GOOD LINIMENT

Essence or extract of wintergreen, one part, and alcohol, two parts, make a most excellent liniment for sprains, lame back, etc., and has been known to cure bad cases of the latter in a single night.

WINDOW CLEANING IN WINTER

To clean windows on the outside easily and quickly, first wipe off the dust with a dry cloth, then with a cloth which has been dipped in kerosene. Polish with a soft cloth. This method is especially good in cold weather, when water would freeze on the glass.

OLD-FASHIONED SALVE

Melt together equal portions of resin and beeswax with twice the quantity of mutton-tallow, and use for boils or inflammation of any kind. Always apply warm. Especially good for gathered breasts.

PITTING CHERRIES

Take a common glass medicine dropper, put small end on blossom end of cherry; push, and you have a perfect cherry with no stone.

TO EXTERMINATE RED ANTS

Remove all eatables and place a plate or saucer slightly greased with lard in the cupboard; this will soon fill with ants, when you can shake them into the fire or hot water and replace your plate. This will soon destroy the nest of ants. I have tried many ways, but found this one the best.

FACTS ABOUT POTATOES

If, when boiling potatoes with "jackets" on, they are done before ready to serve, put in the oven, and when served they will be dry and mealy; I sometimes *purposely* put them to boil half an hour earlier, and then put them in the oven; they can scarcely be distinguished from baked potatoes.

When potatoes burst on the outside before they are cooked in the center, pour in a cup of cold water after they have cooked until the outside is tender; finish cooking and you will be pleased with the result.

When boiling whole peeled potatoes, *add salt to water as soon* as they are put on the stove, and they will stay whole. This also applies to raw potatoes when cut in strips and fried.

NAIL WOUNDS

If unfortunately a nail is stepped on, burn wool *on coals*, hold foot over this for twenty minutes, or until a yellow juice exudes, and pain will cease.

TO FRESHEN COFFEE

When roasted coffee is tough or hard to grind, heat or dry in the oven a few minutes, and it will be easily ground.

TO CURE SOFT CORNS

Take the common green bean leaf and pound to a pulp; apply to the corn at once, binding it on to keep in place. Change as often as convenient, and in a few days the corn will be completely destroyed. If the leaf is hard to get, or it be winter time, plant beans in a jar and raise the same as any house plant.

TO CLEAN A PIANO

Remove finger-marks and dirt from a piano with pure olive oil. Rub the oil on the wood with cheesecloth, then with a fresh cloth remove traces of the oil. For a final polish rub the wood with a soft piece of chamois skin.

TO RENOVATE SHOES

After blacking children's shoes that are rather the worse for wear, give them a thin coat of good varnish and they will not wear rough or need blacking nearly so soon. This will not hurt the leather.

FOR ANT STINGS

Apply common baking soda mixed with sweet spirits of nitre to form a paste. Keep moist with the nitre and it will soon relieve the pain.

GREEN FOOD FOR CANARIES

To keep the canary supplied with something green during the winter, take a large sponge, soak it well, and shake over it every day the sweepings of birdie's cage. In a few days the seeds sprout, and you will have a beautiful green ball which makes a pretty room decoration and affords green food for the canary all winter.

DELICIOUS TEA

Fifteen minutes before serving time place the usual amount of tea in pot with enough cold water to cover; let stand until serving time; then pour on boiling water and serve at once.

TO KEEP GRAPES

To keep grapes fresh for winter use, dip the end of each stem into hot sealing-wax and pack one layer in a shallow box between grape leaves or paper. Be careful to remove all broken or decayed grapes. Keep in a cool, dry place.

CANNED TOMATOES

Canned tomatoes will never spoil if you salt them and add a teaspoonful of pepper corns to be removed when the can is opened for use. Salt to taste and keep in a cool, dark place.

TO KEEP PICKLES

Vinegar will keep better on all kinds of pickles and chow-chow, if a piece of horseradish is added.

TO MAKE WHIPPED CREAM

To make whipped cream, first beat the white of an egg very stiff, then add cream, flavoring and sugar, and stir a moment.

TWO WAYS TO WASH COLORED BLANKETS

Use about two tablespoonfuls of salt in the water in which you wash them, and a little less salt in the rinsing water. Use castile soap.

Use galvanic soap and lukewarm water both for washing and rinsing blankets. Must not be rubbed.

BUTTERMILK FOR BABIES

When nothing seems to agree with baby, and you are actually "up a stump" as to nourishment, try some good fresh sweet buttermilk. It has been known to adjust numerous cases in which the babies began to gain in weight the first week. Some of them will vomit slightly at first, but will tolerate it by a little persistence in a day or two.

AN OBSTINATE FOUNTAIN PEN

When you cannot unscrew your fountain pen to refill it, wind around it one of those little rubber bands in common use; this will give you something to grasp and, instead of sliding round and round in your hands, you will find you can hold it firmly and be able to unscrew it. A foot or two of rough twine can be used in the same way.

USES FOR VINEGAR

The muttony taste is taken from this nutritious meat if a little vinegar is added to the water when boiling.

Vinegar applied to burns will stop the smarting.

Turnips are greatly improved in taste if a little vinegar is added when boiling.

FOR SEA SICKNESS

Place a piece of paper, no matter what kind, over the pit of the stomach next to the body.

TO RID CELLAR OF FLIES

Our cellar was full of big flies until I caught a little toad and put down there. The little fellow repaid me by eating every fly there, and keeping the cellar free from the pests.

MOCK PUMPKIN PIES

Those who are fond of pumpkin pies, and have no pumpkins, should try using carrots. Cook and prepare the same as you would pumpkin, and it is hard to tell which is the better.

HOT WATER WITHOUT A RANGE

I visited recently the home of a friend, who took delight in showing me all the up-to-date wrinkles she had established in her newly purchased house. She took me down cellar, and pointing with pride to a thirty-gallon kitchen boiler attached to her furnace, told me that the house was abundantly supplied with hot water all winter by the heat of the furnace. Connected with the hot water boiler was a small gas heater, by means of which their hot water in summer was obtained. Their cumbersome kitchen range had been removed, and as they cooked entirely by gas, the problem of hot water was thus solved. She informed me that the cost of connecting it to the furnace was quite small, and its absence from the small kitchen was rejoiced over.

BURN POTATO PARINGS

If you will burn all potato parings, it will keep the stove free from soot.

TO CLEANSE THE TEETH

To free the teeth from tartar, moisten a toothbrush and dip in magnesia. A few applications make a decided improvement in them.

TO REMOVE NEEDLES

To remove the needles that have disappeared in a pincushion, brush the cushion hard with a brush-broom.

TO WASH LINEN DRESSES

Linen dresses will not change color if a small quantity of hay is put into the water in which they are washed. Boil and rinse in hay-water, using but little soap.

BREAD AS A DEODORIZER

To keep the odor of onions or cabbage from penetrating the entire house, lay a thick slice of bread on top of the vegetables when you put them on to boil, or a lump of charcoal in the pot will answer the same purpose.

"BLACK JACK" FOR A STOVE

A good way of blackening a stove without getting any of the blacking on the hands whatever: Use "Black Jack" and add a little water to it every time. Have a very small paint brush, to stir the water in with, right in the can, and also to put it on the stove with, then have a larger brush with a handle on to polish with. These are very inexpensive and last forever. If the stove is slightly warm, it is much better. In this way you can be dressed up and blacken the stove without getting any blacking on you.

UNFERMENTED CRANBERRY WINE

Scald five quarts of cranberries until the skins burst. Strain through a fine cloth. Make a syrup of two pounds of granulated sugar, and one quart of water. Mix while hot, and add enough water to make four quarts. Seal tight. When serving, fill glasses with crushed ice and pour the liquid into them. This is a nice drink as well as a tonic.

GRAPE FRUIT WATER

Remove the seeds from the juice, add one pound of granulated sugar to each pint of juice. Stir one pint of the sweetened juice into three pints of boiling water, stirring until sugar is thoroughly dissolved. Set in the ice chest until cold. Serve with bits of broken ice, filling glasses one-third full.

VELVET TO POLISH STOVE

To polish a stove use an old piece of velvet. It will give a gloss that nothing else will and the blacking will not burn off nearly so quickly as when polished with a woolen cloth or brush.

TO PROLONG THE LIFE OF JELLY BAGS

When making jellies, after squeezing the juice out, put the jelly bags in a can of milk either sweet or sour; it will take the stains all out and they can be used repeatedly.

A LAMP HELP

For those who burn oil for light and have lamp chimneys to keep clean, let me say if they will wash them in hot suds, then dip into clean hot water and dry with a warm cloth—use an old gingham apron as there is less lint—they will find it a very easy task.

GOOD WAY TO WASH VEGETABLES

To remove insects, etc., from green vegetables, such as lettuce, greens, green beans, etc., sprinkle a generous handful of salt over them before washing.

TO PRESERVE RAW MEAT

To preserve raw meat for an unusual length of time, tie meat in strong muslin bag or cloth that has been previously wrung out of strong vinegar. Hang bag in the air, out of doors.

BRASS RINGS FOR TOWELS

Tack a piece of oilcloth on the wall near the stove to hang the holders on and so avoid soiling the wall-paper.

Buy at the hardware store brass rings, three-quarters of an inch in diameter, at four cents a dozen, and sew them onto holders, everyday towels and dish-towels and you will find them much handier than loops or buttonholes.

TO SHARPEN SCISSORS

To sharpen scissors hold a coarse sewing needle firmly between the thumb and forefinger of the left hand, and hold the scissors in the right hand and cut smoothly and quickly from hand to point. Unless entirely worn out they are soon sharpened this way.

TO PRESERVE JELLY

Jellies covered with powdered sugar will not mold and will keep for years.

TARNISHED SILVER

If tarnished silver is laid in sour milk it will clean itself.

TO KEEP FRUIT-JAR RUBBERS

To keep rubbers for fruit jars from hardening, cover with flour. When needed, wash well and they will be "as good as new."

SPOTS ON KID GLOVES

To clean spots on kid gloves, make a thick paste of talcum powder and water, apply to spots on glove and let it stand an hour; remove with damp cloth or chamois skin and spots will disappear. This is especially good for white kid gloves.

GRASS STAINS

To remove grass stains from goods in which the color will "run," rub with fresh unsalted butter.

HEALS CRACKED FINGERS

Procure some Venice turpentine from the drug store, and apply as a plaster.

SAGGING SKIRTS

Children's Russian dresses and other styles having a goring side-seam may be kept from sagging when laundered, if they are doubled with the side-seams in the middle and pinned to the line by the hem in the middle of the front and back. This leaves the side-seams in the slack between the pins, and they will not sag.

RELIEF FROM CRAMPS

Rub a little turpentine in the hollow of the feet at bed time, once or twice a week.

DOUGHNUTS MINUS GREASE

To prevent doughnuts absorbing grease, mix three teaspoonfuls of cornstarch with the flour. This is in proportion to one cupful of sour milk.

APPLYING AN EMBROIDERY RUFFLE

Carefully run a strong double thread around the scalloped edge of ruffle; this will prevent the edge from splitting when laundered. Before applying ruffle to garment, neatly roll and whip straight edge; this is a neat finish for the ruffle, besides being a time and money saver, as the ruffle will last longer than the garment and is ready to serve again on another.

TO PREVENT KID GLOVES FROM MOLDING

Before putting away kid gloves for the summer, line a glass jar with blotting-paper, place the gloves neatly inside jar and screw top on tightly. When the gloves are taken out in the fall, they will be in good condition—*unspotted* from the ruinous mold.

MORE ROOM IN THE CLOTHES PRESS

A few coat-hangers with their jackets, waists, etc., seemed to take up so much room in my clothes press that I purchased two nickel towel-racks and fastened them to the under side of the shelf lengthwise and upside down. On these towel-racks I hung my coat-hangers. One rack will hold several coat-hangers without crowding. Those for sale at the ten-cent stores are good enough for this purpose.

FOR THE HAIR

Rub the scalp with glycerine and rosewater; this treatment renews the gloss and increases the growth. Wash the hair and rub the scalp well with a good suds of borax soap or a weak solution of powdered borax, using warm water—*not* hot water. Rinse well, and when the hair is *thoroughly* dry rub the scalp with glycerine and rosewater, not putting on too much. Also put the glycerine on the ends of the hair. If too much glycerine is used and the hair will not curl, it can be easily fluffed by rubbing lightly with a little of the borax solution. Hair that has become slightly gray seems to renew its color.

TO CLEAN A CELLULOID COMB

To clean a celluloid comb or celluloid toilet article, use boraxine, borax or borax soap. Make a stiff lather—as stiff as white of eggs for cake—and put the comb or other articles in the wash basin and cover with the lather. Keep covered for at least ten minutes, and rub with a nail brush. If not perfectly free from soil repeat the process. When clean rinse in warm water and dry.

COCOA SPICE CAKE

One cup of sugar, three scant tablespoonfuls of butter, one egg, one cup of lobbered milk, one level teaspoonful of soda, one-half teaspoonful of cloves, one teaspoonful of cinnamon, two tablespoonfuls of cocoa, one teaspoonful of vanilla, two scant cups of flour. Icing: Six dessertspoonfuls of coffee (left from breakfast), four teaspoonfuls cocoa, one tablespoonful of melted butter. Stir in confectioners' sugar until thick. Flavor with vanilla.

TO REMOVE GREASE FROM PAINTED WALLS

One often spoils a painted wall back of a gas range in trying to keep the grease off it. If the following method is tried no soap or heat is required: Take the cheapest vinegar you can obtain, and with a large sponge wipe over the soiled places. It will remove grease, smoke and dirt from walls and woodwork, making it look like new, and requires very little labor.

GRIDDLE CAKES WITHOUT SMOKE

To avoid smoke in cooking griddle cakes, saturate a cloth with about a teaspoonful of lard, and rub the griddle with this instead of putting on fresh at each baking.

TO CURL HAIR

Olive oil, one pound; oil of organum, one dram; oil of rosemary, one and one-half drams. This is an excellent recipe for curling the hair.

A LUSTROUS BLACK STOVE POLISH

To two ounces of any good polish add one ounce of copperas and mix thoroughly. Polish your range or parlor stove with this and it will not only give a brighter lustre than ordinary stove polishes, but will positively not burn off. A range or stove polished with the above will retain a jet-black lustre from six to nine months without further application. Excellent for stoves not in use during summer or when in storage.

TO CLEANSE THE LIDS OF FRUIT JARS

Cover with sweet milk and let them stand twenty-four hours, and they will look like new if they are not too rough.

TO MEND BROKEN DISHES

Tie dish together with stout cord and boil for two hours in sweet skimmed milk. Set off and let it cool in the milk; remove string, wash the dish, and it will be as stout as it was before it was broken.

APPLE DUMPLINGS

When making boiled apple dumplings put them on in cold water instead of hot, and boil about thirty minutes, and they will not cook to pieces.

AN EASTER DISH

Break the small end out of as many eggs as you would like to fill, empty out contents, make a good cornstarch pudding of milk, eggs and cornstarch and divide in several portions, coloring differently with colored sugar. Fill empty eggshells and stand them in meal or flour to cool. When cool take off the shell and you will have some lovely Easter eggs that will surprise everyone.

TO CLEAN A GRATER

Soon as through grating lemon peel—or the like—take a dry vegetable brush and thoroughly brush off all the peal left on grater, and when through with the pie, or job in hand, the dry juice may be washed off.

RELIEF FOR A TICKLING COUGH

The particularly distressing cough caused by a tickle in the throat may often be quickly cured by gargling with hot water in which a little soda has been dissolved. Use this gargle every half-hour.

TO STOP BLEEDING

When you receive a cut and the wound is bleeding profusely, dust powdered charcoal on the wound and the bleeding will soon stop. This also prevents soreness.

FOR MAGAZINE LOVERS

After selecting the magazines that you wish to bind complete, remove the tins from the "miscellanies" and compile the best stories and illustrated descriptive articles into volumes easily handled—sewing them together through and through the holes left by the tins, with small twine.

Paste in carefully-clipped engravings to hide the "left-over" places, and bind in flexible covers. A cheap bookkeeping set in brown, soft gray and dull green or blue binding furnishes covers easily sewed on with silkaline to match each front cover mounted with a "study" to correspond with a plainly written catalogue of the best stories to be found within. The writer has a dozen such volumes in her library, one of which is bound in mottled brown enriched with a lovely sepia "Angelus." These covers will give better satisfaction than heavier ones.

QUINCE HONEY

To two quinces, peeled, cored and grated, add one and one-half pints of water; boil five minutes, strain and add three pounds of granulated sugar, boiling three minutes. Bottle or can for use.

LOTION FOR THE HANDS

Two tablespoonfuls of quince seed, one ounce of glycerine, one pint of water, six tablespoonfuls of alcohol. Put the seed in water over night on back of stove or where it will keep warm; strain, add glycerine, alcohol and perfume if desired.

SIMPLE WAY TO MAKE CANDY

In a large bowl put the white of one egg, one tablespoonful of soft butter and six tablespoonfuls of maple syrup. Beat all together one minute, then stir in confectioners' sugar until it is like dough and can be rolled on the breadboard. Cut in small squares and dry on plates. It is very nice.

FOR THE CLOTHES WRINGER

When the lower rubber of the clothes-wringer wears out as it invariably does before the upper one, cut the rubber off. Take heavy duck, cut the same width as the rubber, wet it, then turn the wringer and let it run on smoothly until it is the same thickness as the rubber. It will do just as good work and last for years.

IF TROUBLED WITH SLEEPLESSNESS

Try drinking a cup of hot cocoa without sugar just before retiring.

WASH FOR A SORE MOUTH

Golden seal or yellow root, powdered and steeped in water, cannot be excelled as a mouth wash. A little alum in the same is beneficial.

MAKING GRAVY

In making gravy always use cold water instead of hot, and it will be smooth and free from lumps.

TO PREVENT SYRUP FROM SUGARING

In making sugar syrup place the sugar in a basin and pour boiling water over it. Then set where it will keep very hot for a few minutes, but do not let it boil again. If made in this way the syrup will never turn back to sugar.

FOR ACHING EYES

To relieve the eyes when aching from the effects of smoke, or from lime or ashes getting in them, bathe with warm water to which has been added one-half teaspoonful of pure cider vinegar to one teacupful of water.

OLIVE OIL FOR PRICKLY HEAT

To those who suffer the tortures of prickly heat the use of pure olive oil is recommended. While it may not permanently cure, it will immediately relieve. It should be gently but thoroughly rubbed upon the parts affected, and it will bring comfortable and refreshing sleep when all else fails.

By adding a few drops of white rose or any good toilet perfume, it is pleasant to use.

By all means avoid scratching the irritated surface, particularly with the nails, as this is liable to induce blood-poisoning.

PREPARING MUSH FOR FRYING

In preparing mush for frying, put in a tablespoonful of sugar while it is boiling; when sliced it will brown much more quickly and the taste will be greatly improved.

NEW WAY TO BAKE POTATOES

Put potatoes in hot water for five minutes, then grease them and bake. They will bake as quickly as you can boil them, and will pare easily.

UNMARKED HARDWOOD FLOORS

To prevent hardwood floors from being marked, fasten with strong glue pieces of thick felt the exact size of the tips of the chair legs. The felt is far less expensive than rubber tips and will wear much better. Rocking chairs may have a long narrow strip glued on the rocker.

ECONOMIC KINDLING

Potato parings carefully dried are excellent for starting a fire.

TO START SEEDS QUICKLY

To plant seeds and insure their growth, such as onions, parsnips, beets, carrots and salsify, take a piece of flannel or old blanket, wring the cloth out of boiling water, lay on a warm stove, sprinkle your seed on the cloth, and roll up and put in a warm place for twelve hours; then plant in the usual way. You will be surprised to see how quickly the seeds will sprout.

EXTERMINATING ANTS

To exterminate ants it is necessary to destroy the nest. The small red ant usually has its home in the wall or floor. If it is possible to locate it, a liberal application of carbon bisulphide will destroy the ants and larvae. If the nest cannot be found, the most efficient way to protect food stuffs is to stand the legs of tables, ice-box or safe in shallow tins of water, replenishing the water frequently. Poisons or odors have not proved successful in the case of ants. The best means of prevention is to allow no food stuffs, especially sweets, to remain where ants can find them, for if they once begin it is very hard to get rid of them.

EPSOM SALT BATHS

Use a heaping tablespoonful of *Epsom* salts to a pint of as hot water as can be borne with comfort, and apply with cloth or sponge to affected parts, and the result is almost magical. Even the aches of "la grippe" have to succumb to its soothing effect.

TO MEND AN UMBRELLA

When a silk umbrella begins to wear through in the fold, get one inch ribbon the same shade, and with rubber mending tissue, run it down the entire length of each width. A good silk umbrella will last several years longer if carefully mended in this way, and the repairs will scarcely be noticed.

PUMPKIN PIES

A quick method of preparing pumpkin for pies is to put the whole pumpkin in the oven with stem left on. When it is done the stem will fall in, the steam escaping thereby, and the inside will retain its flavor. If the outside should scorch, the inside will be unharmed. When the pumpkin is cool, the inside may be scraped out and used.

TO CLEAN TINWARE

Common soda applied to tinware with a moistened newspaper and polished dry with another, will make it look like new.

TO TUCK CHIFFON

When wishing to tuck chiffon or similar material, lay the tucks on paper while stitching; afterward, the paper may be torn away.

OLIVE OIL FOR BOOK SHELVES

Perfumed olive oil sprinkled on library shelves will prevent mold on books.

CONVENIENCE IN RIPPING

In ripping seams I find the discarded blades of my husband's safety razor more convenient than a penknife.

HOME EXPERIMENTS

A little amusement and considerable understanding of the wonders of chemistry, etc., can be derived from the following experiments:

Fire From Cold Liquids: Put a small quantity of oil of cloves or spirits of turpentine in a stoneware plate and drop into it a little Glauber's spirits of nitre, and it will take fire and be consumed.

Experiments With Sympathetic Inks: *Yellow*—Write with one part of sal ammoniac and one part of sulphate of copper dissolved in water. When dry the letters will be invisible until the paper is heated almost to the point of discoloration, when the letters will become yellow. *Yellow 2*—Write with onion juice, and heat as above. *Brown*—Write with a solution of nitrate of silver, and make visible by heat or strong sunlight. *Purple*—Tar-chloride of gold dissolved in water gives a purple letter when read in the sunlight. Always write in a shady or dimly lighted room.

A NEW WAY OF IRONING

In "doing up" dainty dresses or waists, etc., wring a clean white cloth as dry as possible, spread smoothly on the ironing board over the ironing sheet, laying the piece to be ironed on the wet cloth and using very hot irons. This is much more satisfactory than the old way of sprinkling.

TANGLED EMBROIDERY SILKS

To keep embroidery silks from becoming tangled, cut from cardboard a spool such as darning cotton comes rolled on, cutting the skein of silk where it is knotted and winding on spool in one length. The numbered tag should be saved and pasted on end of spool so that the stock number may be seen at a glance, in case it is necessary to duplicate a shade. This plan is neat and economical, and a short length or more may be cut off as required.

A WHITE HOUSE DAINTY

Cream together two cupfuls of sugar with one cupful of butter. Beat with four eggs. Stir in two teaspoonfuls of baking powder and four cupfuls of flour. Beat well instead of stirring. Flavor with one teaspoonful of cinnamon and one-half teaspoonful of nutmeg. Bake in quick oven.

NEW WRINKLES

A friend, at whose table I was sitting the other day, said, as I was preparing my boiled egg in its glass cup, "Put in a teaspoonful of vinegar as well as the pepper and salt." I did so and liked it so well, I am ready to suggest it to others.

Another helpful item she gave was this: "I found I could easily settle my coffee by a little sprinkling of salt from the shaker, and I have used the method for a long time with good results."

TO KEEP SALT DRY

Instead of using cornstarch with the salt, try two or three lumps of common laundry starch in the salt-shakers.

CANNED STRAWBERRIES

After strawberries are sealed in the jar, lay it flat till cool, then shake till the berries are all through the syrup; they will neither rise nor settle and their flavor will be greatly improved.

TO SET COLORS AND LOOSEN DIRT

To each gallon of warm water use a tablespoonful of turpentine. Colored madras draperies may be cleaned very successfully in this way.

FOR CRAMPS

Tie a bandage very tightly around the leg, just above the knee; breathe forcibly, taking long respirations, thus exciting the action of the lungs.

TO CLEAN A STRAINER

If soap is used on a fine wire strainer, it can be more easily cleaned than by using sand. Fill the meshes full by rubbing with a piece of soap, then wash out with hot water; the wire will be as clean and bright as new.

TO COOK CABBAGE

Chop cabbage very fine; boil in just enough water to cover it; when tender drain as dry as possible, add rich milk or cream, butter, salt and pepper. This is delicious and quite equal to young asparagus.

TO STAMP EMBROIDERY

Embroidery patterns may be reversed by laying on a window-pane and tracing on the back of the pattern with a heavy pencil; if patterns are heavily lined, they may be transferred to the material in the same manner. A good way to stamp when one has no stamping powder.

A DAINTY BOOKLET

For an invalid or friend make the book by folding a paper napkin in fourths; trim the edges to required size, tie the back with baby ribbon bow to match the flower design; then paste in favorite clippings of poetry or prose, bits of wit or wisdom, at various angles, with possibly a child face or flower peeping out cheerily between. More leaves can be added inside if desired.

UNIQUE GARRET CURTAINS

If you have no curtains for your garret windows, whitewash the upper half of the window lights, and from the outside it will look like a neat white curtain covering half of the window.

EASY WAY TO CAN BEANS

Prepare beans (fresh from the vines) as you would for cooking. It is better to cut them in inch lengths as they go into cans more readily. For five pints of beans thus prepared, one small teacupful of salt and sufficient water to cook. Boil ten minutes and seal. When ready to use, drain off the liquor, cover with cold water, bring slowly to scalding, drain and add cream or milk.

TO CLEAN OIL PAINTINGS

Cut a raw potato in half and rub over painting. This will make it like new.

BACON AND APPLES

Fill baking dish with pared and sliced apples, sugar to taste, cover with slices of bacon and bake one-half hour.

A KNITTING HELP

When knitting or crocheting with delicate colors, to keep the ball from getting soiled, seal it up in a large envelope, having an opening at one corner just large enough for the thread to pass through freely.

TO PROTECT MIRRORS FROM FLIES

Wash with a cloth saturated in a solution of Epsom salts dissolved in beer.

TO DRAW ON GLASS, ETC.

Color dissolved white soap with water colors, boil until it will cool hard and mould into crayons. Use to decorate or advertise on shop windows, mirrors, etc.

TO KEEP A BROOM IN GOOD CONDITION

If brooms are wetted in boiling suds once a week they will become very tough, will not cut the carpet, will last much longer, and always sweep like new.

EGGS EASILY SHELLED

If the shell and skin of a boiled egg cling when peeling, hold under water and they will slip off easily.

DUTCH TEN MINUTE PUDDING

To a pint of milk add three well-beaten eggs and a pinch of salt. Thoroughly soak slices of stale baker's bread, and fry in butter to a golden brown. Serve with any sweet sauce.

BROILED SWEET POTATOES

Peel cold boiled sweet potatoes,, and slice lengthwise into two or more parts according to size. Dip in melted butter, and broil to a light brown on both sides. Serve with salt and melted butter.

A NEW USE FOR SHOE HORNS

Many people accustomed to the use of the slipper spoon for slippers, etc., have no idea what a help it may be in managing refractory rubbers. A good hint for the hurried mother or teacher who has so many little feet to dress for rainy days.

TO HELP THE INVALID

Should you have in your home an invalid to whom the noise of emptying coal from the scuttle into the stove is a positive misery, do up coal into bundles, wrapping in paper bags or old papers, quietly deposit coal and paper. The paper burns away leaving your coal in the stove, with no noise to rasp the tender nerves of the sick one.

TO SWALLOW PILLS

Simply place the tablet or pill under the tongue and quickly take a large swallow of water, and the medicine will go down with the water involuntarily

TOO LIGHT BREAD

If loaves of bread are a little too light and in danger of running over, cut strips of heavy brown paper three or four inches wide, grease one side and pin around the loaf, being careful that it does not touch the side of the oven.

MUSTARD IN BEANS

If a generous pinch of mustard is added to beans when baked, they are more easily digested. Two or three tablespoonfuls of rich milk or cream poured over a pan of beans a half hour before they are done, improves the flavor and gives a nice brown crust on top.

A NEW WAY TO ROAST BEEF

Put your beef in the roasting pan and scald well on all sides with plenty of boiling water. Let stand fifteen or twenty minutes and keep turning so that no juices escape. Then pour off all the water but a very little, put the cover on pan, put in oven and bake. When done, sprinkle with salt. You never will have a tough roast if it is prepared in this manner.

A LASTING COMPLEXION

Make a good soap suds with pure castile soap, and as hot a water as can be borne, rub the face vigorously with the suds, then take common table salt and rub all over the face and neck; next take clear hot water and wash off all soap and salt, then dash cold water over face and neck.

EGG PANCAKES

To one and one-half cupfuls of flour take two eggs, yolks and whites separate, stir the yolks in with the flour and enough water to make a batter, as for common battercakes; add about one teaspoonful of salt, then beat whites of the eggs very stiff and add to the batter; fry in lard middling quick—this will make about six cakes, very light and fluffy. Serve with sugar.

FOR APPLE PIES

To make pies of hard, sweet apples, just make them the usual way, but before putting on the top crust, dissolve a half teaspoonful of cream of tartar in one teaspoonful of water and drop it over the apples and sugar. They will cook up juicy and tender.

USE FOR BOTTLES

When a glass is wanted to cover over flower slips, take a beer bottle, tie a cord saturated in coal-oil around it where the bottle slopes to the neck, set the cord on fire and let it burn, then break off top, and you will have a useful glass not easily broken.

A NEW WAY TO COOK BEANS

Cover beans with cold water, let come to boiling point and turn off water; repeat; again cover with cold water, add a pinch of soda, boil ten minutes and turn off water. Cover with cold water, add salt to suit taste, boil until well done and quite dry. Add pepper, butter and cream or milk and serve while hot.

TO POLISH NICKEL

Take ashes from black or white oak, apply to nickel with damp cloth, rubbing off with a dry one.

OLD STOCKINGS

The legs of old black stockings stitched together into any desired size are excellent for cleaning kitchen ranges, sinks and oilcloths.

PUMPKIN CUSTARD

Prepare and season pumpkin the same as for pies; place in a bowl without a pie crust, and bake same as a custard.

CORDIAL JELLIES

To any of the jelly preparations now on sale, add a gill of any sweet liqueur cordial, such as Curacoa, creme de rose, parfait amour, anisette, Chartreuse, Benedictine, etc. Stir with a silver spoon, set in mould and ice until needed. Some of these preparations are of use to people who refuse food when sick.

PARFAIT AU CAFE

Infuse six ounces of roasted unground coffee in a pint of hot sugar syrup for a quarter of an hour. Add the yolks of four eggs, stirring briskly until the mixture thickens. Strain into a dish, set in ice and stir until cool. Add a pinch of cream beaten to a froth, put into a mould and set in ice for two hours.

CRACKERS

Rub six ounces of butter into two pounds of sifted flour, dissolve one teaspoonful of saleratus in a third of a tumbler of milk and strain it on the flour. Add a teaspoonful of salt and milk to roll the dough out. Beat the dough with the rolling pin for half an hour; roll out thin; cut out with a tumbler and bake in a quick oven until crisp and hard.

PURE BAKING POWDER

Mix thoroughly with a fine sieve, twenty teaspoonfuls of cream of tartar and ten of carbonate of soda. Keep in a clean, dry Mason jar tightly closed, and use one teaspoonful of the powder to a quart of flour.

DEODORIZERS

To deodorize a room or shop otherwise clean, burn brown sugar, ground coffee or cotton rags on a fire shovel. A pail of water set in a newly painted room will remove the smell. A flat dish of water, with ice in it if possible, will condense the smoke of cigars and save one's curtains and carpets from the sickly odor. Vinegar boiled with camphor and sprinkled over a room is very refreshing.

FRIED FRESH WATER FISH

Cleanse and scale well, wipe dry with a clean cloth, slightly score the sides of small fish and cut large ones in pieces if necessary; dip in beaten egg or cold milk, roll in flour or cracker crumbs, and fry brown in sufficient boiling lard or oil to float the fish. Serve with tomato sauce.

ENGLISH BACON

Instead of scalding the hog, burn off the bristles with straw, wash and rub smooth with cold water and dress. When thoroughly cold remove the spare ribs and other bones from the sides, and cover with eight parts of fine salt, two parts of brown sugar and one part of saltpeter. Lay the sides (flitches) on each other and turn over the piles daily, resalting as before, for three weeks. Dry and if preferred, slightly smoke.

BARLEY WATER

Soak two tablespoonfuls of pearl barley in a little warm water for half an hour, then stir into two cupfuls of salted boiling water; simmer an hour in a double boiler, or stir frequently to prevent scalding. Sweeten to taste. A good substitute for milk in infantile diarrhœa.

OLD-FASHIONED BROWN BREAD

Take equal parts of new sweet corn meal and rye meal sifted and salted, and mix with scalding hot water to a soft dough. Bake in a hot oven until the crust is half an inch thick and brown. The soft, moist interior is excellent with meat or cheese.

BARLEY SCONES

Mix fresh barley meal with warm water and a little salt to a stiff dough; bake in flat thin cakes and serve while warm with butter. A delicious and healthy bread.

HARD BISCUIT

Rub four tablespoonfuls of butter into two-thirds of a quart of old flour with one-half teaspoonful of salt. Wet with sweet milk until a dough is formed and roll this repeatedly, sprinkling it with flour until an entire quart has been used. Cut into shapes half an inch thick, prick with a fork and bake in a quick oven.

APPLE, PEACH OR APRICOT FRITTERS

Make a batter of half a pound of fine flour, salt, cold water and the yolks of three eggs. Dip the fruit in the batter and fry like doughnuts in plenty of boiling lard. Drain, sprinkle with sugar and serve.

RICH FRUITY LEMON SAUCE

Put in a saucepan the yolks of four eggs, four ounces of sugar, an ounce of fine flour, the juice of two and grated rind of one lemon. Add a pint of boiling milk. Boil until it thickens. Remove and beat until cold.

TO STOP BLEEDING

When a person is bleeding from a cut or punctured wound in any limb, apply pressure at once with both hands, pressing the thumbs on or into the wounds. Twist a handkerchief or cravat into a loose rope and make a hard knot in the middle, tying both ends together around the limb and placing the knot near the wound and between it and the body if the blood comes in jets, showing that an artery is injured. If the blood flows steadily from the veins, put the knot between the wound and the foot or hand. Use a short stick to twist this ligature until the knot bears so nearly on the veins as to stop the bleeding. By encircling the stick and limbs with another handkerchief or a suspender, the whole may be kept in place until a doctor is available. Bleeding from a small cut may generally be stopped by the use of powdered alum, sugar or nut galls and ice or even cold water are powerful styptics.

For bleeding of the throat or lungs, lie in bed with the head raised; take alum (in twenty grain doses for an adult) once in two hours. A mustard plaster on the chest is often prescribed. Use ice cold drinks and a light diet.

When bleeding from the stomach, lie on the back, drink small draughts of iced water or lemonade. If the vomiting is severe, give two teaspoonfuls of vinegar and one of Epsom salts in a wine glass of ice water every half hour until it stops.

Bleeding from the nose is unpleasant, but seldom dangerous, and is sometimes beneficial. It is generally easily stopped by applying ice, ice water, cold keys, etc., to the back of the neck, throwing back the head and raising the arms as high as possible. A little alum dissolved in water, snuffed up the nostril or syringed, may be used. A roll of paper an inch long and as thick as a lead pencil crowded between the upper lip and gum is often effective.

BOILED TONGUE

Simmer for two hours in just water enough to cover the tongue. Remove and peel it and return to the water, adding a half teaspoonful each of whole peppers, mace and cloves, tied up in a small bag. Some add turnips, carrots and rich beef gravy, with fine herbs, so that the tongue may be eaten hot with the vegetables and the liquor in which it is cooked thickened with browned flour. This is economical and delicious. Otherwise let the tongue cool in its liquor and serve cold.

GINGER BEER FOR HARVEST

To one gallon warm water, add two ounces of ground ginger, one pint of molasses or two pounds of brown sugar, and half a pint of good yeast or one-half a yeast cake dissolved. Put in strong jugs, shake up well, and let it stand over night. Then cork and cool for use in the field.

BRUISES

When first received they generally yield quickly to compresses wet with water as hot as can be borne, frequently renewed. One part of tincture of arnica to six of the water used will relieve pain. If very painful and lasting, a bread and milk poultice or cold lotions may be useful. Pieces of raw beefsteak, or brown paper soaked in vinegar, are time-honored remedies for a black eye. When very severe, cold water bandages and proper support forms the "first aid" prior to sending for the doctor. If on the head, and the patient is unconscious, incline the head slightly backward, let him inhale salts of ammonia, or strong cologne, bathe with cold water, and apply hot water bandages to the wrists and ankles. Perfect quiet should be maintained for a day or two at least after head injuries of this nature.

BURNS AND SCALDS

When these are of small extent, and painful, little anxiety need be felt, but when large in area the best medical attendance should be sought at once. Bandage of old linen or cotton over a dressing of either lime water and linseed oil; castor oil; powdered chalk and lard; soap softened to a very thick lather; hot water and milk with a little baking soda, or scraped raw potato. Whatever is used, keep the parts from the air and wet them afresh through the original bandage if possible. If the pain is great, laudanum may be given at intervals of an hour, not to exceed thirty drops in a little water, for an adult, and three drops for a child of ten years or over.

For strong acid burns on the skin, apply lime water, chalk and water, or weak soda water; for quicklime, potash or caustic ammonia, use weak acids. For lime in the eye, wash out with lemon juice or vinegar and water.

SUFFOCATION

Many people die every year from inhaling carbonic acid gas in close rooms, cabins of vessels, etc., especially in very cold weather when everyone tries to save fuel and keep warm. When a patient is found insensible, remove him at once to the open air, dash cold water on the head and chest and induce artificial respiration if breathing ceases. When he becomes conscious, hot coffee, warm wine or brandy and water should be given him. Don't give up trying for hours. I have seen two cases saved after being insensible over twelve hours.

CUTS

Every family in the country should keep on hand sterilized cotton, old linen, iodoform and cotton bandages, one or more soft sponges, needles, thread and adhesive plaster (diachylon) ready for the not uncommon cuts sustained in country life. Where no artery is severed the venous bleeding will usually be stopped as before directed (see Bleeding), and if a clean cut, the edges should be brought together by pressure and secured with strips of the plaster, say two to three inches long and half an inch wide. Apply the plaster warm, the nearer end of the strip some distance from the cut. Carry it across and fasten firmly enough to hold the edges together. Fasten them parallel and near together until the wound is well closed. Place raw lint or sterilized cotton over the cut, or, what is better, sprinkle it freely with iodoform and secure with bandages. If you have to remove the strips take each by both ends and loosen by lifting toward the wound. If a needle, knife or scissors are used to cleanse or trim the wound pass through the flame of a candle or taper before using. If possible the water used should be mixed with a little carbolic acid.

Cuts on the head, if small, should have the hair cut or shorn off near the wound and a fold or two of wet linen kept in place by a bandage.

LIGHTNING PAPER

Take strips of thin unsized paper, eight by three inches, and immerse them without touching each other, in a glass or glazed dish containing four parts of sulphuric and five parts of strong fuming nitric acid, mixed by stirring with a glass rod or long clay pipe-stem. Be careful not to get the acid on your clothes or skin. After lying in the acid bath for ten minutes take up the sheets separately with your glass rods and lay in a dish of soft warm water, or under the flow of a faucet for an hour or so. Take the strips out and you have a form of gun cotton, or pyroxlene. Crumple one of these into a loose pellet, light one corner, toss it into the air, and it will almost instantly disappear in a bright flash. Or give someone a slip to light a cigar or one candle from another, and note the result.

The slips will burn with a colored flame if dipped for five minutes in the following saturated solutions:

Red chlorate of strontium; green chlorate of barium; blue chlorate of copper.

These may be bought or made by mixing equal quantities of a saturated solution of the chloride of strontium, barium, or copper and chlorate of potassium.

PYROTECHNICS

The display of fireworks at suitable times, gives perhaps as general pleasure as any other form of public amusement. Rockets, Roman candles, shells, Saxon wheels, and the like can be bought to better advantage than they can be made by amateurs, but a few hints as to their effective use may be of interest.

The place of exhibition should be ample, both for safety and the accommodation of sight-seers, but a background of forests, beautiful gardens or stately buildings add greatly to the effect. If a pond, river, or narrow bay lies between the audience and the display, its beauty will be doubled by the reflection.

Rockets should always be shot from troughs or tubes large enough to give them way, and set at an angle of about eighty degrees, and pointing away from the audience.

Roman candles, say eight-starred, colored, bought by the gross, are the most effective and cheapest of all. Use them a dozen at a time set in tin cans on cases, as batteries or mines of stars. You will have ninety-six colored stars and a mass of flame equal to two so-called batteries. These mounted on a cart may be used safely in a political torch-light procession.

Colored fires, torches and Bengal lights are splendid to illuminate processions, grounds, vessels, shore lines, and romantic and savage landscapes. It is only necessary to see that the hot scoria is received in sand or ashes, and the light is kept up evenly to the close. These may be easily and cheaply made at home as follows:

Bengal Lights: Make cases about four inches long by one and three-quarter inches in diameter, out of paper strips nine or ten inches long by four inches wide. Use a wooden form, paste the paper only at the first turn and end, and dry thoroughly. To fill the cases have a loosely fitting wooden rammer; over its end place a small square of paper a little larger than the case and push it to the bottom, in this ram tightly *dry powdered clay*, to the depth of an inch or more. Fill with the composition chosen, putting in only a tablespoonful or so at a time, and driving down the rammer with a few blows of a light mallet. Cover with a circle of paper pasted down over the edges. The composition used must be made of dry, pulverized ingredients, thoroughly mixed by passing four or five times through a sieve of brass mesh or muslin. It is best to send to some wholesale chemist for the ingredients, and when received to store them in dry glass jars or large-mouthed pickle bottles thoroughly stoppered.

Brilliant Bengal Fires: Nitre, six ounces; sulphur, three ounces; realgar, one ounce, or nitre, four ounces; sulphur, two ounces; orpiment, one ounce, or nitre, 12 ounces; sulphur, four ounces; black antimony, one ounce, or nitre, eight ounces; sulphur, four ounces; black sulphide antimony, two ounces.

Chertier's White Fire. Nitre, eight ounces; sulphur, two ounces; regulus of antimony, three ounces; red lead, two and one-half ounces.

Special White Fire for Large Landscapes: Nitre, twelve ounces; sulphur, three ounces; regulus of antimony, two ounces; red lead, one and one-half ounces; orpiment, one-half ounce; realgar, one-half ounce; metallic arsenic, one-quarter ounce; shellac, one-quarter ounce.

Golden Yellow Fire: Barium nitrate, five ounces; sodium oxylate, one ounce; potassium chlorate, one and one-half ounces; powdered shellac, one ounce; pure sulphur, one ounce.

Brilliant Red Fire: Strontium nitrate, ten ounces; potassium chlorate. three ounces; sulphur, two ounces; powdered shellac, one ounce; powdered charcoal, one-quarter ounce.

Rich Crimson Fire: Strontium nitrate, sixteen ounces; potassium chlorate, six ounces; pure sulphur, four ounces; sulphide of copper, three ounces; chloride of mercury, two ounces; fine shellac, one ounce; lampblack, one ounce.

Pale Illuminating Green Fire: Barium nitrate, eight ounces; potassium chlorate, three ounces; pure (washed) sulphur, one and one-half ounces; powdered shellac, one-half ounce; powdered charcoal, one-quarter ounce.

Brilliant Green: Barium nitrate, twelve ounces; potassium chlorate, three ounces; pure sulphur, two ounces; powdered shellac, one ounce; chloride mercury, one ounce; powdered charcoal, one-half ounce.

Rich Green: Barium nitrate, sixteen ounces; potassium chlorate, five ounces; pure sulphur, three ounces; barium chlorate, two ounces; chloride mercury, two ounces; powdered shellac, one ounce; powdered charcoal, one-half ounce.

Bengal Lights: In firing Bengal lights the cases should be hung or laid upon the side so that the scoria can fall out, and give the colored flame full egress. For illumination they are the most effective and cheapest lights known.

Campaign Colored Torches: May be made of any of the above fires by taking round turned wooden handles and adding a paper case for the illuminating fires. Two or three thin layers lightly pasted at the first turn and on the outside are enough. Put in a little dry clay rammed hard and fill as for Bengal lights. Strawboard rolls, such as are used for mailing pictures, may be used for handles, but are too thick for cases. The larger cases four by one and three-quarter inches if properly filled ought to burn ten to fifteen minutes.

Salutes: Chlorate of potash and powdered sulphur are very dangerous to mix, unless the sulphur is "washed sulphur" and free of acid. Even then no mortar or mill must be used in mixing them, and the sieve must be used a number of times to secure an intimate mixture. Still it may be used quite safely to fire heavy salutes if used as follows: Procure a heavy iron weight and suspend by a block and tackle from a beam and above a very thick flat stone or sheet of boiler iron. Mix equal parts of chlorate of potassium, pure sulphur, and sharp sand intimately. Spread a tablespoonful thinly on the iron, and drop the weight upon it from a height of four or five feet. The report is very heavy.

The safest way to use large cannon crackers is to fire them from the muzzle of an old cannon or from a mock cannon made by turning a hardwood gun and giving it an open muzzle by driving in a piece of new boiler tube. Shrunk on while hot. This will increase the noise and make it safe to fire. If one of these crackers fail to explode, lay or toss another beside it and both will explode.

There is nothing more beautiful than illuminated boats on a dark night, and a small lake, whose margin is lit up by Bengal lights and bonfires, on which a number of boats decorated with lanterns, and burning colored fires move in unison is more effective than the most costly "set pieces" in a city enclosure. Small boats are easily prepared for decoration by setting hardwood "dowel rods" along each side secured to the gunwale by a strong screw-eye, and braced and connected by soft iron wire. On this frame, about four feet above the gunwale, lanterns and other decorations may be hung, and the occupants may dress and mask themselves "en carnival."

Almost equally effective work may be done by having a skating carnival in winter, with a central bonfire or colored fire beacon, and skaters carrying torches and wearing bright as colors as possible.

JAPANESE PARLOR FIREWORKS

Cover one-half of wooden toothpicks with a mixture of twenty-six parts of gunpowder, eleven parts of pure sulphur and five parts of lampblack. Wet with enough gum arabic mucilage to make a thick paste. The powder should be crushed in a mortar to a fine dust, or "mealed" as it is termed. If they are to be used at once a few iron filings may be added. When lit a small ball of hot scoria will form, giving out a cloud of handsome sparks.

CEMENTS

Alabaster: White beeswax, one part; rosin, one part; powdered alabaster, three-quarter part. Melt the wax and rosin together. Stir in the alabaster dust. Cover with warm water and knead the mass thoroughly. The pieces to be mended must be clean and dry. Melt just enough cement to join them together, bind them tightly and leave for a week.

Cheese for Coarse China: Pound some fresh cheese to a dough and knead it under warm water until only a powder is visible, strain and dry. Mix this powder with half as much powdered quicklime and wet it up with white of egg. Apply at once, as it dries very quickly, and throw the rest of the mixture away.

China Cement: Take a very thick solution of gum arabic and stir into it enough plaster of paris to make a thick paste. Apply to the broken china, and fasten in place. Let stand three days and it will never break in the same place.

Iron Cement: Beat the whites of eggs to a froth; add finely powdered quicklime to make a thin paste and thicken well with iron filings. Use to mend cracks in ironware, stoves, etc.

Japanese Cement: Mix rice-flour with water to a smooth paste and boil it gently for twenty minutes. Add a drop or two of oil of cloves. Very strong, transparent and smooth for light work, as lanterns, toys, etc.

BEDBUGS

In certain localities the neatest housewife in an ill-built house may find it infected. If so, it should be repainted, papered, whitewashed, etc., until the innumerable crevices are thoroughly stopped. Then take a warm day, put out all fires, and saturate the walls, floors, and beds with gasoline. Then go outdoors and let it evaporate. Two "field days" like this will cure the most desperate conditions. For ordinary cases, use the gasoline from a big atomizer on the bedsteads, mattresses, etc., and let evaporate with the same precautions. Or use this: Alcohol, one-half pint; spirits of turpentine, one-half pint; sal ammoniac, one ounce; corrosive sublimate, one ounce; camphor, one ounce. Apply freely with a syringe or sponge.

TO SAVE TREES FROM MICE OR RABBITS

Every fall tack stout brown paper around the base of the tree, and cover the paper with a mixture of tar and tallow. Or apply a strong solution of red pepper with a little starch to the bark of the tree.

HOME-MADE COLOGNE

To each pint of pure alcohol add a teaspoonful each of oil of bergamot, oil of lavender, oil of lemon and orange-flower water. Cork the bottle tightly and allow to mix thoroughly for several days, shaking the bottle from time to time.

TO COOL BEVERAGES WITHOUT ICE

Place in a metal can or glass bottle, cover with several thicknesses of wet cloth and shade from the sun, but keep in a current of air if possible. The cloths should be wet from time to time as the water evaporates. If a little saltpeter is dissolved in the water the degree of cold produced will be much greater. And a charge of gunpowder sprinkled on the neck of a bottle placed in water has long been used in hot countries. Intense cold can be produced by chemicals. Take one pound of muriate of ammonia and two pounds of nitrate of potash to form mixture No. 1, to be kept in closely stoppered bottles.

In other bottles keep three pounds of powdered sal soda, for No. 2.

To use take equal measures of each and *cold* water, and use as a freezing mixture. The mixture will register three degrees below zero.

RAIN WATER CISTERN

When water is scarce or poor, every farmer should have a rainwater cistern midway between his house and barn, and made large enough to hold all the rain shed by his buildings. Such buildings with an area of say 2,200 square feet will gather in a year of about the lightest rainfall known (say fifteen inches) about 20,000 gallons of first-class drinking water. A cistern eight feet in diameter and twelve feet deep would hold this amount, and be equal to the average amount on hand in a year of double the humidity. Such a cistern should be built of concrete or a strong foundation of stone covered with concrete to a depth of several inches.

Where the soil is clay the shape of the cistern can be cut out of the soil, building up the inside wall a foot thick of one part of the best cement to three parts of broken stone and two parts of sand, and keeping it in place by wooden forms. The top may be of stout planking, with an ample hatch to enter and clean if necessary. A wall of porous brick should shut off about one-third part of the cistern into which the water is received and filtered through the brick into the larger part. If the cement lining proves porous, give it a coating of hot clean tallow.

TO CURE A CAT OF FITS

Cut off the very tip of the tail. This is the only sure remedy.

LIMED EGGS

Preserve only strictly fresh eggs. If the shell is cracked it cannot keep long. Take one-half pint unslacked lime, and one-half pint of salt to two gallons of water, dissolve in boiling hot water. Pack the eggs carefully in a stoneware, glass or wooden receptacle; turn in the mixture when cold, and cover closely. Keep in a cool place. The eggs should be good for five months.

TO FRESHEN SALT BUTTER

If your butter is too salt, add a quart of new milk for each pound of butter, and work it over in the churn or if a small quantity is needed with a paddle or large spoon, for at least an hour. Work out the milk, and resalt to taste. Smaller quantities may be worked over in several waters, and thus freshened.

TO BURN LIME

A very good article of lime can be burnt by anyone who can get broken limestone, or plenty of seashells. The stone can be roughly built into the shape of a pyramid, leaving a rude furnace and door at the base, and a chimney flue through the center, cover with sods and earth as for charcoal and start your fire in the center. After it is burning well the draft may be partially closed. Shells must be piled on a large amount of fuel and covered in like manner with soda and earth.

BONE MANURE

Save all the bones procurable, and pack in a hogshead or large tight barrel, in alternate layers between hardwood ashes. When full keep wet with urine, or soft water. Peat soil will do instead of wood ashes if strong sulphuric acid is mixed with the water. When the bones are dissolved, the best chemical fertilizers cannot excel this mixture.

OAT AND WHEAT STRAW FORAGE

Oat straw cut while the grain is in the "dough" and not hardened is as good as most hay, and wheat straw is good forage. Either cut short, wet down and mixed with shorts, wheat bran or Indian meal, will keep a horse or cow in good condition.

DECOCTIONS

In using herbs, roots, barks, leaves, etc., at home, a decoction should be made of one ounce to the pint of boiling water in a covered vessel. The boiling should not be long continued, and the dose should be from one to four ounces, according to the strength of the sample used.

DRINKS FOR THE SICK

Barley Water: Take two ounces of pearl barley to two quarts of water, and boil until soft, strain and mix it with lemon juice, or red or black currant jelly to taste.

Rice Gruel: Six gills of boiling water to each large spoonful of unground rice; flavor with a stick of cinnamon or mace. Strain when boiled soft. Add half a pint of milk, salt to taste and stew a few moments longer.

Water Gruel: Two tablespoonfuls of Indian meal and one of wheat flour, rubbed to a paste with cold water. If wanted thick, add to a pint of boiling water and boil a few minutes; if thin add more water.

Caudle: To rice gruel made as above, add half a wine glassful of ale, wine or brandy. Sweeten with sugar and flavor with nutmeg.

Wine Whey: Stir into a pint of boiling new milk a couple of glasses of sweet wine. Let it boil a moment, take it from the fire and let the curd settle. Strain off the whey and sweeten and flavor to taste.

Egg Wine: Beat together a fresh egg, a wine glass of water and another of Tarragona port, sherry, tokay or other wine (not claret). Sweeten to taste, and drink when well-beaten.

Egg Milk: To one egg well-beaten add two-thirds of a tumbler of fresh *cold* or *hot* (not boiling) milk, any flavor (coffee, tea, lemon, raspberry, vanilla, etc.) and shake well together, adding nutmeg to taste.

Lemonade: Wipe your lemons clean, and rub over them enough loaf sugar to take up the natural oil. Express the juice on the sugar, and add about a pint of boiling water to the juice and flavor of three lemons. This concentrated lemonade may be reduced in strength to taste. The peel of the lemon sliced off very thinly may be steeped if the loaf sugar method is not used.

Tamarind Water: To a large spoonful of tamarind, add a cupful of boiling water. Cool, strain and sweeten to taste. Black currant jelly, or jam can be used in the same way, and are often taken hot for cold, or sore throat.

Beef Tea: To each pound of lean beef cut small, take one and a half pints of cold water, and bring to a boil in a clean sauce-pan, add a pinch of salt, skim it well, cover and let it simmer gently for two or three hours. Strain into a stoneware dish, set away to cool, and when cold skim off every particle of fat. It should be made the day before it is used, and put as much warmed up in a cup for the invalid as is wanted.

Calf Foot Jelly: Boil one calf's foot in two pints and a half of water, until reduced to one-half pint. Strain, cool, remove all the fat, and add a quarter of a pint of milk or wine, the thin rind of one lemon, some nutmeg or cinnamon and sugar to taste. Boil together for five minutes, strain thoroughly and cool.

LITTLE HELPS FOR HOME-MAKERS

TO DRIVE AWAY RATS

Fill their holes and run-ways as fast as discovered with chloride of lime or concentrated lye. Their feet get sore and they will seek other quarters.

TO PACK RIPE FRUITS

Do up in paper bags or parcels and pack in dry bran. If paraffine paper is used, choice grapes can be kept well into the winter.

RESIN CERATE

Resin, five ounces; lard, eight ounces; yellow wax, two ounces. Melt together *with a gentle heat*, and stir until cool. Known as Basdicon ointment and used to gently stimulate blistered surfaces, indolent ulcers, burns, scalds and chilblains.

ESSENCES

Essences of lemon, anise, peppermint, sassafras, etc., should be composed of one ounce of the essential oil to one pint of alcohol. As medicines the usual dose is ten drops of the essence to a teaspoonful of sweetened water.

INFUSIONS

Infusions should be made by pouring boiling water on the substance used, and letting it stand until cool. If a stronger infusion be desired the vessel usually kept covered may stand near the fire or in hot water, but the infusion must not be allowed to boil.

CAMPHOR LINIMENT

For sprains, neuralgia, rheumatism, etc., dissolve six drams of camphor in one fluid ounce of chloroform, and add one ounce of olive oil.

CAMPHORATED SOAP (OPODELDOC) LINIMENT

To three ounces of sliced white soap, add an ounce of camphor; one fluid dram each of oil of rosemary and oil of origanum and a pint of alcohol. Melt the soap in the alcohol using gentle heat, when the soap is dissolved, add the camphor, and oils, and when they are dissolved pour into wide-mouthed vials.

An anodyne liniment for sprains, bruises, painful bunions, etc.

TO REMOVE GREASE STAINS

Soak light fabrics in alcohol, rub as thoroughly as possible, and rinse in lukewarm water.

COMPOUND WINE OF GOLDEN SEAL

Take one dram each of bruised golden seal root, tulip tree bark, and bitter root, half a dram of bruised cayenne pepper, and two quarts of sherry or Tarragona wine. Let the mixture stand for two weeks, shaking the jug occasionally, then express the liquor, strain and bottle.

A pleasant bitter tonic in dyspepsia, etc. Dose from one to two fluid ounces three times a day.

CANKER

Thoroughly mix ten drops of creosote with two ounces of gum arabic mucilage sweetened with loaf sugar. Dose one teaspoonful from two to four times a day, to be held a few moments in the mouth and then swallowed. This has cured many cases which had resisted all other remedies, as it attacks the disease at its center in the stomach.

FOR BURNS

Mix equal quantities of lime water and linseed oil, apply this on cotton (antiseptic if possible) to scalds and burns. This is the best and most available remedy in accidents by fire or explosion where large surfaces are affected.

TO REMOVE BLOOD STAINS

Soak over night and rub or pound in *cold water*, using some first-class washing soda in the latter operations. Rinse out in lukewarm water, and wash in the usual way.

TO REMOVE MILDEW

To one and a half pounds of good washing soda take one pound of chloride of lime. Dissolve the washing soda in four quarts of water. Mix the chloride of lime slowly with a quart of cold water or so much of it as will make a smooth, creamy paste. Add enough cold water to make up the six quarts and mix the two solutions, stirring until thoroughly mixed. Let the mixture stand at least six hours or overnight. Skim off any scum and you will have a pure bleaching liquid. Take one quart of this bleach to five gallons of water, and work in washer or allow the goods to soak, stirring them from time to time until the mildew has disappeared. Use "Wyandotte" washing powder instead of ordinary washing soda for this bleach if procurable.

LITTLE HELPS FOR HOME-MAKERS

TO REMOVE PAINT

If wet rub with benzine. If dried, soften with vaseline, then rub with benzine. Costly silks are best soaked in benzine. Always use benzine by daylight, and, if possible, when there is neither lamplight, gaslight or fire.

TO REMOVE INK STAINS

Dissolve ten grains of oxalic acid in one-quarter pint of water. Keep in well-stoppered bottle, marked *Poison*. Soak the stained article in hot water. Apply the oxalic acid solution to the ink stains, until they disappear, then rinse thoroughly.

Another way (used in laundries) is to cut the ink with chloroform and wash out with strong ammonia. Cover the cloth and press with a hot iron.

TO REMOVE OIL STAINS

Mix thoroughly three ounces spirits of turpentine and one ounce essence of lemon. Scour the stained spots. This will thoroughly remove grease or oil spots.

TO REMOVE COPYING INK STAINS

Make a strong solution of chloride of lime in cold water, and apply to the stain. Follow it *at once* with a solution of oxalic acid in cold water. No time must be lost between the two applications. First dip in the chloride of lime solution, and then in the oxalic acid solution, and rinse in lukewarm water.

TO REMOVE IRON RUST

It is very difficult to remove iron rust stains from some colored goods, as chemical changes take place combining the oxide of iron with the mineral colors employed. Get from your druggist an ounce of hydrochloric acid dissolved in three ounces of water, moisten the stains with this mixture until they disappear, rinse in lukewarm water.

Or apply oxalic acid solution with the finger, lay the article in the sun for a few hours, then rinse, or rub with salt of lemon or Javelle water and wash thoroughly.

PINEAPPLE SHERBET

To the grated pulp of one large ripe pineapple, add the juice and grated peel of one lemon, a pint of sugar, and a quart of water. Freeze with or without straining.

TANKS, CONTENTS OF

Multiply length, width and depth together. If the result is in feet, multiply by the liquid contents of one cubic foot, viz, seven and one-half gallons.

If the tank is round square the diameter and multiply the result by 0.7854, and then again by the depth. If the dimensions include inches reduce all the dimensions to inches before multiplying, and divide the final result by 1728 (cubic inches in a gallon). An ordinary whiskey or cider barrel should hold 4.21 cubic feet, or $31\frac{1}{2}$ gallons.

RAINFALL ON ACRE

Taking the weight of a barrel of water at 200 pounds for $31\frac{1}{2}$ gallons, it will be found that the weight of a one-inch rainfall on an acre of land is between 90 and 100 tons. It is difficult to realize the immense force and effect of the forces which continually pump up fresh water from the salt tropical seas, carry it through the atmosphere and distribute it over the whole world.

CREAM CAKES, PUFFS AND POPOVERS

Mix in an open sauce-pan, one cup of *boiling* water; one-half cup of butter, and two tablespoonfuls of sugar. While still boiling stir in one and three-quarter cups of fine flour. Beat well for four or five minutes until well mixed, and when cool, break five eggs into a bowl (but do not beat them) and add one-half of them to the cool mixture, beating them thoroughly together, then add the rest of the eggs, and beat this batter one-half an hour. Salt to taste.

When very light, drop the batter, about a tablespoonful at a time, on a greased tin or pan, about two inches apart, and bake half an hour in a rather hot oven, and allow to cool.

Fill the hollow cake with whipped cream, sweetened and flavored, or the following filling: One and one-half cups of milk, thickened with two tablespoonfuls of flour, two eggs, two-thirds cup of sugar, one-quarter teaspoonful of salt. Cook in a double boiler for fifteen minutes, stirring thoroughly. When cold flavor with vanilla, lemon, almond, coffee, chocolate, etc., and use a paper cone, confectioner's syringe funnel or small teaspoon to fill the cases. When whipped cream is used it may be mixed with raspberry, strawberry or pineapple in thick syrup, nuts, etc.

Eclairs are baked in the same way except that the cases are larger and narrower. And besides being covered with white or chocolate, the filling is generally richer and flavored like the frosting. Some celebrated confectioners make the cases little more than an inch in width, but very rich and delicious, and others turn out great cakes filled with a thin tasteless paste. Better small flavorsome dainties and fewer of them.

"Popovers" used as puddings are the same cases cooked in cups or gem pans, and served with sweet sauces. All the above are nutritious and easily digested.

THE FAMILY HERBALIST

Some of these simple remedies are undoubtedly found in every State of the Union, and many are still in use, where the doctor is far away, and it is miles to a dispensary. All of the following preparations are indorsed by the best authorities as well as by many local and lay practitioners of the healing art..

Carrot: Both the seeds and the root are good in kidney trouble, as strangury and painful and sparse micturition. Use the seeds in infusion or decoction. Carrot root poultices are antiseptic, soothing and deodorize offensive discharges of the ear and eye.

Turnip: The root of the yellow turnip makes a good healing poultice. That of the white flat turnip may be boiled soft and mashed to express the juice which should be made into a thick syrup for coughs and colds.

Onion: The heart of a roasted onion is often a cure for severe earache. The juice of an onion boiled or raw, with syrup is good for a cough.

Water Melon: Boil down the expressed juice to a thick syrup for coughs and colds or table use. Crush and boil the seeds to a jelly, to relieve urinary difficulties.

Pumpkin: Eat the seeds or boil them to a jelly for kidney troubles.

Cress (Land or Water): Should be eaten freely as a salad by those afflicted with jaundice, liver and lung troubles. Some wonderful cures of consumption have been claimed for this diet. Crush into a poultice for scald head and other scalp eruptions of infancy.

Strawberry Leaves: Make a strong infusion with hot water in a covered vessel, and drink several times a day to promote perspiration and action of the bladder and kidneys. It is also useful for sore throat, chronic coughs, etc.

Sorrel (Garden): Pick, clean and crush the little fleshy leaves and use instead of lime or lemon juice for cool drinks.

Sage: The tea promotes perspiration, and with a little alum makes a good gargle for sore throat, canker, etc.

Blackberry Root: A strong infusion of the root is an excellent remedy for diarrhœa and dysentery. The ripe fruit eaten with sugar and bread and butter often relieves the terrible dysenteries of army life. The fruit juice boiled with sugar and mixed with one-fourth its volume of good rum or brandy, is a famous cordial for similar troubles.

Raspberry: A strong infusion of the leaves is also astringent and tonic, and excellent for the bowel troubles of children. The fruit syrup, sweet or mingled with white wine vinegar, makes a favorite beverage with cold water.

Quince: The seeds boiled with hot water produce a thick demulcent, excellent for inflamed throats or the stomach and bowels in dysentery. Made thin and perfumed, it is an excellent fixatif for the hair.

Spearmint: A tea of the leaves allays vomiting and wind and pain in the stomach and bowels.

Peppermint: The tea helps nausea, griping and wind. The essential oil brushed lightly over the face often relieves neuralgia.

Parsley: The leaves, roots and seeds are all of service in kidney and dropsical complaints when eaten freely with bread and butter. A salad of the finely chopped leaves will be found beneficial, or an infusion may be made from the dried or fresh plant. It is also good in fever and ague.

Lettuce: Eat freely to allay cough, nervousness and insomnia.

Horse Radish: An infusion of the root promotes all the secretions, and when strong is a powerful emetic. Made into a syrup with twice the quantity of sugar it often cures chronic hoarseness. The grated root in vinegar as eaten at table can be spread on linen and used as a counter-irritant instead of mustard.

Figs and Dates: These dried fruits are healing to irritated stomach and bowels, and mildly cathartic. Eaten every morning with a few walnuts they will often remove the bad breath and "dark brown taste" that tell of an over-worked stomach. A fig poultice, made soft and spread on old linen, is one of the most grateful and healing known to medicine.

Prunes: Long soaked to restore their plumpness, gently stewed and not over-sweetened, have few superiors as a gentle and natural laxative. Their syrup boiled down, and blended with liquorice and cubebs makes a cough **remedy.**

PURE ICE CREAM

One quart of new sweet cream; one cup of sugar; vanilla, lemon, or other flavors to taste, freeze.

For strawberry cream, add to above one quart of *ripe sweet* strawberries, and a pint of sugar thoroughly mashed and beaten together, rub through a strainer and freeze.

FRUIT ICES

One pint of sugar to three pints of fresh fruits, and one quart of water, thoroughly beaten together. Strain and freeze.

When the fruit is not strained out and the ice is only partially frozen so that the chilled berries are eaten almost whole, the ice is called a "granate" or "granite" ice.

FOR BURNS

Moisten Epsom salts with just warm water, enough to dissolve thoroughly, add an equal volume of pure glycerine and bottle for use. Soak cotton in the liquid and cover the burn, bandage lightly, so as to keep out the air, moisten the cotton from time to time, and the burn will get well in a remarkably short time. Essence of peppermint applied to slight burns give almost immediate relief.

COMMON SIMPLES

Sassafras: The root-bark and green leaves boiled together make a demulcent, aromatic and carminative jelly, useful in colds, bronchitis, pneumonia and measles, as good or better than those made with flax seed or gum arabic.

Dogwood: The inner bark gathered in the fall or spring, makes a bitter infusion, which is a good substitute for quinine in low fevers and typhoid dysentery.

Thoroughwort or Boneset: An infusion of the leaves drank while hot during the chilly stages of fevers, or when cold as a tonic and preventative of ague attacks, was largely used in the Confederate armies during the Civil War.

Willow or Tulip Tree Barks: Bitters and tea from these have been extensively used for want of quinine.

Pennyroyal: Tea is carminative, antispasmodic and effective against colds, coughs, colics, spasms and female complaints.

Oak Barks: Red, white or black, are very astringent and somewhat tonic. They tend to check agues, chronic diarrhœa, dysentery and cholera infantum. They stop bleeding at the nose and mouth, and if used as a gargle will thicken the lining membrane of the nose and lessen the tendency to chronic nosebleed.

Nutmeg: The tea will relieve nausea, vomiting and diarrhœa, or the nut may be eaten moderately. Patients of an apopletic or paralytic tendency must not use it.

Plaintain: Bruise the leaves into a mass and apply to bites and stings of insects, inflamed sores and swellings.

Cinnamon Bark: Make a mucilage of the ground bark with hot water, sweeten and give freely in diarrhœa and dysenteries. For horses, cattle or fowls, give it in a mash or on wet grain. An infusion of the bark is good but lacks the demulcent quality.

White Pine Bark: The infusion is good in coughs, colds, bronchitis, rheumatism and kidney troubles.

Persimmon: The bark and unripe fruit make very astringent infusions of proven efficiency in ague and bowel diseases. They are also of use as a gargle for sore throat, canker, etc.

Sumach: The bark and young twigs are very astringent. The ripe berries infused in hot water make a pleasant acidulated drink for fevers.

Buckeye: Horse chestnut roots when powdered and macerated in warm water give a soapy, cleansing suds of especial value in renovating fine cotton, woolen and silk fabrics, and a very effective shampoo. The nut kernel contains a very large proportion of starch which will not turn yellow and its flour made into paste is of special value to book-binders as worms will never attack it. Ten grains of the powdered rind of the nut is equal to three grains of opium and may be used to induce sleep, and a strong decoction is recommended for gangrenous ulcers. A strong infusion of the roots held in the mouth will cure toothache.

Creeping Cucumber: The seeds of this vine are a powerful purgative. Half of one is a dose for an adult, and three or four for a horse or hog.

Snake Root: For croup, boil one ounce in one and one-half pints of water until the infusion is reduced to a pint. Dose one tablespoonful every quarter hour until relieved. Also good for asthma of old people, chronic catarrh, etc.

Magnolia: The leaves steeped in hot water or brandy are good for colds, bronchitis, etc. A tincture of the fresh seeds and root-bark in brandy has a reputation for curing rheumatism. A hot infusion of the root bark is a gentle laxative and sudorific, and when cold is a good tonic.

Dill: An infusion of the seeds of this herb are like anise, good for flatulent colics.

Wild Indigo: The root in infusion is an active emetic and purgative. It is also of use as a wash or gargle for ulcers, canker, nursing sore mouths, etc.

Irish Moss: This common sea moss is fully equal in value to the Iceland Moss, long used by druggists. Made into an emulsion or jelly with water, it may be sweetened with sugar or honey, flavored with lemon juice, and used in colds, catarrhs, bronchitis, etc. With milk, sugar and spices or wine it makes a delicate jelly for the supper or sick table. If taken from the shore it should be washed clean, dried and blanched in the sun before using. It is sold as Sea Moss Farine.

New Jersey Tea: The leaves were used largely by the patriotic women of the revolution as a substitute for tea. Two drachms of the powdered root in a pint of hot water, covered closely until cool, are good for canker, nursing sore mouths and fever patients.

Mullein: A tea of the velvety leaves of this weed has long been held useful for coughs, bronchitis, etc., and in chronic diarrhœa and dysentery. When infants are wasting away with such disorders and cannot retain food, it is claimed that mullein tea with milk, given in spoonful doses, has turned the scale from certain death to life.

Marsh Rosemary: A tea made of the root is powerfully astringent and beneficial in diarrhœa, dysentery, etc. As a wash or gargle it is good for canker, sore throat and ulcers.

Sweet Gum Tree: The inner bark or leaf boiled in milk or water is very astringent and used for diarrhœa, etc. The gum with sugar or honey is used for coughs and colds.

Golden Seal: An infusion of the yellow root dyes cotton and other fibres yellow, and when followed by indigo, green. It is a tonic bitter, and a good eye wash, for wenk eyes, opthalmia, etc.

Pond Lily (white or yellow): The astringent infusion of the root is useful in diarrhœa, etc., for gargles, antiseptic washes, etc. The fresh roots pounded to a pulp make a very cooling and grateful poultice for sores or ulcers.

Hops: An infusion is used as a tonic. The hot, wet flowers applied in bags, often relieve neuralgia, rheumatism, toothache, insomnia, etc.

Hawkweed: An infusion of the root is a mild astringent and expectorant in chronic catarrh, bronchitis, spitting blood, etc. It is claimed also that a strong decoction is a sure cure for rattlesnake bite, and experiments made at Philadelphia some years ago tend to justify it, as the man who made the test alowed snakes to bite him which had previously and afterwards killed small animals.

Sweet Fern: A tea made of the leaves is astringent and helpful in diarrhœal troubles, and as a wash or gargle for sore throat, canker, ulcers, etc.

Flowery Elder: Macerate the powdered inner bark and flowers, if in season, in clarified mutton tallow, cocoanut oil or the like, until it is colored a light green, and has a fresh pleasant smell. The ointment will be found very grateful and healing to any eruption or sore.

Red Clover: The tea and fomentation from red clover blossoms have always been considered useful for all diseases of the blood and skin, and especially for cancers, old sores, etc.

Wild Cherry: An infusion of one ounce of the bark to a pint of hot water in doses of a large wineglassful, is recommended to cure asthma, bronchitis, consumption, etc. The gum exuded in wet weather, dissolved in hot water, strained and made into a syrup is also commended.

FREEZING ICES

It is much easier to shave or cut ice than to crush it, and it pays to buy one of those three-pointed hand shavers with which it is mere play to fill a tub with fragments of ice. Take a sharp hatchet, put your ice in a tub and chop off the ice from top to bottom about an inch thick, or get a rude mallet armed with half a dozen sharp points.

LEMON SHERBET

Take the juice of five lemons, and the grated outer peel of one, a pint of sugar and one quart of water. Freeze.

A WEDGEWOOD MORTAR

The Wedgewood mortar and pestle should be found in every pantry, and will be found a great aid in mixing all foods which must become a smooth and homogeneous cream or paste. The Stoneware pestle not only mixes but grinds, dry or wet mixtures, and is as indispensable in the home laboratory as the chemists. With a good sized mortar and several brass wire sieves, the housewife will not only be able to reduce much material to necessary fineness, but will eliminate more foreign substance and imperfect material, tea and coffee dust, etc., than she ever dreamed of in her philosophy.

CEDAR OIL

A tight box, trunk or closet, paneled thoroughly with oil of cedar, and allowed to dry for several days will be found as effectually moth proof as if lined with the best cedar.

POTATO CREAM CANDY

Made without cooking. One medium size mashed cold potato, one teaspoonful of vanilla, one pound pulverized sugar, and one cupful of nuts. Stir this to a cream, then put in buttered plate and cut in squares.

BAKED MILK

Put two quarts of milk into an earthen jar tightly sealed with writing-paper tied down. Let it stand in a moderate oven for eight or ten hours. It will then be as thick as cream and very appetizing and nourishing.

USES OF OLIVE OIL

Thirty years ago few Americans would use olive oil as a food in any shape. Today it is very largely used, and is prized for its nutritious and healing qualities. It should be taken regularly by those who wish to regain nerve force and lost flesh and will be easily taken if used with soft boiled eggs instead of butter, say about a teaspoonful of oil to each egg, or with baked beans, soups, or cereal foods when eaten with cream.

CLARIFIED FAT

Save all fats and fatty scraps from all kinds of food except the fat of mutton, smoked meats, fish or turkey. Reduce to small pieces, cover with cold water, and boil until only a little water is left. Strain and press all the fat from the scraps. If any sediment remains, wash in one or more cold waters until only the clear fat remains; melt and heat in a vessel in which a raw potato cut in thin slices is allowed to brown very slowly. When this is effective, strain the fat and use it instead of lard for any purpose.

FOR WRINKLES

Add to 10 ounces of rosewater, 4 ounces of glycerine and 2 ounces of taurim; or if a small quantity be required half or quarter the above proportions. Apply several times a day with a camel's hair brush, and aid its action by a little facial massage at such application.

WINE WHEY

Stir two wine-glassfuls of port, sherry or any good wine. Boil into one pint of boiling milk a moment longer until the curd forms, take out the curd and sweeten the whey. This is not only nourishing and digestible, but is of value in its effect on the kidneys.

SANDWICHES

CLUB:—Hash finely slices of cold breast of chicken, partridge or turkey, and lay on alternate layers of lettuce, sliced tomato and crisp sweet bacon, with mayonnaise, and between two slices of buttered toast.

SMOKED SARDINE:—Chop fine a box of Norwegian smoked sardines with the pulp of half a lemon, and spread the fish on buttered light biscuit or toast.

EGG AND MINCED HAM:—Scrambled egg with minced ham or egg make fine sandwiches.

CREAM TOASTS

PLAIN TOAST:—Toast stale baker's bread slowly until crisp and brown. Serve with milk, thickened with about one tablespoonful of flour and an ounce of butter to the pint of milk.

BEEFSTEAK HASH CREAM TOAST:—Stir into the cream above made, about one half a pound of finely hashed cold beef, and bring to a boil. Pour the hash cream in a dish and arrange the toast on top.

Turkey or chicken mashed finely may be used as above.

CURRIED EGG CREAM TOAST:—Add to the cream currie to taste and hard-boiled eggs cut in rings.

RASPBERRY CREAM TOAST:—Spread raspberry jam between thin slices of toast, and serve with cream as above.

QUINCE TOAST:—Core ripe quinces and place in a pan, filling the centre with sugar, and flavoring with cinnamon. Bake until tender, and serve in slices of buttered toast with very sweet whipped cream.

MUSHROOM TOAST:—Brush and peel mushroom caps, cut in dice sufficient to fill two cups; then cook in two tablespoonfuls butter five minutes. To one-half a teaspoonful of chopped shallot, add one tablespoonful of butter and cook, stirring constantly, three minutes. Bring one quart can of tomatoes to the boiling point; simmer twenty minutes, then rub through a sieve; there should be one cupful of tomato puree. Add puree to shallot, and season with salt and pepper. Put mushrooms on the toast, and pour over the tomato puree.

CREAMED SPINACH ON TOAST:—Cleanse thoroughly and boil half a peck of spinach in a very little salted water for half an hour. Drain, cut in pieces with a sharp knife, put in a hot pan with two ounces of butter, set on back of stove until the butter melts, add half a teacupful of cream, a small spoonful of sugar, and a little grated nutmeg; arrange some buttered slices of toas' 'n a large dish, and spread the spinach thickly over each slice. Serve h ' boiled egg or some scrambled egg on each piece.

HONEY TOAST:—Beat an egg and add to a cupful and a half c' or half cream and half milk, with a pinch of salt and two tablespoc honey. Beat smooth, dip slices of stale bread and brown quickly ' Serve with plenty of honey.

FOR NAUSEA

Stir into a glass of ice water the white of an egg beaten to a stiff froth.

FLY POISONS

Bicarbonate of potash, one dram, dissolved in two ounces of water. Sweeten with sugar or syrup, and place in a shallow dish and, if possible, where a ray of sunlight strikes it early every morning.
2d: Black cobalt, one dram to two ounces of sweetened water, used as above.
3d: Dissolve ½ dram of formaldehyde in two ounces of sweetened water, and use as above.

HAIR TONIC

For a dry scalp and thinning hair, take 1 fluid ounce tincture of red cinchona bark; 2 drams tincture nux vomica; ½ dram tincture cantharides; 1½ ounce cologne, and one ounce cocoanut oil. Rub in well twice a day at least. A still stronger tonic consists of 2 drams tincture of capsicum; 1 ounce ammonia water; 5 grains hydro-chlorate pilocarpin, and 3 ounces of cologne; mix.

ORANGE ICE

To one quart of water add the juice of six oranges, one tablespoonful of good gelatine, one pint sugar, and the whites of three eggs. Soak the gelatine in one-fourth the water for five minutes; boil the remainder of the water and add the gelatine, sugar and strained juice, and when very cold add the whites of the eggs beaten stiff. Freeze in the usual manner.

HAIR TONIC FOR DRY HAIR

Mix resorcin, 3 drams; fluid extract of pilocarpin, 3 drams; tincture of cantharides, 4 drams; glycerine, 4 drams; spirits of lavender (com.), 4 drams; also castor-oil, 1 dram, and bay rum, 1 pint.
Add the castor-oil to the bay rum and shake thoroughly. Afterward add the other ingredients.

FRUIT PUNCH

juice of three lemons, two oranges, sliced, one grated pineapple ful of sugar. Let stand for one hour to extract the juice, then in into your punch bowl. Add to the juice two quarts of iced slices of pineapple shredded, with or without claret, Rhine wine

PRIVATE THEATRICALS, ETC.

There is no more useful amusement when properly conducted than society and home entertainment furnished by local talent and bringing out abilities and sentiments otherwise dormant. The choice of plays should be worthy and not too ambitious. Simple dialogues, grave and gay, many old comedies, easily procured in pamphlet form, the still popular "Baker Parlor Dramas," and scenes easily adapted from Shakespeare, the Bible, Don Quixote, and modern novels will be more likely to succeed than more pretentious efforts.

The first thing to do is to choose a manager whose decrees in certain matters must be final. He or she may and probably will make mistakes but something will be done and done more effectively, than if everybody is to claim this or that, and do as they please regardless of general results. The play or plays once chosen, the manager should assign the parts and have them read and criticised in accordance with the fitness and abilities of the actors and actresses for them. If any one fails to put vim and character into the reading or is bashful, they should be gently criticised and encouraged to forget self and lose themselves in the character they are attempting to portray. This is the main thing to be kept in view, and the manager should himself thoroughly study the play and the times, customs, events, fashions, dress, etc., etc., of which it is a picture. He should impress on every character, that every part is necessary to the finished design, that it requires as great a genius to picture the fool, dandy, slave, servant, etc., as the hero, heroine, or royalty itself, and that a failure to put life into these subordinate parts will damage and possibly spoil the rendition of the whole play.

Every character should have the full play, or at least his part, typewritten, showing the last words said upon the stage which are his "cues" for appearing or doing or saying something. They should be the first things to be committed to memory and with them the action of the play at those points, and the reason why the actor appears, acts or speaks at those particular times. Particularly in the matter of "cues," the participants must continue to study until every one thoroughly understands their importance.

By the time this is done, the parts should have become "letter perfect" and rehearsals should be frequent and thorough. It will be necessary to repress the ardor and action of some, and to encourage character and force of voice and action in others, until a very fair rendition of what the author had in mind can be given.

Costumes: In many cases modern garments only need be used and, of course, costumes of any kind or period can be ordered of firms in the nearest cities. Still much can be done at home with simple and cheap material. Scriptural characters were usually clad in simple garments such as are frequently illustrated in encyclopedias, dictionaries, commentaries and the like, or in armor with sandals on their feet, with their limbs apparently bare or covered only with greaves or other protection. A helmet is easily made out of any derby or straw hat with the brim cut into a narrow vizor in front and turned down and rounded to cover the back and sides of the head. A few stitches will keep everything in shape and some silver or gold paper, plain or put on in overlapping scales or diamonds, will make a fair basinet. Photographic paste, made by the receipt given, will give clean, smooth, lasting work.

Cheap flesh-colored underwear, doubly sewn at the seams so as to fit tightly at wrists and ankles, are good substitutes for tights; and a Grecian, Roman or Saxon scale armored shirt can be easily made on a gaily dyed loose short-sleeved undershirt with scalloped bands of silver or gold paper overlapping like shingles and fastened with photographer's paste. Greaves, shields, breastplates, etc., can easily be made of stout pasteboard and metallic paper. Spears, swords, battle axes, halberds, antique guns, pistols, etc., are closely imitated in tin or wood covered with silver tin foil and colored paper and will last a long time if properly cared for.

Grecian and Roman dresses are especially effective and should be studied from the engravings. Two sheets or table cloths joined together at the top for six inches or so from the end, then left open for eighteen inches and again closed, then left well open in the center for the head to pass through, stitched together the whole length of the sides, and left open at the bottom, can be gathered into the most graceful and artistic draperies for antique female characters. With gold ornaments, belt, etc., a white costume is very effective.

Wigs are easily made of curled hair, unraveled Manila rope or jute switches sewn upon black or white skull-caps of mosquito netting. Small purchases of colored tinsel, gold paper, etc., will enable the ingenious to manufacture crowns, tiaras, jewels and belts, insignia, etc., which the foot-lights will light up with wonderful effect. Old garrets and trunks will often furnish things that can be used effectively on the mimic stage.

The Stage: In a private house which has potieres or folding doors there is need of little scenery. Folding doors make a fairly good substitute for curtains. Otherwise curtains fastened with rings to a wire and cords so arranged that the curtains can be opened and closed from the sides are the best for home use. There should be a back screen made in two sections having a frame of light wood braced at the corners covered tightly with cotton which is afterwards thoroughly wet with paste and covered with blue or green paper for out-of-door scenery. The wall will hold these up if further secured to ring screws in the door or window casings. From four to six "side scenes," 7x3 feet, made in the same way should set be at the sides with a slight slant toward the rear of the stage to shut off the view of the sides of the room. Three or four "flies" of blue cambric should cross the stage to cover the tops of the side scenes, and shut out the ceiling from the view of the spectators.

Any kind of a rug or carpet, preferably green, of course, or even coarse wrapping or building paper can be used to cover the floor. Very handsome prosceniums or stage fronts can be made on slender frames covered with cloth by using panel work of wall papers, gold or silver paint, etc.

Weather Properties: To make lightning, get a small tube and a few cents' worth of lycopodium. The operator dips one end of the tube into the lycopodium and blows the small quantity taken up into the flame of a candle and away from the stage. A sudden glare lights up the gloom and is followed by the "thunder" which is made by another assistant who is holding and shaking a sheet of Russia iron. A little practice with this will give any kind of a "thunderclap" from a gentle rumble to a tremendous roar. To imitate rain, make a long, narrow box, eighteen inches long by three or four inches through, closed at both ends and traversed by butchers' hardwood skewers set about one inch apart and breaking joints, as it were; a few handfuls of dried peas in this box allowed to fall quietly from one skewer to the other imitates a gentle shower. If shaken violently, a dash of heavy rain, hail, etc. A sudden crash to imitate an accident or great damage to a building or other material, is initiated by dropping a bag loosely filled with broken china and glass.

The home fireside can be easily imitated by setting up a red hearth-frame or simple mantel-shelf projecting from the rear screen with an old-fashioned brick fire place made of red paper marked off with black, and furnished with old handirons and logs previously charred and dotted with bits of crimson tinsel to imitate embers. A dish of unslaked lime hidden by the wood and wet with water will create a very natural smoke and if a candle is placed so as to light this up, it will look very natural indeed. An old-fashioned grate with a fire is made of crimson paper barred with black containing the slacking lime and candle.

When a fire is supposed to break out, the tube used for lightning is turned upon the stage and the burning lycopodium is allowed to follow the edge of the side scenes and a number of tubes should then be used. The flame is harmless against anything but the most inflammable stuff, but should not be used where any of the lady actors are wearing muslin dresses.

In Schools, Halls, Vestries, etc.: Prosceniums should be oblong, about sixteen to twenty feet long according to the length of the stage, leaving room for dressing rooms and for operating the properties, etc., at each end. The side frames should be at least nine feet high, and the top frame the full length possible, and the same width. Both should be strongly but lightly framed, covered with cloth and painted or papered, so as to have a bright and lively effect. Wall papers and borders will give light effect with dark, rich paneling at a very low cost. A little gold paper in strips or pasted over moldings will give an elegant finish.

Strong, upright timber fastened securely to the front of the stage and the floor should be used to secure the proscenium sides and top, and this should be braced by scantlings from either end to the wall at sufficient height to hold the curtain drop curtain, side scenes, etc., etc. The curtains, side scenes, etc. may be made and used as before but should be larger to suit the greater stage. Several interiors can be made by using different wall papers and borders as parlor, chamber, kitchen or cellar and dungeon scenes. Very pretty arbor, garden plots, etc., can be made by cutting out the beautiful vines and flowers now decorating modern wall papers and the woods will often furnish wonderful ferns, dead trees, mosses, etc., which will for a night or two beat the best painted scenery. The curtains covering the dressing rooms and wings, should be of thick dark stuff fastened to strong, tightly-dawn wires. The old-fashioned army blanket made an almost perfect side curtain.

Tableaux: These are very effective and taking, and should be used as often as possible. A loose curtain of black muslin or mosquito netting hung back of the drop curtain and rolled on a light pole should be lowered before a tableau is shown. It lessens [the sharpness of the outlines and blends them like a painter's brush into what the French aptly style "tableaux vivants" (living pictures). Ordinary foot lights are not strong enough for these and red or green fire should be used. Very effective and nice colored fires are now put up in little packages with the fuse which readily lights them. These are the best, but if you can not get them, make your own red and green fire as follows:—

Red Fire: ¼ lb. nitrate of strontia; ½ lb. pulverized confectionery sugar; ⅛ lb. pulverized chlorate of potash.

Have these very fine and dry and mix with a sieve. If not red enough, add more nitrate of strontia; if it burns too slowly, add more chlorate of potash.

Green Fire: ¼ lb. nitrate of baryta; ½ lb. pulverized sugar; ½ lb. chlorate of potash.

These fires will light at once, if a glass rod or a piece of pipe-stem dipped in sulphuric acid touches them. Burn in a tin pan with an inch of sand or loam in the bottom.

Tableaux Concerts: A concert of popular or old songs rendered by a choir, quartette, or soloist, and illustrated by suitable tableaux is easy to organize and always popular. The verse may be sung and the tableaux shown during the chorus or at the beginning and end of the song. Local militiamen, firemen, sailors, mechanics and members of fraternal societies may be used to great advantage at such concerts. The foot lights are now best furnished by a row of incandescent bulbs with a tin reflector behind each one to throw its light on the stage. Ordinary low kerosene lamps with reflectors can also be used to good effect.

Shadow Pictures: A great deal of amusement can be made by placing a white screen across the stage and throwing the silhouette of the actors upon it by means of a single electric bulb, lamp or candle. An easy way to use this is to set up an unglazed window-frame close to the screen upon something opaque enough to darken the screen below it, and show the pictures of one or more characters through the shadow-window.

A man shaving himself; a "painless dentist" pulling teeth; a couple courting; a domestic quarrel; a greedy diner; can all be shown with many more. When the lamp or candle flame is about breast high, the figures are of normal proportion; when lowered they become gigantic; when raised they become dwarfed. The figures must always stay in profile and articles used can be cut out of card board and shown the same way. If an actor steps over a light from the rear, he seems to leap down from the sky upon the stage; if he steps over it and back again, he seems to break through the ceiling and come down again. Comic recitations, rhymes from Mother Goose, sung or recited, old negro melodies, new ragtime songs can all be used to good effect.

Negro Minstrel Performances: The success of these performances depends chiefly upon the originality and spirit of the performers, and also upon their use of costumes. Perhaps the most successful costumes are those which appeared to be in the worst state of dilapidation or which have been mended with prodigious patches of various colors. Much may be done, however, by using the natural gifts of the performers. For instance, whistling when the performer is really a musician and can whistle variations to the playing of a piano or some other instrument seems to be always acceptable to an audience. Performances on the Jewsharp, banjo, xylophone, guitar, mandolin, trombone, ocarina, bugle, drum (if of unusual merit) and other instruments are always a variation and if well performed "take." The songs, "walk arounds" and negro comedies used in the past are almost all easily procured from the music or theatrical dealers.

A few wigs may be bought, and especially what is called a trick wig, which when properly manipulated, demonstrates that the darkey wearing it is frightened out of his life; although the average negro wig can be easily made out of black or gray curled hair. A little grease paint and especially the bright red needed to color the lips and cold cream to anoint face and hands before applying the "essence of black cork" are also necessary. The essence of black cork is easily made by piling clean bottle corks on a fire-shovel or earthenware tiling and pouring over them a little alcohol and burning them until black clear through. The fire must be extinguished and the charcoal mixed with water or vaseline to a thick paste. If rubbed on dry, it is apt both to fall off and to get into the pores and take considerable washing to remove.

A dozen young people from neighboring farms or the members of a country village by these simple means can meet around at each other's houses for the winter and have a good time and learn much in the way of effective speech, self-confidence, graceful movement and a wider comprehension. In a small town, school or church society greater things can be done and if moderate admission fees are charged, some money can be made for charity or greater improvements. These hints will be found to be of practical experience and embody about all that the average performing country troupe uses in its business performances.

A few suggestions will be found elsewhere for the details of public and local celebrations, etc. They have all been personally proven in many places, as have the suggestions for camping out and camp cookery.

Editor.

PARSNIPS, FRIED, STEWED, ETC.

Those which have been left in the earth all winter are sweetest and best. Stewed and served with meats, or allowed to cool, and fried with a coating of egg and cracker crumbs, duly seasoned, they are generally liked. A daintier dish, (Parsnip Rissoles) is prepared by draining the stewed roots, mashing them to a stiff paste, seasoning with salt and pepper, and sometimes a little sugar. Roll into croquettes or small balls, dip in beaten egg, cover with cracker crumbs, and fry in fat as deep as used for doughnuts.

WHITEWASH

Slake eight quarts of good lime in a large tub with enough boiling water to make a paste. Cover until cold, stirring occasionally, to keep it smooth. Dissolve one quart of salt in two quarts of hot water, and half an ounce of indigo in a pint of hot water. Mix and add to the slacked lime. Beat the whole well, and add enough cold water to make the mixture the consistency of thin cream.

TO STEAM VELVET

Place a clean milk pan or other tin dish bottom up over a gas or other stove, and keep it moderately hot. Wring a clean cloth out of water, lay it over the pan and pass velvet or other firm cloth over it with the wrong side next to the cloth. While steaming, brush the nap carefully with a moderately stiff brush.

BANANA PIE

Sprinkle the undercrust with a little sugar, slice in two or three ripe but firm bananas, add about an ounce of butter in small bits, sprinkle over them about half a cupful of sugar, and the juice of half a lemon; dredge with flour and put on the upper crust. A single crust pie is made by baking the under crust by itself, and when cool, adding two thinly sliced bananas. Boil together one cup of milk, one-half cup of sugar, and the yolks of two eggs, thickened with two tablespoonfuls of flour. When cooled, flavor with vanilla and pour over the bananas. If liked, whip the whites of the eggs to a froth for the top of the pie and brown in a quick oven but do not let the pie heat through.

BAKED FISH

Get very fresh, firm bass, pickerel, whitefish, cod, bluefish or shad. Scale and dress, brushing out the settled blood with a small stiff brush; wipe dry with a clean towel or cloth. Stuffing, if used, should be made of bread crumbs, mixed with a little milk, a small lump of butter, and seasoned with salt, pepper and any herb like summer savory, thyme, sweet marjoram, etc. Dredge with flour or corn meal and cover the bottom of the pan with water, to which a little lemon juice may be added to advantage. Bake slowly for forty-five to sixty minutes according to size of fish, basting it frequently. Serve with white sauce, with a little finely chopped parsley.

TO PREVENT FREEZING

Make hay ropes and cover the pump from base to top or make a box around it, and stuff it with scraps of paper well rammed down; or paste layer after layer of paper around the pump until the coating is an inch thick.

The use of paper in barns and sheds will make them warmer at less expense than other material. Two or three layers of wrapping paper on the inner wall, especially if covered with one thickness of tarred paper, will keep man and beast in great comfort, shutting out not only wind but cold.

Many do not like to cover the lower part of their farmhouses with straw, earth or other "banking" because it injures the paint and rots the wood. By tacking tarred paper along the base of the house, and bending out at the bottom, two great purposes are achieved: The protection against wind and frost is doubled, and the house cannot be touched by the material piled against it.

VEHICLE FOR GOLD PAINT

One gill of clear oil, one gill of spirits of turpentine, one gill of Japan dryer; mix well and cork tight. You can mix your gold, silver, or other metallic powder with this and lay it on with a brush, or brush this over the object, let it dry, until "tacky," and lay on the powder dry with a wad of cotton or piece of old velvet. A thin coat of tint varying from white to orange before applying gold paint makes a better job, but is not absolutely necessary.

TO SAVE STOCKINGS

Cut out of thick wrapping paper or thin cardboard inner soles to fit your boots, and throw them away every day or two. They keep the feet warm, absorb perspiration, and save darning.

TO BOIL A HAM

First get a good ham, scrape and clean off any dirt or marking, and soak all night in soft water. Put in a large boiler and cover with cold water, or if possible sweet cider, or pour half a bottle of lime juice into the water. Add some celery leaves and root, an onion stuck with six or eight cloves, a small red pepper, a dozen whole pepper corns, and a couple of bay leaves. If you have neither cider nor lime juice, add a cup of vinegar and three or four tablespoonfuls of brown sugar, or thick sweet molasses. Bring to a boil slowly, then set on the stove to simmer until done. Let it cool in the liquor, then remove the skin; coat with brown sugar, stick with cloves and bake until browned.

TO SAVE COAL

When winter sets in, see that all but one window in each room is made to shut tightly without rattling, wedge them if necessary, and if the house is old cover the joints with strips of white paper neatly pasted down. See to the doors, and if there are cracks between the doors and door-steps, or jamb, make the door fit with strips of thick woolen or sheep-skin with wool on. Storm doors and windows can be made with light frames covered on both sides with cloth oiled with linseed oil or melted paraffine; these will keep out frost and let in light besides being light, cheap and manageable. A very little money spent in this way will save many dollars in fuel, and more in discomfort. Where houses are built in the open Greek fashion, the portieres may be replaced by light frames covered with cloth and finished with small doors of like make and material. When there are platforms and piazzas about a house they often conceal the sources of much discomfort. Take up some of the boards and see if the cold winter winds do not find free access through some hole in the masonry or underpinning. Take out all dirt and fill up with good clean ashes, sand, or dry loam so that no wind or vermin can penetrate.

PRESERVING WHOLE FRUIT

To make whole fruit preserves, boil the syrup until thick before adding fruit, which should be lowered into the syrup with a long-handled ladle to save bruising; the fruit should be solid, not too ripe, and freshly picked.

TO GAIN FLESH

Those who are too thin can add a pound a week to their weight by mixing a teaspoonful of Mellins Food with about a tablespoonful of hot water in a glass, then filling glass with milk; drink before breakfast. Repeat before dinner and supper. This was recommended by a friend of mine, a hospital nurse, and proved very successful in her case and others.

A HARMLESS CLEANER

A good cleaner for oil paintings, furniture, or grained wood, is hot whey, obtained after removing curd from sour milk; it will improve oil paintings that are dimmed with age; also, it is splendid for scullery work of any kind, and will not injure any article, if well rinsed with clear water and wiped dry.

TO SAVE SCREENS

Oil your screens with linseed oil, thus doubling their life and preventing that fine rust dust from drifting into the house. In putting away the screens in the fall, write on each the name of the room and window to which they belong; this saves much time and trouble in the spring.

FOR PLANTING CUCUMBERS

When I first started to raise cucumbers, they were a failure, until one of my neighbors told me of a way which was very successful, a way of propagating that is done in Germany. In the first place, do not be in a hurry to plant them, but wait until the frost is all out of the ground and the nights are warm; second, be sure you get fresh seeds; then soak the seeds in luke-warm water for half an hour or more; next, get a piece of an old cotton sheet or pillow-slip; wet thoroughly in warm water, don't wring; put them in the wet cloth, roll up and put in a dry cup; keep on a shelf in a warm place for two or three days, when they will be well sprouted and ready to plant; do not let the cloth get dry while the seeds are in it; dip it, with the seeds in it, in warm water whenever needed during the two or three days. Plant just before, or right after a rainfall; the ground will then be in the right condition to receive them. I was also told never to put water on the vines, but to leave that to the rain. I planted the "Early White Spine" which is a fine sort, very prolific and suitable for all purposes.

USEFUL BAKING POWDER CAN

One-pound cans make the daintiest little loaves of bread imaginable; so dainty and nice for picnic sandwiches, with a delicate, paperlike crust. You do not need to waste the crust, for, if rightly baked, you would not know there was any. This size of can is also fine for boiled puddings; after greasing the can, put in the pudding and tie up in a cloth and boil; never put the cover on for either bread or pudding. As a potato chopper, this can has no equal; and half-pound sizes make fine soapshakers for washing dishes, cleaning and so forth.

STARCH FOR DARK CLOTHES

To starch dark percales, lawns, laces and so forth, take one ounce of gum arabic and pour one-half a pint of boiling water over the pulverized gum arabic; which has been put in a wide-mouthed bottle; add one tablespoonful of alcohol to solution to preserve same; keep soaked when not in use. Use about a gill of this mixture added to a gallon of boiled starch; the material, when ironed, will have that lovely crisp, fresh appearance of new goods.

USES OF SODA

Flowers may be kept fresh for a long time by putting a pinch of soda in the water.

To promptly and effectually extinguish a fire, use soda. A large package of soda should be kept in every part of any building; home, factory or elsewhere. The entire contents of the package should be thrown, in case of fire, at the base of the flames with a sweeping motion of the hand. The action of the soda on the fire is to extinguish it instantly.

NEW USE FOR A BICYCLE PUMP

A bicycle pump will clean a sewing machine when it is clogged with dust and it seems impossible to reach it with a cloth.

WASHING BLANKETS

For washing blankets, shave and melt one pound and a half of good laundry soap; strain through a colander into a tub half full of luke-warm water; add one-half pound of powdered borax and one tablespoonful of molasses; put in a double blanket and soak twenty-four hours; next morning, pat and wave them through the water, but never rub them; press the water from them and lift into a tub of clean warm water; rinse till the water is clear, using a little bluing for the last; lift them out of the water into a basket and hang in a shady, breezy place; hang *exactly* through the middle, a little full on the line.

TO CLEAN FISH

In dressing fish instead of cutting off the fins, pull them out and thus remove the short fin bones. To do this, hold the fish firmly by the tail, and with a very sharp, pointed knife cut along the sides of the fin, as closely to it as you can, to the depth of half an inch or more; then taking hold of the end of the fin nearest the tail, pull the fin out; the end nearest the head will stick and there will be a few bones which will have to be cut to release it. This is a quicker and more satisfactory way of removing the fins than cutting them off.

FOR INSOMNIA

A napkin dipped in ice cold water, wrung slightly, and laid across the eyes, will cure insomnia.

TESTING MILK

If you wish to know whether the milk has been "watered" or not, take a well-polished knitting needle and dip it in the milk; withdraw it immediately; if there is water in the milk, in the least, the needle will come out quite free of the milky fluid.

BLACK DRESSING

One spoonful sweet oil, two of black ink; mix well and apply with sponge to boots, shoes, black kid gloves and rusty book-covers.

SALT FOR MOTHS

As a preventative of moths, sprinkle dry salt among your furs, under and over fine carpets, upholstered furniture and so forth; they will give you a wide berth.

FOR DISORDERED NERVES

When you have been on a nervous strain and are at a loss what to do, and know that lying down will not bring rest, try putting something in order; it may be a room, a box, a drawer, a desk—anything which really needs having order brought out of chaos; no matter what it is, and no matter how tired you feel, go at it quietly and systematically and you will find that by the time you have restored order, you are restored yourself. I have tried this often since discovering, and hope it will benefit others as much as it has me; at any rate it is worth trying, even if nothing else is gained, for you have the satisfaction of feeling that something has been accomplished.

DEODORIZER

Equal parts of ground cloves and cinnamon. Put a hot coal on a shovel and sprinkle over it one-half teaspoonful of the mixture. This is a fine deodorizer.

FOR SMALL BATHROOM

If you are unfortunate enough to have a *very* small bathroom with no room for a permanent stand, you can have quite a good substitute by taking a board, covering it with white enamel cloth and putting across the tub.

This is very handy to hold the bowl, soapdish and so forth and can be easily removed when bathtub is needed. A cleat on under part of the board will keep it in position.

COOKIES WITHOUT SHORTENING

One cup of sugar, one and one-half cupfuls of New Orleans molasses, one teaspoonful of ginger, one tablespoonful of vinegar, four eggs, and one teaspoonful of soda. Mix as stiff as possible with flour. If the molasses is cold, warm it, otherwise enough cannot be worked in; the only possible failure with these cookies is in not getting in enough flour.

BREAD STICKS

Cut strips of bread which has risen the second time one-fourth inch wide and three inches long, and fry in deep fat till a delicate brown. Fine to serve with salad or soup.

CRISPLETS:—If the above bread sticks are dipped in a thick syrup, made by boiling a teaspoonful of cinnamon in a cup of granulated sugar till it spins a thread, they make a dainty accessory to a luncheon.

HOW TO CLEAN COMBS

The easiest and neatest way to clean a comb of dandruff, is to take a discarded booklet or pamphlet and gently, but firmly, strip the comb through the leaves.

WHEN THE BUCKET LEAKS

When a bucket leaks, wash it with hot water and soda and dry thoroughly; then take a small paint brush and some ordinary house paint and paint over the part where the hole is, afterward placing a small square of white material over the paint and pressing it well into position with the brush; when this is dry, add another piece of cloth in the same way· let the second patch dry and then give the pail a coat of paint inside and out.

TO EXTINGUISH GASOLINE FIRE

Wheat flour will quickly extinguish gasoline fire.

GERMAN WAYS OF COOKING CARROTS

Slice, parboil with a pinch of soda for five minutes, then stew in milk until done and salt to taste.

Slice, parboil with a pinch of soda for a few minutes and drain, add boiling water and, when almost done, one-third the amount of raw potatoes, sliced. Cook until done, then drain off all liquid, mash, season with salt, pepper and sweet cream or milk and butter.

HOW TO COOK BEANS

In cooking navy beans that are old, parboil with soda until skins shrivel, then drain, add boiling water and a tablespoon of vinegar, and the beans will cook done in half the time required otherwise, and be just as palatable.

GASOLINE IN THE LAMP

If the blaze pops or sputters, turn down the wick and put out the light immediately; then learn whether or not gasoline has, by mistake, been put in the bowl instead of kerosene.

SALT IN ALUMINUM

Salt will draw dampness and eat up an aluminum vessel quicker than rust will destroy iron. Keep salt out of aluminum when not in cooking use.

POTATOES FRIED IN COTTOLENE

Potatoes fried or stewed slowly in cottolene so as not to harden them, the surplus poured off when the potatoes are nice and soft, will digest easily in a stomach which will not tolerate lard at all.

CANNING BERRIES

To can berries that incline to rise to the top of can, leaving juice in bottom (especially strawberries): As soon as sealed, lay cans on their side and roll occasionally until cold, and berries will plump out and remain scattered through juice.

TURKEY FAT FOR BUTTER

I find turkey fat and fat from hens, after it has been tried, far ahead of butter in cookies.

TO MAKE HAM TENDER

To make ham nice and tender, put about one tablespoon of vinegar in the frying pan while cooking the meat.

DRY SODA FOR BUCKWHEAT CAKES

In putting soda in buckwheat cakes, mash the soda fine and put in dry; you will find this method far better than dissolving soda in water.

NAIL KEG FOR WOODBOX

A handy device for carrying wood is made from a nail keg. Two of these baskets can be made from one keg. Remove the ends and saw the hoops, leaving the keg in two halves. Fasten the ends of the hoops securely to the staves and nail a hoop across the center for a handle. If the baskets are wanted for short wood the ends might be left in.

NEWSPAPERS FOR PRESSING

Use newspapers instead of cloths for pressing trousers; they make a good substitute.

TO TINT FEATHERS, RIBBONS, ETC.

You can tint white feathers, ribbons, lace, or artificial flowers any color you choose by dipping them in gasoline to which has been added a little tube paint; use a glass fruit jar for the purpose, shaking the material in it.

TO REVIVE WILTED ROSES

Wilted roses may be completely revived and freshened by putting the stems of the roses in a tumbler of water, and then place the tumbler of roses in a vessel of sufficient size to allow the entire bouquet to be covered.
Cover the vessel tightly and leave undisturbed for twenty-four hours. By that time the roses will be found all fresh and invigorated, as if just plucked from the bushes, with every petal covered with artificial dew. Wilted lettuce may also be freshened and kept in excellent condition for weeks if treated in the same way.

A USEFUL SUGGESTION

Keep bits of cloth handy for wiping greasy dishes and skillets—it saves so much grease from the dish water.

FRESH JELLY IN WINTER

I often can fruit juices of different kinds in the summer. It is so easy then to make a glass of fresh jelly as you want it in the winter. In putting up tomatoes I like to strain some and bottle all ready for tomato soup.

TO FREE HOUSE OF COOKING ODORS

If a kitchen window is kept open two inches at the top while frying foods, boiling cabbage or other odorous vegetables, the unpleasant odor will go out of the window instead of spreading through the house.

RELIABLE RECIPE FOR PRESERVING EGGS

There is probably no method which is more simple and effective in preservation of eggs than the use of water glass (sodium silicate). Take ten quarts of water which has been previously boiled and add to it one pint of water glass. This may be placed in a jar or tub and fresh eggs added from time to time, always being careful to have at least two inches of the solution over the eggs.

STARTER FOR BREAD

Put three tablespoonfuls of granulated sugar and a compressed yeast cake into a pint of the water potatoes were boiled in. Let it rise and use two-thirds of it for your bread, keeping one-third for the next time, when it is added to potato water and the three spoonfuls of granulated sugar. If kept in a cool place you need never be out of yeast. It is much better than any of the dry yeast cakes. Do not add salt to the starter as that has caused many failures.

THE VALUE OF CHARCOAL

Charcoal has great value as an antiseptic. Smoked ham will keep for years packed in charcoal. A few lumps of it in a cistern will keep the water pure and sweet. A quantity of it in a cellar will absorb the odors, and a small lump boiled with cabbage or onions will do the same. Butter put into small vessels completely surrounded with charcoal will keep sweet a long time. A paste of powdered charcoal and honey makes a good dentrifice. It not only cleans the teeth, but disinfects them and sweetens the breath. Taken inwardly it is good for the digestion and relieves constipation.

VINEGAR TO WHITEN THE HANDS

If the housewife is troubled with rough hands, try bathing in cider vinegar after washing and rinsing free from soap, and let the vinegar dry in. This will soften and whiten the hands.

HOME-MADE FIRE EXTINGUISHER

A simple fire extinguisher may be made at home, and if kept always on hand, will sometimes prove of great value. Take twenty pounds of common salt and ten pounds of sal-ammonia (nitrate of ammonia), which can be bought at any drug store. Dissolve these in seven gallons of water. Put in thin glass bottles holding a quart each, cork tightly, and seal to prevent evaporation. When a fire breaks out, throw one of these bottles so that it will break in or near the flames, or if this is not possible, break off the neck of the bottle and scatter contents on the fire. This has been tested. Sometimes it is necessary to use several bottles.

SUGAR FOR TURNIPS

Season boiled turnips as usual, then add a tablespoonful of sugar a few minutes before serving. This makes them more palatable, removing that disagreeable strong taste, and giving them a delicious flavor.

TO STOP BLEEDING

One way of stanching the flow of blood from a cut, or other wound, given by a physician, has been found very effective. Press the thumb, finger, or fingers, upon the wound tightly. Continue the heavy pressure several minutes until the blood coagulates.

NEW CALENDARS OUT OF OLD

If handy with the paint brush, take the old calendars that are mounted on heavy boards, remove the date block from the bottom and paint the whole frame around the picture in tints harmonizing with the picture. Place a new date block on the bottom and you have a very pretty gift for a friend.

STUFFED WARM BISCUIT

Carefully remove the top from nice, large warm biscuit. Take out the center and fill the shell with creamed oysters thickened. Replace the top and put a spoonful of the dressing over the whole. Creamed chicken may be used instead of oysters, if preferred.

TO BOIL EGGS

When boiling eggs, be sure the water is boiling when you drop the eggs in, and you will have no trouble to remove the shells.

HOW TO GET RID OF ANTS

The little red ants came in multitudes into my store-room this summer. I removed the sugar pails and soaked a large sponge in sweetened water, putting it in a shallow tin where the sugar had stood. Two or three times a day I dipped it in hot water, killing quantities each time.

BASTING THREAD PULLER

An old shoemaker's awl, fixed in a convenient handle, makes the best basting thread puller.

MARKER FOR FANCY WORK

Use a crimped "invisible" hair-pin as a marker in knitting or crocheting wool yarn. It stays in place and is not in the way.

TO SAVE THE HOT WATER BAG

Before, or even after the rubber hot water bag begins to show signs of the sides sticking together, take this precaution. Drain well, then inflate the bag somewhat with the breath, and quickly screw in the stopper. The sides will be held apart, and consequently cannot stick together.

HOW TO WASH A LAMP GLOBE

In washing glass lamp globes, if they are first washed in warm soap and water, then rinsed in cold water and placed on the top of a hot range until the moisture is nearly gone, they will need very little polishing, and will be found to have a beautiful luster. The globes will not crack if first placed on the back of the range until tempered by the heat.

TO REMOVE PAINT FROM GLASS

To remove paint from glass, make a paste of saleratus moistened with water, apply with a cloth, then rub it off and rinse with clear water. Every particle will come off easily.

A CHEAP MOUSE-PROOF MORTAR

Take one cupful of wheat flour, two cupfuls of common wood ashes and boiling water enough to make a thick paste suitable to spread with a knife while warm; fill all cracks with this and the mice won't gnaw it. This makes a very good mortar in place of common lime mortar, when this falls off in little pieces.

A MOUSE TRAP

Take a good-sized thimble, fill it with cake or cheese and lay it on the side with the filled end under a bowl—a common bowl will do. Use a glass cover, then you can see the mouse. Set the bowl on the small end of the thimble as near the edge as you can get it, and when mousie goes under to nibble, down goes the bowl and he is in a trap. If you set it on a piece of board, it can be easily carried out.

CORNCOB SUGGESTIONS

Corncobs furnish the most excellent material for smoking meat.

Corncobs placed in musty syrups and the latter brought to a scalding heat will impart a palatable flavor.

Corncobs immersed in syrup and baked brown will make a change in cereal coffee.

Corncobs broken in bits and burned will make an agreeable disinfectant.

Corncobs dipped in molasses and given to cows improves their flow of milk and general condition.

OYSTER SHELLS FOR TEAKETTLE

If you are troubled with lime settling in the bottom of your kettle, just put in two oyster shells. When these are covered with lime put in new ones.

SALT FOR BEATING EGGS

A little salt added to an egg before beating it makes it very light and much easier to beat.

MATTRESS PADS

A satisfactory mattress pad may be made from a lightweight cotton blanket and four pounds of cotton. Spread the latter out between the two thicknesses of the blanket, then tie it here and there. Lastly loosely overcast it around the edges, so that it will be an easy matter to take it apart to wash the outside covering.

TO KEEP HOLDERS HANDY

On the kitchen apron put a pocket about eighteen inches from the bottom, large enough to hold the holders used about the stove when baking.

On the lower corners of the kitchen apron put pads, to be used for holders when baking.

RAIN-SPOTTED VELVET

My hat was a sight, dotted all over with tiny rain spots. I brushed it carefully the usual way with no results, then I tried brushing it against the grain and the spots all came out.

VINEGAR INSTEAD OF GLOVES

In winter weather you can hang out the weekly wash with perfect comfort if you wet your hands well with vinegar, letting it dry on before going out.

FOR DARK CELLAR

If your cellar is dark, whiten the bottom step. You will then be able to see when you reach the bottom and will thus avoid a fall.

CLOTHESPIN FOR APPLE CORER

To core apples use an ordinary clothespin. To pit cherries use a shoe-button hook.

MOLASSES AND WATER FOR ANTS

A good way to exterminate ants is by placing an oatmeal dish partly full of molasses and water where they congregate; as only one colcry of ants infests the house at a time, it is not long before that colony is exterminated by drowning. You will not be troubled until another season.

SUBSTITUTE FOR CASTOR OIL

An effective substitute for castor oil is made as follows: Take a quarter of a pound of figs and stew them slowly in olive oil; when they are swollen add honey and lemon juice to taste, and put into an earthen jar or glass. Should medicine be required by either adult or child, one fig will have the same effect as a dose of castor oil, and is much more pleasant to take. It will leave the skin clear and fresh.

SOAP SAVER

As a soap saver I take a thin cake of soap nearly used up and soak it in hot water a few moments and place it on a new cake; it soon adheres and will last as long as the rest.

TO DRY RUBBER BOOTS

When your little boy comes in with wet rubber boots, try pulling them on sticks that will stand up against the wall. In a short time boots will be nicely dried on inside. The sticks should reach nearly to ceiling where the heat is.

A NEW USE FOR SALT

Occasionally put a handful of kitchen salt in the washbowl to keep the waste pipe from filling up. That same salt if rubbed on the dirty bowl will clean it beautifully and easily.

FOR PLANTING HORSERADISH

When setting out horseradish roots put a board about six inches below the roots and your horseradish roots will be shorter and thicker and not so scraggly as is usual.

TO RID GREENS OF INSECTS

If lettuce is first put into quite warm water, the insects will come out and be found at the bottom of the water. By being transferred then to cold water, it becomes crisp and fresh. This will prove effective in cleaning all kinds of "greens."

A "SHORT CUT" IN BREAD-MAKING

Mix the bread at night in the usual proportions of warm water (or milk), salt, sugar, shortening, flour and yeast—only instead of a thin "sponge" make the mixture as thick as can be stirred with a big spoon. Beat and stir it thoroughly for five minutes, then cover it and place where it will be in no danger of chilling. Early in the morning beat it again, dip it into well-buttered baking-pans, let it rise, and bake it with the same fire that cooks breakfast. This is the entire-wheat bread which is used so much. Make white bread in the same way, except that you add a little more flour in the morning, just enough to permit the dough to be formed *very quickly* into loaves, ten minutes being ample time for four loaves. Why spend half a day over the work—wasting time and fuel—when a "short cut" leads to perfectly satisfactory results?

FRYING DOUGHNUTS

A tablespoonful of vinegar put in the hot lard before frying doughnuts will prevent their taking up the lard.

BETTER THAN A WHETSTONE

Scissors and knives can be quickly sharpened with a small fine-cut file. It is superior to a whetstone for taking the "nicks" out of knives.

POTATOES KEPT FROM ROTTING

To keep potatoes from rotting in the cellar, drop or dust dry lime among them.

POULTRY FOOD

Roast to a crisp several ears of corn and chop up to feed the hens. There will soon be a noticeable increase in the number of eggs.

A HINT TO THE LAUNDRESS

Cover scorched places with ordinary starch, dampen, lay in the sun for an hour and every vestige of scorch will disappear.

BACKGROUND FOR A COUCH

Nearly every housewife knows how soiled wall-paper behind a couch often becomes, especially where there are children. Tack a piece of fancy matting to the wall, extend the lower edge to the baseboard, and put a narrow picture-molding at the upper edge. When the pillows are arranged the effect is very pleasing.

TO TAKE STAINS FROM THE HANDS

One part alcohol, five parts lemon-juice; mix and put away in bottle; rub on the hands when they are stained from fruit or vegetables. Use before doing any fine needlework; it makes the fingers smooth so they will not fray material. It will keep indefinitely.

RELIEF FROM PRICKLY HEAT

Dissolve a tablespoonful of Epsom salts in cold water and apply to afflicted surface; it will relieve all irritation and prevent any further trouble.

GRATE LEMONS WHEN WET

If when grating lemon rind the lemon is kept wet, it will not stick in the grater.

TO REMOVE EGG STAINS ON SILVER

Salt will remove the stains from silver caused by eggs, if applied dry with a soft cloth.

TO ERADICATE PAINT STAINS

Equal parts of ammonia and turpentine will remove paint from clothing, no matter how dry and hard it may be. Saturate the spot two or three times, then wash with soapsuds.

TO FRESHEN WRINKLED SILK

To make silk which has been wrinkled and "tumbled" appear exactly like new, sponge it on the surface with a weak solution of gum arabic or white glue, and iron it on the wrong side.

FOR SALAD DRESSING

In making salad dressing mix the eggs, mustard, etc., together, but before putting in the vinegar, add a couple of tablespoonfuls of cold water so that it will not curdle.

CHOPPED INSTEAD OF GRATED CHEESE

When preparing macaroni and cheese, put the cheese through your food chopper instead of grating it. It is much quicker and easier.

SHIELD FOR A WIND-SWEPT PORCH

It may help some of the Home-makers who have a wind-swept porch to know of a simple protection for little plants, like seedling flowers or tomato or cabbage plants, which they start early in the house, transplanting when the ground gets warm enough. Make a shield of a light, foot-wide board, about three feet long, two triangular boards for braces, and three or four laths. Nail the triangular boards upright against the ends of the long board like brackets on a shelf, and nail the laths across the other side. Set the pan of little plants in the half-box thus made, on the laths, with the board up against the wind. The little plants will smile in the sunshine and the winds beat against their firm background to no purpose.

A SAFE WAY TO TAKE OUT INK STAINS

Soak the articles in quite warm water to which has been added several spoonfuls of gasoline; rub and squeeze with the hands, and wash in the usual way.

TO CLEAN A WATCH

To clean your watch, open up the face and back and immerse it in gasoline for a short time. Leave it open till the gasoline has evaporated, and then oil it with the best oil you can procure. This does not injure the watch, and the settlings in the gasoline will show that it removes dirt.

TO TOUGHEN A BROOM

Immerse the brush of the broom in boiling suds occasionally—say as often as once a week. This will prevent the broom from cutting the carpet, and will make it last longer.

NEW USE FOR A PAINT BRUSH

Try putting your frosting on the cake with a small paint brush (kept expressly for that purpose) and see if it will not lessen the work and be more satisfactory.

PICKLED APPLES

When pickling apples you will find the task much easier to put apples in a two or three gallon jar, then pour the liquid (one part vinegar to two parts brown sugar and spices) over apples, set jar in boiler of water and cook till fruit is tender.

EASIEST WAY TO REMOVE IRON RUST

The easiest, quickest and surest way of removing iron rust from white material is to place on the spot of rust a generous quantity of powdered alum and hold over the spout of the boiling teakettle; very soon the rust will disappear.

WASHING MEN'S WORKING CLOTHES

When washing men's or boys' working clothes, such as pants or coats, hang them on the line without wringing, directly from the rinse water, and they will dry nicely without being streaked.

NEW-FASHIONED MOTH BALLS

Balls of cotton dipped in oil of cedar and placed in boxes become a good moth preventive, and, unlike the old-fashioned detestable moth balls, they impart a delightfully clean and fresh odor.

AN EXCELLENT TOOTH POWDER

This can be made at home at a small cost and of sufficient quantity to last a family a year. Buy prepared chalk in bulk, and to one-eighth part of ground castile soap add seven-eighths part of the chalk, mixing thoroughly. Add a little wintergreen or peppermint essence, and fill any tooth-powder bottles or jars you have.

A "PROBABLE HISTORY"

A great many of my most appreciated gifts of last year were made by utilizing a stack of old magazines—the illustrations and advertisements. All of us who anticipate a quiet summer at home or at some as yet "undiscovered" resort, can arm ourselves with a lavish supply of magazines and "prepare for war in time of peace." The booklet, of twenty-five or fifty leaves, may be made either for a gentleman or a lady, and is called a "Probable History." Letter paper may be used if no other sort is obtainable, but the leaves from a drawing tablet are much more artistic looking. Lace together with ribbon or fasten the leaves with art clasps. If your chum is a college man or woman, use ribbon of the college colors. Cut from the magazines pictures of all sizes of boys, girls, pets, men, women and a goodly number of Cupids. If the friend for whom you make the history is especially fond of any kind of sport,—hunting, boating or other fad—have a good supply of pictures representing their particular hobby. On the cover write "Probable History" of————, giving the name in full and any hand decorations to make the cover more attractive. Then begin with the baby pictures—the first short dress, and the proud mamma showing "the little dear" off in various and sundry ways. To make the "history" seem more real than probable, if the person has brothers and sisters, put in the required number, writing fitting remarks or explanations under each picture. Step by step, always by means of well-chosen pictures, carry the subject up to college, cunningly introduce Cupid and the sweetheart days, amid a great round of gaieties, receptions, parties, dances, etc. And now comes the most delightful and realistic part of the history—they meet their fate, fall desperately in love and become engaged. The wedding pages can be made most attractive with pictures of the bride and groom under which lines from "Lohengrin" may be written, and one who is handy with paints or pen and ink can sketch in wedding-bells and other appropriate embellishments. The wedding trip and honeymoon come next, and finally they are brought home to a tiny cottage where they keep house and decide "There's no place like home," and "Two's company and three's a crowd." This is an inexpensive and a very unique gift.

AN IMPROVISED SHADE

When a subdued light is necessary in a sick room, place the handle of a palm-leaf fan in a vase and set on the table near the lamp. This is an easy and effectual shade for the patient's face.

FOR IN-GROWING TOENAILS

A correspondent of the *British Medical Journal* says of the treatment of in-growing toenails:—"I have for many years used tannin for the purpose, and do not find rest necessary. A concentrated solution (an ounce of perfectly fresh tannic acid dissolved in six drachms of pure water with a gentle heat) must be painted on the tender parts twice a day."

A SIMPLE DEODORIZER

Pieces of orangepeel if placed on a hot stove and allowed to burn to a crisp will remove any objectionable smell of cooking, besides cleansing and purifying the air in a remarkable degree.

CHEMISTRY AS APPLIED TO AN OMELET

Few housekeepers have any knowledge of the chemistry of food, and therefore do not realize that pepper and salt should not be added to an omelet until just before it is taken from the fire, when a thread of vinegar should be dropped at one side of the pan and allowed to run around the edge; thus is made an omelet famous for its tenderness, while if the salt is mixed with the eggs while they are being beaten, it serves only to toughen them. Omelets should be eaten as soon as cooked.

A "BUNNY" CLOAK FOR BABY

Instead of making the usual baby or infant's long cloak, try making the "Bunny" coat. Bind with satin ribbon one and one-half inches wide a yard square of eiderdown or material of that nature. When ready to take baby out, put on the hood as usual, and lay the little one about in the center of the square; then turn end up over feet and sides toward center, leaving loose corners at the baby's head which can be turned away from the face. Use safety-pins to secure these sides and end, and fasten a pretty rosette of same ribbon as was used for binding where the outside safety-pin comes. It is not customary to make any coat before the wee one's arrival, and later there is the dread of making a coat, but this is so simply fashioned and so easily done by hand, that the mother can do it shortly after sitting up. There is the comfort of not having to put sleeves on baby when ready to start out.

ASBESTOS ON THE RANGE

For ten cents you can buy a piece of asbestos as large as is necessary to lay over the range, and you will find it very helpful, as it keeps the range clean and will prevent food from burning or boiling over. Small sheets of asbestos are also useful to lay over or under the tins in the oven when baking, according as the oven gets too hot above or below. In hot weather lay paraffine paper over asbestos sheets and roll out cookies on them, shaping the cakes with a sharp knife, and baking without removing from the asbestos. This process requires less heat than it takes to bake in pans.

HAND-MADE TRIMMING WILL RETAIN ITS FRESHNESS

If the thread is skeined over the hand and knob of a chair, and the skein covered with boiling water, after which dry and wind again on spool. The trimming made from thread thus treated loses none of its original beauty after laundering, as is the case when made from spool direct from the store.

WHEN HOT DISH STICKS TO OILCLOTH

When a hot dish sticks to your new oilcloth, empty the dish and add hot water; keep adding as the water cools, until the dish is sufficiently heated to loosen itself.

A HELP FOR WASHING DAY

When rinsing clothes, shake the towels smooth, fold as you would to iron and run through a tight wringer; by unfolding carefully when you hang them on the line, they retain the smoothness and creases and are ready to fold and put away as soon as dry. The same is true of many coarse flat things.

MOIST CAKE

To keep cake from drying out, beat a tablespoonful of hot water with the sugar and butter; it makes it easier to beat besides keeping your cake from getting dry.

BAKED GREEN PEPPERS

Select large peppers; cut in halves lengthwise and remove seeds; rinse in cold water. Use any cold meat and chop it up with stale bread as for hash; moisten with tomato juice and season with salt, pepper and melted butter; put a thin layer on each pepper; lay in a dripping pan with a very little water; bake an hour, until done. These are delicious for any meal.

FLAT INSIDE POCKET

You will find a flat pocket on the inside of your kitchen apron very handy for handkerchief, small change and note book; being on the inside, it cannot catch on any projection and tear.

DOUGHNUTS FREE FROM GREASE

No more greasy doughnuts! And why? Because, when frying them, have a kettle of boiling water near and dip each cake instantly in and out of the hot water as you take it out of the fat; this makes the cakes keep moist longer as well as removing the extra fat.

FOUR GOOD SUGGESTIONS

1—You may save many a mealy potato by using a hatpin, instead of a fork, to ascertain when they are done.

2—Shell your peas as soon as you can after picking, whether you cook them or not, as much of their sweetness is absorbed by the pod. The same principle applies to husking corn.

3—Drain your fine china and glass dishes on a Turkish towel; by so doing, you not only save noise, but many a nick, crack and possibly a break.

4—Put a small pinch of salt in each bottle of milk for baby; the salt makes the milk digest more easily and is more strengthening.

SLIPPERY ELM BARK SALVE

Shred the bark and soak in warm water until a thick mucilage is made. Excellent for nail wounds, old sores, boils and scratches on horses; it cleans the wound and heals quickly.

FOR SUN-BONNETS

After ironing a bonnet, pin it around a gallon syrup pail and place near the stove; when dry it is round on top and fits the head.

TO DRIVE AWAY FLIES AND MOSQUITOES

A drop of oil of lavender in a small dish of water will drive away flies, and a little dabbled on one's stockings at the ankles makes it possible to sit on a "mosquito-y" piazza with comfort—a condition absolutely impossible, ordinarily, even with joss sticks or the "friendly nearness" of a cigar.

QUICKLY PATCHED OVERALLS

Rip the inside seam, lay on a generous patch and sew on the machine; re-sew the seam, and a great bugbear is easily vanquished.

STOCKING KITCHEN RUGS

Ladies, take the family's worn stockings, cut them round and round, each in one long strip, and have them made into rugs. Overalls make fine rugs, too.

CUTTING BROWN BREAD

Try cutting warm brown bread with a strong thread.

SANDPAPER FOR "SHINY CLOTH"

To remove the "shine" of wear on cloth or dress goods, use fine sandpaper and press.

FOR THE PRIMROSE

To keep a primrose in bloom, set the pot in a saucer of water; never water the soil directly and they will bloom indefinitely

TO KEEP CRANBERRIES FRESH

When they are your own growing, do not remove the chaff by winnowing; take to a cool upstairs place and stir lightly with the hand occasionally, till dry; then leave them to freeze, as it happens, and they will keep both color and flavor as long as they last.

NEW WAY TO BAKE JUICY PIES

Place half the amount of sugar used on bottom crust with a slice of bread, cut into small squares; then put in the fruit and the other half of the sugar with bits of butter on top; put on top crust. The bread will absorb the juice.

LIGHT DUMPLINGS

To insure light dumplings, drop them in the stew and leave the cove off the kettle until they are twice the size they were when dropped in; then place on the cover and boil fifteen minutes.

TO CLEAN PATENT LEATHER SHOES

Use the white of an egg to clean patent leather shoes.

FOR EMBROIDERY SILK

Wrap each skein in tissue paper, and your silk will never become rough or tangled.

IN FRYING DOUGHNUTS

Try using a spoon egg-beater to remove doughnuts from the hot grease; it is a great improvement on the fork.

AN AID TO DIGESTION

Take the lining of a chicken gizzard, scrub clean, then dry. Eat a small portion at a time, several times a day; it is most effective in the morning before breaking your fast. A lady troubled very much with indigestion found permanent relief after using two of these linings.

BLUING DISTRIBUTED EVENLY

When rinsing clothes in hard water, the bluing will distribute as evenly as in soft water, if a half to two-thirds cup of sweet milk is added—according to the amount of water.

SUBSTITUTE FOR BEESWAX

In the absence of beeswax or paraffine, sad-irons, heated by gas-flames, or otherwise, may be rendered perfectly smooth by a particle of lard on a sheet of brown paper.

REMOVING STONES FROM PEACHES

When peaches cling to the stone, cut around the peach with a knife before peeling, give it a little twist with the fingers and the peach will open withou any trouble.

RHUBARB AND FIG SAUCE

Take one package of figs and one orange or lemon, cut in very small pieces, cover with water and cook until tender; stir this into four quarts of stewed rhubarb, add sugar to suit the taste and cook until thick. Very good and rich.

CANDLE HINT

Run a wax candle several times through hot starch, which has had a pinch of salt added to it.

"CAMP" BOILED EGGS

To boil eggs when camping, boil briskly while singing the four stanzas of "My Country, 'Tis of Thee," then "Let all that breathe partake."

TO SCREEN BATHROOM WINDOWS

If you wish to screen bathroom windows, or any others, without excluding the light, paint them with the preparation made by dissolving pulverized gum tragacanth in the white of an egg for twenty-four hours. Apply to the window panes with a soft brush.

WHITE INSTEAD OF BLACK FOR SCREENS

It is not generally known, that if window-screens are painted with a thin white paint, instead of with black, as they often are, those inside the house may look through the screens the same as before, while outsiders cannot see inside.

NEW SHOES MADE WATERPROOF

Warm the soles of new shoes and while they are warm, paint them with copal varnish; when it dries, paint them again; three such coats will not only make the soles waterproof, but will make them last twice as long.

SENSIBLE SUGGESTIONS

Always pin stockings and socks on the line by the tops, as the pins help wear holes in the toes. When taking off soiled stockings, pin them together, at the top, with small safety pins, before putting them in soiled clothes bag. Wash, hang up to dry, press and darn before unpinning them; then roll them up and put away; saves time matching up stockings after mending day.

FOR THE NASTURTIUM

To make your nasturtiums bloom, pull off nearly all the leaves; they grow so large and shade the vines so, they do not bloom as well as they will if you pull off many of the leaves; also never let seed-pods form, as they stop the blooming as well.

TO PREVENT TOMATOES CURDLING

If adding milk or cream to tomatoes, add first a pinch of baking soda; it will prevent curdling in every instance.

WASHLESS CHIMNEYS

Merely breathe through lamp chimneys and polish with paper; they never require washing.

NEW RUBBERS EACH TIME IN CANNING

It is a mistake to use can rubbers the second time to save a little additional expense. Use a new rubber each time and you will be assured of success.

SALAD DRESSING WITHOUT OIL

Salad dressing without oil for potato, nut, apple or any vegetable salad:—
One egg, one teaspoonful of sugar, one teaspoonful of salt, one-fourth teaspoonful of pepper, one teaspoonful of mustard, two teaspoonfuls of flour; mix till smooth; add slowly one-half cup of boiling vinegar; let come to a boil; thin with cream till right consistency.

CURE FOR CHIGGER BITES

When suffering from bites of the "chigger," take common sulphur and vaseline and mix together and apply to affected parts; it will give almost instant relief. This remedy will relieve almost any skin irritation caused by insect bites, sun-burn, heat, etc. A small box should be in your "kit" on every trip to the woods or water.

SKIRT-HANGING MADE EASY

To turn up evenly the bottom of a skirt for hemming try this method: place the end of a yardstick on the floor close to the skirt and at the top of the stick place a pin in the skirt; move the yardstick little by little around the body, placing a pin in skirt at top edge of stick each time it is set on the floor. After going thus all around the skirt, lay it on a bed and place one end of the yardstick at the line of pins, and at the lower part of skirt, place a pin as far from the end of yardstick as desired around in this manner, then turn the hem at new line of pins and baste it. This method insures a perfect-hanging skirt and makes it possible to hang a skirt on one's own person unaided and without difficulty.

SMOKELESS LAMPS

Boil your lamp wicks in vinegar, dry them thoroughly, and your lamps will not smoke.

TO KEEP FRUIT JELLIES A LONG TIME

Fruit jellies of all kinds will keep for years, if covered with pulverized sugar to the depth of a quarter of an inch.

SLIPPER HELP

Line the back of low shoes and slippers, that slip down, with velvet, carefully pasted in.

HOT GRIDDLE CAKE HELP

Try adding a tablespoonful of melted lard to your batter for griddle cakes; also a spoonful of dark molasses; grease griddle pan for the first cakes only.

CURRANT WORMS

For worms on currant bushes, cover the ground at the base of the bushes with coal ashes

A VIRGINIA DISH

In a baking dish place alternate layers of sliced apples and sliced boiled sweet potatoes, each layer sweetened and flavored with nutmeg; add a lump of butter, pour over it a little water and bake slowly until the top is nicely browned; serve in dish in which it is baked. Delicious!

SLIP FOR SUIT-CASE

Make for your suit-case a heavy duck slip cover, neatly "boxed" like a mattress, and fastened securely with strap and buckles each side of the handle. This will keep the suit-case from being scratched and marred.

OLD-FASHIONED DYES

The more durable vegetable and mineral dye-stuffs of "ye olden time," are again coming into favor, and many lovers of fancy work will find the following hints of service, even if only used to dye carpet rags, or color Easter eggs.

YELLOW: Steep saffron in an earthen dish and use more or less to give a deep or light straw color. The dry outside skins of onions steeped as above give a richer yellow. Peach leaves when full-grown, or the inner bark and roots of the barberry, give a fair tint. A rinsing of the colored goods in weak alum water helps to set the above colors.

BROWN: White maple bark boiled in a brass kettle and a little alum added gives a light brown. Lye of wood ashes with half an ounce of copperas to the pailful boiled in it until dissolved dyes cottons a fast nankeen shade. Birch bark covered with water and boiled in brass or tin with copperas as above gives a nankeen tint; if alum is used instead of copperas, it dyes a slate. Black tea boiled in iron with copperas dyes slate. Logwood boiled in iron with cider or water and vinegar and a little copperas gives a good black. Any rusty iron boiled in vinegar with copperas makes a black dye.

LIGHT RED: In two gallons of water, boil for two hours six ounces cochineal; eight ounces logwood; four ounces fustic; six ounces tin crystals; one ounce cream of tartar. Let the material to be dyed simmer two hours. Handle with rubber gloves.

DARK RED: Boil in two gallons of water eight ounces fustic, one pound of cochineal, one pound of logwood for two hours. The material to be dyed must soak for twenty-four to forty-eight hours in a solution of five ounces of alum and five ounces of cream of tartar, boiled until dissolved. Drain the material and boil in the dye until it takes the desired shade.

ORANGE: Prepare (mordant) as above, and immerse in a boiling bath of eight quarts of water, one pound of madder and one pound of fustic. For a dark orange mordant, as above, and boil for two hours in eight quarts of water with one pound of madder, two ounces of logwood and a half pound of fustic.

YELLOW: Powdered yellow dock root, boiled in eight quarts of water.

BROWN: Boil four ounces of copperas two hours in eight quarts of water. Use while hot.

VIOLET: Boil one pound of logwood, four ounces of cochineal and one ounce of alum in eight quarts of water.

SNAKE BITE

Besides the rattlesnakes of several varieties found in some degree in every section of the Union, the moccasin, the copperhead and water moccasin of the Eastern and Southeastern states, there is but one dangerously poisonous species, the coral snake, found in the Southern states from southern Virginia to the Rio Grande. The last named is a small and slender reptile, with a black nose and rings of red and black, the black rings being bordered with narrow bands of yellow.

The bite of very poisonous snakes leaves only the punctures of two or possibly one fang, while the bite of less dangerous species show, with or without the deeper punctures, the bite of other teeth.

Recent experiments with antivenenes, that is, a serum that can be hypodermically injected into or near the wound, has shown that special serum must be prepared for each species. Therefore, if a specific serum for rattlesnake bite is desired, it can be secured at the Rockefeller Institute, New York city, of Professor Noguchi, or in Chicago. About one-third of an ounce of antivenene injected under the skin (abdomen preferred), has saved life fifteen or twenty hours after being bitten.

Where antivenene is not at hand, and indeed in any case, the first thing to be done is to prevent the absorption of the poison. If bitten on a finger, the immediate amputation of the finger is a sure defense, but when any limb is bitten, a handkerchief, necktie, small cord or shoe string must be tied around the limb between the wound and the heart, and twisted so tightly as to prevent the return of the poisoned blood to the heart. Some place several ligatures one above the other. Then the wound should be squeezed in such a way as to express as much of the venom as possible, and the fang punctures should each be enlarged by two cuts at least as deep as they have penetrated. The blood and venom may be sucked out by anyone whose mouth is unwounded, but cupping can be used in most cases. A bottle filled with boiling hot water, emptied and placed over the wound, will usually bring a flow of blood and venom, and this may be repeated frequently until satisfied that nothing but blood is drawn. A common clay tobacco pipe bowl thus heated and placed over the wound with the stem closed will "draw" very strongly.

Permanganate of potash crystals should always be kept on hand in a "snake country," as that is the great reliance in India, where myriads die yearly from snake bite. After washing the wound with clear water, use water in which permanganate of potash has been dissolved until it is of a deep wine color. Then use the antivenene, but if not at hand, rub powdered permanganate of potash into the wound, and if a hypodermic syringe can be procured, inject a strong solution of the permanganate of potash into a series of punctures surrounding the snake bite, and apply over the wound a cloth saturated with the same solution. Every half-hour the dressing should be raised and more of the solution poured over the wound.

A solution of chlorinated lime (chloride of lime), one ounce of chloride of lime to twelve ounces of water, is thus used by some physicians after an elastic constriction (an India rubber ligature) is placed above the wound. Just before being used, nine ounces of water are added, and of this weakened mixture about an ounce is injected above the bite. The gases disengaged neutralize the snake venom.

After all has been done that can be done to remove and neutralize the poison, the ligatures should be loosened by degrees, beginning first of all with those furthest from the wound and nearest the body. It will not do to long continue the stoppage of circulation, and the patient must fight out his fight for life. To maintain his vitality, use hot water bottles and hot bricks; hot drinks—water, milk, soups, beef tea, but no whiskey—should be given. If too weak to swallow, the drinks may be injected. If possible, he should walk about, but if too weak, the limbs may be rubbed. Alternate applications of hot and cold wet compresses to the spine, or a wet sheet rub and hot baths have been used to good effect.

The wounds should be kept open by bits of sterilized gauze, and frequently dressed with the permanganate solution for several days. After that time, it may be allowed to heal by the end of a week, but it is not unlikely that for months after a bite from a mountain rattlesnake, the patient will feel a twinge or two of pain to remind him of the great ophidian.

It should be said that the general consensus of experts condemns the free use of whiskey as an antidote for snake bites, nor does there seem to be a confident belief in the healing power of the snake's skin or small chicken split open and used as a plaster on the wound.

OLD-FASHIONED MOLASSES CANDY

Take equal quantities of brown sugar and Porto Rico molasses, boil and skim well, and if necessary, strain it; then boil until a few drops poured into cold water are brittle and do not stick to the teeth when bitten. Pour out on a well-greased stone slab or shallow dish, and, as it cools, turn the edges in upon the centre until the whole mass is cool enough to handle. Flour the hands and work until a bright golden color, then pull into sticks and cut to length. Sprinkle plates with powdered sugar and between the sticks of candy, if piled on each other, to prevent sticking together. A little oil or essence of peppermint, anise, cinnamon or clove may be added to a part of the candy, and pulled only enough to incorporate the flavor. Good molasses, if sweet enough, may be used without the sugar, as above, but will need more "pulling" and will not look so bright.

White Chewing Candy: Boil very carefully until the cooled syrup cracks like glass, one and a half pints of golden syrup and two and a half pounds of white moist sugar. When poured out to cool, work in any flavor, and pull until white.

Corn Balls: Boil one quart of molasses, as above, until it is only waxy when dipped in water. Have one-half bushel of corn nicely popped and free of hard kernels, and laid several inches thick in a dripping-pan. Add to the molasses candy one-half cup of thick gum arabic solution made the night before, stir well and pour over the corn, lifting it up and mixing it as you go; then with your hand slightly buttered, roll the balls into shape, or with a knife cut into squares to be broken apart when set. Brown or white sugar may be used instead of molasses, adding a cupful of water before boiling. The proportions given should make eight or nine dozen balls.

Nut Candy: Before cracking pecans or walnuts for making candy, pour boiling hot water over them the night before and let them soak all night. In the morning or the next evening, they will crack easily and leave most of the kernels unbroken. Old-fashioned molasses candy filled full of walnut or pecan kernels is a dainty for a king, and all kinds of "fudge" should be filled with nut meats.

Fig Cheese: Take good figs, dip in boiling hot water to soften, flatten and split, laying the halves skin down on a slab or tin, sprinkled with powdered sugar, inside a tin ring the size and depth of the cheese. Sprinkle the first layer thickly with chopped nuts and cover with another layer of split figs, and alternate

LITTLE HELPS FOR HOME-MAKERS

thus, until the forms are full. Sprinkle with confectioner's sugar, and press the cheese under a weighted board over night. When served, cut like a pie or tart.

Nut and Fig Strips: Butter thinly some rolled-out pie crust and strew with a paste of equal parts of dried figs and nuts. Cover with a thin crust. Cut into strips and bake in a quick oven.

ARTIFICIAL HONEYS

People living out on the ranches and farms of the Northwest, where fruit is not plentiful, will find these preparations harmless and toothsome:

Sugar, ten pounds; water, three pounds; Bent's cream of tartar, two ounces, or in like proportion. Dissolve the sugar in luke-warm water, add the cream of tartar, a wine-glass of vinegar and the well-beaten white of an egg. Continue to stir until the sugar is nearly melted, add one-half pound of genuine honey, if it can be had, and stir until boiling for a few moments. Take it off and when only fairly warm, strain and stir in two tablespoonfuls of extract of rose, or half a teaspoonful of white rose or honeysuckle perfume. This is a very fair and perfectly harmless imitation of honey.

Or: Make a syrup of four pounds of sugar and a pint of water; boil and add one-fourth ounce powdered alum. When thoroughly dissolved, remove and add one-half ounce of cream of tartar, and when nearly cold, a little extract of rose or honeysuckle as above.

ARTIFICIAL JELLIES

Dissolve in one pint of water one-fourth ounce of alum, and when boiling, dissolve four pounds of sugar and strain while hot. When nearly cold, flavor to taste with lemon, strawberry, raspberry or any other desired flavor. While it is not honest to sell this for "fruit jelly," it is wholesome and palatable, and resembles fruit jellies so closely that few can detect the difference. When people crave a sauce for their food, these are cheap substitutes for the real thing.

RHUBARB WINE

Express the juice from any amount of rhubarb stems, using a clean clothes wringer for the purpose. Strain and to each gallon of the clear juice add one gallon of water, in which seven pounds of sugar have been dissolved. Let this mixture stand in a keg or barrel, laid on the side and unstoppered, keeping it filled with sweetened water until it works clear; then bottle or barrel tightly as you desire. The wine is a beautiful straw-colored sherry, and is superior to most purchased wines.

Another Recipe: Pour one gallon of boiling water on four pounds of stalks cut fine, and four pounds of brown or white sugar, with a little bruised cinnamon, allspice, cloves and nutmeg. Cover and let it stand one day, strain, let it work until clear and bottle for use.

FLOWER SALVE

Melt together new unsalted butter and clear mutton tallow, one-fourth of a pound each, and simmer slowly in the mixture a handful each of leaves of sweet clover, live-forever and camomile and the inner bark of sweet elder. When the leaves and bark grow crisp, press and strain out the menstruum, and add to it enough beeswax to form a thin salve. Spread very thin on thin cloth for burns, frost-bites, eczema, heat blisters, etc. If no other ingredient can be had, the green inner bark of the elder alone will furnish a most grateful and delicate salve.

GINGER CORDIAL

Bruise well one ounce of Jamaica ginger root, and macerate for one week in one quart of full-proof chemically pure alcohol, with five grains of cayenne pepper and one-fourth ounce of citric acid; filter or strain well. Add to one gallon of boiling water two pounds of white sugar, and when cold, put in the other ingredients, strain or filter and bottle for use. Taken hot for a bad cold or stomachic pains, it is very effective in easing pain and promoting perspiration.

HONEY CORDIAL

To one gallon of boiling water add three and a half pounds of honey. Boil in a pint of water, the peel of half a lemon, one-fourth ounce of ginger, a bit of mace and a few cloves. Strain and add to the other mixture. When quite cool, add a teaspoonful of yeast, and leave the jug uncorked until the fermentation is over. Bottle and keep as long as possible before using.

TO REMOVE GLASS STOPPERS

Warm the mouth of the bottle, and with a feather brush a little sweet oil about the stopper, letting it stand near the fire, and from time to time trying, not too harshly, to remove the stopper. When warm, strike the stopper gently with a small wooden mallet or ruler, first on one side and then on the other. Add more oil from time to time, and continue as before, until the stopper is loosened.

FIRE-PROOF PAINT

Take six quarts of slaked lime, one quart of rock salt, four quarts of water, boil and skim clean; then dissolve four ounces pulverized alum, two ounces sulphate of iron, three ounces potash; add one pound fine sand, or marble dust. Add any desired coloring matter, and apply with a brush. It will dry hard, stop small leaks and resist any ordinary shower of cinders and brands.

FREEZING MIXTURE

Where ice cannot be obtained, water or wine may be cooled by the use of freezing powders. The first is composed of one ounce of sal ammonia and two ounces of saltpeter, both of which must be finely powdered, intimately mixed, and kept in stoppered bottles. The other powder consists of three ounces of powdered soda, also kept separately in stoppered bottles. When used, put the liquid to be cooled in a glass bottle, wrap it in a woolen cloth, dissolve the two powders in just enough cold water to dissolve them, and pour the mixture upon the wrapping, placing the bottle in a jar or crock that will contain the bottle, wrapping and mixture. A pint and a half of the mixtures and the water in which they are dissolved, should cool two bottles of water, wine or milk in the hottest weather.

FRUIT WINES

Cherries, currants, gooseberries, wild cherries, raspberries, blackberries and elderberries make good wines. Express the juice, then pour an equal quantity of boiling water on the pressed fruit, let it stand from two to four hours, strain and add to the juice. Add one pound of sugar to each quart of juice, and keep in unstoppered vessel or barrel, with gauze over the mouth, until it works clear. Then bottle or bung for keeping and use. Tomato juice needs no water and makes a highly colored wine. White currants require less sugar, and give a very clear and delicate wine. All fruit should be dead ripe and the sugar should be added before fermentation. Wild grapes give the best-bodied wines.

CHEAP PAINT FOR FENCES, ETC.

Dissolve in four quarts of water one-half pound of sal soda, and when boiling, add gradually one pound of gum shellac. When cold this will blend with any good paint in equal quantities. Cover surface well, and it will wear well and considerably reduce the cost. This was patented years ago, and large sums were paid for the right to make and sell it.

Old paints and paint skins, if soaked in the sal soda and water for two or three days, and then boiled and strained, may be restored to good condition, adding more oil and drying fluid, if necessary.

FAINTING FITS

Loosen all the clothes and lay the patient's head lower than the feet. Where men are treated in the public service, they are sometimes simply held up by the feet for a few seconds to determine the blood to the head, an effectual, if rough remedy. Dash cold water in the face. Hold hartshorn salts to the nostrils. A burned feather is sometimes used when this is lacking. A hot bath to the feet is also effectual. If persistent, a doctor should be called.

EARACHE

Pains in the ears are frequently the symptoms of nasal or neuralgic troubles, which must be cured by regular treatment, regimen and diet. Oftentimes, however, simple home remedies will ease or drive away the local pains, and a few of these have been proven for generations. Among them are:

Hot applications to the outer ear include: Flannel bags filled with hot salt; hot steeped hops, or camomile flowers; hot water bags, compresses, or warm soapstones or irons.

Applications to the inner ear include: The heart of a roasted onion or fig; cotton pledgets wet with a mixture of warmed sweet oil and laudanum, or either alone, warm steam or tobacco smoke guided into the ear by a funnel.

The use of electrical or manual massage is often of benefit when the pain is local and of a nervous origin. Rest and warm applications will generally effect a cure, and if brought on by cold, the ears should be filled with cotton for a day or two to prevent a return.

CARE OF THE EYES

It is not well to use eyewaters and crude remedies on such a delicate organ as the eye. Cold or warm water, milk or tea may be used to cleanse and soothe an ordinary inflammation. Foreign bodies are often removed by overlapping one eyelid over the other, or by turning the eyelid inside out over a knitting needle or clean toothpick. If the foreign body is not imbedded, it can easily be removed with a wet handkerchief or, what is better, a camel's hair paint brush. The tip of the tongue is largely used by mechanics, who frequently suffer from small and sharp metallic filings, etc.

When a large factory is near at hand, there will often be found a workman, whose constant practice in removing such objects make him more skilful than most physicians, even when a sharp particle is imbedded in the eye.

THE EYELASHES

If the tips of the eyelashes are carefully trimmed once a month, they will grow longer and thicker.

SWEET PICKLE FOR MEAT

To each four quarts of water, add one and a half pounds salt, one-half pound sugar or molasses, one-half ounce saltpeter, one-half ounce potash, boil together and skim off all impurities; then pour into a barrel or vat to cool. Cut up the meat, sprinkle lightly with salt and let it stand a day or two before pickling. Pack in a barrel or vat and pour the pickle over it. Let it stand for four or five weeks, turning the meat over once or twice, so that the upper and lower layers change places.

SOFT SOAP

Take one pound of bar soap and dissolve it by boiling in a gallon of water, adding one-fourth pound of sal-soda. When well mixed, pour into a jar and let it cool.

TRANSPARENT TOILET SOAP

Dissolve in one quart denatured alcohol, three pounds of good soap cut into shavings, heat slowly in a tin or copper kettle until dissolved. Add one-half ounce of any perfume desired, pour into pans to about the depth of an inch and a half, and when cold, cut into squares or pour it into small tin moulds if desired.

CHARRED FENCE POSTS

If posts are charred at a fire or covered with coal tar, as far as they are to be set in the ground, they will defy dry or wet rot for many years.

TO DESTROY WEEDS

Slake ten pounds of lime in ten gallons of water, add two pounds of flour of sulphur, and boil together in an iron kettle. When cold and settled, draw off the clear liquor and sprinkle freely on weedy walks and drives. It will destroy all vegetable life and for some time prevent its recurrence.

CLEANING AND POLISHING MIXTURE

Mix one-eighth ounce of prepared chalk and one ounce of aqua-ammonia, and keep closely corked. To clean and polish smooth jewelry apply with a cloth, and rub dry with chamois leather or old silk. Use a brush to apply the mixture to rough and broken surfaces. Shake well before using.

BUTTERMILK COSMETIC

Buttermilk applied often to the hands and face is one of the best and safest cosmetics known. It may be warmed but not boiled. If some scraped horseradish is added to the buttermilk, the mixture, strained after standing eight or ten hours, will remove freckles. Taken as a drink it is good to increase flesh, and is of value in kidney complaint.

WHITE HOUSE STUCCO WHITEWASH

This celebrated wash, formerly used on the east end of the President's mansion at Washington, D. C., has been known to retain its brilliancy for from twenty to thirty years. It is probably, all things considered, the cheapest and most effective coloring mixture used on buildings.

Slake one-half bushel of carefully chosen lime with boiling water, covering the tub or box to keep in the steam. Strain the liquid wash, and add one peck of salt dissolved in water. Three pounds of rice or rice flour, boiled to a thin paste and stirred in boiling hot, one-half pound of Spanish whiting, one pound of clean glue, also dissolved. Add five gallons of hot water to the whole, mix well and let it cool and stand for several days, carefully covered from the dirt.

When used, it must be applied hot, and the main supply kept in a kettle on a portable furnace or kerosene stove. It is most effective as a brilliant and glossy white, but may be tinted to suit.

Coloring matter should be dissolved in denatured alcohol and stirred in for the whole job at once. Spanish brown will give a reddish-pink. Yellow ochre or chrome yellow give pretty shades of that color. Green does not work well, spoiling both the wash and the color.

TO DRIVE AWAY RATS

Stop their holes with cement, first putting into their runways Scotch snuff, cayenne pepper or wet potash, or leave one or more of the holes open, but treated in like manner. They will soon leave the house.

ANTI-RUST FOR FARM MACHINERY

Take one pound of fresh tallow, one-half pound of rosin, melt and strain, and keep in a jar or tin. Warm and apply a thin coat to machinery, tools, etc., when stored for the winter.

MOTH BAGS

With two ounces of powdered orris root, mix one ounce each of cinnamon, cloves, nutmeg, mace, camphor and caraway seed. Fill little flannel bags and place them among the goods to be protected.

WHISKEY GLUE

Fill a bottle two-thirds full of good glue with cheap whiskey. Cork tightly and set in a moderately warm place for some days. It will not spoil, and is always ready for use, although in very cold weather it may be well to set the bottle in warm water before using.

FIRE KINDLER

Melt together any quantity of resin, adding to each pound of resin eight ounces of tallow or paraffine wax, and when fluid and hot, stir in as much pine sawdust or finely chopped straw as it will take. Pour it out while hot on boards covered with sawdust, or on greased sheets of iron, and when cold, cut into inch squares, each of which will ignite readily from a match and start any wood fit to burn.

A GOOD WHITEWASH

Dissolve two ounces of white glue in cold water over night, and pour into one gallon of boiling water into which stir four pounds of whiting. When thoroughly mixed, add sufficient warm water to thin it properly. Apply with a common whitewash brush.

FARMERS' PAINT

To four ounces of freshly slaked lime reduced with skim milk to the consistency of cream, pour the balance of four quarts of skim milk and ten pounds of fine whiting. Stir thoroughly to a smooth paint, and apply with a brush. It will be found insoluble when dry, and better than white lead paint for outdoor use.

RICE PAINT

Boil rice or rice flour until a thin gruel is formed. Strain and add to the hot solution air-slaked lime pulverized and sifted until a smooth whitewash is formed, and add to each four gallons one quart of linseed oil. When cold, apply like other paints on outdoor or inside work. It has been used on sea and land, and stands the test of time and weather.

PRAIRIE WHITE PAINT

Mix your whitewash with skim milk from the separator, instead of water, and paint your fences, sheds and barns. After proving this, you will use it on your house. The lime makes the cheesy constituents of the milk insoluble when dry, giving an extra hardness and gloss to the wash. It may be tinted if desired.

LIQUID GLUE

Dissolve one ounce of tragacanth in soft water, also three ounces of good clean glue; mix and add enough soft water to make six ounces, and stir in one ounce of commercial acetic acid. If not thick enough, add a little more glue.

POISON ANTIDOTES

Generally speaking, an emetic should be taken. The best and most easily procured is made by mixing two tablespoonfuls of made mustard with a pint of warm water. Tickling the throat with a feather or the fingers will often save life, where other emetics are not procurable. Draughts of warm milk or water mixed with oil, melted butter or lard are also of service.

Arsenic: After severe vomiting, administer lime water, chalk and water, and, if procurable, the hydrated sequi-oxide of iron.

Alkalies, Soda, Potash, Ammonia: Give vinegar, lemon or lime juice and water, olive oil, almond oil, butter, etc.

Corrosive Sublimate: Give white of egg and water, milk and cream, decoction of cinchona, infusion of galls.

Sulphate of Copper (Blue Vitriol): Sugar and water, white of egg and water.

Antimony, etc.: Warm milk, gruel and barley water, infusion of galls, infusion of cinchona.

Nitrate of Silver: Drink freely of warm water and salt.

Sulphate of Zinc: Carbonate of soda in warm milk and water, gruel, flaxseed or slippery elm bark tea, etc.

Acetate of Lead: Emetics, sulphate of soda in water, white of egg and water, warm milk.

Opium, Morphine, Laudanum, Paregoric, etc.: Emetics followed by strong black coffee, dashing cold water on the face and breast, forcing patient to walk and keep awake, slapping with towel dipped in cold water, electric massage.

Prussic Acid: Hartshorn and ammonia cautiously held to the nostrils, ammonia in repeated small doses in water, small doses of solution of chlorine in water, small doses of chloride of lime in water. This subtle and dangerous poison may be taken by eating peach pit kernels, drinking Eau de Noyau and eating or drinking preparations flavored with synthetic "bitter almonds" or benzine, which is a most dangerous preparation in the laboratory or the kitchen.

Strychnine and other Alkaloids: Infusion of gall nuts, decoction of cinchona, emetics.

A LASTING PERFUME

In one-half pint of alcohol dissolve one drachm of ambergris, one drachm of civet, three drachms of oil of lavender, three drachms of oil of bergamot, one-fourth ounce of camphor; cork and shake well for ten days, then strain and bottle for use.

TANNING DEER SKINS

Remove the hair by liming the skin, putting each deer skin in a bucket of water in which one quart of lime has been slaked, and let soak three to four days. Rinse until clean, scrape off the hair and grain; soak in clear water to remove the gelatine, and scour and pound in good soapsuds for half an hour. Dissolve a tablespoonful each of white vitriol, alum and salt for each skin in just enough water to cover them, and let them stand for twenty-four hours; wring dry and spread on one-half pint of currier's oil, or some fresh butter, and hang in the sun for two days. Scour out the oil with soapsuds and dry in the sun; then pull and work each skin until it is soft; if not soft the first time, scour out in suds, working in yellow ochre with a stiff brush. Sheepskins may be worked in the same way.

HUNTING

In shooting cranes, swans, geese, ducks plover, etc., it is far better to manage so as to have them fly near the gunner than to tramp in search of them and chance shots. All birds of passage have favorite haunts or feeding grounds at the several points where they alight on their way from North to South in the fall, and from South to North in the spring. These should be studied by every fowler who expects to vary his food or earn a few dollars by his trusty double-barrel.

A good supply of decoys should be made at odd seasons, and outline decoys are the easiest to make, to carry and handle. Having made a good outline of a goose, duck or plover, a dozen of each can be secured and during the winter painted like the originals and fitted with pegs or wires for feet. If they are painted even approximately like the real bird, they will do good service, but it may be said that much better work will be done if the decoys are first painted white, and allowed to dry before the next darker color is laid on and shaded into the white. The darkest or most pronounced color should be left until the last. If it is desirable to have floating decoys, make a triangular grating of wood with holes into which the legs of the decoys may fit tightly, and arrange these so that they seem to be resting naturally, as a flock lit on the water.

If there is a point where birds feed, and the wind blows toward it, float the decoys near it, or arrange them along its margin and have a natural-looking cover or "blind" not further than half-gunshot from the decoys.

If an expert at "calling," use a call, but if not, let the decoys and the feeding ground attract the coming flock, and trust to the wind to sweep them a little nearer than they would ordinarily venture. Keep out of sight until at the moment of firing, and fire rather farther ahead of your birds than drag on your aim and shoot behind them.

If you find birds already "haunted," don't shoot at them if you intend to put your decoys out at that place. Walk up quietly, let them fly away quietly, and get ready to receive them when in smaller flocks they fly back again.

Where black ducks haunt along the Atlantic coast, there are a number of small springs and pools near the harbors, to which they fly to drink after feeding on the flats. By watching at these pools in the fall evenings, many have been killed by the expert gunners of the past. One and sometimes two ducks always come in first to see if the coast is clear. If these are shot or frightened away, there will be no more of their comrades seen that night. The wary old Bayman used to keep perfectly still and out of sight until the drakes and their companions were gone, and erelong often saw the pool so full of ducks that a score or more were killed at a discharge.

Sandhill cranes are best decoyed amid the cornstalk piles of a great cornfield. They are very good eating. Green decoys will do almost anywhere, but the best prairie cover is a pit about thirty inches deep and wide by sixty inches long, dug in the ground.

Grain-eating birds can be fed to advantage by strewing corn or wheat every day at some point easily approached under cover. Many black ducks, mallards and teal are thus taken in some localities.

SHEEPSKIN MATS

Take long-wooled handrana skins and make a strong suds with hot water, but do not wash the skins until it is cold, getting out all the dirt in the wool. Then wash out the soap with clean cold or lukewarm water. They may now be dyed with Diamond Dyes or other methods. Dissolve in hot water one-fourth pound each of alum and salt for each skin, and pour into a tub containing cold water, enough to cover the skins; let them soak twelve hours, drain and dry. While still a little damp, sprinkle on the flesh side of each skin about an ounce each of saltpeter and alum, rubbing it well in; then lay the flesh sides of two skins together and hang in the shade for two or three days until perfectly dry. Then scrape the flesh side with a blunt knife and rub it smooth with a piece of pumice stone.

WELL-SET TABLES

Nothing so pleases one's guests as to be received at a table not only laden with good things, but tastefully arranged and originally decorated. Thus a Hallowe'en lunch served at a table decorated with tiny peanut owls perched on sprays of autumn foliage, lit by bright candles set in pine-cone candlesticks and by Jack-o'-lantern imps with pumpkin faces, with napkins stencilled with medieval witches, and black cats and wizards glaring at one from the cards and favors, is always a source of pleasure and a pleasant memory.

Thanksgiving suggests a table whose size and array of snowy napery, choice china, silver and steel, permits little decoration during the early courses. The dining and dessert knives and forks, the spoons and glasses are all in place, as are the spoon ladles, slicers, etc., to be used by the host and hostess. The Blue Points, daintily iced with a slice of lemon, if served instead of soup, are already awaiting each guest and the fish comes on in due season, if it comes at all at a Thanksgiving dinner. To most of us the great turkey, with his gaily colored attendant dishes of celery, turnip, white and sweet potatoes, crisp celery and glowing cranberry jelly, leaves little room for special decoration. The favors and cards may remind one of old Colonial days, or bear scme hearty greeting or jovial welcome to enjoyment and good fellowship, and old-fashioned flagons, pitchers or dishes may break the ordonnance of modern table equipage; but until the dessert comes in, beauty must yield place to the bounty and good living of the day. Then, indeed, ancient candlesticks with shades of autumn leaves, low cutglass dishes or high vases with rare flowers, epergnes laden with gorgeous fruits, delicious confections and exquisite cakes and tartlets, can make up a picture worthy of the day and the era which brings together from the ends of the earth the luxuries of every clime.

The round tables now in use are often set for breakfast with a drawn-work cloth, whose corners barely touch the rim of the board. A square serviette under each plate is flanked by the napkin and forks on the left, and the spoons, etc., on the right. Where there is no maid, the grapefruit or melon is already in place, and the hostess serves the coffe , the host serving the cereal and breakfast dish in due course. A low glass dish in the centre has a wire mesh cover, through which the short stems of the flowers reach the water, allowing great taste and originality in their arrangement.

At a family dinner, the table is fully draped, and a dish of fruit replaces the flowers. The soup, vegetables and the dessert are served by the hostess, the host carving and serving the other vegetables.

A luncheon table recently arranged in New York for four guests was crossed by two bands of ferns in the centre, of which the flower bowl glowed with colors in accord with the color-scheme of the room. On the right of each plate were glasses and knives; on the left, the forks and spoons; and the plate bore an unfolded serviette and a roll.

An evening dinner, at which skilled waiters serve every course, is often a mass of flowers, epergnes, vases, candlesticks, etc., in the centre, around which the plates and their equipage are arranged like a converging army, each pushing forward into the glittering maze in the centre, a phalanx of exquisite goblets and glasses. Just now it appears that the real artist avoids regularity in his central scheme of shape and color as much as possible, and vases, candelabra and gay shades are placed in little coteries here and there.

A novelty for the Christmas dinner table is made by opening the shells of walnuts with a knife, taking out the meats and fastening the shells together again after inserting some tiny toy, witty couplet, weird prophecy or the like. A little mucilage fastens them, and a green paper seal at the large end makes it impossible to tamper with them, unless these are torn. Every guest should be made to display his or her prize, and the variety of small objects that can be used insures lots of fun.

It is suggested that raisins, figs, dates and other dried fruits when used for dessert, should be rinsed in boiling hot water and dried in a napkin before being sent to the table, not only for sanitary reasons, but because the lyes, sulphur fumes, etc., used to cure the fruit are no addition to the taste of these dainties.

WINTER ECONOMY AND COMFORT

In the late fall, it is time to prepare for cold weather, to put on the double windows and storm doors, and make other preparations to save fuel and economize warmth. Not everyone has the means to furnish the extra windows and doors in a home of his own, and many rent houses whose owners will make no improvements and few if any repairs. Much may be done with little money to make up for these deficiencies.

To Tighten Old Windows: If the windows rattle in the casing, wedge them tightly with pieces of the thin end of a shingle; then procure some strips of strong paper to match the paint, an inch and a half to two inches wide. Make some flour paste (by the recipe on page 247,) and be sure to have it smooth and rather thick. Wet the strips quite thoroughly with the paste, and neatly cover every joining between the casing and the inner frame, as well as that at the junction of upper and lower frames. Don't tighten all the windows; leave the lower or upper half of one for ventilation and airing, but if most of the windows of an old house are thus tightened, it will make a great difference in the consumption of fuel and the amount of comfort secured.

To Tighten Doors: It is often necessary to go over the doors of a house that have swelled, and need a little trimming and shaving to fit properly. Sometimes the threshold is so worn that a mouse can easily run in and out under the door. A new well-fitting sill should be at once put in, and will more than pay for itself in coal-saving. When the doors fit loosely, and the housekeeper does not feel able to pay for rubber weather strips, she can supply their place with various substitutes tacked on the inner edge of the door itself, so that enough of the strips of material used is bent in between the door and jamb, when it is closed to prevent any draught of air. Very thick woolen cloth, old felt hats and boots, strips of sheepskin with the wool on, green baize—any of these may be used according to the width and shape of the crack to be closed. There are many people who allow the outer doors of a house to become so ill-fitting that it is almost impossible to keep the rooms near them warm in a winter storm. Make them tight for all winter, and don't wait until a storm comes, and you have to put a rug across the threshold to keep the snow out.

To Bank Up a House: Many people bank up their houses with seaweed, sedge, barn refuse, etc., but the best banking is paper. Take good tarred sheathing paper and fasten the upper edge to the baseboard of the house, with laths and lath nails, allowing the lower ends to bend outward at the ground and fit the paper well against the wall, breaking joints well and covering the lower edge with sods or earth. If you can build a sod wall against this up to the edge of the paper, or pile sand or earth against it, you will have a perfect protection against mud or frost, keep your house paint clean and can use the paper for several successive years. Any other material may be used for banking, but earth or sods is the best. Care should be taken to close up the openings under platforms and piazzas; very often there are openings clear under the sills of the house that keep the floors cold the winter through.

LITTLE HELPS FOR HOME-MAKERS

Unfinished Attics: Very often a roomy attic, or even a part of the chamber remains unfinished for years, making the house cold and a source of annoyance to the housekeeper, who longs for finished rooms, but somehow never feels able to afford the cost of finishing them. Where a room is lathed but not plastered, it can be nicely finished by pasting the tough mottled building paper used on outside walls over the lathing of walls and ceilings. Be sure and use thick strong paste, and lay the paper on the table and thoroughly wet it with hot water, taking off the excess with a sponge; then paste thickly and fit to the wall, overlapping the edges about half an inch. It will dry as smooth and hard as a board, and is superior to plaster in a cold or very hot climate, for it is the poorest conductor of heat known. Any wall paper may be put on over it when once thoroughly dried, and will look just as well as on the most costly plaster wall.

Where an attic is unfinished, paste the building paper between the rafters, having first stained, painted or covered the rafters to suit the taste. The chimneys and partitions may be papered or painted, and if the rafters run unbroken to the roof, finish them to the ridgepole. It is better, however, to have a light ceiling thrown across, above the top of the end windows, and to cover this to match the rest of the room, which will be as warm as if plastered, and if the paste used has a proportion of glue in it and dries thoroughly, will not be greatly affected by an ordinary leak. This finish has been proved in the Northwest by years of trial by temperature over fifty degrees below freezing and terrible blizzards.

USES FOR AMMONIA

To clean brushes put a teaspoonful of ammonia in a quart of water, wash your brushes and combs in this, and all grease and dirt will disappear; rinse, shake and dry in the sun or by the fire.

Keep nickel, silver ornaments and mounts bright by rubbing with a woolen cloth saturated with ammonia.

Equal parts of ammonia and turpentine will remove paint from clothing, even if it be dry and hard. Saturate the spot as often as necessary and wash out with soapsuds.

One teaspoonful of ammonia in a teacupful of water will clean gold or silver jewelry.

A few drops of clear ammonia poured on the under side of diamonds will clean them immediately, making them very brilliant.

A few drops in a cupful of warm water, applied carefully, will remove spots from paintings and chromos.

Ammonia inhaled will often relieve a severe headache.

White kid shoes can also be cleaned by dipping a perfectly clean white flannel cloth in a little ammonia and then rubbing the cloth over a cake of white soap. After doing this, rub the soiled places gently and they will be white again. As the flannel becomes soiled change for a clean one.

RENOVATING, REPAIRING AND PRESERVING BOOKS, PRINTS AND WATERCOLORS

Books, prints, maps, etc., cost a great deal of money, but are less intelligently cared for, and repaired than any other household possessions. One reason for this is the difficulty of finding workmen who can do this class of repairing, and even in large cities extortionate charges are made by the few experts in the business. As a result millions of dollars worth of valuable and indeed almost priceless books are allowed to fall to pieces until they become an eyesore to the dainty housekeeper, and are consigned to the stove or the dustman.

The following directions will enable the patrons of the National Magazine to put into complete repair, and creditable condition most of their literary and artistic treasures, unless valuable books have reached a condition that can only be remedied by rebinding.

THE CARE OF BOOKS

Leather bindings deteriorate rapidly in overheated libraries and especially when gas is used for lighting. A very little vaseline rubbed in with a soft cloth should be applied at least three times a year. A very little olive oil on the hinges will keep the leather from cracking. Be sure and don't saturate the leather or you will stain it.

Books should never be closely packed on the shelves or piled upon one another. If the air cannot circulate between them and there is any moisture in the air, they will surely mildew or "fox" which means the formation of dry brown patches which break away in time.

To prevent mildew, go over the covers very gently with a soft brush dipped in alcohol, or in some essential oil as clove, neroli or cinnamon. Book worms, not the human kind, may be destroyed by keeping in the closed presses a saucer containing a little benzine. The vapor will destroy both the insects and their larvae and eggs.

To preserve libraries and public records against insect foes it is recommended:

That no wood be used in binding, or, if it can be avoided, in shelves and cases, and when used, to finish it in oil or lac varnish.

To use laths one inch apart or wire netting instead of solid wood in making bookshelves.

To remove all wafers and paste from papers kept in drawers or cover the same with lac varnish.

To air and dust books frequently.

To use glue mixed with alum instead of flour paste.

To brush over calf bound books with thin lac varnish.

A saucer of quicklime kept in a press or drawer will absorb humidity and prevent mildew.

Vellum bindings or deeds may be cleansed by gentle sponging with benzine.

Mildew once present can only be thoroughly dried out and the book kept from further damage in a strictly dry case.

RENOVATING AND REBINDING

A valuable old book which has lost its back and hinges should by all means go to the skilled binder; direct him to save the old sides and to match the new back to the old lettering, coloring and tooling if possible. Don't let him cut down the margins any more than is absolutely necessary; many a valuable book has been ruined in appearance and lessened in value by some workman who did not realize the value of broad margins.

Less valuable volumes may be greatly improved by amateur treatment; the first process being of course to cleanse the old leather coverings.

One part of muriatic acid to six of water will remove the ink spots. Then rinse thoroughly in cold water. Take out grease spots with a soft cloth and benzine or ether; or hold a hot flat-iron near but not touching the stain.

When cleansed, if there are white spots left on the leather, it may be stained to match the original shade. Grease or wax spots are removed by holding a hot iron near but not on them; or by gentle "dabbing" with a soft cloth or cotton ball dipped in ether or benzine.

When the corners or edges are broken or frayed, brush in some good clean glue and allow it to become "tacky." Then hammer the corners or edges into shape and bring the broken leather into place; see that all holes and cracks are filled up, wipe clean, and dry thoroughly. When stiff and hard, brush off any dust and sponge over with the beaten yolk of an egg, and when dry polish with a clean hot iron.

Or instead of the egg apply brown or ox-blood boot polish with a soft woolen pad; brush thoroughly with a clean boot or clothes brush, and finish with a soft duster or velvet pad.

Black Calf Bindings: can be renovated with book-binder's varnish to which Brunswick Black thinned down with spirits of turpentine to the required shade is added in the proportion of about one teaspoonful of the varnish to twenty of the black tint. Apply with a soft brush or sponge, and dry out of reach of the dust.

To Re-Gloss Fine Bindings: Brush or sponge them with a mixture of six ounces of Canada Balsam; six ounces of the best White Resin; and a quart of Oil of Turpentine.

To Bind, or Rebind Books and Papers: A volume, not too thick, may be neatly bound at home, by first forming a smooth firm pack. Near the side which is to form the back of the book drive a thin chisel through the pack about half an inch from the edge making three or four slits at equal distances apart. Run strong tapes through these slits, leaving ends about two inches long; draw these tightly and glue them down to the outside of the strawboard covers whose inner edges should come to the slits, and the others should project say a quarter of an inch beyond the leaves. Cut a piece of thin leather wide enough to cover the back of the book and lap over an inch on either cover. "Skive" or cut the edges of the leather slanting, so that the edges are very thin and paste down over the covers; fold the ends in so as to form a neat end and lap the end of the back over the boards on the *inside.* Cover the sides with paper, cloth, or any other material, and finish the work by pasting down the blank leaves inside.

Charred Books: The leaves should be taken from the covers and the threads clipped so that the leaves are only held by the charring. Then soak several hours in clean water and dry rapidly in a current of hot air; the leaves will separate, but handle with great care.

CEMENTS, PASTES, VARNISHES, ETC.

Cement for Leather and Cloth: Take four ounces gutta percha; one ounce clear India Rubber; one-half ounce pitch, and one-quarter ounce shellac; mix with one-half ounce linseed oil; dissolve thoroughly, and apply while hot.

Transparent Cement: Dissolve twelve and one-half drachms of best Brazil rubber in ten drachms of chloroform; cutting the rubber very fine. Keep in a cool place, in a well-stoppered bottle, and when dissolved add two and one-half drachms mastic and macerate for ten days. This cement should be perfectly white and very adhesive.

Copying Ink: Add one tablespoonful of glycerine to three of jet black writing ink and write with firm even letters on glazed paper. The writing will not dry for some time, and will make several copies on absorbent paper by the mere pressure of the hand.

Glue, To Test: If dry glue tastes salt or acid it will not stand dampness. If glue is soaked in water for twenty-four hours, and when thoroughly dried again is of exactly the same weight, it will stand all the tests of time and wear. A little salicylic acid will prevent it from turning sour.

Dry Pocket Glue: English recipe: Boil twelve parts of best glue until completely dissolved and add five parts of sugar or rock candy. Evaporate, and turn out on a greased surface to cool. Use as "mouth glue" or dissolve in warm water for use on paper.

Glue: Insoluble: Add about two per cent of bi-chromate of potash to a small amount of made glue just before using it; expose the glued article to strong sunlight, and it will not melt in warm water.

Liquid Glue, or Cement: Dissolve four ounces of gum shellac in three ounces, liquid measure of naphtha. Keep in a wide-mouthed, well-stoppered bottle. It should be about as thick as new cream and will mend almost anything.

Gum or Elastic Mucilage: Mix in a wide-mouthed bottle, twenty parts alcohol; one part salicylic acid: three parts soft soap; and three parts glycerine. When mixed, add a mucilage composed of ninety-three parts of gum Arabic, and 180 parts of water.

Gum for Labels: To twelve ounces of hot water, dissolve four ounces sugar candy; one and one-half ounces gum Arabic, and three ounces good glue which has been soaked in cold water for twenty-four hours. Spread this mixture on the backs of labels and allow to dry.

Ink: Ancient Record (from a receipt of the Seventeenth Century): To a pint of filtered rain-water, add one and one-half ounces coarsely powdered galls, six drachms sulphate of iron and ten drachms gum Arabic; expose in a closely-stoppered bottle to the sunlight, and stir occasionally until all is dissolved. Add ten drops of carbolic acid to prevent mould, and at the end of a month you will have a brilliant and unfading ink.

Liquid Pastes: To six pounds of water add five pounds of starch and four ounces of pure nitric acid; keep in a warm room for forty-eight hours, stirring frequently. Boil until thick and translucent, and thin if necessary to strain before using.

Or, add to the starch paste above-described, five pounds of gum Arabic and one pound of sugar dissolved in five pounds of water to which one ounce of nitric acid has been added, and bring the whole to the boiling point. This liquid paste will not mould and dries on paper with a gloss. It may be used on labels, wrappers and fine book-work.

Polish for Fine Old Carvings, etc.: Mix half a pint of linseed oil, half a pint of old ale, the white of one egg, and one ounce of muriatic acid. Apply with a soft cloth and rub lightly until polished.

Varnish, Book Binder's: Mix in three pints of alcohol (40 per cent) eight ounces shellac; eight ounces sandarach; two ounces mastic in drops and two ounces Venice turpentine. Apply very lightly with a varnish brush or a soft sponge.

Varnish to Revive Leather Bindings: Dissolve one and one-half ounces gum benzoin by suspending it in a muslin bag in one pint of wood alcohol. Filter through paper and apply with a soft brush or pad.

Cleaning Prints or Leaves of Rare Books: Examine the print carefully in a strong light, before commencing operations as no one method will remove every kind of dirt. Unless very dirty such valuable old curios are better left alone. But if you decide to clean a print or page, first rub lightly with a silk handkerchief. Do not use an erasive, as it will leave a rough surface. Grease spots must be removed first, by laying the print face down on a sheet of glass and dabbing the spots with clean white blotting-paper or a cotton pad dipped in benzine, sulphuric ether, turpentine, ammonia or naphtha. These must be applied to the *back* of the picture only, beginning at the edge of the spots and working toward the centre. Indian ink stains can be removed with hot water. Pencil marks may be taken out with very soft spongy rubber if not too deep. Sealing wax dissolved by hot alcohol may be removed by gentle "dabbing." Blood stains yield to chloride of lime, whose yellowish stain may in turn be removed by diluted acid. "Fox marks," or brown spots, are the results of dampness and if deep-seated should be let alone. If slight, dampen with alcohol and when dry touch with a weak solution of oxalic acid. A few drops of ammonia in a cupful of rainwater will sometimes remove them. After removing these stains lay the print face upwards, in a leaden trough or large dish absolutely free from grease, and just cover it with clean, cold water. Let it stand in the sun two days, and all dirt will disappear. Then reverse the print very carefully and leave it in a water bath for two days more. Dry very carefully in the shade, on a flat surface.

Sometimes having soaked the print in cold water the front and back alternately are flooded with one part of chloride of lime, in forty parts of water. The print should bleach out white, and if any spots are left they may be dabbed out with nitro-hydrochloric acid, or pure liquor of chloride of lime. When thoroughly cleansed the print must lie for some time on a clean board or sheet of glass, and under a gentle stream of cold water until all traces of the acids and chlorines are washed away. Dry in the shade, and never near a fire.

The fretted surfaces which a print presents under the microscope, may be removed by pressing between two sheets of blotting-paper with a flat iron, not too hot. If too glossy, hold in the smoke of a small fire of green wood which will also stain the print to the proper shade.

Another Process: 1st. Soak the print in clean water. 2nd. Pour off the water. 3d. Flood with a solution of one quart liquor Calcis Chloratae to thirty parts of soft water. 4th. If there are any spots touch them with pure Liquor Calcis Chloratae or with dilute nitro-muriatic acid. 5th. Rinse thoroughly with clear water to remove all traces of acid. 6th. Place the print in a very weak solution of glue to restore the surface of the paper. 7th. Dry between sheets of white blotting-paper and smooth with a warm flat-iron.

A Third Process: 1st. Wet with pure, clean water. 2nd. Soak in the dilute solution of chloride of lime. 3d. Pass print through water slightly soured with hydrochloric acid. 4th. Wash away all traces of acid in running water. 5th. Finish in the usual way.

Mounting Prints, Chromos, etc.: Prints should not be "laid down"; that is, pasted on another piece of paper or cardboard, unless they can be preserved in no other way. Then use good paste, bring the edges of any torn places as closely together as possible, and if any portions are missing connect the broken lines using Indian ink and a very fine pen. Heavy shadings may be laid in with the brush, using ink sparingly. Dry under pressure.

Mounting Prints on Cloth: Stretch the cloth on a frame, tacking it well at the edges. Size it with starch or thin paste and let it dry until as tight as a drum-head. Paste on your print, using for choice photographer's paste and rolling it down with a photo-roller. A print with its margin thus laid down on cloth stretched on a frame made of narrow, thin wood is in ideal condition for framing as soon as dry. Otherwise, cut out the print and save the frame for future use.

To Mount Colored Prints: Soak for fifteen minutes between two wet sheets of paper; paste to the panel of wood, cardboard or canvas, and rub smooth with the hand roller. Use only perfectly smooth and for choice best photographer's paste.

New Margins for Old Prints: To do this work neatly, one requires a nice cutting board or sheet of plate glass (a marble-topped table is just right); a metal straight-edge, say a strip of printer's brass furniture; a keen cutting knife, finely pointed pencil; pot of good paste and small soft brush. Trim prints carefully with straight edge and knife; saving the plate marks if possible, as these are the evidences of age and value. If you cannot save these, trim to the edges of the picture. Choose paper to match your print as nearly as possible and lay your print in position leaving your widest margin at the bottom. Trace with a pencil the exact shape of the print and cut out the paper about one-sixteenth of an inch inside the traced lines making the opening a little smaller than the print. Carefully paste the edges of the print at the back only, and also paste the inside edge of the cut in the mount. Lay the print face upward, in position, and press evenly under clean paper. Dry under a heavy weight. By using an oval form, prints may be inserted in pages to illustrate books, etc.

To Copy Prints: Coat unsized writing paper on one side with ten grains Bichromate of Potash, and twenty grains Sulphate of Copper dissolved in one ounce of distilled water. When dry lay the print face down upon it and cover with a sheet of clean, good glass. Expose to the sun's rays for an hour and you will have a pale yellow impression. A solution of twenty grains of Nitrate of silver in one ounce of distilled water will turn the color to red and lastly to brown if exposed to the sunlight.

To Restore Old Writing: Dampen the paper or parchment with clean lukewarm water, and then brush over the writing with a solution of Sulphide of Ammonium. The writing should become legible at once. On paper the color fades, but may be renewed. On parchment it is more permanent.

TO KEEP SILVER BRIGHT

Silver will keep brighter much longer if wrapped in dark-brown canton flannel.

"BROWNIES"

Two eggs beaten; one cup of sugar beaten in eggs; one half cup of butter melted in two squares of chocolate; beat all together; stir in one-half cup of flour and one cup of broken walnuts; bake in a tin so that it will be one-half inch thick; cut in strips two inches long while warm.

I think the home-makers will find this the best of all recipes for "Brownies." I buy the walnuts in the shell, for I find them fresher and of a more delicate flavor than those already shelled. These "Brownies" are a pleasing addition to fancy crackers when serving refreshments and will keep some time, if you hide them.

FOR SQUASH AND PUMPKIN

If the "National" housekeepers will try putting their squash and pumpkins, after being steamed and cooled, through the meat chopper, using No. 3 knife, I feel sure they will find it a much easier and quicker way than using a colander.

TOMATO SOUFFLE

To a pint of fresh or canned tomatoes (if canned, drain off part of the juice) add one well-beaten egg, a cup and a half of cracker crumbs, butter size of a hickory nut; salt and pepper to taste; stir together thoroughly and put in a well-buttered frying pan; do not stir but allow the lower side to brown, then turn without breaking; when both sides are brown, serve immediately with croutons or toasted crackers.

TO CLEAN STICKY DISHES

Dishes in which food has dried or burned on, may be cleansed easily as follows: Scrape with a knife what will come off easily; then fill with potato parings and water; let boil hard for twenty minutes or more; when taken out the dish will be nearly, if not wholly, free from any burnt or sticky substance.

A FINE FURNITURE POLISH

One quart of soft water; two tablespoonfuls of linseed oil; soap the size of a walnut; boil till the soap is dissolved; apply with a soft flannel and rub dry with another.

CHERRY DUMPLINGS

Cherry dumplings to be served with meat: One quart of cherries, seeded; one cup of sugar; two cups of water; set on the stove and when boiling, add dumplings made of two cups of flour, two heaping teaspoonfuls baking powder, one teaspoonful salt and one cup of milk; beat to a very stiff batter, drop by spoonfuls in the cherries and cook ten minutes, covered. These are fine. Canned cherries may be used, but use one pint only, for it is equal to a quart of fresh ones.

FOR THE GAS STOVE

I wonder if any of your readers know that to save heating the gas oven, potatoes for a small family can be baked on the burner of the top of stove by placing them on an asbestos griddle and covering with a granite basin, size of the griddle; turn the potatoes once or twice.

A POT ROAST

A three or four pound roast can be cooked upon top burner by first taking the iron skillet, or spider, putting in small quantity of water, little more than to just cover bottom of skillet; let come to a boil; have the roast well seasoned, place in the skillet and cover with granite pan to fit; now and then add hot water, just a tiny bit to keep from burning; turn the roast same as when in the oven, but you do not need to baste it; the result is fine.

WINTER WASHING

To protect handkerchiefs and fingers in cold weather, fasten handkerchiefs and small fine pieces to a long strip of cotton, and pin the strip to the clothes-line.

A DUSTLESS DUST-CLOTH

To make a dustless dust-cloth, saturate a piece of cheesecloth with turpentine; dry thoroughly and the dust will not fall from it until thoroughly shaken.

TWO-STORY BISCUIT

For baking-powder or soda biscuit, try rolling the dough only half as thick as usual, spread with melted butter, cut out biscuits and lay in buttered pans, two deep; prick the top with a fork, to press the layers together; sprinkle on a little sugar; have oven very hot for five minutes. The tops will be crisp and brown, and the layers will break apart in a very appetizing manner. "Two-story biscuit" is the name given to them by one of our friends.

A WARNING

Do not have an electric light within reach of the bath-tub. There is great danger of a shock should one attempt to turn on the light while standing in the tub, owing to the metal pipes that connect the tub with the ground.

HOT WATER TO RELIEVE PAIN

Pain, no matter where located, will be quickly relieved if one drinks several cups of hot water. While suffering greatly from severe muscular rheumatism, nothing seemed to avail until I began drinking freely of very hot water; the effect was magical and I was able to lie down in comfort, when it had been agony to move before trying the simple remedy; had I but learned this long ago, I would have been saved much unnecessary suffering. It is well worth passing along—a remedy so simple and so effective.

TO KEEP MILK FROM SCORCHING

First, boil a little water—enough to cover the bottom—in the vessel in which the milk is to be heated, and add to it the required amount of milk.

The main thing is to be sure that the water actually boils before the milk is added.

GOOD BATH TOWELS

When crocheted bedspreads become worn in spots, give them a new lease of usefulness by cutting apart and hemming for bath towels; mine have worn well and are well liked by the family.

IMPROVED COTTAGE CHEESE

Remove the objectionable acid taste from cottage cheese, by washing through two or three waters and draining carefully, before seasoning for the table.

"DOWN PUFFS"

How many of the sisters have feather-beds which have been discarded and know not what to do with them? Try my plan:—

Make a tick of muslin the size of your bed and put a portion of the feathers in it, spreading them evenly and thinly; put the case in your quilting frames, cover both sides with some pretty cloth and tack or tie exactly as you would a comforter, making the tufts quite close together.

You will find it a warm, soft "down puff" at practically no expense.

PIE HINTS

In cooling pies, it is necessary to let the air circulate under the pan, which is done easily by setting them on a wire rack, or small sticks, any way so the air can come in contact with the bottom of the pan. This is sure to prevent a soggy undercrust.

Again, if the cream, or milk, for pies is brought to a boil and added to the eggs the last thing before putting in the oven, it expedites the baking, as crust and custard will bake in the same time.

AN EXCELLENT SALVE

Take one-half as much lard as the amount of salve required, then add equal parts of tree turpentine and beeswax; melt, mix thoroughly and set away to cool.

FOR CHAPPED HANDS

The best remedy for chapped hands I have ever tried, is to sprinkle them with common corn-meal, while yet damp after washing, then rub briskly; those, who have to do work which roughens the hands will find that this simple remedy whitens and softens them wonderfully.

BRIGHT LIGHT

To make the lamp give a better light,
Be sure and put it on something white.

AIDS TO DIGESTION

For indigestion use cayenne pepper on your food. Buttermilk is good for acidity of the stomach.

NEW CARPET STRETCHER

When tacking down a carpet, if no carpet stretcher is handy, an excellent substitute will be found by having someone, either child or adult, put on a pair of rubber overshoes, taking care that the bottoms of the shoes are not worn smooth, and shuffle across the carpet. This stretches it as smooth as by using a machine.

PENNSYLVANIA DUTCH NOODLES

Beat two eggs thoroughly; add pinch of salt and enough flour to mix as stiff as dough can be rolled; roll like thin pie crust into three pieces; leave on moulding board to dry about an hour, turning occasionally; lay together and cut in two-inch lengths; then cut across fine, a little coarser than for slaw; throw into boiling salted water five minutes; drain in colander; while draining fry brown in butter one heaping cupful of stale bread cut in dice; when nice and brown throw over the bread three cupfuls of sweet milk and salt to taste; when ready to serve pour milk and bread over noodles, which have been placed in a covered dish, and serve hot. This is excellent and enough for family of eight. Is very nice warmed for lunch the next day.

GERMAN GRIDDLE CAKES

At supper time scald one heaping teacup of flour with water in which pared potatoes have been boiled; mash one medium-sized potato very fine and mix with scalded flour; have one-half yeast cake soaking in enough warm water to cover; when soft and batter is cool enough, add yeast and stir thoroughly; let stand covered in warm place until morning, when, first thing you do, add one teaspoonful of salt and one of sugar and three well-beaten eggs. By the time the rest of the breakfast is done the batter will be ready to bake as griddle cakes. Will serve family of six.

GASOLINE CLEANSING

To clean a handsome silk or wool garment, put into a tub of gasoline, rub all soiled parts with Ivory soap (if necessary, rub on washboard) but do not use water. Rinse in clear gasoline. A number of garments may be done in the same gasoline, if one works quickly, as it evaporates so rapidly, but it is amazing how the soap and gasoline combined do the work! I have seen garments of all kinds (baby's white wool coat, ladies' silk gowns, men's dress suits) cleaned beautifully, having the soap rubbed on them. One friend became so delighted, she filled a washing machine and cleaned handsome portieres, evening wraps and many heavy things. The soap brings out all that the gasoline will not touch.

TO RAISE FLOWERING BULBS

In raising gladiolus, plant them about four inches deep, from four to six in a hill, and hoe them just as you would your potatoes; when they begin to blossom, cut the stalks and put them in water; all the buds will gradually open.

You will then have strong fat bulbs at digging time. When the flowers are allowed to open and fade on the stalk, they cause the bulb to weaken, and they will gradually become worthless.

NEW IRONING WAX

A good substitute for wax for rubbing on the bottoms of irons will be found in the inside wrapper of bar soap. Use in the same manner as beeswax.

DAHLIAS

Dahlias are quite expensive where you buy the bulbs. One can buy mixed seed and have several colors at small expense. I have planted the seed in the open ground the middle of May and had the flowers the following September. The last time, I planted them the first of April in the house; then transferred them to the open ground when there was no danger of frost; my reward was very gratifying in numerous blossoms.

TO SET COLORS

To set colors of prints, put a handful of common salt and two large tablespoonfuls of turpentine in a pail of rain water; place the soiled garments in the pail and let soak all night; this sets the color in any kind of goods which is liable to fade; I have used this for many years and found it the best of anything I ever tried.

A BOILED DINNER

To prepare a boiled dinner, take a deep pan with a flat rim; in this put the vegetables, then pour on the meat liquor, which must be boiled the day before (keeping the meat in a warm place).

Cover this over with another flatrimmed pan; this is to prevent steam from escaping: set on top of stove just long enough to get it to boiling; then place it in a hot oven and cook all the morning; it will come out beautifully done and saves all odor, usually unpleasant; be sure the vegetables are all covered with the liquor when placed in the oven; this prevents drying out and disturbing them till done.

TO RENEW SHINY SILKS

It is very discouraging to the economical woman when her best black silk gown turns shiny before it is in the least worn, and comparatively few are aware that this state of affairs is easily remedied. One ox gall placed in a basin containing two or three quarts of cold water will be required. This will turn the water inky black. Take a piece of soft dustless black cloth, dip it into the liquid, squeeze it moderately dry, then carefully sponge all the shiny places with it. This will entirely remove the shine. Powdered ox gall is kept at drug stores and may be used, but it is better to get one from a butcher if possible.

HOME-MADE FIRELESS COOKER

Having an old-fashioned commode, I first lined the upper part, cover too, with several thicknesses of newspapers, tacking on with tacks. In the space made for the pitcher, put in hay and thin board to prevent burning; heat two soapstones (Tilo, or bricks will do) piping hot; then, after I get whatever food I am preparing, which must be in tightly covered dishes, like lard pails, bean pots, and the like, boiling hot, place dishes on one soapstone and the other on top of the dishes; then pack in papers around it all and weight down the covers to prevent air getting in; I have cooked my baked beans this way all summer; they are fine; the secret is to give everything plenty of time and just water to cover.

TO SAVE STOCKINGS

If your stockings wear first at the heel, put a piece of chamois inside of the heel of your shoe. This will prevent friction on the stocking and greatly prolong its wear.

SACHETS AND ODORS

Many women think they have no time for such trifles as sachets for the linen closet or drawers in which clothing is kept, yet it is possible for the very busiest of them to have all of their household linen and laundered clothing impart something vastly more pleasing than the odor of laundry soap so often left in them. A sachet made with dried rose petals mixed with half their quantity in equal parts of allspice and calamus root imparts a delightfully elusive fragrance. Place the mixture thickly between sheets of thin wadding and finish by tacking it between cheesecloth, then lay the sachet or sachets between the clean linens in the closets or drawers. The faint sweet odor will be delightfully refreshing. By using china silk or thin silk of any kind these sachets may be made very dainty indeed. An easier way as well as a very satisfactory one is to tie some arrowroot in a piece of strong cotton and boil it with the linens and cottons when they are laundered. This imparts a delicate refreshing fragrance.

Little cheesecloth bags filled with powdered Florentine orris root hung among the gowns and coats in the closets will give a faint pleasing violet fragrance.

A cheap and delicate violet perfume may also be made with the orris root. Cut half an ounce of it into small bits, put it into a bottle, and pour over it one ounce of spirits of wine. Cork tightly and let stand for a week or ten days. A few drops sprinkled on the hair or the pocket-handkerchief will have a smell as sweet and delicate as fresh violets.

TO DRIVE AWAY SPARROWS

If bothered with sparrows, put a little molasses on their roosting place and they will leave.

USES FOR BARREL HOOPS

I wonder how many of the "National" readers know that plain barrel hoops can be transformed into two useful articles!

Cut the hoop in half round the edges and you have two very excellent coat-holders, ready to hang up; of course, these can be beautified in the usual way by covering with scented cotton batting and then with pretty silk or ribbon and hang up with a big bow of the same material.

Another way to utilize the hoop is to gather a bag over it and then hang it up by strong tape, and you have a most useful bag for soiled clothes for the bathroom; the top being so open makes it very convenient, doing away with the drawing-strings nuisance.

CHOCOLATE FROSTING

Instead of boiling the chocolate with the syrup, add it just before placing it on the cake, but while still hot. You will be pleased with the result.

TO WHITEN YELLOWED LINEN

Fine linen, such as pocket handkerchiefs, collars and infants' clothing, that have become yellow, may be whitened by boiling for half an hour in strong suds, made with yellow soap and milk and water (half water and half milk), then wash in ordinary suds—hot; rinse first in clear hot water, then in cold blued water.

TO WASH CORDUROY

Wash with a good white soap, making a suds; then rinse in plenty of clear water and hang without squeezing or wringing, as either will ruin the goods; when dry, do not iron, but rub smooth with the fingers to restore the silky look.

CHRYSANTHEMUMS FOR WINTER

Break off budded branches of chrysanthemums, which you are afraid Jack Frost will take, keep in jars of water in a cool (not freezing) place; bring them into a warmer room as you want them and you will have blossoms as long as the branches last.

TO POLISH GLASS

Wash glass in warm soapsuds, rinse in cold water and wipe dry.

TO SAVE ASTERS

To rid asters of maggots, which destroy so many fine plants, work wood ashes into the soil, and remove a little soil immediately about the base of each plant, then scatter tobacco-dust there liberally; it is best to change the location of the bed yearly, but the liberal use of wood ashes and tobacco-dust will help much to keep the maggots away.

NEW USES FOR LEMON JUICE

A little lemon juice added to cream when whipping it, will make it thickish faster, as well as add to the flavor. When someone has carelessly scratched the painted wood with matches, rub with a cut lemon; the juice will remove the marks.

MOTH-BALL PREVENTIVE

Try tying moth-balls in thin cloth and tying them among the roses and grape-vines to rid the shrub of rose-bugs. Put two or three balls in each hill of cucumbers, squash, etc., to rid the plants of pests. Moth-balls placed in mole-runs are said to drive the moles away.

TO KEEP HAMS AND BACON

Farmers' wives can keep ham and bacon through hot weather, if they will half fry it and pack in a crock, covering with hot lard; after taking out slices to use, pour over hot lard again to cover and keep out the air.

TO CLARIFY LARD

The lard can be clarified by cooking sliced raw potatoes in it until brown, and skimming all impurities that rise.

GLEANED FROM ONE HOUSEWIFE'S EXPERIENCE

One or two tablespoonsful of sugar added to strong turnips when cooking, will greatly improve their flavor.

If tough meat is rubbed with a cut lemon before cooking 'twill make it nice and tender.

Stove-blacking, if mixed with a little ammonia will have a brighter luster and will not burn off.

MOCK MINCE PIE

One cup of chopped rhubarb; one cup of sugar; one-half cup of chopped raisins; one egg; a little salt and a little ground clove.

TO REMOVE SCORCH

If your iron scorches take a clean cloth, dip in vinegar and rub on the spot until it disappears; then use clean water the same way and re-iron.

TO PREVENT A BURNT TASTE

If anything scorches when cooking, remove from fire and set the vessel in another containing cold water; let it remain a few moments, then put the contents in a clean vessel and continue cooking; you can clean your burnt vessel more easily, too, as well as saving the food.

TO REMOVE ODOR

A few drops of oil of lavender in a cup of hot water will remove the smell of cooking from the house.

A GRIDDLE GREASER

For a good pancake griddle greaser, take a potato, long and narrow in shape; cut a knob in one end for a handle when greasing the griddle, make the other end flat and dip it in lard and apply to the griddle; you will be much pleased with the result.

TO REMOVE GREASE FROM WOOLENS

I thought my new wool dress was ruined with wagon grease, until a neighbor told me to use cold water and wool soap, or any white soap. I did so and the grease disappeared as if by magic.

WET FLOUR FOR BURNS

Take a cloth and put plenty of flour on it, wet slightly with cold water, then place it on the burn; you will feel almost instant relief; this remedy also keeps the worst burns from blistering.

THE PERPETUAL LAMP

Many people wish to keep a dim light, but a turned-down kerosene lamp has a very bad odor, which is very unhealthy, besides the danger from explosion. Try this: Take of dry phosphorus, one part; olive oil, six parts; put them in a phial, cork it and place in warm water for three hours; for use, remove the cork. The time by a watch may be seen by this light, and it will last for years if kept carefully corked when not in use. This is called the "Old Pioneer's artificial light."

SIX GOOD SUGGESTIONS

Keep tacks in bottles; it saves opening many boxes to find a particular kind.
Large red apples, when served whole at the table, are polished with olive oil.
If a shoe pinches, wet a cloth in hot water and place it over the tight spot when the shoe is on; it will soften the leather and enable it to stretch to fit.
A package or envelope sealed with the white of an egg cannot be steamed open.
Burning oil is spread by the use of water; to extinguish it, throw flour, sand or earth upon it—anything to prevent the oil from spreading.
A good grade of ink can be made by taking a short piece of indelible pencil and placing it in a bottle of water.

YEAST

When the bread will not "rise," and the yeast seems to have lost its strength, add a little ginger and notice the effect.

TO CLEAN A PANAMA HAT

Take a nail brush and scrub the hat with castile or Ivory soap and warm water; rinse in plenty of tepid water, then re-rinse in tepid water, to which has been added one and one-half tablespoonfuls of glycerine.
Use a Turkish towel to press out all water and dry in the sun for three hours, resting it upon the towel; it will be thoroughly clean and retain its shape.

GROUND COFFEE

If the housewife who buys her coffee ground will put it in a dripping pan, then beat an egg and stir it into the coffee, put it in a warm oven and dry, then return it to the can, she will have her coffee always ready for use and it will be clear and mild; besides the economy on eggs will be distinctly appreciated by many.

OYSTER SHELL SCRAPER

An oyster shell is the very best thing to scrape saucepans and kettles; when once you have used them, you will never return to a knife, a spoon, or a link dishcloth; they, the oyster shells, are sharp and lend themselves to all corners.

TO REMOVE IRON-RUST

To remove iron-rust, dampen cloth, and rub cream of tartar on the spots well; let stand an hour, then wash; if not all removed, repeat the process.

KEEP CAKE FROM BURNING

To prevent cakes from burning place a little bran on the bottom of the tins.

TO KEEP AWAY RATS

Sprinkle cayenne pepper in the corn bins, and your barn will be free from the rats.

TO SAVE LEMONS

If when using lemons you need only half of it, put the other half on a plate and cover with a glass; this excludes the air and prevents it from getting dried or mouldy.

FOREIGN BODIES IN THE EYE

A celebrated oculist recommends in any case where dirt, lime or a cinder gets into the eye, that the sufferer should use pure olive oil; the remedy is quite painless and never fails to remove all foreign substances.

FOR DAINTY WAISTS

To prevent the buttons from tearing out of sheer lingerie waists, stitch a piece of narrow tape (No. 0) on the under side of the hem on the line of the buttons and sew them on this.

POTATO SALAD

For six cupfuls of cold boiled potatoes cut into small cubes, take a tablespoonful of grated onion, three tablespoonfuls of minced parsley, a teaspoonful of salt, half a teaspoonful of pepper, and mix them thoroughly with the potato. Beat until thick and smooth one pint of sweet heavy cream and four tablespoonfuls of tarragon vinegar. Mix with the salad and serve at once.

TO KEEP GRAPES

Pick out perfect bunches of not over-ripe grapes, clip the stems afresh and dip them in melted paraffine. Line wooden boxes with dry paper, lay the bunches in carefully so as not to crowd each other, cover with paper, then with fruit and so on until the box is full. Cover well with paper and keep in a cool place.

TO MEND A LAMP CHIMNEY

When a glass lamp chimney cracks or a small piece falls out it may be made useful for a time with a piece of muslin saturated with alum or soda or borax, dried and pasted over the break. Such a patch will not burn out, and is sometimes a most convenient resource.

SPRINKLE CLOTHES ON THE LINES

A garden hose with a very fine spray nozzle can be used to sprinkle a whole washing on the line. The plain clothes can be rolled and laid in the basket as they are taken down, and starched goods sprinkled a little more by hand if necessary.

FEATHER AND DOWN COMFORTERS

If ducks and geese are killed in cold weather the down should be picked and saved separately, exposed to oven heat to kill vermin, and used to fill quilted skirts and coverlets, which have no equal for lightness and warmth. Old feather beds and pillows should be used to make coverlets or "comforters," using silkaline or fine cotton, and knotting with worsted or narrow ribbon.

CORNSTARCH PIE

Beat the yolk of an egg with one cup of sugar and one and one-half tablespoonfuls cornstarch (wet the cornstarch with a little milk); put all into one pint of boiling milk, stir constantly until a nice custard; when it is only warm, flavor with lemon and fill in a crust already baked; when baked, frost it and set in the oven till a delicate golden brown.

INDEX

AIR: to purify, 100.
ANTI-RUST: for farm machinery, 334.
ANTS: Black, to get rid of, 124, 160.
ANTS: Red, 23, 39, 50, 55, 70, 158, 232, 239, 242, 251, 253, 312.
ALUMINUM: vessels eaten by salt, 306.
AMMONIA: uses of, 1.
AMUSEMENTS: Christmas, 14; probable history, 317.
APPLES: baked, 118; cooked with sweet potatoes, 325; baked with cranberries, 135; sundry dishes, 35; sauces, 31, 132; substitutes for, 35.
ARTIFICIAL FLOWERS: 23.
ARTIFICIAL HONEYS, 329.
ARTIFICIAL JELLIES, 329.
ARTISTS: care of brushes, 64; fixative for drawings, 153.
ASTERS: to save, 355.

BAKING DEPARTMENT

BARLEY SCONES: 273.
BISCUIT: hot, 231; hard, 274; graham, 36; railroad bread, 233; two-story, 348.
BREAD: brown, 31, 42, 321; old-fashioned, 273, 308; a short cut, 313; baking, 124, 140, 391; keeping fresh, 59, 92.
CAKES: made with water, 63, 74; without eggs, 76; frosting, 76; to mix with freezer, 93; new, 19; fruit, 140; Lady Baltimore, 231; cocoa spice, 261; cream, 286; to keep, 214, 319; nut, 249; Aunt Dinah's recipe, 66; poor man's, 3. to prevent burning, 358.
CRACKERS, 272.
DOUGHNUTS: light, 98, 260, 314, 320, 322; with vinegar, 23; to sugar, 40; to keep, 3.
FLAVORING EXTRACTS: to make, 96, 142; to use, 73; to use in custard, 217.
FRITTERS: fruit, 274; batter, 325.

FROSTING: maple sugar, 94; cooked, 124; for cakes, 213; boiled icing, 50; not boiled, 58; to spread, 242, 316; 54, 134, 320; pure baking powder, 272; chocolate, 354.
PIES: apple, 271; blueberry, 160; custard, 272, 350; plum, 232; pumpkin, 74, 231, 242, 266; pumpkin, crustless, 54; mock pumpkin, 256; rhubarb, 80, 129; syrup, 156, 321; winter, 38; cornstarch, 359; fruit, 41; mock cherry, 4; buttermilk, 72; banana, 300; to cool, 350; mock mince, 356.
PIE CRUST: single, 21, 167; double, 48, 104, 125, 134, 218, 249; soggy, to prevent, 70.
PUDDINGS: Easter, 262; popover, 286; Dutch, ten minute, 270; preventing burning, 44, 79, 164; mother's, 50; mother's sauce, 274.

BACKGROUND: to save wallpaper, 314.
BASTING THREADS: to remove, 310.
BEDBUGS: to extirpate, 8, 279.
BEE-KEEPING: hints, 154; to separate wax, 155.
BLACKING: to make it waterproof, 12.
BLEEDING: to stop, 309.
BOOKS: care of, 342; to renovate and rebind, 343; to clean leaves or prints, 345.
BUGS AND WORMS: to kill; on cucumbers, 84; currant bushes, 325; plants, 119, 120.
BUNNY CLOAK: for baby, 318.
BURDOCKS: to kill, 94, 243.
BUTTER: care of milk, 75; substitute for, 307.
BUTTONS: that stay on, 74; to cover, 241.
CALENDARS: new from old, 309.
CAMP RULE: for boiling eggs, 323.
CANNED GOODS: spoiled, to detect, 231; peas, to freshen, 29.

INDEX

CARBON PAPER: substitute, 255.
CEMENTS: alum cement, 9; grafting wax, 9; aquarium, 9; Armenian, 9; label, 9; lamp ring, 9; leather, 9; Chinese blood, 9; liquid label and mouth glues, 9; alabaster, 277; with coal ashes, 56; to cork, 17; china, 9; 217; rice flour, 247; iron cement, 279, 9; Japanese rice flour, 279; transparent, 344; leather and cloth, 344.
CHARCOAL: uses of, 308.
CHARRED FENCE POSTS: 333.
CHEAP PAINTS: farmer's, 335; rice, 335; prairie white, 335.
CHICKEN CHOLERA: cure for, 105.
CIDER: sweet, 99, 119.

CANNING, PRESERVING AND PICKLING

APPLES: to core, 312; to polish, 357.
BEANS: to can, 246, 269.
BLACKBERRIES: 160.
CORN: 240.
FRUIT: to can, 28, 216.
FRUIT JARS: to seal, 46.
PEAS: with oranges, 57.
PIE PLANT: 79, 213, 249.
STRAWBERRIES: 269, 306.
TOMATOES: to can, 48, 215, 255; to pare, 245.
USE NEW RUBBERS: 324.
WINTER VEGETABLES: to can, 99.

APPLE PICKLES: 316.
BERRY JAMS: 78.
CHERRIES: to pit, 310.
FRUIT BUTTERS: 105.
GRAPES: spiced.
JELLIES: 54, 118, 162; rhubarb, 215; cordial jellies, 272; to keep, 239, 325; to make fresh in winter, 309.
PEACHES: to stone, 322.
PRESERVING WHOLE FRUIT: 302.

PICKLES: 38; in oil, 79; syrup for sweet, 96, 123; sweet apple, 239; to keep, 255.

QUINCE HONEY: 263.
RHUBARB AND FIG SAUCE: 322.
TOMATO CATSUP: 20, 324.

CHRYSANTHEMUMS: late blooming, 354.
CISTERN: a unique, 17.
CLOTH: thin, to cut, 36; to tell right side of, 127.
CLOVES: value and uses of, 30.
COLLARS: to make, 92, 126.

CLEANSING DEPARTMENT

AMMONIA: uses of, 9.
AXLE GREASE: 232.
BATH TUBS: 189.
BED LINEN: 39, 178, 229.
BLACK GOODS: 205.
BLOOD STAINS: 8, 284.
BOOKS: 174.
BOTTLES: 240.
BRASS: 158.
BROOMS: 174.
BURNED SAUCEPANS: 7.
CARPETS: 154, 157, 181; carpet sweeper, 28, 46, 168, 183, 261.
CELLULOID: 261.
CHIMNEY: 101, 229, 220, 324.
CLOTHING: 220.
CLEANING AND POLISHING: mixture, 333.
COAL SOOT: 193.
COFFEE AND TEA POTS: 203.
COMBS AND BRUSHES: 106, 119.
DRY CLEANSING: 113.
DUSTING: with old silk, 166; with paint brush, 165.
ENAMELLED WARE: 64.
FLUIDS: for cleansing, 77.
FURS: 236.
GALVANIZED WARE: 11.
GASOLINE: 242, 351.
GILT FRAMES: 164.
GLASS: 169; to polish, 354.
GRATERS: 262.
GREASE SPOTS: 47, 284.
HARMLESS CLEANSER: 302.

INDEX

HATS: straw, 142; Panama, 61, 169, 357.
IRON STAINS: 316, 358.
IVORY: 216.
KEROSENE: 233.
KETTLES: 94, 106, 134, 177, 258, 324.
KID GLOVES: 254, 260.
KNIFE HANDLES: 234.
LACES: 79, 117.
LAMP CHIMNEYS: 176, 258, 310, 324; lamp burners, 34, 240, 325.
LEMON JUICE: to cleanse with, 358.
LINOLEUM: 117.
MARBLE: 106, 175.
MATCH MARKS: to remove, 5.
MILDEW: 26, 27, 241, 284.
MILK STAINS: 17.
MIRROR VELVET: 164.
MUD STAINS: 97.
NICKEL: 272.
OIL PAINTINGS: 269.
OYSTER SHELL: scrapers, 358.
PAINT: brushes, 159; stains, 315; to remove, 310.
PATENT LEATHER: 322.
PEACH STAINS: 5.
PERSPIRATION STAINS: 78.
PHOTOGRAPHS: 189.
PLAYING CARDS: 153.
RUGS: 241.
RUSSIA IRON: 221.
RUST: 250.
SEWING MACHINES: 105, 240.
SHELVES: 94.
SILKS: 115; to renew, 352.
SILVER: 129, 158, 219, 225, 251, 259.
SOAP: soft, 333; transparent toilet, 333.
STAINS: sundry to remove, 5, 11.
STEEL: 224; steel pens, 185.
STICKY DISHES: 347.
STOVES: 188, 221, 226, 228, 258, 259.
STRAW MATTING: 64, 155, 174, 221.
TEA STAINS: 70.
TIN: 174, 210, 266.
TRIMMINGS: 38.
TURPENTINE: uses of, 6.
TYPEWRITER: 19.
VELVET: 225, 194, 300, 312.
WALL PAPER: 96, 218.
WATER BOTTLES: 230.
WHITE SINK: 5.
WINDOWS: 187, 238, 253.
WITH CHALK: 205.
WOODWORK: 227, 228, 261.
WRINGERS: 188.

COOKING DEPARTMENT

APPLES: sweet, 232; apple dumpling, 262; with sweet potatoes, 325.
BAKING POWDER CANS: uses of.
BACON: 104, 269; English bacon, 273.
BEANS: baked, Boston style, 164; with olive oil, 75; mustard in, 270; cooked quickly, 212, 271.
BEEF: pot roast, 103; roast, 271; beef tongue, 114, 275.
BISCUITS: 229; biscuits, pan, 245; stuffed, 309.
BOILED DINNER: 352.
BREAKFAST FOODS: 100, 306.
BRIEF SUGGESTIONS: 241.
BROTH: remove fat, 92.
BUCKWHEAT CAKES: with soda, 307.
CABBAGE: boiled, 184, 268; digestible, 73; odorless, 45; to keep, 121.
CAPE COD: fish chowder, 191; Cape Cod sea pie, 192.
CARROTS: 19, 306.
CELERY LEAVES: 116, 143.
CHEESE: chopped, 315; cottage, 122; cream cheese, 206; dreams, 32.
CHERRIES: to stone, 253; in dumplings, 348.
CHESTNUTS: boiled, 166.
CHICKEN: boiled, 49; to season, 87; oil for salad, 24.
CHOCOLATE DIP: 57; with cornstarch, 116.
COCOA: 121; quickly made, 141.
CODFISH BALLS: 115.
COFFEE: to freshen, 254, 337.
CORN: cakes, 29; meal, 171; Kentucky pone, 97.
COTTAGE CHEESE: improved, 349.
CRANBERRIES: 248; to keep, 321.
CREAM: to whip, 27, 42; to use sour 226.

INDEX

CROQUETTES: potted tongue, 217.
CUSTARD: baked, 130; custard, curdled, 18.
DATES: to cleanse, 198; fairy stuffed, 94.
DUCK: to dress, 35.
DUMPLINGS: light, 321.
ECONOMICAL MEAT DISHES: 82.
EGGS: baked, 137; boiled, 68, 136, 316, 323; to peel, 3; fried, 142; poached, 8, 223; for invalids, 142; in dumplings, 133, 321; pancakes, 271.
ENGLISH MEAT PIES: 190.
FINNAN HADDIES: to make, 181.
FISH: to fry, 273; to scale, 42, 304; baked, 300.
FROSTED ONIONS: to fry, 105.
FRUIT JAR RUBBERS: use new, 259.
FURNACE: to utilize, 18.
GAME: to choose, 92.
GERMAN GRIDDLE CAKES: 351.
GRAVY: rich, 80, 222, 264.
GREASE: substitute, 28; spilled on stove, 51, 96; to grease griddle, 356.
GREEN CORN: 268.
GREENS: to prepare, 313.
GRIDDLE CAKES: 261, 325.
HAM: fried and freshened, 53; tender, 301, 307.
HASHED MEAT: baked, 4, 193.
HINTS: general, 68, 114, 161; cooling the oven, 133, smoked kettle, 141, 142, 320.
ICE BILL: to save, 4.
LARD: scorched, 32; suet substitute, 43, to keep, 47; to render, 136, 142, 188.
LEMONS: to grate, 316.
LIVER: fried, 137.
MADE MUSTARD: 12.
MAYONNAISE: 248.
MEAT: to keep fresh, 24, 63, 255, 234; dishes, 86; crust for meat pies, 127; meat souffles, 226; sweet pickle for, 332.
MILK: to test, 304.
MINCE MEATS: crab-apple, 58; temperance, 91; tomato, 207.
MUSH: fried, 51, 184, 264.

NEW DISHES: 6.
NOODLES: 175.
NORTHAMPTON OYSTER TOAST: 191.
OATMEAL: 106.
ODORS: to kill, 48, 356.
OKRA AND TOMATOES: 206.
OMELETTES: tender, 125, 318.
ONIONS: to peel, 221; salad, 346.
PANCAKES: 107, 151, 207; batter, 20; oyster, 78.
PARSNIPS: 299.
PEPPERS: green baked, 319.
PENNSYLVANIA DUTCH NOODLES: 351.
PINFEATHERS: to remove, 249.
PORK: to cure, 134, 176, 186; pork chops, baked, 25; coating, 6.
POTATOES: baked, 37, 48, 56, 156, 166, 168, 206, 264; boiled, 188, 253; browned, 18; cakes, 213; fried in cottolene, 306; frozen, 101; to keep, 64; mashed, 105; mealy, 31, 135; salad, 2; soup, 34; steamed, 218; to bake on gas stove, 348.
POT ROAST: 348.
PRUNES: laxative, 90, 130; spiced, 167.
RADISHES: 150.
RICE: 204, 239.
SALAD: 61; winter, 109; Terra Alta, 211; hot weather, 180; potato, 339.
SALAD DRESSING: 164, 315; without oil, 174, 239, 324; for fruit salads, 315.
SANDWICHES: to keep, 29; bread for, 52; picnic, 70; salmon loaf, 216; sardine, 190.
SARDINE TOASTS: 1.
SAUERKRAUT: 111, 215.
SAUSAGES: ginger in, 70.
SCORCHED TASTE: 89, 209, 356.
SHORTCAKE: 120.
SHORTENING: 351.
SOUP: stock, 137, 144; tomato, 15; vegetable, 182.
SOUR FRUIT: 177.
SQUASH: fried, 77, 91; boiled, 347.
SUETS: 46, 137.

INDEX

SUGAR SYRUPS: 31, 49, 131.
SWEETBREADS: 149.
SWEET POTATOES: broiled, 270: to keep, 63; with apples, 325.
TAPIOCA: jelly, 161.
TEA: 255.
TOMATOES: 185, 324; souffle, 347.
TROUT AND BACON: 195.
VEGETABLES: to season, 89; wash, 258.
VINEGAR: to make, 59; uses of, 256.
WITHOUT FIRE: 56.
WORTH TRYING: 235.
YEAST: to improve, 357.

CONFECTIONERY, ETC.

APPLE FUDGE: 17.
BROWNIES: 347.
CANDIES: Christmas, 84; maple, 263; sea foam, 251.
CORN BALLS: 328.
ICES, FRUIT OR SHERBET: 288.
ICE CREAM: pure, 288; strawberry, 288.
JAM: 7.
MARSHMALLOWS: 7.
MOLASSES CANDY: 328.
NUTS: to crack, 123; nut candy, 328; nut and fig strips, 328; fig candy, 328.
PARFAIT AU CAFE: 272.
PEACH STONES: to remove, 322.
PINEAPPLES: 74, 285; to cut, 5, 73, 118.
SHERBETS: see ICES.
TURKISH DELIGHT: 38, 130.
WHITE CANDY: 328.

DAHLIAS: to raise, 352.
GLUE: to test, 344; dry pocket, 344, insoluble, 344; liquid, 344.
ELECTRIC LIGHT: dangerous when, 349.
FLOWERING BULBS: to raise, 354.

HOUSEWORK DEPARTMENT

AMMONIA: uses, 128.
APRONS: for washing, 71.
ASBESTOS: stove covers, 319.
ASHES: to handle, 154.

BABY: table for, 248; buttermilk for, 255.
BAG: sunshine, for invalids, 60.
BARREL HOOPS: to utilize, 354.
BASKETS: hanging, 132.
BASTING CLIPS: 13.
BATCH OF LITTLE HELPS: 97.
BATH TOWELS: to make, 349.
BATTER: to save, 60.
BEAD WORK: 7.
BED: making, 168, 169; gown, 168.
BEETS: to keep, 126.
BEVERAGES: cool without ice, 280.
BIRDS: canaries, etc., 155.
BLANKETS: to comb, 169.
BLUING: to test, 22.
BOILING OVER. to prevent, 44.
BOOKLETS: dainty, to make, 268.
BOOKS: care of, 124, 126, shelves, 266.
BOTTLES: to cut, 114, 271.
BOWLS, WOODEN: to strengthen, 97.
BOXES: for clippings, 131.
BRIDE GIFTS: 98.
BRIGHT LIGHT: 350.
BROKEN DISHES: 261.
BROOM: to cover, 218.
BUDGET OF HINTS: 170.
BUTTER MAKING: 141.
BUTTER: to freshen, 281.
BUTTONHOLES: 29, 31, 90.
CAKE: to keep moist, 319.
CANARY: green food for, 254.
CARPETS: to stretch, 350.
CATS: to physic, 153.
CELLARWAY: 168; damp, 59.
CHAIRS: wire-seated, 25, 74.
CHAMOIS SKINS: to wash, 94, 115.
CHICKENS: to water, 169.
CHIFFON: to tuck, 266.
CHIMNEY: to clear, 80, 220.
CHINA: to mend, 24, 53, 114.
CISTERN: an unique, 17; rainwater, to build, 280.
CLOSET DOOR: as a washstand, 176.
CLOTHES: to mend, 125; press, more room, 260; sprinkler, 38; racks, 117.
CLOTHES PINS: as apple corers, 312.
COAL: to save, 301.

INDEX

COAL ASHES: for cleaning, 41.
COFFEE: should be washed, 171.
COLLARS: old, uses of, 136.
COLORS: to set, 243.
COOKER: The Fairy, 95.
COOKING: to prepare material for, 90.
COPPERAS: for plants, 99.
CORK: to remove, 153.
CORNMEAL: for cleaning, 165.
CORNSTARCH: for the hands, 22.
COUPLES: newly-married, 59.
COVERS: bed, made of old blankets, 41.
CRANBERRIES: to keep, 000.
CRANBERRY WINE: 257.
CROCHETING: marker, 310.
CROCKING: to prevent, 218.
CUCUMBERS: to plant, 302.
CURCULIO: to drive from plum-trees, 219.
CURIOS: to preserve, 104.
DARNING: cotton hose, 243; dress goods, 92: stockings, 67.
DEODORIZERS: 273, 308, 318; coffee, 46.
DISH-DRAINER: uses of, 89.
DISH-TOWELS: to keep white, 60.
DISH-WASHING: 231.
DOILIES: to pack, 461.
DOORS: to secure, 156.
DOWN PUFFS: to make, 349.
DRESSMAKER'S HOME HINTS: 101; dress shields, 29; dresses for growing girls, 29.
DRINKS: eleven for the sick, 282.
DUSTING: 107, 160, 165.
DUSTLESS DUST CLOTH: 348.
DYEING: to set colors, 352.
DYES: old-fashioned, 326.
EGGS: frozen, 40, 110; to beat, 102, 167; to keep, 24, 125, 308; to save, 116; to test, 158; limed, 281; easily shelled, 267.
EMBROIDERY: silks, care of, 287, 322; ruffle to apply, 260; to stamp, 268; marker, 310.
ERASER: novel, 175.
FEATHERS: pillows to wash, 43, 62; to handle, 252; to color, 306; comforters, 359.

FILE: fine for sharpening, 314; flat in side pocket, 320.
FIRE EXTINGUISHER: 309.
FIRE KINDLERS: 335.
FIRELESS COOKER: home-made, 353.
FLIES: to kill or drive away, 28, 62, 138, 146, 220, 256, 320.
FLOORS: to renovate, 36, 46; to polish, 219.
FLOUR: to test, 22; sacks for clothing, 64.
FLOWERS: artificial to renovate, 34, 69, 307; cut, to keep fresh, 30, 58; arranging, 146; hints to growers, 80, 148, 323; bone and charcoal fertilizers, 147.
FORAGE: wheat and oat straw, 281.
FORK: good garden tool, 235.
FOUNTAIN PEN: to open, 152, 256; to fill, 53.
FREEZING MIXTURES: 331.
FROSTED: plants, 155; windows, 49.
FRUIT JARS: to cleanse, 262.
FUNNEL: 172.
FURS: care of, 165; mending, 145; storing, 44.
FURNACE HEAT: 155.
FURNITURE: to dust, 106, 159; to make new, 218; to polish, 158, 245, 347; to remove scratches and white spots, 27.
GARRET: false window curtains, 268.
GASOLENE: to cleanse with, 54; to detect in the lamp, 306; to extinguish, 30.
GATHERING: new way, 242.
GLASS: to bore, 67; to draw upon, 269.
GLASS JARS: for food, 214.
GLASS STOPPERS: to remove, 330.
GLEANINGS: 335.
GLOVES: tinted, to cleanse, 55; long, to save, 67.
GLUE: dry, to soften, 45; to keep sweet, 104, 107; with whiskey, 334; liquid, 335.
GOLD PAINT: 300.
GRANITE WARE: to mend, 104, 107.
GRAPES: to keep, 255, 359.
GRAPE FRUIT WATER: to make, 258.

INDEX

GRATER: to make, 33, 331.
GREASE: to remove from woolens, 356.
GREEN VEGETABLES: to keep fresh, 73, 74.
GUESTS: to keep book of, 35; unexpected, to provide against, 18.
HAMMOCK: home-made, 162.
HAMS: to keep in hot weather, 355.
HARD WATER: to soften, 129.
HARDWOOD FLOORS: 268.
HENS: to set in mid-summer, 92, 101; nuts as food, 100.
HOLDERS: twine, 50; ticking, 100; handy, 247, 312.
HORSE RADISH: to plant, 313.
HOSIERY: 36.
HOT DISH: to remove from oilcloth, 319.
HOT WATER: without a range, 256; bottles, leaky, to use, to fill properly, 171.
HOUSE-PLANTS: to protect, 88; purchase, 108; drive away insects, 78; raise slips, 42.
ICE: to prepare for invalids, 106.
ICES: see CONFECTIONERY.
INSECTS: to kill, 42; on smoked meats, 55.
IRONING: wax for, 352.
JELLY BAGS: to preserve, 258.
KEROSENE: lamps, safety, 81, 87; to clean, 83, 87; uses of, 86; cure for toothache, 88; fire to extinguish, 18.
KITCHEN: hints, 134; rugs, 321; shears, uses of, 60; table to cover, 103; work stool, 113.
LABELS: to paste on tin.
LACES: to color ecru, 62; insertion, 122.
LAMP: wicks to trim, 17; to prevent smoking, 76, 163, 325; chimney, to mend, 359.
LARD: to clarify, 355.
LAWN BORDER: 123.
LEAD PIPE: leaks, to stop, 22, 122.
LEMONS: boiled, 91; dried to freshen, 131; heat before using, 36; uses of, 8, 116; to economize, 358.
LETTER: to seal securely, 152.

LETTUCE: to keep fresh, 232.
LIGHT: reflected, 145; white light, 145; cheap reflector, 145; night light, 125.
MAGAZINE BOOKLETS: 263.
MAGNETS: to pick up tacks, etc., 48.
MATS: felt, 26.
MATTRESSES: to preserve, 33; to handle, 49; pads for, 311.
MEDICINE: to drop, 19; glass covers for, 247.
MENDING: coat lining, 239; gloves, 47; overalls, 321; stockings, 126; clothes wringer, 267.
MICE: to drive away, 157.
MILK: to detect chalk in, 112; to keep, 3, 63; to scald, 23; to prevent scorching, 30, 349.
MIRRORS: spoiled by sun, 159.
MITTENS: looped, 127; for numbness, 112.
MOSQUITOES: to drive away, 120, 152; chair for invalid, 51.
MOTHS: to exterminate, 107; in carpets, 250; mothballs, 317; salt for, 304.
MOTH BALLS: to make, 334.
NAILS: to drive easily, 129.
NASTURTIUMS: to promote flowering, 322.
NEEDLES: to thread easily, 35, 91; to prevent rusting, 91.
NERVES: tired to rest, 37.
NEWSPAPERS FOR PRESSING: 306.
NEW WORDS: to teach children, 138.
NEW WRINKLES: 267.
NIGHT LAMP: 3.
NUTMEG GRATER: new uses, 176.
ODORS: to remove, 103.
OILCLOTH: apron, 52; to mend, 94; table mat, 71; wall pocket, 71.
OLD CLOTHES: uses, 307.
ONIONS: eat parsley with, 31; to deodorize, 257.
OVEN: to heat quickly, 122.
OYSTER SHELLS: in kettles, 311.
PADS: blotting paper, 214.
PAINT: white to clean, 47; brushes to clean, 53.

INDEX

PALETTE KNIFE: uses in the kitchen, 247.
PANCAKES: turner for, 240.
PANTRY SHELVES: to make, 244.
PASTES: to make, 11, 37, 71, 156, 247.
PASTILLES: to make, 18.
PATENT LEATHER: care of, 128, 129.
PEPPERS: ornamental, 315.
PHOTOGRAPHS: to preserve, 72; paste for, 120.
PIANO: to clean, 254.
PIN CUSHION: to recover needles from, 251.
PLASTER CRACKS: to mend, 10.
PORCH: wind-break for, 315.
POTATOES: to keep, 314; for sweeping, 3.
POCKET: flat inside, 320.
PUMP: to prevent freezing, 300.
QUASSIA CHIPS: for insects, 42.
RAINCOAT: buttons for, 244.
RATS: to drive away, 283, 334, 358.
RIBBONS: child's, to secure, 147; to renovate, 110.
REFRIGERATOR: cheap, 161.
RESTAURANT: making home a, 65.
RIPE FRUITS: to keep fresh, 283.
ROACHES: to drive away, 251.
RUBBER BOOTS: to dry, 98; 168, 313; to mend, 219.
RUGS: to prevent "creeping" of, 61.
RUST: to prevent, 77, 111; to remove, 131; in water pail, 152.
RUSTY SCREWS: to loosen, 131.
SAFETY PIN: use as bodkin, 244.
SAFETY RAZOR: blade utilized, 171, 266.
SALT: old sacks used, 140; water baths, 32; cellars to fill, 70; rice in, 139; starch in, 267; excess corrected, 234.
SALTPETER PAPER: to make, 41.
SANDPAPER: for rust, 252; shiny cloth, 321.
SASH CURTAIN RODS: 174.
SAVINGS: roast meat drippings, 57; potato parings for fuel, 257; soap scraps, 40, 108.
SCISSORS: to sharpen, 259.

SCREENS: to make convenient, 176, 323; to save, 302.
SCRUBBING BRUSH: new uses, 24, 33.
SEWING MACHINE: 171, 176; hints on using, 78; to cleanse, 303.
SHEARS: use, 236.
SHEEPSKIN MATS: 10, 338.
SHIRT WAIST: belt, 250.
SHOES: to stretch, 27, 50, 72, 162; ties, 98, 154; soles to preserve, 33, 116 rough to line, 21; to soften, 24, 69; slippery, 155; renovate, 216, 254; tight, 251; to waterproof, 323.
SINK: to clean, 97.
SIX SUGGESTIONS: 357.
SKIRT: to hang, 324.
SLIPPERS: to keep in place, 325.
SILVER: to keep bright, 347.
SOAP: household, 62; improves with age, 88; perfumed, 195; saver, 313; substitute for, 47; to cut, 70; home-made, 13.
SODA: in gruel, 38; for cut flowers, 303.
SPECTACLES: to clean, 20.
STARCH: 28, 160; cold, 35; dark lawns, 303, 159; soap in, 213; on fringed goods, 174; black dresses, 7.
STOCKINGS: long wear, 50; fast black, 165; to join, 215; uses for old, 34; to save, 301, 353.
STORM DOORS: substitutes.
STOVE: fine polish, 129, 261; with coffee, 58; to black pipe, 57.
STOVEPIPE: to fit, 171.
STRAINER: to clean, 268.
STRAWBERRIES: government distribution, 133.
SUGGESTIONS: 120, 323.
TABLE SYRUP: 19; hygienic, 39.
TEA: punch, cold, 34; stains, to prevent, 70.
THIMBLE: loose, tightened, 220.
TIGHT COVERS: to remove, 214.
TIGHT SHOES: to stretch, 357.
TINWARE: to keep from rusting, 14.
TOWELS: rings for, 258.
TRIMMINGS: hand-made, 319.
UMBRELLAS: to mend, 265.

INDEX

VEIL: to keep dainty, 56.
WAISTS: to strengthen, 358.
WALL PAPER: mats, 245.
WALL POCKETS: for stove covers, 27.
WALNUTS: to hull, 14, 50.
WARE: enamelled, to repair, 32.
WATER-CRESS: a tonic, 48.
WELL-SET TABLES, 338.
WHITEWASH: to paper over, 100.
WINDOW GARDEN: December work in, 83.
WINDOW SCREENS: 325; painted white, 323.
WINDOW SHADES: renovated, 215.
WINTER ECONOMY: 340, 348.
WOOD-BOX: made of nail-keg, 307.
WORSTEDS: worn smooth, to renovate, 321.
WRINKLED SILKS: to freshen, 315

LAUNDRY DEPARTMENT

BEESWAX: substitute for, 322.
BLANKETS: colored to wash, 303, 316; to comb, 161.
BLUE GOODS: to wash, 26.
BLUING: to use, 322.
CLOTHES: easily folded, 161; men's, to wash, 316.
COLD STARCHING: 127, 213.
COLORS: to restore, 28; to set, 26, 268; delicate colored fabric, 89, 244.
CORDUROY: to wash, 354.
CURTAINS: lace to wash, 21, 26, 57, 235.
FINE GOODS: to wash, 143.
HANDKERCHIEFS: to bleach, 26; to wash, 69.
IRONING: 20, 116, 213, 267.
LAUNDRY HINTS: 101.
LINEN: to whiten, 354.
SKIRTS: to wash, 168; to dry, 93; to hang up, 157.
SPRINKLING: with hose, 359.
STAINS, TO REMOVE: blood, 284; grass, 248; iodine, 43; ink, 10; 110, 251; in colored clothes, 216; oil, 285; paint, 243, 285; perspiration, 78; rust, 23, 139, 285, 316; scorching, 159, 248, 314, 356; table linen, 233, 284; tar, 234.
STARCH: to dry, 320.
STARCH: wax in, 323; thin waist, to starch, 37.
STOCKINGS: to dry, 323.
SUNBONNETS: to dry, 320.
WASHING: dress, to make, 39; fluid, 102; evening shawls, 127; linen, 49; to lustre, 91; new process, 33; silks, 132; white silks, 124; stockings, to dry, 323; sunbonnet, to dry, 323; sundry points, 115, 319.
WHITE FABRICS: to prevent yellowing, 175.

HUNTING: 337, 338.
INKS: copying, 344; record ancient, 344.
KID GLOVES: to remove spots on, 259.
LEATHER: to glue to metal, 245.
LIGHTNING PAPER: to make, 276.
LIME: to burn, 281.
MANURE: made of bones, 281.
MORTAR: mouse-proof, 311.
MOUSETRAP: 311.
MUCILAGE: fruit tree gum, 245; elastic, 344; for labels, 344.

PHARMACY AT HOME

COMMON SIMPLES: sassafras, dogwood, thoroughwort or boneset, willow bark, pennyroyal, tulip-tree bark, oak bark, nutmeg, cinnamon, white pine bark, persimmon, sumach, buckeye or horse-chestnut, creeping cucumbers, 89. snake root, magnolia, dill, wild indigo, Irish moss, New Jersey tea, mullein, marsh rosemary, sweet gum tree, golden seal, pond lily root, hops, hawkweed, 290.
CORDIALS: ginger, 330; honey, 330.
DECOCTIONS: how made, 282.
DEODORIZERS: 273.
DRINKS FOR THE SICK: 282.
ESSENCES: how made, 283.
FAMILY HERBALIST, GARDEN REMEDIES: carrot, turnip, onion, melon and melon seeds, pumpkin seeds,

INDEX

FAMILY HERBALIST—*Continued*.
cress, strawberry leaves, sorrel, sage, blackberry (fruit and root), raspberry (fruit and leaves), quince seeds, spearmint, peppermint, parsley, lettuce, horse radish, figs, dates, prunes, 287 to 288.
FLOWER SALVE: 330.
HOME EXPERIMENTS: 266.
KNITTING: to keep clean, 269.
POULTRY: food, 314.
PRIMROSES: to bloom, 321.

REMEDIES

ACHING FINGERS: 142.
ANT STINGS: 254.
APPENDICITIS: 175, 228.
ASTHMA: 37, 127.
BACKACHE: 53.
BARLEY WATER: 273.
BED SORES: 44, 151.
BED WETTING: 188.
BLEEDING: 274.
BOILS: 70.
BRAN BAG: 55.
BREATHING: difficult, 56.
BRUISES: 236, 275.
BUNIONS: 236, 275.
BURNS: 34, 58, 80, 107, 115, 173, 288; alum, 48; egg, 68, 284, 275; wet flour, 356.
CAMPHOR LINIMENT: 282.
CAMPHORATED SOAP LINIMENT: 283.
CANCER: violet leaves for, 122.
CANKER SORES: 44, 103, 130, 264, 284.
CAR SICKNESS: 227.
CARE OF INVALIDS: 270.
CASTOR OIL: to take, 24, 217, 224, 244; substitute for, 312.
CATARRH: inhalants, 100, 220; German cure, 115.
CERATE: resin, 283.
CHAPPED HANDS: 140, 350.
CHIGGER OR CHEGO BITES: 324.
CHILBLAINS: 22, 248.
CHOKING: 21.
COLDS: 141, 162, 234; glycerine for, 252; to prevent, 207.
COLIC: catnip tea for, 68.
COMPOUND WINE OF GOLDEN SEAL, 284.
CONSTIPATION: 53, 169.
CONSUMPTION: 77.
CORNS: 43, 131, 142, 216, 254.
COUGHS: 173; hot water, 37; syrup, 46, 62, 178; horses, 10.
CRACKED FINGERS: 250.
CRAMPS: 27, 178, 260, 268.
CROUP: 61, 67, 159; membranous, 22; liniment, 44.
DANDRUFF: 52.
DEAFNESS: 234.
DIGESTION: weak, 25, 179, 236, 322.
DIPHTHERIA: Russian government cure, 1, 234.
DYSPEPSIA: old remedy, 44.
EARACHE: 62, 117, 244, 332.
ERYSIPELAS: cranberry, 227.
ESSENTIAL OILS: to make, 102; care of, 332.
EYES: object in, 36, 101, 358; aching, 264.
FAINTING FITS: 331.
FELON: to prevent, 67.
FEVER: 235; thirst in, 51.
FLESH: to gain, 302.
FOREIGN BODY: in nostril, 158; in throat, 138.
FROSTED LIMBS: 43, 329.
GOITRE: 252.
GYPSY MOTH POISON: 183.
HAIR TONIC: 245.
HAY FEVER: 243.
HEADACHE: 123, 167, 173.
HEMORRHAGE: cut, 262.
HICCOUGH: 61, 62, 104, 126, 160, 220, 227.
HOT WATER CURE: 172, 173, 349.
INDIGESTION: 350.
INFLAMMATION: 178.
INGROWING NAILS: 36, 318.
INSOMNIA: 53, 61, 263, 304.
IVY POISON: 119, 167, 221, 229, 246.
JAUNDICE: 47, 67.

INDEX

KEROSENE: : antidote, 46.
LA GRIPPE: 63, 265.
LOCKJAW: 32, 41.
MALARIA: 125.
NERVE TONIC: 241, 304.
NEURALGIA: 163.
NURSING MOTHERS: 179.
PERSPIRATION: feet, 207; body, 225, 250.
PILLS: to swallow, 270.
PIMPLES: 42.
PLASTERS: 221.
POISON: general antidote, 6, 336.
POWDER BURNS: 172.
POWDERS: to take, 250.
PRICKLY HEAT: 264, 314.
PUNCTURED WOUNDS: nails, etc., 75, 76, 163.
RHEUMATISM: 138, 150.
RUN-AROUND: 67, 80.
SALVE: 253, 350.
SEASICKNESS: 48, 122, 256.
SICK HEADACHE: 35, 19; beverage for, 19.
SIMPLE REMEDIES: 129.
SLEEPLESSNESS: 7.
SLIPPERY ELM BARK SALVE: 320.
SNAKE BITE: 184, 238, 326.
SNEEZING: to prevent, 147, 207.
SORE JOINTS: 27.
SPLINTERS: to remove, 106.
SPRAINS AND BRUISES: 24, 37, 52, 249, 253.
SUFFOCATION: 276.
TEETHING: 169.
TIRED FEET: 8.
TONIC: 233.
TONSILITIS: 43, 178, 179, 228.
TOOTHACHE: 228.
TUBERCULOSIS: 151.
VOICE: weakness of, 249.

WARTS: 217.
WEAK EYES: 68.
WHOOPING COUGH:
WOUNDS: 242.

PYROTECHNIC DEPARTMENT

BENGAL LIGHTS: to make, 277.
COLORED TORCHES: 278.
CRIMSON FIRES: 278.
DISPLAYS: 277.
GREEN FIRES: 278.
JAPANESE PARLOR FIREWORKS: 279.
RED FIRES: 278.
ROCKETS: to fire safely, 277.
SALUTES: 278.
SKATING CARNIVAL: 279.

PAINTS: fireproof, 330; cheap for fences, 331.
PASTES: liquid, 344.
PERPETUAL LAMP: 357.
PLANTING CUCUMBERS: 312.
PLASTER ADHESIVE: for mending books, 219.
POLISH: for old carvings, 345.
POTATOES: to keep from sprouting, 5.
PRIMROSES: to bloom, 321.
PRINTS: to copy, 346; to mount, 346; to make new margins for, 346.
PRIVATE THEATRICALS: 295, 296, 297.
PUTTY: to soften, 17.
RAINFALL: estimate of, 286.
ROSES: to keep fresh, 31; to revive, 75, 307; to propagate, 96, 176; to kill bugs on, 128, 353.
ROUGH CARPENTERING: 12.
SALT: new use for, 246.
SCREEN: for cylinder stove, 240; lamp, 318; bath window, 323; to be painted white, 323.
SEEDS: to start quickly, 265.
SHADOW EMBROIDERY: to iron, 45.
SHAWL, TWO-COLOR: to knit, 278.
SHOE SOLES: to waterproof, 78.
SILK: underwear, to wash, 76; to sew, 106; to keep white, 175; to cleanse and preserve, 19, 132.
SKIRTS: braid for, 30; to prevent sagging, 259.
SPARROWS: to drive away, 355.

INDEX

STAINS, TO REMOVE: copying ink, 285; grease, 284; ink, 10, 210, 251, 285; on colored goods, 216.
STOCKINGS: old, uses for, 272.
STRAW HATS: to cleanse, 52; to dye, 160.
SUGAR: in teapot, 220.
SUIT CASE COVER: 325.
SYMPATHETIC INKS: 266.
TANNING: deerskins, 331.
TANKS: to estimate contents, 286.
TREES: to save from mice, 280.

TOILET AND TOILET ARTICLES

BABY SHAMPOO: 166.
BAKING SODA: 68.
BATH: 238; bags, 217.
BELT: to keep in place, 18, 165.
BLACKING FLUID: 304.
BUTTERMILK COSMETIC: 333.
COLOGNE: homemade, 280.
DEODORIZER: 318.
DENTIFRICE: 317.
EYEGLASS: 247.
EYELASHES: care of, 332.
FACE WASH: 217, 250, 271.
FEET: blisters, to relieve, and prevent, 74.
HAIR: to curl, 261; receipts, 24, 233, 252; tonic, 245, 250, 260; Indian wash, 20.
HANDS: care of, 31, 89, 117, 159, 250, 314; lotion, 263; use of vinegar, 309, 312.
JEWELRY: care of, 152, 153.

NAILS: to soften, 232.
PERFUME BAGS: 30.
PERFUME: lasting, 336.
PERSPIRATION: 234, 250.
SACHETS AND ODORS: 353.
TEETH: to preserve, 87; to cleanse, 257.
TIGHT RING: to remove, 341.
TOILET WATER: 217.
TOOTH POWDER: 317.

UDDER: cows to relieve, 40.
UMBRELLA HANDLES: to mend, 242.
VARNISH: book-binders, 345; to revive leather bindings, 345.
WAISTS: to measure, 25; to use old, 249.
WALKING SKIRT: to get length, 214.
WASHING: see LAUNDRY.
WATCH: to clean, 97, 119, 316.
WATER: to test for purity, 11; to increase flow, 11; to cleanse in wells, 13; in cisterns, 13.
WATERPROOF BLACKING: 12.
WATERPROOF CLOTHING: 12.
WEEDS: to kill, 123, 33.
WESTERN WIFE: a poem, 84.
WHALEBONE: to cut easily, 51.
WHIPPED CREAM: 253.
WHITE HOUSE DAINTY: 267.
WHITE HOUSE STUCCO WHITEWASH: 334.
WINE: rhubarb, 329; fruit, 331.
WHITEWASH: 11; for barns and sheds, 11, 299; good, 335.
WORMS, EARTH; to drive away, 58; to collect for bait, 61; currant, 325.

www.ingramcontent.com/pod-product-compliance
Lightning Source LLC
Chambersburg PA
CBHW051626230426
43669CB00013B/2198